SPORT, FITNESS, AND THE LAW

North American Perspectives

Second Edition

**MARGERY HOLMAN,
DICK MORIARTY,
and JANICE FORSYTH**

Canadian Scholars' Press Inc.
Toronto
2001

Sport, Fitness and the Law: North American Perspectives
edited by Margery Holman, Dick Moriarty, and Janice Forsyth

First published in 2001 by
Canadian Scholars' Press Inc.
180 Bloor Street West, Suite 1202
Toronto, Ontario
M5S 2V6

Copyright © 2001 Margery Holman, Dick Moriarty, and Janice Forsyth, the contributing authors, and Canadian Scholars' Press. All rights reserved. No part of this publication may be photocopied, reproduced, stored in a retrieval system, or transmitted, in any form or by any means, electronic, mechanical or otherwise, without the written permission of Canadian Scholars' Press, except for brief passages quoted for review purposes.

Tables 4.1 to 4.11 in Chapter 4: Legal Responsibilities of the Meet Director, are taken from "Track and Field Curriculum for Physical Education," copyright © 1995 Professor Robert J. Vigars, The University of Western Ontario, London, Ontario, Canada N6A 3K7. Reprinted by permission.

Every reasonable effort has been made to identify copyright holders. CSPI would be pleased to have any errors or omissions brought to its attention.

CSPI acknowledges the financial support of the Government of Canada through the Book Publishing Industry Development Programme for our publishing activities.

Canadian Cataloguing in Publication Data

Main entry under title:

Sports, fitness and the law : North American perspectives

2nd ed.
First ed. published under title: Canadian/American sport, fitness and the law.
First ed. edited by: Dick and Mary Moriarty ... [et al.].
Includes bibliographical references and index.
ISBN 1-55130-190-3

1. Sports – Law and legislation – Canada. 2. Sports – Law and legislation – United States. I. Holman, Margery Jean. II. Moriarty, Dick. III. Forsyth, Janice Evelyn. IV. Title: Canadian/American sport, fitness and the law.

KE3792.Z85C36 2001   344.71'099   C00-933133-6
KF3989.C36 2001

Managing Editor: Ruth Bradley-St-Cyr
Production Editor: Jo Roberts
Marketing Manager: Linda Palmer
Marketing Assistant: Renée Knapp
Page layout: Brad Horning
Cover design: Jean Louie

00   01   02   03   04   05   06   6   5   4   3   2   1

Printed and bound in Canada by AGMV Marquis

TABLE OF CONTENTS

LIST OF TABLES AND FIGURES ix

PREFACE xi

CONTRIBUTING AUTHORS xvii

Chapter 1
PHYSICAL ACTIVITY AND LEGAL LIABILITY
by Dick Moriarty 1
    What to Do in Case of a Lawsuit
    Critical Path in a Law Suit
    How to Avoid Legal Litigation
    Variables and Relationships in Negligence
    Liability for Injuries in Sport Activities
    Traditional Sources of Litigation
    Abbreviations of Court Titles
    References
    Canadian Table of Cases
    (Abbreviations of Court Titles)
    American Table of Cases

Chapter 2
A PRACTICAL LOOK AT RISK MANAGEMENT
by Mike Mahoney, Janice Forsyth, Margery Holman, and Dick Moriarty 19
    Introduction to Risk Management
    Risk Categories
    Conclusion
    Questions for Class Discussion
    Relevant Cases

Endnotes
References

Chapter 3
VOLUNTEER SCREENING: LEGAL RESPONSIBILITIES FOR SPORT ORGANIZATIONS
by Janice Forsyth and Brenda Gallagher 33
    The Importance of Volunteer Screening
    Overview of Volunteer Screening
    Step 1—Determining the Risk
    Step 2—Position Design and Position Description
    Step 3—Recruitment Process
    Step 4—Application Form
    Step 5—Interviews
    Step 6—Reference Checks
    Step 7—Police Records Checks (PRC)
    Step 8—Orientation and Training
    Step 9—Supervision and Evaluation
    Step 10—Participant Follow-up
    Questions for Class Discussion
    Relevant Cases
    References

Chapter 4
LEGAL RESPONSIBILITIES OF THE MEET DIRECTOR
by Dennis Fairall, Dick Moriarty, and Margery Holman 51
    The Meet Director
    Review of Cases
    Tort Liability
    Reducing the Risk
    Safety Factors in Track and Field Competitions
    Conclusion
    Questions for Class Discussion

Chapter 5
RISK MANAGEMENT FOR TRIATHLON DIRECTORS
by Tony Nurse and Margery Holman 75
    Introduction
    Managing the Risk
    Cases Relevant to Triathlon Directors
    Characteristics of a Triathlon
    Safety Concerns for the Swim Section
    Safety Concerns for the Bike Section
    Safety Concerns for the Run Section
    Safety Concerns for the Transition Area
    Medical Requirements
    Conclusion

Questions for Class Discussion
References

Chapter 6
PERSONAL TRAINING: LEGAL LIABILITY AND RISK MANAGEMENT
by Carrie Czichrak Lancaster 87
Personal Training
Legal Liability
Negligence
Risk Management
"At Home" Personal Training
Questions for Class Discussion
References

Chapter 7
THE RIGHTS OF ATHLETES, COACHES, AND PARTICIPANTS IN SPORT
by Hilary A. Findlay and Rachel Corbett 101
Introduction
Contract
Procedural Fairness
Right to a Hearing
Rule against Bias
Administrative Appeals
Judicial Review
Dispute Management
Conclusion
Questions for Class Discussion
Relevant Cases
Footnotes
References

Chapter 8
NATURAL JUSTICE AND SPORT: ATHLETES' RIGHTS, DRUG TESTING, AND AGENTS
by Edward W. Ducharme 121
Introduction
Principle #1—Natural Justice and Fairness in Sport
Principle #2—Athletes' Rights and Mandatory Drug Testing
Principle #3—The Role of the Agents
Questions for Class Discussion
Endnotes
References

Chapter 9
MANDATORY DRUG TESTING IN ATHLETICS
by Charles Palmer 131
The Problem
Preventing Drug Abuse in Sports

In the Short Run—Drug Testing
　　Conclusion
　　Questions for Class Discussion
　　References

Chapter 10
GENDER EQUITY IN SPORT BY LEGISLATION AND LITIGATION
by Margery Holman 139
　　Understanding Equity and the Law
　　Organizational Policy
　　Participation
　　Sex, Sexuality, And Discrimination
　　Questions for Class Discussion
　　Endnotes
　　References

Chapter 11
AIDS, SPORTS, THE LAW, AND EDUCATION
by Helen Mickens 151
　　What We Need to Know
　　What is HIV? What is AIDS?
　　Is There a Relationship Between Sports and AIDS?
　　Well-known Athletes and AIDS
　　Discrimination: How Does the Law Relate to AIDS Issues and Sports?
　　Other Legal Issues
　　AIDS, Sport, and Drug Testing
　　The Sports Risk
　　Athletes: Anti-HIV/AIDS Hygiene
　　Should an HIV Infected Person Participate in Sports?
　　The Health of the Infected Athlete
　　Trainers, Coaches, and the HIV-infected Athlete
　　What is the Role of Sport Organizers and Institutions?
　　Education and Policy Formation
　　Athletes Contracting AIDS Outside of Sports
　　The Job Ahead
　　Questions for Class Discussion
　　Endnotes
　　References

Chapter 12
LEGAL INTERVENTION IN SPORT FOR PEOPLE WITH DISABILITIES
by Jennifer Larson 163
　　Canadian Legislation
　　American Legislation
　　Protection of Athletic Involvement Through the IEP
　　Risk Management and People with Disabilities

Disabled Sport in Canada
Summary
Questions for Class Discussion
Table of Cases
Endnotes
References

Chapter 13
SPORT AND THE LAW OF DEFAMATION
by Raymond E. Brown **179**
Introduction
The Cause of Action for Defamation
Defenses to an Action for Defamation
Actual and Express Malice
Damages
Conclusion
Questions for Class Discussion
Table of Cases
Endnotes
References

Chapter 14
INSURANCE FOR SPORT AND FITNESS ORGANIZATIONS
by Gina M. Jefferson and David L. LaBute **199**
Introduction
The Insurance Crisis
Liability for Negligence
Negligence in Sport
Risk Management
The Retention of Risk
The Transfer of Risk
The Insurance Contract
General Liability and Accident Insurance
Workers' Compensation Insurance
Protection of Property, Finances, and Operations
Summary
Appendix 14.1: Tort Laws and Negligence
Appendix 14.2: Contract For Use of School Facilities: School District of Owen-Withee [WI]
Appendix 14.3: Release Form: 2000 USA Cycling
Appendix 14.4: HPAC Liability Insurance Coverage Summary
Appendix 14.5: Liability And Sports Accident Insurance Policy: Softball Manitoba
Appendix 14.6: Club Sport Liability Policy: Indiana University
Appendix 14.7: Non-Owned Automobile Insurance: Windsor-Essex Catholic District School Board [ON]
Questions for Class Discussion
Relevant Cases
Endnotes
References

Chapter 15
TURNING CONFLICT INTO COOPERATION: ALTERNATIVE DISPUTE RESOLUTION
by Margery Holman, Rebecca Mowrey, and Dan Bondy 237
    Conflict
    ADR and the Law
    What is ADR?
    ADR and Sport/Physical Activity
    Current Sport Use of ADR
    Questions for Class Discussion
    References

CITATION FORMAT 247
    Canadian
    American

LIST OF ABBREVIATIONS 249

GLOSSARY OF TERMS 251

TABLES AND FIGURES

Chapter 1
Physical Liability and Legal Liability
    Table 1:1 What to Do in Event of Potential Lawsuit 3
    Table 1:2 Steps in Legal Trial 5
    Table 1:3 Negligence—the Basis of Tort Liability 6
    Table 1:4 Variables in Law 7
    Table 1:5 Liability—Rules of Thumb 8

Chapter 2
A Practical Look at Risk Management
    Table 2:1 Participant Readiness Table 20
    Table 2:2 Categories of Potential Users and the Duty of Care Owed 25
    Table 2:3 Providers of Equipment Have Four Responsibilities 26
    Table 2:4 Considerations when Developing Policies and Procedures 28

Chapter 3
Volunteer Screening: Legal Responsibilities for Sport Organizations
    Table 3:1 Key Terminology 35
    Table 3:2 Acceptable and Unacceptable Practices in Recruiting and Interviewing 39

Chapter 4
Legal Responsibilities of the Meet Director
    Table 4:1 General Risks of Track Events 57
    Table 4:2 Risks of Hurdle Races 59
    Table 4:3 Risks of Steeplechase 60
    Table 4:4 Risks of High Jump 61
    Table 4:5 Risks of Pole Vault 62
    Table 4:6 Risks of Long Jump 64
    Table 4:7 Risks of Triple Jump 65

Table 4:8 Risks of Shot Put 66
Table 4:9 Risks of Discus Throw 67
Table 4:10 Risks of Javelin Throw 68
Table 4:11 Risks of Hammer Throw 69

Chapter 6
Personal Training: Legal Liability and Risk Management
Figure 6:1 Legal Liability 89
Table 6:1 Risk Analysis 95
Figure 6:2 Negligence Defenses 96

Chapter 11
AIDS, Sports, the Law and Education
Table 11:1 Minimizing Exposure to HIV-infected Blood 158

Chapter 14
Insurance for Sport and Fitness Organizations
Table 14.1: The Liability Crisis: Reasons for an Increase in the Number of Lawsuits 201
Table 14.2: Liability Insurance and Sport 212
Table 14.3: Sport Classification Chart 215
Table 14.4: Crime Insurance 216

Chapter 15
Alternative Dispute Resolution
Figure 15.1: ADR Process for Sport/Physical Activity Organizations 240
Table 15.1: CIAU Guideline for Alternative Dispute Resolution 243

PREFACE

This book is intended for use by university and high school students, as well as other individuals involved as executives, administrators, teachers/coaches, or players/participants in school sport, amateur athletics or fitness activities. It consists of a series of chapters that can be read independently or consecutively. Of necessity, there is some redundancy; however, the legal points reiterated are those that should be internalized by anyone involved in sport or fitness activities. The range of authors includes university professors, administrators, practicing lawyers, and teachers and coaches from elementary to university level. These authors include a founder of the Centre for Sport and Law, the former manager of Leadership Development for Windsor's United Way (currently Chair of the Institute of Learning and Teaching for St. Clair College), a former Coaching Development Coordinator with the Ontario Special Olympics, and an administrator with Volunteer Canada. Also included as authors are graduate students who have been enrolled over the years in Canada's first graduate course, and subsequently undergraduate course, on Sport, Physical Activity and the Law, which is offered at the Faculty of Human Kinetics at the University of Windsor.

Our first book, *Sport, Physical Activity and the Law*, was published by the Canadian Association for Health, Physical Education and Recreation, and sold out two printings, attesting to the need for books in this area. Likewise, our second book, *Canadian/American Sport, Fitness and the Law*, published by Canadian Scholars' Press Inc. sold out. The current text offers some new material that reflects the increased legal challenges faced by those within the various fields of physical activity as well as the foundations that are essential in understanding the law as it applies to sport/physical activity.

The sport litigation trend that began in the United States continues to encroach upon Canadian culture. Lawyers have taken over the sports pages to a degree that cannot go unnoticed. Each new wave of legal action takes the form of both criminal and civil litigation. Increased government legislation and statutes related to human rights, government intervention and/or regulation of organizations further complicate comprehension of the world of sport, athletics and fitness. Since ignorance of the law is no excuse for violation of the law, those involved as executives, administrators, teachers, coaches, instructors, spectators, and competitors owe it to themselves and those with whom they interact in the sport and fitness world to gain some insight into the types of legislation and litigation most likely to affect them. We hope that by surveying the chapters in this book, answering the questions, reading, reciting, and reviewing, the reader will be put on the road to "legal literacy." The topics are given in a macro, generic way (nature, formation and application in general), as contrasted with the micro, specific way (detailed substantive rules and regulations). The text is designed for non-lawyers who wish to have an understanding of the law and its application in sound policy and procedure. It is not to be read in a passive way, but rather as a guide to active study and participation in individual or group projects. Numerous Canadian and American cases are referred to in the text so that the reader can understand the application of the law to sport/physical activity. These cases provide precedent that is more important for what it portends for the future, than for what it has meant in the past. Remember to follow cases through to their conclusion and appeal, for in the law, as in sport, "it's never over 'til it's over."

At the end of each chapter, there are questions and suggestions for discussion, debate, and worthwhile projects such as interviews or visits. A glossary has been provided in an appendix at the end of the book, so you will not require access to a legal dictionary while reading.

As John Barnes (1983) has pointed out:

> Lawsuits and sport contests have much in common: competing parties striving for victory according to rules under the control of an arbitrator, the urge to win, damaged pride, the luck of the draw, practiced skills and the gambling of costs, play equal parts in law games and sport games. The spirit and practice of play are alive in the courtroom.
>
> (Barnes, 1983: v)

In other words, every lawsuit is a horserace, with different horses for different courses. Lawsuits are a very expensive way, however, to gain the enjoyment of victory and the agony of defeat, and a blunt instrument for running amateur and school sport. It is hoped that by studying this text you will improve your performance as a wise and prudent person and never have to experience the difficulty of legal litigation as an actual participant. The school of hard knocks is a painful one, but as the old saying goes, "Fools will learn by no other way!" In view of this fact and the litigious nature of our North American society, the probability of being involved in a lawsuit increases daily. Nonetheless, by familiarizing yourself with the principles of law and natural justice you reduce the probability of being sued, or at least increase the probability of prevailing if you are sued.

Chapter by Chapter

Chapter 1, dealing with "Physical Activity and Legal Liability," is written by Dick Moriarty, who served as a university athletic director for approximately thirty years and a professor of sport and the law for fifteen. This chapter compares and contrasts the way lawyers and educators see the world and deal with differences of opinion. Information is provided on what to do in case of a lawsuit, the critical and arduous path of a lawsuit, and how to avoid legal litigation. Some of the major variables in the law as they relate to physical activity are listed and some handy rules of thumb are provided to guide behavior. Typical sources of litigation, such as injury to participants, spectators, use of waivers, coach's liability, and liability for injury in physical education classes, faulty medical treatment, or for defective athletic equipment are discussed. Numerous cases are cited.

Chapter 2, "Risk Management: Prevention, Not Litigation," Mike Mahoney works with the editors of the book to provide a definition of Risk Management. The chapter continues with comment on the components of a Risk Management Program, such as feasibility of establishing a Risk Management Program, risk identification, risk treatment, safety inspection and investigation, risk program implementation, and evaluation. Strategies are presented to determine whether risks can be avoided completely, reduced, transferred or retained when considering variables such as real risk presence and participant readiness, or when comparing accident severity and accident frequency. Samples of risk management checklists, waivers and agreements, accident procedures, and insurance coverage are included. Cases are cited in the chapter and the appendix contains checklists for facility equipment safety in a variety of areas in sports.

In Chapter 3, "Responsible Volunteer Hiring," Janice Forsyth, who was heavily involved in volunteer training with the United Way has teamed up with Brenda Gallagher of Volunteer Canada to explain the legal implications of selecting and working with volunteers. The chapter provides the steps involved in sound management of a volunteer base within an organization from the search for individuals to selection, training and evaluation. Sport and recreation require a large complement of volunteer services to maintain and operate their programs. Proper management of the volunteer sector within an organization is critical as a risk management strategy and avoiding litigation.

In Chapter 4, "Legal Liability of the Meet Director," Dennis Fairall, one of Canada's top university and amateur track and field coaches, joins with Dick Moriarty and Margery Holman to look at the risk involved in conducting one of sports most challenging events — a track and field meet. No other sporting event involves as many competitors, coaches, officials, spectators and media in such a wide variety of individual and team events that are fraught with potential risk of injury. Safety factors in track and field competition include a full range of physical layout of the facility, equipment safety, schedule, surfaces, spectator safety, officiating competence, medical and first aid treatment, and sanctioning and insuring of the meet. This chapter, through track and field as an example, provides guidance on how to administer sport events while minimizing risk to all participants.

In Chapter 5, "Planning For A Triathlon," Tony Nurse, a graduate student who currently is a triathlon competitor, joins with editor Margery Holman to outline the idiosyncrasies of organizing a triathlon. Although much of the planning parallels the responsibilities of a meet director of a track and field event, there are also a number of unique features. Precautions must be taken to ensure safety for the participants during wave starts, within transition zones, while swimming or contending with traffic on foot or bike. Safety can be affected in each component of the competition by weather variables to which meet managers must be attentive. With triathlon experiencing relatively new popularity, this is a must read for those who assume responsibility as a Triathlon Director.

Chapter 6, "Personal Training: Legal Liability and Risk Management," is written by Carrie Czichrak Lancaster, a personal trainer who studied the risk factors in the profession while doing graduate work. The growth of the fitness industry, and hence the need for clients to seek a knowledge source for the development of personal fitness programs, has made this issue relevant. This chapter extends the study of risk management for personal trainers to the home environment. With restricted time schedules, increased disposable income, and availability of home equipment, the demand for personal trainers to come into the home for fitness tutoring is likely to increase. This chapter alerts the reader to some to the cautions that need to be taken.

Chapter 7, "The Rights of Athletes, Coaches and Participants in Sport," is written by two leading associates with the Centre for Sport and the Law, Hilary Findlay and Rachel Corbett. Their extensive work in the area of sport law provides the reader with valuable information about the rights of participants within a sport organization. Amateur athletics has become a setting in which litigation has increased. The responsibility of an organization to provide equitable opportunity, adhere to procedural fairness in decision making and establish fair appeal processes are examined in this chapter.

In Chapter 8, "Natural Justice and Sport: Athletes' Rights, Drug Testing and Agents," Ed Ducharme, a practicing lawyer and former professor at the University of Windsor, relates the principles of due process with the pedagogical practices of those involved in sports. Three areas are addressed: (1) natural justice and fair play in sport, athletes' rights and (2) mandatory drug testing and (3) the role of agents. The Canadian Charter of Rights and Freedoms (Sec. 7 & 8) and the U.S. Constitution and Amendments (4th, 5th, and 14th) are reviewed and compared to popular belief and procedure in terms of mandatory drug testing.

In Chapter 9, "Mandatory Drug Testing in Athletics," is written by Charles Palmer, a law professor from the Thomas M. Cooley Law School in Lansing, Michigan. This chapter deals with the contemporary problem of drugs in sport and society. The major athletic drugs of choice are described and discussed as a threat to the moral and social justice for sport. Drug testing in sport is contrasted with drug testing in criminal law and the associated issues are addressed.

In Chapter 10, "Gender Equity in Sport by Legislation and Litigation," Margery Holman deals with legislation and litigation in Canada and the United States aimed at providing equal opportunities for female participation in sport, as competitors, coaches, officials and administrators. Margery is the University of Windsor's first Employment Equity and Sexual Harassment Officer and a prominent teacher and coach at both the high school and university levels. This chapter reveals the different influences of legislation with the Canadian approach of using generic non-discrimination laws to ensure equity in sport while the American primary success has been through the use of specific law that has targeted educational equity. Landmark cases from Canada and the United States are presented. American cases provide an example of the way in which litigation has shifted from appeals for equal opportunity to participate as athletes to a broader range of issues such as harassment, pay equity and hiring and retention of sport leaders.

In Chapter 11, "AIDS, Sports, the Law and Education," Helen Mickens, a practicing lawyer from Lansing, Michigan, deals with the interesting legal issues that have developed in sports, fitness and recreation areas as a result of the AIDS epidemic. Ongoing issues of whether well known athletes who have tested positive for HIV should participate, and the effect such participation might have on their own health and that of opposing players is analyzed. Questions and cases related to discrimination, torts, drug testing and employee torts involving trainers, coaches, instructors, and administrators are addressed. Finally, the job ahead in terms of education, legislation and policy formation is presented.

In Chapter 12, "Legal Implications in Sport for People with Disabilities," Jennifer Larson relates how Canadian and American legislation and litigation have advanced equal rights participation by disabled athletes in sport and recreation activities. A distinction is made between physically, mentally, and emotionally disabled. Cases have been woven throughout to assist the reader in understanding how the complexities of the law have been applied to the diversity of barriers with which disabled athletes must contend to experience sport and develop their potential as athletes. Jennifer is a Windsor graduate who has worked extensively, both as a volunteer and as a professional with disabled athletes.

In Chapter 13, "Sport and the Law of Defamation," Raymond E. Brown, law professor at the University of Windsor, compares and contrasts Canadian and American treatment of slander and libel over the years. Canada's strict liability is compared with the constitutional protection provided in the United States. Seven sport-related scenarios are presented and related to the causes for action (defamation, publication, identification, and distinction between libel and slander) and the defenses to an action for defamation (justification, consent, absolute privilege, protected privilege, qualified privilege, peer comments and expression of opinion, actual and expressed knowledge, damages) among the American and Canadian constitutional considerations. Landmark Canadian and American cases from school, amateur sport and professional athletics are included.

In Chapter 14, "Insurance for Sport and Fitness Organizations," University of Windsor Human Kinetics graduate Gina Jefferson joins with David LaBute to present the theory of insurance and how it works. Gina's current experience in the insurance industry provides an insider's knowledge to the benefits and limitations of insurance for those in sport management. This chapter makes the link of negligence, liability, and risk management with the need for insurance. "The liability insurance crisis," "deep pocket syndrome," and "hazard insurance index" as they relate to risk rates and availability are considered. Major areas of insurance coverage appropriate for a variety of physical activity environments are addressed.

In Chapter 15, "Using the ADR Approach in the Sport Organizational Environment: Alternative Dispute Resolution," Margery Holman, Dan Bondy and Becky Mowrey team up to suggest that sport organizations consider a variety of means for settling disputes of all kinds without litigation. The chapter provides an introduction to ADR, offers one of many strategies for using ADR techniques, and develops scenarios in which ADR would benefit the organizations and those involved in a dispute. ADR is a new trend using old techniques adapted for modern day conflict. With an increase in litigation in amateur sport, this chapter encourages sport managers to commit to the ADR process, learn the techniques of ADR and apply the process to disputes that might otherwise end up in the courts.

Useful Publications for Further Research

There are a number of excellent U.S. publications that give students topics of interest. Unfortunately, there is a lack of Canadian counterparts but the common trend is that, whatever is happening in the USA will undoubtedly happen in a few years in Canada.

The oldest source in our field is a publication entitled *Sport and the Courts,* which has an index. The index gives title and reference to the case and also the volume number and page of the summary. For example, the first alphabetically listed case in the index for Volume 18 — 1997 falls under the descriptor "abusive conduct" and provides the following information for the researcher:

Title IX action against university dismissed for failure to state a claim. *Brzonkala v. Virginia Polytechnic and State Univ.*, 935 F. Supp. 772 (W.D. Va. 1996), Vol. 18, No. 5, p.3.

You can locate the actual case in the library for specific and complete details (including precedent setting cases). You may have to read a case several times to understand the legalese. Similarly, *The Sport, Parks, & Recreation Law Reporter* has an index and publishes volume numbers and copy. For example, the Annual Index for March 1996 — March 1997 provides the content of Volume 10, Issues 1–4, Pages 1–64.

Also useful are:

1. *The Exercise Standards and Malpractice Reporter*, a publication of PRC Publishing Inc., 4418 Belden Village Street, N.W. Canton, Ohio, 44718-2516;
2. *Your School & the Law: Incorporating Athletic Director & Coach*, published by LRP Publications, 747 Dresher Road, P.O. Box 980, Horsham, PA, 19044-0980; and
3. *The Sports Lawyer: The Bimonthly Newsletter of the Sports Lawyers Association*, an SLA publication with information at www.sportslaw.org/sla/.

Finally, the *Journal of Legal Aspects of Sport* is published by the Society for the Study of Legal Aspects of Sport and Physical Activity Incorporated, c/o Executive Director, 5840 South Ernest Street, Terre Haute, IN 47802-9562 or by phone, 812-237-2186. Details are also available on http://www.ithaca.edu/SSLASPA. The *SSLASPA Newsletter* contains references to excellent articles in law journals and current case reviews. Andrew Pittman is the editor of the newsletter and can be contacted for further information at the Department of HPER Baylor University, Waco, Texas, 76798-7313, by email at andy_pittman@Baylor.edu.

On the Canadian scene, The Canadian Bar Association (Continuing Legal Education) occasionally includes Sport and Recreation in their topics for published conferences. Check your local Law Library. Also, relevant topics such as insurance crisis, pay equity, civil litigation, labour law, marketing, appeal procedure, harassment, fiduciary duties, incorporation, and so on, can be related to physical activity.

Fitness Canada, a department of the Government of Canada, in Ottawa has produced a number of publications that may be useful. The publication *Legal Liability* is of benefit to fitness leaders. Volunteer Canada produced the manual and program *Safe Steps: A Volunteer Screening Process for Sport and Recreation*. The Canadian Association for the Advancement of Women in Sport and Physical Activity produced *An Introduction to the Law, Sport, and Gender Equity in Canada*. These publications are examples of those available from Fitness Canada.

Various provinces put out summaries of cases such as *Selected Cases on Negligence Liability in Parks, Recreation and Sport*, published by Recreation Resource Centre in Nova Scotia which index case summaries by province, legal aspect (signage, product liability, voluntary assumption of risk, et cetera) and activity (i.e., school, park, sport).

Topics and sources are much more plentiful than may be first imagined. Use your local library to search various subjects. Books, proceedings, journals, newsletters, papers, and law cases are all invaluable sources of reference.

Do not give up searching after one try. You need to dig and use various topics. Issues are often indexed under legal topics, not colloquial topics. It is great fun to search, find sources, and read and understand them (cases, once understood, read like a murder mystery). If it is hard to research a topic, then tell yourself that you are doing pioneering work. Don't just give up and pick a topic of convenience on which there is plenty of information readily available as it has probably been well researched and offers old knowledge. If you do pick a topic like this, be creative and take a different approach. Remember you must give definitive answers to minute well-worn topics but tentative solutions will do for significant new topics. Easier to be a critic of the old than creator of the new! Good luck with this text, the classes that you take in sport and the law, and the projects in which you engage.

A final word of caution: As you read this text and pass from neophyte on your way to expert in sport and the law, you may experience some fear and paranoia. There is no need to become frightened, overcautious and overprotective, as long as you use common sense and act as a wise and prudent professional. It is our sincere wish that you enjoy reading and studying this book to reduce the probability of your being included in the case references in some future text.

Acknowledgements

The editors would like to thank all of the authors who took time from their busy schedules to research and write their chapters. We would also like to acknowledge the assistance provided by Mr. Paul Murphy and Ms. Laurie Brett from the Law Library, University of Windsor and from Mr. Soong, recently retired from the Law Library, University of Windsor. Their ongoing support is greatly appreciated.

Most significantly, very sincere thanks to the undergraduate and graduate students who participated so enthusiastically in class activities, rummaged through the library to locate cases, conducted surveys with sport and fitness agencies, and interviewed experts from the law and sport communities over the years. We wish that all of their names and all of their writings could be included; however, both space and the nature of this particular text make that impossible. Rest assured, however, that the editors and authors are conscious of their contributions and express sincere thanks.

Margery Holman
Dick Moriarty
Janice Forsyth
Windsor, Ontario
January 2001

CONTRIBUTING AUTHORS

Dan Bondy graduated from the University of Windsor with an Honors degree and a Masters degree in Physical and Health Education. He obtained his Teaching Diploma from Althouse College in London, Ontario. He will soon retire from secondary school teaching, with thirty years of experience in teaching, coaching, and administrative work. He has recently completed an ADR Course (Alternative Dispute Resolution), from the University of Windsor and York University, and will be starting a new career in this field.

Raymond E. Brown received his BA degree from Seattle University (1956) and his LL.B. from the University of Washington (1961). He is author of the two-volume book *The Law of Defamation in Canada*, published by Carswell, and co-editor of *Sports, Torts and the Courts*, as well as the first edition of *Sports, Fitness and the Law*. He has also written on "Tort Liability as a Form of Social Control over Violence in Sports" for CAHPER's Administrative Committee Monograph series. His areas of specialization are torts, labour law, trial advocacy, civil liberties, and defamation.

Rachel Corbett is a professional planner and risk management consultant with experience in sport, recreation and non-profit management. Ms. Corbett has worked with national and provincial sport and recreation organizations, educational institutions and municipalities on a variety of planning, policy, research, and risk management projects. Ms. Corbett is Managing Director of the Centre for Sport and Law based in St. Catharines, Ontario and is the principal author of the Centre's ten-volume sport and law handbook series.

Edward Ducharme holds B.A. and M.A. degrees from the University of Windsor, a Ph.D. degree from the University of Michigan, and an LL.B. degree from the Faculty of Law at the University of Windsor. Dr. Ducharme is former Associate Professor in the Department of English at the University of Windsor, and remains affiliated with the University as an Adjunct Professor. He is a partner and head of the employment and labour law department at the Windsor firm of Ducharme Fox LLP. He has published in a number of legal fields, including personal injury and employment law, medical malpractice, and environmental law.

Dennis Fairall is currently in his seventeenth year as head coach of the University of Windsor track and field team. During his seventeen years he has served as meet director of over one hundred track and field competitions ranging from local elementary school meets to international track and field competitions.

Hilary Findlay is a lawyer licensed to practice in both Ontario and Alberta. She is the Chair of the Department of Sport Management at Brock University, where she is also an Associate Professor. While practicing law in

Edmonton Professor Findlay taught courses in sport and law at the University of Alberta. She has continued to teach at Concordia University in Montreal and at Algonquin College in Ottawa. Before turning to law, Professor Findlay was an Assistant Professor and coach at the University of Manitoba, and is also the founder of the Centre for Sport and Law, based in St. Catharines, Ontario.

Janice Forsyth is the Chair of the Institute of Learning and Teaching at St. Clair College in Windsor, Ontario. She received a Ph.D in Instructional Technology from Wayne State University's College of Education in 1997, and a BHK (1983) and an MHK (1989) from the University of Windsor. She has lectured in the Communication Studies Department at the University of Windsor and for the Sport Management program at Brock University in St. Catharines.

Dr. Forsyth managed the Leadership Development Services at the United Way/ Centraide Windsor-Essex County for twelve years; in addition to her local involvement, she is a national trainer for the United Way/ Centraide Canada and a trainer for Volunteer Canada. At the provincial level she is a master trainer for the Fitness Ontario leadership program and the Skills program for management volunteers.

Brenda Gallagher has worked at Volunteer Canada on the screening portfolio since November 1997. She is currently working on the Ontario Screening Initiative, a project promoting and developing effective screening strategies for people in positions of trust. She has served as the Director of Communications at the Canadian Wheelchair Sport Association and as the communications and domestic Development Coordinator at Speed Skating Canada.

Ms. Gallagher has a Bachelor of Science degree in Exercise Science from Concordia University in Montréal and a Masters degree in Sport Administration from the University of Ottawa.

Margery Holman is an associate professor in the Faculty of Human Kinetics at the University of Windsor. She served as Director of the Women's Sport program (1970-89), and variously as coach for the swimming, synchronised swimming, and volleyball teams. She has served with Ontario's Provincial Girls Team for the Canada Games, and as an official at the World Student Games in England and Japan. She has received numerous awards for her contributions to the development of volleyball and the advancement of women's sport in her community. Former president of the Ontario Women's Inter-university Athletic Association, Professor Holman was also the University of Windsor's first Employment Equity Co-ordinator and Sexual Harassment Advisor (1989–92).

In 1995, Professor Holman earned a Ph.D. from Michigan State University. She has her B.A. (1968) and B.P.H.E. (1969) from the University of Windsor and M.Ed. from Wayne State University. Professor Holman has presented and published widely in her various areas of specialization.

Gina Jefferson received her Bachelor of Human Kinetics degree from the University of Windsor in 1997, specializing in sport management. She has been employed in the insurance industry for fifteen years, where she has worked in both the personal and commercial insurance sectors. Ms. Jefferson is an Associate of the Insurance Institute of Canada (1999), and is the head of the personal lines department at Blondé & Little Insurance Ltd., in Windsor, Ontario. Ms. Jefferson is currently pursuing her Certified Human Resources Professional designation. This is her first published work.

David LaBute received his Bachelor of Arts (Honours Mathematics) (1992) and Bachelor of Education (1993) degrees from the University of Windsor. He has been teaching for eight years, and is currently the head of the mathematics department at St. Thomas of Villanova Secondary School in LaSalle, Ontario. Mr. LaBute was the lead writer for the Ontario Grade Eleven Functions and Relations Course Profile. He is currently involved in the writing of the Grade Twelve provincial course profiles.

Carrie Czichrak Lancaster received a Bachelors degree in Kinesiology from McMaster University (1999). Specializing in the area of sport management, she graduated from the University of Windsor with a Master of Human Kinetics degree in 2001. During her time at Windsor, she was awarded with the Human Kinetics Graduate Alumni Award for top academic student in sport management and a tuition scholarship for Graduate Studies. Ms. Lancaster has been active in the fitness industry as a group fitness instructor since 1996 and is currently working as a Divisional Manager Assistant for GoodLife Fitness Clubs.

Jennifer Larson has a B.H.K. (co-op) in Sport Administration from the University of Windsor (1996), and over twelve years experience in sport for athletes with disabilities as a coach, official, support staff, and board member. An international referee for the Paralympic sport of boccia, she is also the High Performance Chair of the Canadian Cerebral Palsy Sports Association and past Sport Technical Chair of the Ontario Cerebral Palsy Sports Association. She coached the Ontario Boccia Team from 1997-2000 and was a member of the 1996 Canadian Paralympic Team. Ms. Larson is currently the director of Marketing and Partnership Development for High Five, a program of Parks and Recreation Ontario.

Mike Mahoney is a recent Master of Human Kinetics graduate from the University of Windsor, Ontario. Through working with post-secondary athletics and/or campus recreation programs, Mr. Mahoney aspires to continue researching various aspects of risk management in sport and the organizational effectiveness of campus recreation and post-secondary athletic programs. This is Mr. Mahoney's first published work.

Helen Pratt Mickens is a Fellow of the State Bar of Michigan, and a member of the state bars of Michigan and Louisiana. She served as a member of the Michigan Supreme Court Task Force on Gender Issues in the Courts, and as a member of the State Bar of Michigan Committee on Legal Education. She has been a franchise and securities examiner with the Michigan Department of Commerce, and a member of the board of directors of the Ingham County Bar Association. Professor Mickens has served on the board of Trustees for Kalamazoo College and Olivet College, as well as on a number of community and corporate boards. She served as an Associate Dean at Thomas M. Cooley Law School from 1982-1996.

Professor Mickens currently teaches Torts and Professional Responsibility.

Dick Moriarty is a retired professor from the Faculty of Human Kinetics, University of Windsor. From 1956 to 1985, he served as the first University of Windsor Director of Athletics (1956-1970) and Director of Men's Sport (1970-1985). He is Director of SIR/CAR (Sports Institute for Research/Change Agent Research), which he founded in 1970.

Professor Moriarty has a Ph.D. from the Ohio State University (1971), M.Ed. from Wayne State University (1966), M.A. from Assumption University of Windsor (1958) and a B.A. from Assumption College (1956). In 1985 he was awarded both the J.P. Loosemore Award for contribution to inter-university sport in Ontario and Canada, and the R. Tait MacKenzie Honours Award from the Canadian Association for Health, Physical Education and Recreation (CAHPER) for his contribution as a teacher, administrator and researcher. In 1993 he was named CAHPER Scholar for the year. Professor Moriarty has published and presented throughout his career.

Rebecca J. Mowrey is Assistant Director of Women's Athletics and an Associate Professor of Sport Management at Millersville University, Pennsylvania, USA, where she teaches in the area of legal issues of sport and recreation and risk management. She received her D.P.E. from Springfield College; M.S. from West Virginia University; and B.A. from Mount Union College. Professor Mowrey was formerly Chair of the Exercise and Sport Sciences Department at the University of Pittsburgh-Bradford (1984-1996) where she co-ordinated the Sport and Recreation Management undergraduate degree program. She is an active member of the Society for the Study of Legal Aspects of Sport and Physical Activity, AAHPERD, NASSM, NIRSA, and NACWAA. She has presented and published internationally and nationally in the area of sport law.

Tony Nurse received his Master's degree in Human Kinetics, with a major in Sports Management, from the University of Windsor. He has two Bachelors degrees from Dalhousie, one in History and the second in Sports Management. He has worked in the Campus Recreation programs at both Dalhousie and Windsor Universities. Mr. Nurse hopes to pursue a career in Athletics and Recreational Services.

He has been involved with triathlons and duathlons for three years, focussing particularly on duathlons. He placed third overall in the twenty-five to twenty-nine age group in the Ontario duathlon series last summer, and hopes to complete a Ironman triathlon in the next three years.

Charles A. Palmer is a professor of law at the Thomas M. Cooley Law School. He has written in the fields of entertainment and sports law.

CHAPTER 1

PHYSICAL ACTIVITY AND LEGAL LIABILITY

Dick Moriarity

The law surrounds, guides, restricts, and if necessary, punishes all of us without exception, from birth to death, and sometimes has its effects upon us before birth and after death (Post, 1963).

The pursuit of the law is relentless from the cradle to the grave and occasionally beyond; however until recent years (before 1980), the world of sports/athletics considered itself exempt from its restraint. Sports/athletics consisted of players, coaches, administrators and fans interacting on a basis of mutual trust and respect with the ethics and professional behaviour of voluntary mutual-benefit or service organizations. Even in nonvoluntary professional athletic organizations, or in the world of big-time government international competition, involvement or intrusion of the law was rare. Professional athletic organizations and athletes had their lawyers, but for the most part their business was contracted in private, with rare exceptions, and to a truly extraordinary degree even those directly involved seldom paid attention to legal issues related to potential liability associated with the activities of the game. Certainly athletic directors and coaches in educational institutions were blissfully unaware that legal concepts and machinery concerned them in any way and very few lawyers had occasion to deal with sports as anything but a form of entertainment. In actual fact, the amount of legal business involving sport or athletic organizations a couple of decades ago was very small, particularly in view of the ubiquitous nature of sport or athletic activities.

Things are radically different today. Not a week goes by without producing a major story involving the law on the sports pages of the daily paper. Few major decisions are made by sports/athletics authorities without prior advice of legal counsel. Legal fees have become a major operating expense for organizations ranging from little league baseball to professional football. In general, the more commercialized the athletic activity, the higher degree of legal involvement, however, amateur/school sport does not escape legal involvement and a heavy responsibility on those involved in amateur/school sport is an understanding of the role of the law in sport and athletics and a professional obligation to disseminate this knowledge to players, coaches, fans and administrators involved in sport activities.

The increase in legal action in the sporting world has been followed by an explosion in both the public and professional literature. In the past every once in a while something appeared concerning baseball and the anti-trust laws; a parliamentary/congressional investigation might bring famous athletics and lawyers before the cameras; an inquiry or investigation was commissioned periodically at the national or provincial/state level; and only rarely did an article appear reporting litigation in the amateur/school sport world (Koppett, 1973; Moriarty, 1978). Within the legal profession, and especially in law schools, articles or discussions of some legal aspect of sports (usually anti-trust) would surface periodically in the '50s and '60s (Brennan, 1967; Keith, 1958; Schulman & Baum, 1969; Comment, 1969; Note, 1970, and Comment, 1953). The entire number of single articles dealing with sport and the law in America and Canada in the 1960s has been more than duplicated by entire issues devoted to sport and law in the 1970s (see e.g. Ottawa Law Forum and Proceedings, 1977; Johnson, 1976; Bayles, 1978 — Canadian; "Athletics," *Law and Contemporary Problems*, 1973; "Symposium on Sports Law," *New York Law Forum*, 1973; "Symposium: Sports and the Law," *WSTUI Review*, 1976; "Symposium — Professional Sports and the Law," *William and Mary Law Review*, 1977; "Sports, Torts and Courts," *Trial*, 1977; "Sports and the Law," *Connecticut Law Review*, 1978; and Sobel, *Conference on Women's Sport and the Law*, 1976 — American). Added to this is a plethora of books and monographs in the '70s (Appenzeller, 1970, 1975, 1978; Weistart & Lowell, 1979; Sobel, 1976, 1977 — American; and Dewar and Moriarty, 1977 — Canadian), and a deluge in the '80s and '90s and beyond (see bibliography). The list of individual articles published throughout Canada and the United States is too lengthy to recount, however, it can readily be identified through Sports Information Resource Centre (SIRC) and the Educational Resource Information Center (ERIC) in Eugene, Oregon.

The intervention or intrusion of the law in sports has met with considerable hostility on all sides. For the most part, players, coaches, administrators, parents and spectators in amateur/school sport find it repugnant to have to resort to the law to secure natural justice, on the one hand, or compliance with rules or regulations, on the other hand. In high-level amateur and professional athletics, producers and consumers feel that they are involved in a "special, peculiar business" where game-result considerations take precedence over ordinary business, including legal considerations (Koppett, 1973: 816). To fans and to the journalists who are their extension, sports/athletics is appealing precisely because it is fun and games, essentially escapist entertainment in which "good guys" and "bad guys" are gloriously identifiable, and win-lose decisions satisfyingly clear cut (Coleman, 1964). When real-life questions of equity, compromise, search-for-justice, logical reasoning, restraining orders, and legal status impinge on this fundamental and emotional entertainment, the fun is spoiled. In general, those involved in sports/athletics know (or are convinced they know) everything significant about sport and the people involved; when sports/athletics veers off into legal areas, the sense of certainty is lost, and those involved resent it. Even lawyers are thoroughly bewildered and somewhat frustrated by the increased involvement of the law in sport or athletics.

Educators involved in sport or athletics are probably more concerned and frustrated by legal litigation than any other single topic in physical education today. Some of this concern derives from the lack of clear-cut direction or advice (or in some cases too much) from either the courts of law or educational institutions. More confusion and concern is often generated by the sensationalism of some press reports but a large portion is possibly caused by lack of knowledge on the part of educators of the process of law and an inability to understand the reasoning involved. As pointed out in the legal edition *Newsletter of the Ontario Association of School Physical and Health Educators* (Johnson, 1979), this confusion and frustration in part "arises from the fundamental difference between education and the law" (Johnson, 1979: 3). Education is, by its very nature, constantly changing and bringing about change. In education not only is the pupil changed, and in such a manner that it is impossible to forecast the degree of change, but the teacher is changed, the school is changed, the whole world is changed. Law, which is founded on precedent and assumes regular behaviour, must be at odds with this ever-changing educational process. This fundamental difference between education and the law is further confounded in sport or athletics, where participants and administrators are fundamentally problem-solvers and are inclined to weigh the practical realities of the situation with an eye to working out a resolution. Lawyers, on the other hand, are gladiators, rather than conciliators, and their adversary stance is fundamentally at odds with the idea of settling lawsuits by cooperative give-and-take (Solomon, 1979). Lawyers, indeed, can become obstacles to a settlement, especially during the pre-trial discovery phase of legal action, when they often skirmish over what documents and depositions are relevant as potential evidence. Moreover, a by-the-clock fee system, minimally $200 to $300 per hour or more for a partner's time, and perhaps more to secure specialized legal representation, rewards the protracted jousting that characterizes large-scale litigation. This fee and format is particularly frustrating for those involved in voluntary activities such as school or amateur sport. Lawyers do settle most suits before they go to trial, but usually not until both sides have wearied of the escalating costs and the disruptive effects on operations. More cases could probably be settled at an earlier stage if those involved in sport or athletics understood the distinction between the confrontation of litigation versus the cooperation of negotiation or problem solving. Note the trend to Alternate Dispute Resolution (ADR) and refer to the Chapter in this text. Those who have been involved in legal action generally agree that it is better to deal with conflict by problem solving, compromise or peaceful co-existence, rather than engaging in a win-lose power struggle through legal litigation. The cost in human and physical resources is staggering when sport or athletic organizations play Russian roulette with a judge and jury.

What to Do in Case of a Lawsuit

Since anyone can file a lawsuit against anybody for just about anything, those involved in sports/athletics should know what to do and what to expect if involved in a lawsuit. The question may arise, "What do I do when something happens that may lead to a lawsuit?" The answer is simple — call your insurance carrier and your lawyer, in that order (Ross, 1978). This will assure a prompt investigation of the entire case when all events are still fresh in everybody's mind, so that the actual facts may be accurately preserved for presentation later, perhaps years later. It will also protect you against taking any action that could prejudice your position at a later date.

Be sure to keep detailed notes on everything that happened, including the names and addresses of all pertinent witnesses, even those people who say they don't know anything. Many times, under skilful questioning, they may recall useful facts.

Be reluctant to discuss any aspects of the case without the advice of your attorney; this applies particularly to the news media. This should not imply that you are trying to "cover up" or "hide" anything, but merely that any public statement should be delayed until all the facts are known. Many times statements are made at or about the time of an incident, which later turn out not to be the true facts at all, after an investigation has been completed. In short, keep your mouth shut; for in a court of law it is logic, not emotion, that will decide the issue. Trials resulting from lawsuits are actually relatively simple mechanisms to understand, while being difficult and expensive to use.

Table 1.1
WHAT TO DO IN EVENT OF POTENTIAL LAWSUIT

1. CARE OF VICTIM
2. EMPLOYMENT OF A SCRIBE
3. CONTACT YOUR EMPLOYER
4. CONTACT INSURANCE AGENT AND LAWYER
5. AVOID DISCUSSION OF THE ISSUE
6. TRY TO SETTLE OUT OF COURT

Your chances of being involved in litigation are greatly reduced if you conduct your activities as carefully, discreetly, and conservatively as possible. Act like a wise, prudent and caring parent and as a competent professional educator using sport or athletics as an educational vehicle. Before liability can be established in a typical case, a breach of duty, or violation of a right must be proven by the allegedly aggrieved party. This proof comes in almost all cases at the trial of the lawsuit, anywhere from six months to five years after the lawsuit is started.

Fortunately, most legitimate claims are settled before trial, some even before a lawsuit is filed.

Critical Path in a Law Suit

Lawsuits are conducted pursuant to Rules of Civil Procedure. These Rules are very specific and technical; however, they are extremely valuable and helpful in charting the course that a lawsuit will follow.

A critical path for the first six months to five years includes:

1. A "pleading," usually called a "complaint" in the United States and "statement of claim" in Canada, setting forth the material facts that the aggrieved party — the plaintiff — alleges gave rise to his or her injury is prepared and sent to the defendant and filed with the court. Notice of the lawsuit gives the defendant an opportunity to respond and rebut the allegations in an "answer." Frequently, the best defense is a good offense and, therefore, the answer is frequently a "counter-claim" indicating the defendant has been libelled and/or adding additional parties so that all people and institutions who may be liable are within the jurisdiction of the court.

2. Once the initial pleas are filed and everyone is "in court," the "discovery period" follows (several weeks to several months depending upon the magnitude or complexity of the case).

3. During the "discovery period" as many facts as possible about the lawsuit are ascertained, i.e., how the event developed, who the witnesses were, how much damage has been sustained, and similar matters of a factual nature. This is accomplished either through (a) "interrogatories" to the other party, a series of written questions that must be answered under oath, or (b) "through depositions" where the party to be questioned is physically present with attorneys for all parties. The attorneys ask questions that are answered by the witnesses, plaintiff or defendant, and the answers are taken down verbatim by the court recorder and transcribed and added to the record in the court file. These documents can be used at the trial as part of the evidence to refresh the memory of the plaintiff, defendant or witness, or to attack the credibility of those involved in the event if any answers have changed. What you say is important, but even more important in a deposition is what you do not say. For the most part, the statements will not be used to support your position, but rather will be used to attack your position.

4. After the period of discovery there are several alternative courses of action such as (a) a "summary judgement" where the facts are not in dispute and the outcome of the case depends solely on which law is to be applied or (b) a trial if there is a genuine dispute over material facts.

5. Development of a "trial brief" prior to the beginning of the actual trial during which the lawyers prepare for every contingency that could occur at the trial, reviewing all the facts, talking in detail to all witnesses and potential witnesses, completing the legal research necessary to present the client's legal position as favourably as possible, and to assist the judge in grasping the essence of the case.

6. A trial has several distinct parts, such as selection of a jury, and the presentation of opening statements to the jury, during which the lawyers tell the jury what they are attempting to prove or disprove.

7. After the opening statement the plaintiff then presents their case and if the plaintiff cannot offer sufficient evidence to prove his or her case, then it can be dismissed by the judge, on proper motion by means of a directed verdict.

8. If the plaintiff does offer sufficient evidence to establish a *prima facie* case, then the court case proceeds. The defendant is judged innocent or liable, and if they are liable, damages must be determined. The defense will argue damages are not as large as they are claimed to be by the plaintiff.

How to Avoid Legal Litigation

The majority of cases that appear in the American and Canadian courts related to school/amateur sports or athletics are cases involving:

basis of "vicarious liability" and may be held liable because of the master-servant relationship between the coach and the organization. In general, as we pass from voluntary mutual-benefit or service organizations that are private in nature, to public business or government organizations, of either a non-profit or for profit nature, the probability of litigation increases. Of course, all involved in sport or athletics are responsible for their behaviour; however, the courts do allow more freedom and flexibility for those involved in voluntary non-incorporated organizations as opposed to those involved in public incorporated organizations.

Sport or athletic litigation is usually examined in law under the law of torts, although hockey violence has occasionally been subject to criminal sanctions. In examining the law of torts (civil wrongs), there are five areas of concern that can be applied to charges of negligence.

1. A "duty of care" existing between the representatives of the sport or athletic organization and the players.
2. A "standard of care" to which the executive or coach is expected to conform in relation to the participants.
3. "Injury" or "damage" (physical or personal) resulting to the participants.
4. A causal "connection" between the conduct of the executive or coaches and the injury to the participant ("proximate cause").
5. The "defendant's part" in his/her injury ("contributory negligence").

Liability in broad terms refers to one's legal responsibility for incurred injury, physical or otherwise, that usually arises out of negligence. Negligence in this sense is legally defined as "failure to act as a reasonable and prudent person would act under the circumstances" (Coaching Association of Canada, 1979). In addition to the "reasonable and prudent person" responsibility, coaches and officials in school/amateur sport are increasingly being subjected to responsibility to act as a "competent instructor." Recently, there has been increased litigation based on "instructional incompetence and infringement of individual rights." Schools and professional associations who offer certification as

---

Table 1.2
STEPS IN LEGAL TRIAL

1. CHARGE
2. SERVING OF WRIT
3. PLEADINGS   STATEMENT OF CLAIM
                       STATEMENT OF DEFENSE
4. EXAMINATION FOR DISCOVERY PERIOD
5. TRIAL — SUMMARY JUDGEMENT
6. TRIAL BRIEFS
7. TRIAL   PLAINTIFF
                 DEFENDANT
8. WITNESSES
9. CLOSING STATEMENT   PLAINTIFF
                             DEFENDANT
10. JUDGEMENT   INNOCENT
                          GUILTY
                          MISTRIAL
11. SENTENCE/ASSESSMENT OF DAMAGE
        SPECIAL — PHYSICAL INJURY
        GENERAL — TRIAL EXPENSES
                          PAIN/DISABILITY
                          LOSS OF EARNINGS
                          LOSS OF AMENITIES
                          LOSS OF LIFE
                             EXPECTANCY
                          FUTURE LOSS OF
                             EARNINGS
                          FUTURE PAIN &
                             SUFFERING
                          FUTURE CARE

---

1. Negligence,
2. "Due process" regarding eligibility and discrimination,
3. Violence (assault and battery).

The disposition of these cases is related to the nature of the organization (private voluntary association versus public non-voluntary organization), precedent and public statute, and the relationship that exists between the participants in the school/amateur sports or athletics organization. In cases involving negligence on the part of the coach, the organization may also be joined on the

Table 1.3
NEGLIGENCE — THE BASIS OF TORT LIABILITY

1. A DUTY OF CARE OWED BY THE DEFENDANT TO THE PLAINTIFF, REQUIRING THAT THE DEFENDANT MEET A CERTAIN STANDARD OF CARE.
2. A BREACH OF THE ESTABLISHED STANDARD OF CARE OR A FAILURE TO CONFORM TO IT.
3. ACTUAL INJURY(IES) SUFFERED BY THE PLAINTIFF.
4. A PROXIMATE CONNECTION BETWEEN THE DEFENDANT'S CONDUCT AND THE PLAINTIFF'S INJURY(IES).
5. NO CONDUCT BY THE PLAINTIFF THAT WILL BE PREJUDICIAL TO HIS ACTION (i.e., VOLUNTARY ASSUMPTION OF RISK).

---

coaches and administrators should ensure that their training experiences leading to certification embody sufficient practical and up-to-date knowledge to avoid claims of negligence in training or qualification (Coaching Association of Canada, 1979: 3).

Generally, the following precautions should be taken to avoid damage suits:

1. Provide a safe environment for the activity,
2. Provide safe equipment and apparatus,
3. Provide adequate supervision of activities,
4. Provide adequate qualified medical assistance,
5. Provide suitable competition/activity taking individual preparation and differences in size and skill under consideration,
6. Provide qualified properly-trained instructors,
7. Provide due process in dealing with coach/athlete conflicts,
8. Provide clear, written rules for training and general conduct, and *most important*
9. Obtain appropriate general liability insurance coverage (see Chapter 14 on insurance).

School/amateur sports are replete with situations that may, or have already resulted in legal action involving coaches, executives and officials. Competitive sports and the high level of physical challenge and emotional excitement that accompany them, are an attraction for children/youth but offer a Pandora's box of potential problems for individuals and groups involved in sponsoring these activities. Increased participation, inherent physical danger, new activities and potentially dangerous equipment in sports/athletics create unusual risks and hazards that require closer supervision, better instruction, and regular inspection of equipment and facilities.

If the safety implications of judicial statements are fully comprehended, sponsors of sports/athletics activities will understand that the best way to avoid serious financial or personal sacrifice because of decisions is to act in a non-negligent or responsible manner. Guidelines for teachers and coaches as spelled out by Robert Forester, reporting to the Toronto Metropolitan Board, provide excellent guidance for coaches involved in school/amateur sports/athletics (Forester, 1979: 1-3).

As Forester points out, historically torts were avenged in blood. Hammurabi's law code of "an eye for an eye" was a social step forward since it limited the amount of revenge and ultimately led to the concept of the use of money as a method of compensating for damages and injury.

The great majority of sport tort liability cases rest on alleged failure to safeguard a child or youth involved in sport or athletics from foreseeable harm. Did the executive or coach act as "a reasonable and prudent man would act under the same or similar circumstances." Indeed, courts may demand a higher level of caution and competence, since sport or athletics provide an allurement for children and youth.

The test for negligence consists of four consecutive questions that the courts usually ask if the coach acted as a normal, prudent parent would have acted under the same or similar circumstances:

1. Did the defendant or defendants owe the plaintiff a duty?
2. Was there a breach of the duty owed?
3. Was the breach the proximate cause of the injury?
4. Was there actual loss or damage resulting to the interests of another?

Where all four questions can be answered in the affirmative, the courts will rule, as a matter of law, that negligence was present. Where there is no negligence, there is usually no liability. Within the broad framework of existing law, it may be suggested that the broad duties of those involved in children/youth sports or athletics are:

1. Anticipation of foreseeable risk,
2. Reasonable steps to prevent those risks from occurring,
3. Warning and care addressed towards those risks that for whatever reason cannot be reduced or averted,
4. A duty to aid the injured,
5. A duty not to increase the severity of injury.

Variables and Relationships in Negligence

The expectations of the court for sport or athletic organizations are based on a number of factors:

1. The "age" of the player;
2. The "nature of the activity";
3. The "amount of instruction" received by the player and/or coach or official;
4. The coach, official or player's "general awareness of risk" and harm;
5. The "approved general practice";
6. The "foreseeable risk," damage or harm; and
7. "Previous accidents" in similar circumstances (Johnson, 1979:4).

Table 1.4
VARIABLES IN LAW

1. AGE
2. NATURE OF ACTIVITY
3. AMOUNT OF INSTRUCTION
4. GENERAL AWARENESS OF RISK
5. APPROVED GENERAL PRACTICE
6. FORESEEABLE RISK OF DAMAGE/HARM
7. PREVIOUS ACCIDENTS IN SIMILAR SITUATIONS

In general the following relationships exist:

1. There is a negative correlation between age and responsibility, i.e., the younger the players, the higher the demand for responsibility and care. It is not likely that the courts would rule favourably upon treating children and youth in school/amateur sports in a way that is appropriate for employees of professional athletic organizations. Is your program commensurate with the age and ability of the players?
2. There is a positive correlation between the degree of danger in the nature of the activity and the degree of responsibility required. The duty of supervision as a careful, responsible parent increases as we go from non-contact individual and dual sports (tennis and badminton) to collision team activities (football and hockey). Some activities, such as swimming and gymnastics, carry with them specific demands for vigilance in supervision and coaching. Is your equipment safety-checked regularly and is it appropriate for the needs and abilities of participants?
3. There is a negative correlation between the quality and amount of instruction given, and the supervision required. A high school age student who has been taught the drive block in football as outlined in the coaching certification program is less likely to hurt himself or someone else, than a player who has not been taught the fundamentals of blocking and is simply told to "take the opposing player out." The more instruction given, the less supervision may be necessary. Coaches will not be held liable merely for conducting an activity that contains an element of danger. Has coaching instruction followed a logical progression from simpler to more complex activity?
4. There is a negative correlation between players' general awareness of risk and danger and the liability of the coach, i.e., the more explicitly and accurately the coach describes inherent dangers or elements of danger, the

more likely the courts will rule that the player has accepted the risk involved in the activity. Are safety factors explained fully and are they insisted upon?

5. There is a positive correlation between the approved general practice of supervision and the expectations of the courts for that supervision, i.e., if it is general practice to have a doctor and ambulance in attendance at high school football games, it is more likely that the courts will find negligence on the part of organizations not providing this precaution. Is it reasonable to place a high school student trainer in charge of first aid and medical assistance in a high risk sport?

6. There is a positive correlation between the foreseeable risk of danger and the need for supervision, i.e., in a high-risk sport such as hockey there is higher expectation of the court for coaching and medical expertise than in a low-risk sport such as softball. It should be cautioned that in activities where the risk of an accident is small and the consequences of such an accident are severe, or catastrophic extra precautions to prevent such an accident must be taken. This judgement has special bearing on such activities as gymnastics and trampolining. Is there a skill-training program for participants and leaders before the sport or athletic activity begins?

7. There is a positive correlation between previous acts and incidents in similar circumstances, and the expectations of the court for vigilance, i.e., if there is a high incidence of eye or tooth injury in hockey and lacrosse, it can be expected that the courts will expect school/amateur sport organizations, executives and coaches to take precautions to prevent such incidents. This is particularly true where research studies have been conducted and valid, reliable and objective data is available on the incidence of injury associated with particular practices. Is there a regular review of injuries as to their nature and causes, and is in-service instruction provided for coaches and officials to refresh them on existing techniques and methods and/or innovative techniques and methods?

**Table 1.5
LIABILITY — RULES OF THUMB**

1. - r AGE, DEMAND OF CARE
2. + r DEGREE OF RISK & DUTY OF SUPERVISION
3. - r QUALITY & AMOUNT OF INSTRUCTION AND SUPERVISION
4. - r AWARENESS OF RISK & LIABILITY "INFORMED CONSENT"
5. + r APPROVED GENERAL PRACTICE AND SUPERVISION
6. + r FORESEEABLE RISK & NEED FOR SUPERVISION
7. + r PREVIOUS ACTS & INCIDENCE OF VIGILANCE

+ r = Positive correlation, as factor goes up, liability goes up.
- r = Negative correlation, as factor goes up, liability goes down, or factor goes down, liability goes up.

Liability for Injuries in Sports Activities

John Barnes of Carleton University pointed out at the University of Ottawa Law Forum that "Canada is not particularly litigation conscious and it is the rare incident that gives rise to potential liability. The law fairly clearly recognizes that the person engaged in a sport voluntarily "assumes the risks" that are inherent in the sport" (Barnes, 1988). On the other hand, there is no immunity from civil or criminal action simply because the injury has occurred in a sport's setting. The rash of criminal actions against National Hockey league players precipitated by Attorney General Roy McMurtry of Ontario attests to this fact (Moriarty, 1993). The 1980s have also seen a rash of negligence cases in our schools, fitness and parks and recreation settings.

To be actionable a sports injury must be attributed to some sort of fault, and civil action will succeed only where a causal connection can be shown between some fault on the part of the defendant (coach, instructor or executive) and the injury that is sustained by the claimant (player or participant). The claimant or plaintiff has very difficult problems of proof and the burden is on the claimant to prove his/her case. The legal remedy where liability is determined is most often in the form of monetary damage in order to "put a person who is injured in the position he would have been but for the injury, insofar as money can compensate" (Barnes, 1988; Wong, 1994; Hronek & Spengler, 1997). Generally, the judgement is compensatory with damages awarded for such things as earning, pain and suffering, medical expenses, and in extreme cases loss of amenities to compensate for a person's diminished or denied opportunities to engage in his or her favourite activities. Punitive damages can be awarded in cases where there has been a deliberate or flagrant invasion of the plaintiff's interests as in cases of assault and battery. Punitive damages are defined as "damages in excess of what it would take to compensate the plaintiff" (ibid.).

There are a variety of types of actions that might arise out of a sport's situation. The injuries arising out of the ordinary rough-and-tumble of a particular sport are not actionable; however, anything that goes beyond the implied consent of the participants is actionable. For example, a fistfight in a hockey game would probably be within the implied consent of the sport; whereas, a kicking incident would not. Similarly, a spectator at a hockey game, for instance, might reasonably expect to be struck by a flying puck, but not by a stick in the hands of a player. Theoretically, even when an injury occurs unintentionally, an athlete or spectator could take action against another for negligence. Again, the burden of proof is on the claimant (plaintiff) and a causal connection must be shown between the defendant's conduct and the injury sustained by the claimant.

Traditional Sources of Litigation

Listed below are some typical liability actions related to sports/athletics:

Liability for Injury to Participants

The most direct type of liability resulting from sport activity is that which arises as a consequence of injury suffered by a participant. The most frequent allegation and claim for relief is that the person or institution from whom recovery is sought was negligent. The most frequent defense is "contributory negligence and/or assumption of risk." Assumption of risk may arise in any of four circumstances. The first is where one by expressed consent relieves another of the obligation to exercise care for his or her protection, and agrees to take the chance of injury from unknown or possible risk. The second is where one enters a relationship with another that involves a known risk, and is deemed to have relieved the person of the responsibility for that risk. The third occurs when one is aware of the risk caused by potential negligence of another and yet proceeds to encounter it voluntarily. Finally, one may proceed to encounter a risk that is so unreasonably great as to render the party guilty of contributory negligence, so that the recovery is barred by both assumption of the risk and the contributory negligence principles (Weistart & Lowell, 1979: 935-936; Van der Smissen, 1990; Nygaard & Boone, 1989).

The courts have imposed liability where an injury is caused by an athlete's having been required by a coach to compete while injured; by failure of the coach or team physician to render proper medical attention; by failure of the coach to provide proper equipment; and by negligent instruction of a coach. Liability has also been imposed when injury is a result of the negligence of a referee in not detecting the use of an illegal wrestling hold, or failing to properly supervise a game (ibid.).

Liability for Injury to Spectators

There is always danger that sports activities will cause injuries to spectators when errantly hit or thrown balls escape the playing field, or when over-eager tacklers pursue their game into the sidelines. The courts have evolved the general rule that spectators at sports activities assume, as a matter of law, all of the ordinary inherent risks of the sport that they are observing. This is frequently framed in terms of a "common knowledge" rule, i.e., risk of injury posed to spectators that any person of reasonable intelligence could not help but realize and is deemed to have accepted or assumed. The degree of popularity and time of exposure of a sport is significant.

In California, during the 1970s, the courts decided that the common knowledge rule applied in baseball cases, but did not apply in hockey injuries (ibid.) since it was a recently introduced pro sport.

Waiver and Release of Liability

In light of the extensive liability inherent in the conduct of any sporting enterprise, it is not surprising that those who sponsor sporting events, being aware of significant risk of injury to participants or spectators, seek to acquire release from any liability arising therein. Immunity from such liability is almost impossible. Negligence is negligence, or as one judge put it, an injury caused by negligence is not strictly speaking an accident (Barnes, 1988).

Liability for Injuries in Educational Programs

The most common context in which sports activities take place is in public and private educational institutions sponsored by either school or amateur sport organizations. With respect to athletic activities conducted under their auspices, educational institutions have the duty to exercise reasonable care to prevent reasonably foreseeable risks and where such risks are foreseen, take sufficient precautions to protect the students in their custody. This general duty can be translated into several specific obligations, namely: (1) establishment and enforcement of rules for the maintenance of discipline in sport and recreational activities; (2) provision of adequate supervision; (3) exercise of due care in the selection of supervisors and coaches; (4) the provision of suitable equipment and facilities for the conduct of sport and recreational activities.

Most liability suits involve litigation against the coach and the sponsoring school or amateur sport organization. The principle of *respondeat superior* or master-servant suggests that the sponsoring organization is responsible for the behaviour of the coach. Relief from this responsibility has been sought by arguing that (1) its institutional statutory duty is fully discharged if its own duties are satisfactorily performed; or (2) institutions are not subject to negligence liability as a result of the sovereign and/or (3) charitable immunity doctrine; or (4) that teachers and coaches are not ordinary employees. Since the 1970s the trend is away from court's recognition of these arguments; in other words, if the coach fails to perform the supervisory duties properly, then the employer-institution will be vicariously liable (ibid., 974; Johnson, 1978: 2; Hronek & Spengler, 1997).

In light of the potential liability that confronts institutions that conduct sports activities, it may be well to ask whether the assets of the institution may be insulated from sports-related liability by forming a separate corporation through which the activities will be conducted. Incorporation provides asset-insulation because it is a legal entity separate and distinct from its shareholders. Thus, when injury recoveries are awarded the only assets available for their satisfaction are those of the corporation, and the shareholders are liable only for the limited amount of capital that they have exchanged for their shares of stocks.

If an educational institution or an athletic organization is authorized to form such a corporation, the basic legal question that it will present is whether the corporation will be a viable legal entity. As a general rule, a corporation will be recognized as a separate entity. If the facts in a given case, however, indicate that the corporation is merely the alter-ego of its organizers and is not in fact operated as a separate entity, then it might be disregarded, with the result that there would then be no limited liability advantage to its shareholders (Gillespie, 1989: 363). A corporation formed to conduct sports/athletics activities will normally be recognized as a viable entity so long as it has control of its own decision-making and is independent of the educational institution that is responsible for its initial organization. To the extent, however, that the corporation is subject to control, either financial or administration, of the institution, or is set up with the evidently dominant purpose of avoiding specific tort liability, the corporation's separate identity will be more likely to be disregarded (Weistart & Lowell, 1979: 978-979, Moriarty, 1993). A sports-governing body is likely to be causally quite removed from the actual incident in a specific facility that brings about an injury. There are, however, certain circumstances under which a sports-governing body might be liable. If, for instance, an association operates an event of some sort, then it would probably be subject to occupier's liability. It would, in other words, be responsible for the general safety of the facility, the supervision of crowds, the conditions of equipment, and so on. Sports-governing bodies using coaching manuals, coaching training programs and coaching certification, and/or involved in the sale of sporting equipment are also liable to be sued by athletes, although the plaintiff would probably have difficulty providing a causal connection and hence negligence on the part of the sports-governing body (Barnes, 1988; Van der Smissen, 1990).

Liability of Coaches

Since coaches normally have the most direct control of the activities of athletes, it is not surprising that they are frequently named as defendants in suits brought by injured athletes. In these cases, the critical inquiry will be whether the coach has fulfilled his duty to exercise reasonable care for the protection of athletes under his or her supervision, which duty will be satisfied by providing proper instruction on how to play the game and by showing due concern that the athletes are in proper condition and suitably equipped. The coach is not, however, an insurer of the athlete's safety and the duty of care will be satisfied if the coach takes all reasonable steps to minimize the possibility of their injury in games that involve an inevitable amount of physical contact (ibid., 980; McGee vs Board of Education of the City of New York, 1962). Thus, a coach who has properly instructed the players will not be liable for injuries caused when a first baseman hits another participant with a wild throw (McGee, 1962), or when a slightly injured player is sent home without first receiving medical aid (Dutter vs Gaines, 1951). Similarly in Vendrell vs School District #26C, Malheur County (1962) where a high school football player suffered a broken neck and became a permanent paraplegic, when he charged headfirst into approaching tacklers the court ruled:

> No one expects a football coach to extract from the game the body clashes that cause bruises, jolts and hard falls. To remove them would end the sport. The coach's function is to minimize the possibility that the body contact *may result in something more than slight injury*. The extensive calisthenics, running and other forms of muscular exercise to which the ... coaches subjected the ... subjects were intended to place the students in sound physical condition so that they could withstand the shock, blows and other rough treatment with which they would meet in actual play (Vendrell vs School District #26C, Malheur County, 1962).

On the other hand, liability has been found where the coach required a player to compete when he or she knows, or in the exercise of ordinary care should have known, that:

1. The player was already suffering from serious injury to his back or spine (Morris vs Union High School District A, King County, 1952);
2. Directed that a severely injured player be carried from the field without awaiting the arrival of medical assistance (Welch vs Dunsmuir Joint Union School Dist., 1958);
3. Allowed a team to compete against an opponent whose players are grossly disproportionate in size and ability (Vendrell vs School District #26C, Malheur County, 1961);
4. Allowed spectators to congregate so close to the playing field as to pose a danger to the players (Domino vs Mercurio, 1963);
5. Failed to instruct wrestlers properly in the use of and defense to certain holds that may pose danger of physical injury (Stehn vs Bernarr MacFadden Foundations, Inc., 1970); or
6. Instructed one team member to drive others home after practice, although the driver was known to be "a reckless driver of an unsafe jalopy" (Hanson vs Reedley Joint Union High School Dist., 1941).

Coaches are frequently liable for making demands which exceed their role as coach, i.e., (1) conducting initiation services (DeGooyer vs Harkness, 1961), and/or (2) demanding behaviour outside of the general physiological, psychological, or (3) social demands of the sport activity in question (see below, due process).

Liability for Providing Medical Treatment for Athletic Injuries

Generally, under the common law system, a person is not under a duty to administer first aid to a stranger.

This seemingly callous rule has its origin in the concept that it is not the purpose of the law to dictate morality. But if a special relationship exists involving a responsibility to supervise or take care of people in one's charge as in the relationship between the coach and the athlete, then one is under a duty to administer first aid.

Different standards of care are expected of different individuals. A physician is bound to professional standards; whereas a coach is not expected to provide the same standard of care as a doctor. The coach, however, is held to a duty more demanding than the ordinary person since, presumably, the coach has had some experience with sports injuries and their treatment (Barnes, 1988; Weistart & Lowell, 1979: 982; Nygaard & Boone, 1989; Hronek & Spengler, 1997).

In a relationship where one is under a duty to administer first aid, then one is liable for "worsenment" or deterioration that treatment might cause. It should also be noted that some jurisdictions have what is known as a "Good Samaritan status" under which persons providing gratuitous assistance to someone who is injured are not liable for any injury their treatment may cause, or their liability will depend upon conduct in excess of ordinary negligence.

Trainers are particularly susceptible to litigation related to liability for providing medical treatment. The Ontario Drugless Practitioners Act under RRO 1960 REG 121S.6/ states that the restrictions regarding physiotherapy treatment such as ultrasound, shortwave diathermy, microwave, "does not apply to or affect trainers for athletic or sporting clubs or associations so long as they confine their services to members of such clubs or associations during their training or playing seasons." At the Royal Military College in Kingston, Ontario the right of the athletic trainer to use any rehabilitation techniques, electromedical or otherwise is being questioned by the Chief Medical Officer at the base. The latter, but not the trainer, is a registered physiotherapist (*Journal of Canadian Athletic Therapists Association*, 1979: 23-25). Initially, the athletic trainer was restricted to immediate care (first aid) and prevention (taping, exercise, etc.) and subsequently this was liberalized to include rehabilitation treatment when (a) the team physician is present in the clinic and (b) under specific direction from the base physiotherapist.

The persons and/or organizations in charge of sports activities will have a duty to secure or provide reasonable medical assistance to injured participants or spectators as soon as possible under the circumstances. Thus, liability would presumably not be found where coach, trainer and attendant provided first aid or secured medical assistance as quickly as reasonably possible (Ryan, 1973; Van der Smissen, 1990). The decision to summon medical aid or transport the injured player to a hospital should be made by a competent medical authority. A football coach was held liable for serious injuries suffered by one of his players when, despite suspicions that the player had suffered a severe neck or back injury, he directed that the player be carried from the field by eight of his teammates without awaiting the arrival of a physician (Welch vs Dunsmuir Joint Union High School district, 1958). It is best to have a doctor in attendance at collision or high injury incidence sport activities. Even a doctor may be liable if negligence can be shown (W. Proser, 1971: 162); it should be noted that the standard of care is not altered by the fact that a doctor is acting gratuitously, though "Good Samaritan statutes" have been enacted in some states/provinces that would limit liability to situations involving intentional misconduct or grossly negligent practice (Harney, 1973: 1.5; Van der Smissen, 1990).

Treatment of injured athletes is particularly liable when the injured person questions the medical competency of the coach or trainer (Weistart & Lowell, 1979: 982); or the patient has not provided "informed consent" (Harney, 1973: 58; Nygaard & Boone, 1989).

It is axiomatic that the doctor-patient relationship is a "fiduciary" relation in which the doctor will have a duty to maintain the confidence of disclosures made by the patient during the course of treatment (Harney, 1973: 1.6; Van der Smissen, 1990). This relationship takes precedence over the responsibility of the doctor to the school or sport organization. Additional candidates for liability in doctor-athlete cases are schools vicariously liable for the conduct of the doctor (Fahr "Legal Liabilities for Athletic Injuries," 1963: 220-221; Nygaard & Boone, 1989). Such liability may be imposed on the school only if the doctor is acting as an employee of the school as opposed to an independent contractor, i.e., the school doctor may make the institution liable, whereas a community doctor contracted or gratuitously performing may alleviate the institution of responsibility.

Liability for Defective Athletic Equipment — Negligence Liability

Product liability is an up and coming area of the law. When you use a sports product, you accept the ordinary risks that are incidental to such use. But you do not accept the risk or defects or inherent danger that might be in the product itself. To some extent the manufacturer is under a duty to accept some misuse or light deviation from the standard use. If an injury is attributable to extraordinary use of the product, there will be no liability on the supplier. Additionally, the seller or renter of a product is liable if goods are not fit for the purpose for which they are sold or rented (Barnes, 1988).

The school or athletic organization that supplies equipment to participants is liable for physical harm caused by the use of the product in the manner for which it was supplied if (1) it has reason to know that the product is dangerous for the use for which it is supplied; (2) it had no reason to believe that those who use the product will realize its dangerous condition; and (3) it fails to exercise reasonable care to inform them of the product's condition or the facts that make it likely to be dangerous (Kelak vs Maszczenski, 1968: 434).

These principles were applied in Vendrell vs School District #26C, Malheur county (1962) where an injured high school football player brought an action alleging, *inter alia*, that the equipment that had been given to him was defective. The evidence showed that the player had selected the equipment from a table on which it had been placed the day after he reported for practice, and that it consisted of the usual helmet, pads and uniform used for competitive football. Thereafter, the helmet originally selected developed a crack and the player selected another helmet from several that were available. He used the helmet although he knew that it was "just a bit loose" as were the shoulder pads, and he also knew that others were readily available. The courts held that there had been no negligence in the provision of equipment and noted that the player.

> conceded that he did not mention to the manager, the coaches or any other school representative the fault that he found with the gear. He also conceded ... that he had the privilege of returning any of his equipment and of selecting a substitute ... we have studied the evidence with care and have found no indication that the plaintiff's equipment, if it was not proper, had any bearing on the happening of his injury. (Further) if it was in any way unsuitable to the plaintiff's needs, he was immediately familiar with the fact and voluntarily decided to proceed. This, we believe, is the proper case to employ the rule denoted by the phrase *volenti non fit injuria* (assumption of the risk) (Vendrell vs School District #26C, Malheur Count, 1962: 412).

Manufacturers are particularly liable for litigation related to inferior equipment. Although the rule was once followed that only those who dealt directly with the manufacturer could recover for the injuries caused by its products (Winterbottom vs Wright, 1842: 302), that rule has been generally repudiated (MacPherson vs Buick Motor Company, 1916: 1050).

It is now clear that any user whom the manufacturer should expect to use the product may recover from injuries caused by excesses or omissions of the manufacturer (Quova vs Harley-Davidson Motor Company, 1979: 800).

The courts also note that the mere fact that the product meets or exceeds the requirements of the industry is not conclusive of its reasonable safety. Negligence has been found for failure of a manufacturer to properly test vaulting poles that it sold to pole vaulters (McCormick vs Lowe & Campbell Athletic Goods Company, 1940: 866); and to make shatterproof the sunglasses it sold to baseball players (Filler vs Rayex Corporation, 1970: 336).

The sellers of athletic equipment may also be held liable for defective products. One who sells a product that is unreasonably dangerous because of a defective condition is subject to the liability for the physical harm caused thereby to the ultimate user or consumer, provided the seller is in the business of selling such products and the product has not been substantially changed (Weistart & Lowell, 1979: 1001; Wong, 1994). School boards or athletic organizations that sell or resell equipment may liable for product liability.

Canadian Table of Cases

Definition of the Standard of Care Owed by Teachers to Their Pupils
Williams V. Eady, (1893) 10 T.L.R. 41 (CA)

Cases Involving Extra-Curricular School Activities
Edmondson V. Board of Trustees for the Moose Jaw School District, (1920) 3 W.W.R. 979 (SASK. CA)
Gard v. Board of School Trustees of Duncan, (1946) 1 W.W.R. 305 (BCCA)
Moddejonge v. Huron County Board of Education (1972) 2 or 437 (Ont. H. CT.) (Outdoor Education-Field Trip)

Cases Involving Games, Races, Etc.
Boese v. Board of Education of St. Paul's Roman Catholic Separate School District No. 20 (Saskatoon), (1976) Q.B. 607 (QBD)
Dunn v. University of Ottawa [1995] O.J.No.2856 (QL)
Eaton v. Casuta, (1977) 75 DLR (3rd) 476 (BCSC)
Jones v. London County Council, (1932) 96 J.P. 371 (CA)
Ralph v. London County Council, (1947) 111 J.P. 246 (KBD) affirmed by Court of Appeal (1947) 111 J.P. 548

Cases Involving Class Wrestling Matches
Hail v. Thompson (1952) OWN 133 affirmed (1952) OWN 478 (ONT. CA)
Piszel v. Board of Education for Etobicoke, (1977) 16 O.R. (2nd) 22 (ONT. CA)

Cases Involving Vaulting Over a Box-Horse
Butterworth v. Collegiate Institute Board of Ottawa, (1940) 3 D.L.R. 466 (ONT. S. CA.)
Gibbs v. Barking Corporation, (1936) 1 all er 115 (CA)
Tomlinson v. Manchester Corporation, (1947) 111 J.P. 503
Wright v. Cheshire County Council, (1952) 2 ALL ER 789 (CA)

Cases Involving Other Gymnastic Exercises
McKay v. Board of Govan School and Molesky, (1968) S.C.R. 589 (S.C.C.)

Murray v. Board of Education of the City of Belleville, (1943) 1 D.L.R. 494 (ONT. H. CT.)
Myers v. Peel County Board of Education, (1977) (ONT. S. CT.)
Thornton, Tanner, et al. v. Board of School Trustees of School District NO. 57 (Prince George), Edamura and Harrower, (1975) 3 W.W.R. 622

Abbreviations of Court Titles
1. CA — Court of Appeal (England)
2. KBD — King's Bench Division
3. Ont. H. Ct. — Ontario High Court
4. Ont. CA — Ontario Court of Appeal
5. BCBS — British Columbia Supreme Court
6. SCC — Supreme Court of Canada
7. Ont. S. CT. — Ontario Supreme Court
8. BCCA — British Columbia Court of Appeal
9. QBD — Queen's Bench Division

American Table of Cases

Assmus v. Little League Baseball, Inc., 70 Misc. 2d 1038, 334 N.U.S. 2d 982 (1972).
Barnhart v. Cabrillo Community College, 90 Cal.Rptr.2d 7009 (Cal, App. 6 Dist. 1999).
Barretto v. City of New York and New York City Board of Education, 655 N.Y.S.2d 484 (N.Y.App. 1997).
Bauder v. Delavan-Darien School District, 558 N.W.2d 881 (Wis. App. 1996).
Behagen v. Intercollegiate Conference of Faculty Representatives, 346 F Supp. 602 (D Minn. 1972).
Bingler v. Johnson, 394 U S 741, 75122LEd695, 895 Ct 1439 (1969).
Blanco v. Elmont Union Free School District, 687 N.Y.S.2d 235 (Supp. 1999).
Brayton v. Monson Public Schools, 950 F. Supp.33 (D. Mass. 1997).
Brenden v. Independent School District 742, 477 F 2d 1292 (8th Cir. 1973).
Brenden v. Independent School District 342 F Supp. 1224 (D. Minn. 1972).
Brown v. Board of Education of Topeka, 347 U S 483, 493, 98 L Ed. 2d 873, 74 S. Ct. 686 (1954).
Brown v. Wells, 288 Minn. 468, 181 N.W. 2d 708 (1970) noted in 36 *Missouri Law Review*. 400 (1971).

Bucha v. Illinois High School Association, 351 F Supp. 69 (N.D. Ill. 1972).

Buckton v. NCAA, 366 F Supp. 1152, 1158 (D. Mass. 1973).

Bunger v. Iowa High School Athletic Association, 197 N.W. 2d 555 (Iowa, 1972).

Corrigan v. Musclemakers Inc., 686 N.Y.S.2d 143 (N.Y. App. Div. 3 Dept. 1999).

Cova v. Harley-Davidson Motor Co., 26 Mich. App. 602, 182 N.W. 2d 800 (1970).

Crisp County School System v. Brown, 487 S.E.2d 512 (Ga. App. 1997).

Daniel v. City of Morganton, 479 S.E.2d 263 (N.C. App. 1997).

Davis v. Meek, 344 F. Supp. 298 (N.D. Ohio 1972).

Domino v. Mercurio, 17 App. Div. 2d 342, 234 N.Y. S. 2d 1011 (1962).

Duda v. Gaines, 12 N. J. Super 326, 79 A. 2d, 695 (1951).

Dumez v. Louisiana High School Athletic Association, 334 S. 2d, 494 (La. App. 1976).

Dunham v. Pulsifer, 312 F Supp. 411 (D. Vt. 1970).

Dunn v. Blumstein, 405 U.S., 330, 335, 92 S. Ct. 995, 31 L. Ed. 2d 274 (1972).

Egger v. St. Dominic High School, 657 N.Y.S.2d 85 (A.D. 2 Dept. 1997).

Filler v. Royex Corp., 435 F. 2d 336 (7th Cir. 1970).

Frontiero v. Richardson, 411 U.S. 677, 36 L. Ed. 583, 93 S. Ct. 1764 (1973).

Gilpin v. Kansas State High School Activities Association, 377 F Supp. 1233, 1224 (D. Kansas, 1973).

Hanson v. Reedley Joint Union High School District, 43 Cal. App. 2d 643, 111 P2d 415 (1941).

Howard University v. National Collegiate Athletic Association, 510 F. 2d 213 (D. C. Cir. 1975).

Jones v. National Collegiate Athletic Association, 392 F. Supp. 295 (D. Mass. 1975).

Kelley v. Metropolitan County Board of Education of Nashville, 293 F. Supp. 485 (M.D. Tenn. 1968).

King v. Little League Baseball, Inc., 505 F. 2d 264 (6th Cir. 1974).

Lee v. Florida High School Activities Association, 291 Se 2d 636(Fla. App. 1974).

Long v. Zapp, 476 F 2d 180 (4th Cir. 1973).

Louisiana High School Athletic Association v. At. Augustines High School, 396 F. 2d 224 (5th Cir. 1973).

MacPherson v. Buick Motor Co., 217 N. Y. 382, 111 N.E. 1050 (1916).

Marjorie Webster Junior College v. Middle States Association of Colleges and Secondary Schools, Inc., 432 F Supp 650 (D.C. Cir. 1969).

McGee v. Board of Education of the City of New York, 16, App. Div. 2d 99, 266, N. Y. S. 2d, 329 (1962).

McCormick v. Lowe & Campbell Athletic Goods Co., 240 Mo 708,144 S.W. 2d 866 (1940).

Mitchell v. Louisiana High School Athletic Association, 430 F. 2d 1115 (5th Cir. 1970).

Moran v. School District No. 7 Yellowstone County, 350 F. Supp. 1180 (D. Mont. 1972).

Morris v. Concord School District, 59 Mich. App. 415, 228 N.W.2d 479 (1975).

NAACP v. Button, 371 U.S. 415,438, 9 L. Ed. 2d 405, 83 S. Ct. 328 (1963).

Oklahoma Secondary School Activities Association v. Midget, 505, P 2d 155 (Okla. 1972).

Parish v. National Collegiate Athletic Association, 506 F 2d 1028 (5th Cir. 1975).

Parson's College v. North Central Association of Colleges and Secondary Schools, 271 F. Supp. (N.D. Ill. 1967).

Reed v. Reed, 404 U.S. 71, 30 L Ed 2d 225, 92 S. Ct. 251 (1971).

Robinson v. Illinois High School Association, 45 ILL. App. 2d 277, 195 N.E. 2d 38 (1963).

Roventini v. Pasadena Independent School District, 981 F. Supp. 1013 (S.D. Tex. 1997).

Samara v. National Collegiate Athletic Association, 1973 Trade Cases 1174, 536 (E. D. Va. 1973).

Sewell v. Southfield Public Schools, 576 N.W.2d 153 (Mich. 1998).

Shapiro v. Thompson, 394 U.S. 618, 22 L. ED 2d 600, 89 S. Ct. 1322 (1969).

South Dakota High School Activity Association v. St. Mary's Inter-Parochial High School of Salem, 82 S.D. 84, 141 N.W. 2d 477 (1968).

Stehn v. Bernarr MacFadden Foundations, Inc., 434, F. 2d 811 (6th Cir. 1970).

Strurrup v. Mahon, 261 Ind. 463, 305 N. E. 2d 877 (1974).

Taylor v. Alabama High School Athletic Association, 336 F. Supp. 54 (M.D. Ala 1972).

Taylor v. Wake Forest University, 16 N.C. App. 117, 191 S.E. 2d 379 (1972).

University of Denver v. Nemeth, 127 Colo. 385, 257 P. 2d 423 (1953).

University Preparatory School v. Huitt, 941 S.W.2d 177 (Tex. App. 1997).

Van Horn v. Industrial Accident Commission, 219 Cal. App. 2d 457, 33 Cal. Rptr. 169 (1963).

Van Horn v. Industrial Accident Commission, 219 Cal. App. 2d 457, 33 Cal. Rptr. 169 (1963) noted in *UCLA Law Review* 11 (1964) 645.

Vendrell v. School District No. 26C, Malheur County, 233 Ore. at 15, 376 P. 2d at 413.
Welch v. Dunsmuir Joint Union High School District, 326 P. 2d 633 (Cal. Appl. 1958).
Willaims v. Eaton, 468 F. 2d 1079 (10th Cir. 1972).
Winterbottom v. Wright, 10 M & W 109, 52 Eng. Rep. 402 (1842).

References

Appenzeller, Herb. (1975). *Athletics and the Law.* Charlottesville, Virginia: The Michie Company.

Appenzeller, Herb. (1970). *From the Gym to the Jury.* Charlottesville, Virginia: The Michie Company.

Appenzeller, Herb. (1978). *Physical Education and the Law.* Charlottesville, Virginia: The Michie Company.

Appenzeller, Herb and Thomas Appenzeller. (1980). *Sports and the Courts.* Charlottesville, Virginia: The Michie Company.

Appenzeller, Herb. (1998). *Risk Management in Sport: Issues and Strategies.* Durham, North Carolina: Carolina Academia Press.

"Athletics." (1973). *Law and Contemporary Problems,* 38: 1-171.

Avoiding Legal Liability Problems, (1976). Manual 5, Canadian Sports Administration Association, Ottawa, 1976.

Barnes, John. (February, 1979). "Soccer and the Law." Canadian Soccer News in *West Side Newsletter,* 5-6.

Barnes, John. (1988). *Sport and The Law in Canada (2nd Ed).* Toronto, Ontario: Butterworth Press.

Bayles, Audrey (ed.) (1978). *Legal Liability in Physical Education.* Ottawa, Ont.: Experience 78 Ontario.

Brunt, R. Thomas. (1969). "Tortious Liability of Canadian Physical Education and Recreation Practitioners." Unpublished MA Thesis, University of Alberta.

Buck & Orleans, (1973). "Sex Discrimination — A Bar to Democratic Education: Overview of Title IX of the Education Amendments of 1972." *Connecticut Law Review* 6: 1.

Clement, Annie. (1999). *Law in Sport and Phyical Activity (2nd Ed).* Tallahassee, Florida: Sport and Law Press Inc.

Coaching Association of Canada. (circa 1976). "Legal Liability" prepared by Robert Neil and Cameron (Joe) Blimkie. Ottawa, Ont.: Coaching Association of Canada, Item #4.

Coleman, J. (1967) *Abnormal Psychology and Modern Life.* (3rd Ed.), 103.

Comment (1976). "New Regulations Under Title IX of the Education Amendments of 1972: Ultra Vires Challenge." *Brigham Young University Law Review,* (1976): 133.

Comment (1974). "Sex Discrimination in High School Athletics." *Syracuse Law Review,* 25: 535.

Cox. (1977). "Intercollegiate Athletics in the Wake of Hew Regulations Under Title IX of the 1972 Educational Amendments." *George Washington Review,* 46: 34.

Cross. (1973). "The College Athlete and the Institution." *Law and Contemporary Problems, 171: 163-66.*

Dewar, John and Dick Moriarty. (1978). *Sport and the Law.* Windsor, Ont.: Sports Institute for Research.

Dobbyn, E. Latty. (1971). "A Practical Approach to Consistence in Veil Piercing Cases." *Kansas Law Review,* 19: 185.

Gilbert and Williams. (May 28, 1973). "Women in Sport, Part 1: Sport is Unfair to Women. *Sports Illustrated:* 92-95.

Gillespie. (1969). "The Thin Corporate Line: The Loss of Limited Liability Protection." *North Dakota Law Review,* 45: 363.

Grayson, Edward. (1978). *Sport and the Law.* London, England: Sunday Telegram Publication.

Hanford, George. (1974). *An Inquiry Into the Need for and Feasibility of a National Study of Intercollegiate Athletics.* Mission, Kansas: National Collegiate Athletic Union (NCAU).

Harney, D. (1973). *Medical Malpractice.*

Hawley, Donna Lee. (1974). "Legal Liability of Canadian Physical Education Teachers." Unpublished MA Thesis, University of Alberta.

Hronek, Bruce R. & J.A. Spengler. (1997) *Legal Liability in Recreation and Sports.* Champaign, Illinois: Sagamore Publishing.

Hudgens, H.C., Jr. and Richard S. Vacca. (1979). *Law and Education: Contemporpary Issues and Court Decisions.* Charlottesville, Virginia.

Johnson, Barbara (ed.). (1978). *Ontario Association of School Physical and Health Education Legal Edition Newsletter.* Mississauga, Ont.: The Peel Board of Education.

Koch. (1976). "Title IX and the NCAA." *Western State Law Review,* 3: 250.

Koppett, Leonard. (1973). "Sports and the Law: An Overview." *New York Law Forum XVIII*, 4 (Spring): 815-839.

Kuhn. (1976). "Title IX: Employment and Athletics Are Outside HEW Jurisdiction." *Georgetown Law Journal*, 65: 49.

Moriarty, Dick. (1978). "Comparing Canadian-American Sport/Athletic Policy and the Law." *Crime and Justice*, 6, 1: 22-30.

Note (1974). "Equality in Athletics: The Cheerleaders vs the Athlete." *South Dakota Law Review*, 19: 428.

Note (1972). "Judical Review of Disputes Between Athletes and the National College Athletic Association." *Stanford Law Review*, 24: 909-916.

Note (1973). "The Case for Equality In Athletics." *Cleveland State Law Review*, 22: 570.

Note (1975). "The Emerging Bifurcated Standard for Classifications Based On Sex." *Duke Law Journal*: 163.

Note (1971). "Sex Discrimination and Equal Protection: Do We Need a Constitutional Amendment?" *Harvard Law Review* 84: 1499, 1515-1516.

Note (1972). "Sex Discrimination in High School Athetics." *Minnesota Law Review*, 57: 339, 351-357.

Note (1975). "Sex Discrimination in Intercollegiate Athletics."*Iowa Law Review*, 61: 420.

Nygaard, Gary & Thomas H. Boone. (1989). *Law for Physical Educators and Coaches* (2nd ed). Columbus, Ohio: Publishing Horizons, Inc.

Post, C. Gordon. (1963). *An Introduction to the Law*. Englewood Cliffs, N.J.: Prentice-Hall, Inc.

Prosser, W. (1971). *The Law of Torts*. (4th ed.): 162.

Report on Experiment: Girls on Interscholastic Athletic Teams. (1972). New York Department of Education and Recreation. 477 F.2d at 1300-1301.

Ryan. (1973). "Medical Practice in Sports." *Law and Contemporary Problems*, 38: 99.

Sobel, Lionel S. (1976). *Conference on Women's Sport and the Law*. Los Angeles, California: University of Southern California.

Sobel, Lionel S. (1977). *Professional Sports and the Law*. New York: Law-Arts Publishers, Inc.

Solomon, Stephen. (1979). "A Businesslike Way to Resolve Legal Disputes." *Fortune* February 26: 80-82.

"Sports, and the Law." (1978). *Connecticut Law Review*, X, 2 (Winter): 251-254.

"Sports, Torts and Courts." (January, 1977). *Trial*, 21: 21-48.

Stroud. (1973). "Sex Discrimination in High School Athletics." *Indiana Law Review*, 6: 661, 666-669.

"Symposium on Sports Law." (1973). *New York Law Forum*, 18: 815.

"Symposium: Sports and the Law." (1976). *WSTUI Review*, 3: 185.

"Symposium: Professional Sports and the Law." (1977). *William and Mary Law Review*, 18: 667.

Thomas, Alan M. (1976). "Accidents Will Happen: An Inquiry into the legal liability of teachers and school boards." *The Interaction of Law and Education Series*. Toronto, Ont.: Ontario Institute for Studies in Education.

Ottawa University. (1976). "Sport Policy and the Law." *Proceedings of the University of Ottawa-Faculty of Law Common Law Section Annual Symposium*.

Van der Smissen, Betty. (1990). *Legal Liability and Risk Management for Public and Private Entities*. Cincinnati, Ohio: Anderson Publishing Co.

Weistart, John C. and Cym H. Lowell. (1978). *The Law of Sports*. New York: The Bobbs-Merrill Company, Inc. Publishers.

Wise, Dave. (March 1,1979). "Association Business Report (CATC)." *The Journal of the Canadian Athletic Therapists Association*, 6: 23-25.

Wong, Glenn M. (1994). *Essentials of Amateur Sport Law (2nd Ed)*. Westport, Connecticut: Praeger Press.

CHAPTER 2

A PRACTICAL LOOK AT RISK MANAGEMENT

Mike Mahoney, Janice Forsyth, Margery Holman and Dick Moriarity

Prevention of injuries and accidents are a concern for sport and recreation professionals. The development of a comprehensive risk management program can help reduce this concern. The purpose of this chapter is to explain the importance of a sound risk management plan and how it can provide an essential safety barrier between the potential risks in a sport or recreational setting. The chapter is divided into three sections: Introduction to Risk Management, Risk Categories, and Conclusion. A list of study questions and legal cases related to risk management concludes the chapter.

Introduction to Risk Management

Definition of Risk Management

In its simplest form, risk management is the management of risk. It is a proactive process, which attempts to prevent accidents before they occur. Risk Management is not achieved solely by purchasing extensive insurance policies and covering the walls of the facility with warning signs. It is a total program that analyzes where and why accidents may occur and how the hazards might be controlled. There is no one ideal risk management plan that can be implemented for every facility and program. Although it may be possible to develop a risk management plan based on similar facilities and programs, there are situations unique to each facility. It is important not to simply copy a risk management plan, but to model and create a plan best suited to meet the unique requirements of the facility or program.

Importance of Risk Management

There are numerous organizational considerations when developing a risk management plan. In addition to providing for the safety of participants, an organization may protect itself against potential lawsuits and reduce the cost of insurance. Moreover, most insurance companies will not sell a policy to an athletic-related organization without proof of a risk management plan. Ultimately, a risk management plan has four main goals:

1. To prevent the occurrence of injuries;
2. To prevent possible lawsuits;
3. To prevent the lawsuits from being successful;
4. To minimize the amount of damages.

Reducing Risk

There are strategies that can be used to reduce risk in sport and recreation environments. However, it is first important to identify the risk involved. One of the most convenient ways to identify the risk would be to use the Participant Readiness Table (see Table 2.1).

Table 2.1
Participant Readiness Table

HIGH		
Real	Avoid	Transfer
Risk	Reduce	Retain
LOW	Participant Readiness	HIGH

Forsyth & Moriarty, 1994, p. 114

The Participant Readiness Table assists in the identification of risk based on the participants readiness to participate versus the real risk present in the activity. If the real risk is high and the participants readiness is low (not ready for the potential risk) the activity should be avoided. If risk is low and the participants readiness is low, reduce the activity risk. This can be accomplished by developing progressions. Always ensure that the activity is being offered at a level that is equal, if not lower, than the participants' level of readiness. If the activity risk is high and the participant's readiness is also high, the risk can be transferred to the participant through informed consent forms and waivers. The transfer of risk is used in many high-risk activities such as sky diving and mountain climbing. Finally, retaining an activity indicates the risk level is low and all foreseeable risks have been identified and either eliminated or controlled. The participant is made aware of these potential risks and the activity is maintained in a protected environment (Forsyth and Moriarty, 1994).

Impact of Increased Litigation

Although litigation is not a welcomed action, it can have both positive and negative impacts. There are many negative impacts of liability on sport and recreation planning. One negative impact would be the increase of cost, both to the participant in the way of increased participation fees and for the organization due to increased insurance costs. Similar to car insurance, when an accident occurs, there is often a major increase in insurance costs. An insurance company does not favor a lawsuit that could have been avoided. Lawsuits drain sport and recreation programs of valuable financial resources, resulting in program cancellations.

On the positive side, when an accident happens in a sport and/or recreation facility, it increases the awareness of existing risks. An improved standard of care will evolve from increased litigation in attempts to do everything possible to prevent a lawsuit from reoccurring. Finally, the realization of the importance of risk management is brought to the forefront, as without a sound risk management plan, the recreational setting could become an accident waiting to happen.

Protection from Liability

The primary factor that prevents total protection from liability is a participant's preference to partake in activity where there is a preferred high level of risk. Many people compete for the thrill of competition and the inherent risk. Two examples of high risk, thrill-seeking activities are extreme skiing and sky diving. These activities are a concern to sport organizations because of the potential for liability. In some cases, the level of risk may prevent an activity from being offered. A second factor is the lack of human and financial resources required to conduct high-risk activities. The responsibility rests with the sport organization to determine the feasibility of the activity within available resources.

Risk Management Team

The development of a risk management team is essential to effective risk management. One person should be designated as the leader the risk management team with the assistance of a competent and effective risk management team. Each risk management team member should have sufficient background experience in the areas of sport, recreation and safety and, possess a basic knowledge of risk management. Each person on the risk management team should be assigned specific duties, which match their knowledge and skills. Potential team members might be lawyers, doctors, parents, coaches, participants and/or teachers. The background experience of the risk management team is critical to the effectiveness and success of the risk management plan. Team members experience might not be directly related to sport but specific to one aspect of the risk management plan (i.e., lawyers' knowledge would be useful in contracts and waivers).

The allocation of resources for risk management is essential. Risk management is a proactive practice that requires time and money for team meetings and program evaluations. The team approach ensures the implementation of the plan is manageable.

Finally, it is key that the risk management team has the power to execute the plan. The risk management team must have the authority to make decisions and oversee the enactment of these decisions. Otherwise the risk management team will not succeed. Through the cooperation and support of others, and adequate resources and training, the risk management team will be able to develop a sound risk management plan with a common goal to provide a safe environment for participants.

Risk Categories

Sport and recreation programs have a number of risks and liabilities inherent to their programs and activities. Six categories of risks and liabilities will be discussed in this section: People (Employment); Programs and Services; Facilities; Equipment; Transportation; and, Emergency Action Plans.

People (Employment)

There are three main concerns of sport and recreation professionals in employing qualified personnel: hiring, supervision, and retention (Sharp, 1993). Hiring suitable employees does not mean looking at a resume and making a decision. Negligent hiring occurs when the employer knows, or should have known, of an applicants propensities, hires the individual, and gives the employee the opportunity to repeat the inappropriate behaviour (Levin, Smith, Caldwell, & Kimbrough, 1995).

"Negligent hiring places liability on the employer when the doctrine of *respondeat superior*[1] applies. The doctrine of respondeat superior places liability on an employer for acts of the employee performing duties within the defined job description (Miller, 1998, p.407). Two cases represent this issue. First, in *D.T. by M.T. v. Independent School Dis.* (1990)[2], charges were laid, alleging a school had neglectfully hired a 30-year-old teacher-coach who had previously molested three elementary students. The second case, *Doe v. British Universities North American Club* (1992)[3], involved allegations that the defendant be held liable for negligently hiring a camp councilor who sexually abused a camper. Before hiring employees, the administrator needs to consider if the potential employee has the required qualifications and certifications. There should also be an investigation into the applicant's background and employment history, especially if the supervision of younger children is involved (see Forsyth & Gallagher chapter on volunteer screening). The employer should also ensure that the potential employee possesses sufficient technical skills and the knowledge required in administering first aid and cardio-pulmonary resuscitation.

The second personnel concern, supervision of employees, is a critical aspect of sport and recreation programming. The main reason for hiring staff is to disperse the workload and ensure that all activities are properly supervised. There are a number of ways to ensure that proper supervision of an activity is taking place. Once the hiring has taken place, training sessions should be held to ensure that the roles and responsibilities of the employees are expressed and fully understood. A written job description, including all duties and expectations should be documented and given to the employee. A job description should be created specifically for each position. The job description should include organizational policies and procedures, and outline the evaluative and monitoring procedures for employees. Periodic evaluative meetings throughout the year where employees update their supervisor on the progression of the programs and activities are also an opportunity for the supervisor to provide constructive feedback to employees.

Retention of employees is the third personnel concern. After there has been adequate selection of employees and their training has been completed, any problems or concerns that may arise from an employee must be addressed. Once a concern is brought forward, the supervisor must immediately investigate the situation. Feedback provided to an employee will enhance their contribution to the organization. However, in the event that an evaluation exposes issues of concern that put the safety of program participants at risk, the supervisor must consider termination of that employee. This must be done incorporating the principles of due process.

Programs and Services

Recreation programs and services must be well researched and presented to the participant in a risk free environment. There are a number of considerations to be addressed when organizing and delivering sport and recreation activities. The first is the protection of the participants. Rules and regulations should be developed and implemented to ensure the safety and satisfaction of the participants. The key to developing rules and regulations is to create an environment where the participants are not out of their element; meaning they are not involved in an activity that is beyond their physical ability and physical preparation to the point where they could be endangering themselves. The utilization of informed consent forms, waivers and participant readiness forms can: (a) create an awareness of the potential risks inherent to an activity; and, (b) act as an indicator of participant readiness.

A second consideration is the voluntary assumption of risk. This indicates that risk is an inherent, but accepted, part of an activity in which an individual is about to engage. Some people actually take part in some activities because the risk is a desirable characteristic. However, those activities that pose an unreasonable risk due to the nature of the activity must be managed through the utilization of proper forms, instruction and supervision. It is essential that the participant be alerted to all potential risks.

Adequate supervision during all activities and programs is essential to ensure the safety of the participants. In the case of an accident, the supervisor will know how to handle the incident and administer an appropriate Emergency Action Plan (EAP). There are different levels of supervision required based on the age of the participant, the level of risk of the activity, the skill level, amount of instruction required, and the approved general practice and supervision (Moriarty et al., 1994). Foreseeable risk, the need for supervision, and previous acts and incidents of vigilance must also be considered. Respecting these factors, there are three levels of adequate supervision (Adams, 1990):

1. **Specific** supervision, which is the direct overseeing of any activity involving a small group or an individual;
2. **General** supervision, which involves observing a larger group and a larger area, and is not instructional in nature; and,
3. **Transitional** supervision, which takes place as the participant increases in knowledge and the ability to move toward general supervision, but still requires some instruction.

Within these three levels of supervision, the following list of recommendations helps to ensure adequate supervision (adapted from Merriman, 1993: 20):

- Supervisor must be within the immediate vicinity;
- If required to leave, there must be an adequate replacement in place before departing;
- Supervision procedures must be pre-planned and incorporated into daily lesson plans;
- Procedures should include what to look for, listen for, where to stand, and what to do if a problem arises;
- Supervision requires that age, maturity, and skill level of the participants must always be considered, as must the inherent risk of the activity;
- Know the risks involved before offering any activity;
- Develop rules and regulations for all activities;
- Hire qualified personnel;
- Supervision should be equal to or greater than that required for the activity;
- Provide proper training in any Emergency Action Plans (EAPs);
- Know the abilities of the participants;
- Know documentation procedures;
- Create a risk management team; and,
- Be proactive in maintaining the supervision of activities.

Another sound decision in preparing for program safety, is the development of checklists. A checklist can be an extremely effective risk management tool if used correctly. Checklists can be used for inspection of the following areas:

- General work schedule
- Maintenance
- Inventory
- EAP Equipment
- Building structure
- Signage
- Water
- Safety
- Communication
- Accident report
- Documentation
- Special events
- Crowd control
- First aid equipment
- Events off campus

The guidance presented thus far is intended to assist in the provision of a safe environment for the participants as well as to protect the organization from fault or negligence in the event of an injury.

There are four areas that must exist to establish negligence:

1. Duty of care;
2. Breach of the standard of care;
3. Actual damage, and;
4. Proximate cause of injury (Moriarty et al., 1994).

If the defendant can prove that just one of these areas is absent, then they can not be found guilty of negligence. All four steps must be proven in a court of law to establish the presence of negligence.

In the United States, negligence is discussed as a failure to act as a reasonably prudent person would in the same or similar circumstance. Negligence could be found in a person's (or organization's) actions or in the person's (or organization's) failure to act. The key consideration is whether or not the person causing the injury could foresee the possibility of the hazard (Moriarty, 1994). In Canada, the Criminal Code of Canada[2] defines criminal negligence as follows:

Everyone is criminally negligent who (a) is doing anything, or (b) in omitting to do anything that is his duty to do, shows wanton or reckless disregard for the lives or safety of other persons.

Facilities

It is important for the risk management team to be familiar with every possible aspect of the facility in order to be aware of the potential risks. Seidler (1998) suggests that everyone who enters a facility has the right to expect that the facility will be reasonably safe. Sport and recreation professionals have a legal duty to provide a safe environment to all patrons. Seidler (1998) discussed five safety duties that should be carried out to provide a safe environment:

1. Keep the premises (inside and outside) in safe repair;
2. Inspect the facility for unusual or hidden hazards;
3. Remove hazards or at least warn patrons of potential hazards;
4. Anticipate foreseeable uses and activities by the patrons and establish precautions to protect from foreseeable dangers; and,
5. Conduct operations on the premises with reasonable care for the safety of the patrons.

The three key areas of liability with respect to facilities are foreseeability, facility inspection, and maintenance. Foreseeability is the ability to identify a potential risk and deal with it appropriately before an injury occurs. Seidler (1998) further discusses the concept of notice (actual and constructive), in relation to foreseeability. **Actual notice** suggests that the facility manager (and/or an employee) had direct knowledge of a hazard from either routine inspection, a report from a patron or staff member, or a past injury. **Constructive notice** is considered to have occurred when the facility manager (and/or employee) should have and would have known about a hazard, had a proper inspection taken place.

Notices are important aspects of foreseeability because some courts use these notices as timelines to justify whether or not the facility had enough time to fix or eliminate the hazard before further injury occurred. Ultimately, once any form of notice has been made about any form of hazard, it is expected that the appropriate steps will be taken quickly to remedy the situation.

A second area of liability is facility inspection. Both inside and outside facility checks should be completed to identify potential risk areas. Studies have revealed that athletic fields that have also been used for intramurals, physical education and other school functions tend to receive more wear and tear and therefore, more injuries and the need for more frequent inspection (Kanoy, 1992, p.11). Therefore, inspection of all potential user areas should be examined and all concerns should be attended to appropriately. These areas could be, but are not limited to, seating for spectators, fencing around outdoor facilities, padding surrounding basketball back boards, leaks in the ceiling, and sufficient, accessible, entrance and exit doors that are properly maintained. Facility developers may not have foreseen all the potential risk concerns when the facility was created.

A schedule of periodic inspections should be developed once the initial inspection has been completed (i.e., inspection of facility before a varsity game or another highly populated activity). There should be checklists for general (water on the floor, garbage on the ground, broken windows) and specific (damage to weight machines, cracked diving boards) inspections. The general inspections should be done daily and the specific inspections should be done when most appropriate and suggested by the manufacturers. All checklists should be easy to understand and to complete. Specific, yet appropriate, rules and regulations should accompany the checklists, and should be posted in clearly marked, easy to read areas. It is also important to remember that the facility manager and other employees should not only enforce the rules, but also follow the rules themselves.

The third area of concern involves the maintenance of the facility. Maintenance would include equipment, activity areas and any other potential hazard to the participants or spectators. A facility manager has a duty to provide a safe environment for the users of the facility for which they are responsible. This includes prohibiting programming of activities for which the facility was not designed and cannot accommodate.

After identifying the risks, the rules, and the protocol, it is essential that the facility manager and the risk management team develop specific documentation and incident forms to provide the necessary written records when an accident occurs. This is of particular importance if an incident is taken to court for settlement. The facility manager must prove an appropriate standard of care was maintained. The utilization of checklists and periodic inspections are a definite asset to providing a safe environment. If a potential hazard has been identified and needs repairs, Goodman and McGregor (1997) suggest that the next step would be to prevent the participants and spectators from injuring themselves by providing some form of protection against the hazard in one the following four ways: warnings, isolation, signage, and elimination.

Warnings can be used in a number of ways (verbal, loud speaker, pamphlets). Verbal warnings can be done on a one on one basis as people are entering the facility. Loud speakers can be offered during an event such as announcing a warning about the possibility of a puck flying into the spectators areas within the arena. General warnings are usually complemented with signage and written information. Pamphlets and information on the back of tickets are usually accompanied with a verbal warning. The pamphlet/ticket contains information that further explains the potential risks that the entrant should be aware of upon entering the facility.

Isolation should be used when a hazard has been identified and it cannot be eliminated or repaired immediately and a warning does not provide sufficient protection. The concern in such instances is the creation of an attractive nuisance, something that, because it is off limits or presents a potential danger to someone, becomes attractive to investigate, regardless of the potential danger. When possible, ensure that the hazard has been removed, the unsafe area is secured and supervised, and the hazard receives immediate corrective attention.

Signage provides a visual warning to anyone who may come into contact with the potential hazard. "Broken: Do Not Use," "Construction Ahead," and "Unsafe: Keep Out," are examples of potential signs, warning people of conditions that may put them at risk. However, there is a problem with signage if a participant or user is not able to read and/or understand the message (eg. age, ethnicity). The facility manager (and/or employees) must know the characteristics of the facility patrons from which the most appropriate signage strategy can be determined. It should be noted that utilizing universally identifiable symbols/signage when possible to notify people of risk can overcome many of the misunderstandings. The following four guidelines will provide effective assistance when creating effective signage: (1) be a specific as possible; (2) do not clutter signage in one area; (3) keep it simple; and, (4) make sure the sign is prominent and readable.

Elimination is the safest and best way to take care of a potential hazard. This means completely removing it from the environment by either repair or replacement. By eliminating the hazard, the risk is removed and eliminating the hazard reduces the chances of injury.

The final risk management issue to be discussed concerning facilities is **Occupier's Liability.** According to Goodman and McGregor (1997), an **Occupier** is a person who is in physical possession of premises or who has the responsibility for and control of the condition of the premises. We can estimate that most of the patrons who come through the facility doors will be invitees. Invitees are owed the highest possible standard of care. That standard of care should be equal to, and no less than, that provided by a reasonable, prudent and careful facility manager. Table 2.2 outlines the categories of the potential users of a facility and the duty owed to these users. If the category of a user is unknown, owing them the highest possible standard of care is the best way to ensure safety.

Table 2.2
Categories of Potential Users
and the Duty of Care Owed
(Adapted from Goodman & McGregor, 1997)

Occupier Category	Duty Owed to the Category
Contractual Entrant/Invitee — any person who has paid for the privilege to be on the property of another; any person with the expressed or implied permission to be on the property and the occupier stands to gain some economic advantage.	Take every step reasonable to make the premises as safe as possible for those who have paid to come onto the property and to take reasonable care to protect from **unusual** dangers of which the occupier **ought** to be aware.
Licensee — a person who is on the property with the implied or expressed permission of the occupier, but from whom the occupier will not receive any economic benefit.	Take reasonable steps to protect the licensee from any **hidden** dangers or conditions of which the occupier is **actually** aware.
Trespasser— a person on the premises without permission of the occupier does not have permission to engage in activity that is not allowed on the property.	Duty of care is minimal, but an obligation not to deliberately cause an unsafe environment to harm or injure the trespasser. The duty of common humanity.

Equipment

Sport managers have a responsibility for the equipment that they provide (see Table 2.3). Liability for programs related to equipment generally fall into four categories (Brown, 1993):

1. Modification of, or misuse of a product;
2. Failure to follow manufacturers guidelines related to selection, fit, maintenance or replacement of products;
3. Inadequate instruction of athletes related to use of products; and
4. Failure to warn athletes and parents of the limited ability of products to reduce the risk of participation.

Modification of product indicates that the provider altered a piece of equipment and thus prevents the piece of equipment from properly functioning in the manner for which it was developed. Consider cutting the ears off softball helmets, or removing padding from a football helmet. By altering these pieces of protective equipment, there is now a greater chance for injury, as the equipment no longer provides the pre-existing level of safety. Another example of misuse of equipment is the operation of a gymnastics springboard as a diving board for a pool. The equipment is not designed to be used in a damp environment and cannot be suspended over the water, therefore the potential for injury is high.

Table 2.3
Providers of Equipment Have Four Responsibilities

1. Make sure the equipment is safe; inspect new equipment for possible defects.
2. Offer participant appropriate sized equipment (i.e. Right sized softball helmet).
3. Ensure equipment is used for its intended purpose.
4. Instruct participant on how to use the equipment properly.

(Brown, 1993)

The importance of a well-developed and documented process for maintaining a current and detailed equipment inventory is recommended. It must be stressed that the manufacturer's guidelines related to selection, fit, maintenance or replacement of products be followed. Mouth guards and protective eyewear should be mandatory for activities where the potential for injury is high such as squash, racquetball, hockey, and even basketball.

Inadequate instruction to athletes related to use of products could be one of the least thought about liabilities for sport and recreation programs. Instruction on the proper use of any piece of equipment is essential, as this instruction is a proactive measure in the prevention of injury. Failure to warn athletes and parents of the limited ability of products to reduce the risk of participation is another concern. All participants and parents, when appropriate, must be made aware of the inherent risks involved in an activity in spite of the protective measures taken.

The next step of a risk management program with respect to equipment involves developing specific policies and procedures for the equipment usage, repair, replacement and inspection. Written procedures ensure that all communication is clear and the potential risks inherent in the activities are outlined. Providing an alternative while equipment is being replaced or repaired is key. There should never be a time when a decision has to be made between using below standard equipment or not offering the activity at all. If a problem arises regarding equipment, or any area of the program, an alternative should already be pre-planned to prevent cancellation and ultimately, unhappy participants. If this is not possible, a program should be cancelled rather than using sub-standard equipment.

For sport and recreation programs, the equipment used should meet the criteria of the Canadian Standards Association (CSA), or the American equivalent in the USA, and a thorough periodic evaluation of the equipment should be completed. To prove negligence in the area of Product Liability, it must be shown that the equipment in question was defective and that the defect was the cause of the injury. Some of the defenses of product liability are (Goodman & McGregor, 1997):

- Improper manufacturing;
- Over use;
- Worn out equipment;

- Improper installation;
- Improper use; damage during shipping or storage;
- Improper instruction; and,
- Improper maintenance/defective material.

Risk-proofing equipment involves a complete and documented inventory of all equipment. The inventory includes when it was purchased, any problems or repairs, and a periodic evaluation schedule describing the inspection of all equipment. The instructions that come with the equipment should be readily available for program staff.

Used equipment should never be given to other sport or recreation facilities. Donation of used football helmets is an example. A football team has a number of helmets, which are missing padding, chinstraps and a couple of screws and the team gives the helmets to a local junior high school. One of the students using one of the old helmets suffers a fractured skull and is hospitalized for months. The liability will rest with the donor of the equipment because it was known the equipment was damaged and it was not disposed of accordingly.

All information and evidence following an injury, which may relate to the usage of equipment should be collected immediately and properly documented. This will ensure that, in case of a potential lawsuit, the information and evidence will be at hand and ready for the defense.

Transportation

There are a number of classifications of vehicles to consider when discussing transportation. Four classifications of relevance to sport/physical activity are independent contractor, school vehicles, employee owned vehicles, and non-employee owned vehicles (Van der Smissen, 1990). An independent contractor is a taxi or bus service that is contracted to transport people from point A to point B. The independent contractor is the best option for transporting people. However, the inhibitor is the cost. Independent contractors are covered by their own insurance policy and the standard regarding drivers' qualifications. Further, their vehicles are subjected to preventive maintenance and kept up to standard. An independent contractor should always transport injured participants, if at all possible. This way if further injury should occur on the way to the hospital (i.e., an accident) the further injury would be covered under the independent contractors insurance and would not be the responsibility of the sport or recreation program.

School vehicles are the second option for transportation from a liability perspective. In most cases, it is extremely expensive to own school vehicles for transportation, due to the insurance and the maintenance of the vehicle. However, having school vehicles requires organizations to document the vehicle's condition and history of repairs as well as the record of the vehicle's drivers. Care must be taken to provide adequate maintenance and qualified drivers for the school vehicles.

Employee owned vehicles (i.e., teachers, staff, faculty, coaches), if being used for work related purposes, will still be held liable under the doctrine of *respondeat superior* (Pittman, 1993). If the employee uses a personal vehicle without the consent of the school and an accident occurs, that employee will be held personally responsible for any injuries caused. Use of a personal vehicle with consent of the school may need an added clause or rider for insurance purposes.

When non-employee owned vehicles (student, volunteers, and sometimes coaches) are used, there should be a thorough mechanical examination and a complete review of the driver's insurance and driving record. Van der Smissen (1987) suggests that student drivers present a high risk because of their youth and relative lack of driving experience. Using students to drive to and from activities to save some money for the department is not a suggested practice, due to the increased exposure to liability.

Sport and recreation programs must develop policies and procedures that are tailored to the specific needs of the programs and services offered. The following considerations can assist in the development of policies and procedures:

- Student drivers;
- Private cars;
- Route plans;
- Arrival times;
- Departure times;
- Number of passengers per vehicle;
- First aid kits;
- Seat belts;

- Use of alcohol;
- Drowsiness;
- Driver background; and
- Release forms.

Each of these areas should be given consideration in the development of transportation policy.

Emergency Action Plans

An accident has occurred during the last game of the intramural basketball tournament. The official rushes to the administrative office looking for assistance. People are panicking and the injured party is lying unconscious on the floor with their leg bending in a way that seemed only possible in cartoons. What do you do?

This incident would not occur if the sport or recreation program had an Emergency Action Plan (EAP). When developing an EAP, it is always better to err on the side of safety because ultimately, as sport and recreation professionals, the safety of the participants is our responsibility (Ondracka, 1999). The best way to prepare for any emergency is to train staff with emergency training drills. This training should also include the roles and responsibilities required for each staff member in the event of an emergency. Each person should also be aware of any potential responsibilities beyond the immediate area where they are working.

In addition to training, first aid kits should be available and easily accessible at every event. An inventory should be maintained of every kit. Emergency equipment (i.e., spinal boards and neck braces) should be placed in areas that best suit the situation, depending on the risk level of the activity. A directory of critical phone numbers should be listed and posted near every phone in the facility. A documentation procedure that records every minor and major accident is necessary to complete the EAP.

If an injury occurs, it is essential that the situation is handled in a calm manner. This will decrease the anxiety of the injured party and others observing the incident. An injury could be aggravated and additional injuries can occur if an accident is not managed properly. Comforting the injured is essential to develop a good rapport with the participant. Concern for their well being may also discourage legal action. Again, documentation describing the event, with eyewitness accounts and contact information is always a good practice. Finally, a follow up telephone call to inquire about the injured person's recovery completes the required documentation.

Conclusion

A generic risk management plan will *not* work for all facilities and programs. Rather, each risk management plan should be individually developed and tailored to the facility or program. Goodman and McGregor (1997) have developed six steps in the development and tailoring of a risk management plan for individual programs.

The first step is the development a risk management committee. The second step is an audit of self-risk, including the evaluation of policies, procedures and current forms (i.e., waivers, informed consent). The third step involves an independent professional who assesses the risk management plan. The fourth step would be to develop new, or revise existing, policies and procedures according to identified needs and associated risks.

Table 2.4 provides a list of considerations when developing a facility's policies and procedures.

Table 2.4
Considerations when Developing Policies and Procedures

- Definition of terms
- Objectives of recreation facility and grounds
- Agreements with other departments
- Methods of acquisitions – purchases
- Repay procedures
- Emergency reports
- Complaint handling
- Required supervision standards
- Inventory procedures
- Staff recruitment, selection and training and evaluation procedures
- New employee training protocol
- Disciplinary actions
- Staff expenses
- Maintenance
- Certification and qualification requirements
- Insurance policies

The final two steps in developing a risk management plan are implementation and evaluation. These include providing the proper training; scheduling periodic evaluations and monitoring the overall program on an ongoing basis to ensure that the plan adequately serves the needs of the organization and its members.

Questions for Class Discussion

1. Why is risk management important?
2. What are the four primary goals of risk management?
3. List two negative impacts of increased litigation.
4. What are some common causes of injuries to participants?
5. List and discuss the five categories of risk.
6. List and discuss the four ways to deal with hazards.
7. List and discuss the steps in developing a sound risk management plan.
8. What are the skills required of an effective risk manager?

Relevant Cases

Bitterman v. Atkins, 458 SE 2d. 688 (Ga. App. 1995)

Parents of student and the student brought personal injury action against the schools principal for allegedly failing to supervise adequately the installation of lockers as the student was injured when school lockers fell on him. The superior court, Douglas County, denied the principal's motion for summary judgment, and the principal appealed. The Court of Appeals held that: (1) sovereign immunity extends to school districts, and (2) sovereign immunity applied to principals' discretionary act in ordering new school lockers.

Ronk v. Corner Kick. Inc. 850 F. Supp. 369 (D. Md. 1994)

Patron who slipped on wet spot on racquetball court sued owners and operators of the court for his resulting injuries. On the defendant's motion for summary judgment, the District Court, held that the owners and operators of the racquetball court were not liable for injuries sustained by patron, given complete lack of evidence that they had created wet spot or had actual or constructive knowledge thereof.

Davis v. Savona Central School District, 675 N.Y.S. 2d 269 (A.D. 4 Dept. 1998)

High school student, who was injured after striking an unpadded portion of the school gymnasium wall during interscholastic basketball game, sued the school district, architects, and contractor, and the athletic equipment company was made a third party defendant. The Supreme Court, Appellate Division, held that the student assumed the obvious risks inherent in playing basketball in the school gymnasium.

Checchia v. Port Washington U.F.S.D., 678 N.Y.S. 2d 367 (A.D. 2 Dept. 1998)

Pupil allegedly injured when another student collided with her during a basketball game. A claim was brought against the school district to recover damages for personal injuries. The Supreme Court, Appellate Division, held that the pupils injury resulted from a spontaneous and unforeseeable act committed by a fellow student, which, under the circumstances, could not have been anticipated in the reasonable exercise of the school's legal duty to the pupil.

Alexander v. Sportslife, Inc., 502 S.E. 2d 280 (Ga. App. 1998)

A player in a pick-up game of basketball who was involved in a fight with another player at an athletic facility brought action against the other player for battery, and against the facility's owner in tort and breach of contract. Defendant player filed counter claim against plaintiff and a cross claim against owner. The Court of Appeals, Smith J., held that no conduct by any employee of the owner of the facility proximately caused the injuries suffered.

Phillipe v. City of New York Bd. Of Education, 678 N.Y.S. 2d 662 (A.D. 2 Dept. 1998)

Survivors of deceased student injured during the course of a spontaneous pick-up game of football that took place in a schoolyard brought suit against city board of education to recover damages for personal injuries. The Supreme Court, Appellate Division, held that, inasmuch as the accident occurred before the start of the school day, no duty of supervision had arisen.

Paone v. County of Suffolk, 674 N.Y.S. 2d 761 (A.D. 2 Dept. 1998)

Basketball player sued school for injuries sustained when he stepped into a hole or depression on paved surface of the court. The Supreme Court, Appellate Division, held that the player assumed the risk of injury since he chose to play basketball on court surface with faulty conditions that were open and obvious.

Dunne v. Wal-Mart Stores, Inc., 679 So. 2d 1034 (La. App. 1 Cir. 1996)

A woman, who was injured when the stationary exercise bike she was using collapsed underneath her, brought a product liability suit against the manufacturer and seller of the bike. The Court of Appeal, held that (1) use was reasonably anticipated for purposes of Louisiana Products Liability Act (LPLA), (2) failure to include warning that bicycle was not designed for use for people over 250 pounds rendered the bicycle unsafe, (3) failure to warn was the sole proximate cause of the woman's injuries, and (4) woman was entitled to awards of $10,000.00 in general damages and $469.72 for past medical expenses, but not to award for past lost income or future medical expenses.

Ferone v. Sachem C.S.D. at Holbrook, 639 N.Y.S. 2d 43 (A.D. 2 Dept. 1996)

A softball player brought negligence action for injuries incurred when he ran into a soccer goal post. The Supreme Court, Appellate Division, held that the risk of running into the goal post was not a concealed one, and the player assumed that risk by voluntarily participating in the game.

O'Leary v. Coleman (1980 NFLD 70, 26 Nfld., & P.E.I.R. 271, 72 A.P. R. 271)

14-year-old high school boy suffered an eye injury during a warm up exercise for volleyball when a fellow player struck him in the eye with his hand. The case was dismissed as the Newfoundland Supreme Court stated that such games always involve some risk and the boy did not injure him intentionally or negligently.

Drodge v. St. John's Young Men and Young Women's Christian Association (1985 No. St. J. (D.C.) 1487)

The plaintiff member of the defendants YM-YWCA was injured when he slipped and fell on a patch of water on the defendants gymnasium floor while playing a scheduled game of floor hockey. The floor was wet from a leak in the roof, which the defendant knew about, but did not warn the plaintiff about. The Newfoundland Supreme Court, Trial Division, allowed the action. The court held that the plaintiff was using the gym pursuant to contract and the defendant breached his duty to permit the plaintiff to enjoy the premises without risk of danger so far as reasonable care could make the premises safe.

Sanchez v. Ballets Total Fitness Corporation 68 Cal. 4th 62; (1998)

Sanchez sued for negligence for injuries sustained during a slide aerobic class. She suffered a wrist injury due to a slip on a slide used for aerobics (she had also unsuccessfully sued the Reebok Corporation, manufacturer of the mat). Plaintiff claims that she received no prior instruction on how to cross the slide and if she had, it never would have happened. Plaintiff claimed the contract was not sufficient because it did not disclose the word negligence. The plaintiff was senior real-estate agent and her professional knowledge shows that she knew what she was signing at the Fitness Club. She admitted signing and reading the contract and understood the three day rescind clause. It was believed that the injury was within the contemplation of both parties, based mainly on the plaintiff's professional knowledge and her admission to signing and understanding the contract. It was obvious that patrons of health clubs sign release forms and assumption of risk provisions in contemplation of injuries that might occur in the course of using the facility for the primary use of exercising and using the exercise equipment. Case dismissed.

Nydegger and Nydegger v. Don Bosco Preparatory High School, Zawacki and Cunningham 202 NJ 535; 495 A.2d 485; (1985)

Plaintiff suffered serious injury during a soccer game versus the team of which Zawacki was the coach. Contention that Zawacki coached his players to be aggressive and intense and should be responsible for the actions of his players. Case was dismissed against the coach. Court stated that unless there is direct instruction from the coach to intentionally harm or commit a wrongful act against another player on an opposite team, or instruct procedures that would increase the risk of harm, the coach is not responsible to a player who gets hurt on another team. It was also stated that interscholastic sports are voluntary and that with twenty-two players on a field, accidents are bound to happen.

Endnotes

1. Respondeat Superior: an employer is responsible for all the acts of employees done in the course of employment (Moriarty, Holman, Brown & Moriarty, 1994).
2. D.T. by M.T. v. Independent School Dist. No. 16 of Pawnee County, Okl. 894 F.2d 1176 C.A.10 (Okl. 1990).
3. Doe v. British Universities North American Club, 788 F.Supp. 1286 (D.Conn. 1992).

References

Adams, S. H. (1993). Duty to properly instruct. *JOPERD Journal*, 64(2), 22–23.

Brown, S. B. (1993). Legal obligations related to facilities. *JOPERD Journal*, 64(2), 33–35.

Forsyth, J. & Moriarty (1994). Risk management. In Moriarty, D., Holman, M., Brown, R. & Moriarty, M. (Eds.) (1994). *Canadian/American sport, fitness and the law*. Toronto, Ontario: Canadian Scholars' Press Inc.

Goodman, S. F. & McGregor, I. (1997). *Legal liability and risk management (2nd ed.)*. North York, Ontario: Risk Management Associates.

Kanoy, R. (1992). The duty to provide safe facilities. *Journal of Legal Aspects of Sport*, 2(1), 10–11.

Levin, D. S., Smith, E. A., Caldwell, L. L. & Kimbrough, J. (1995). Violence and high school sports participation. *Pediatric-exercise-science*, 7(4), 379–388.

Merriman, J. (1993). Supervision in sport and physical education. *JOPERD Journal*, 64(2), 20–21.

Miller, R. D. (1998). Campus recreation risk management. *NIRSA Journal*, 22(3), 23–25.

Moriarty, D., Holman, M., Brown, R. & Moriarty, M. (Eds.) (1994). *Canadian/American sport, fitness and the law*. Toronto, Ontario: Canadian Scholars' Press Inc.

Ondracka, S. (1999) Personal Interview.

Pittman, A. T. (1993). Safe transportation — A driving concern. *JOPERD Journal*, 64(2), 53–55.

Schofield, J. K. & Atkinson, J. A. (1995). The four As = A+ recreation: Adaptive, alternative, ambulatory and accessible. *NIRSA Journal*, 20(1), 48–49.

Seidler, T. L. (1998). Elements of a facility risk review. In Appenzeller, H. (ed.), *Risk management in sports: Issues and strategies* (283–295). Durham, North Carolina: Carolina Academic Press.

Sharp, L. A. (1993). Employment of qualified personnel. *JOPERD Journal*, 64(2), 18–19.

van der Smissen, B. (1990). *Legal liability and risk management for public and private entities*. Cincinnati, OH: Anderson Publishing Company.

van der Smissen, B. (1987). Transportation considerations. In Baker, B. (ed.), *Current issues in sport law*, (43–65). Sport Law Symposium conducted at the AAHPERD National Convention, Las Vegas, NV.

CHAPTER 3

VOLUNTEER SCREENING: LEGAL RESPONSIBILITIES FOR SPORT ORGANIZATIONS

Janice Forsyth and Brenda Gallagher

Adapted from Volunteer Canada's "Safe Steps: A Volunteer Screening Process for Recreation and Sport"

Recreation and sport organizations rely heavily on the goodwill of volunteers to implement programs and services in the community. From the local little league to provincial sport organizations, volunteers fill vital roles such as coaches, administrators, trainers, and instructors. Ensuring that volunteers are appropriate for these roles can be facilitated with an effective screening process. Screening volunteers is challenging for recreation and sport organizations due to the unstructured nature of volunteer management. Screening is a poorly understood and relatively new concept in organizations that are predominantly volunteer-driven. This is magnified in organizations that utilize a large number of parent volunteers and work with hundreds of thousands of children. The recreation and sport community is characterized in all of these ways.

The Importance of Volunteer Screening

Why screen? The answer is simple. We want to do a better job protecting participants from abuse and harassment. Both human and financial resources are wasted when problems arise due to poor recruiting. Organizations are not obliged to accept everyone who wants to volunteer. However, organizations are legally required to do everything that is reasonable to protect participants.

Educating participants, coaches, managers, leaders, and volunteers about abuse and harassment is very important. However, it is not enough! As soon as an organization opens for business whether run by staff and/or volunteers it has a responsibility to screen any person appropriately who will have access to vulnerable people. This responsibility is both moral and legal; it is not only the "right" thing to do but it is legislated under the "duty of care" concept.

"Duty of care" is a legal principle that identifies the obligations of individuals and organizations to take reasonable measures to care for and protect their participants. If participants are vulnerable the "duty of care" is more rigorous and the standard of care is higher. It is important to understand that Canadian/American courts will uphold organizations' responsibilities to screen carefully. In this way, Canadian/American courts also have a "duty of care."

The "duty of care" concept is supported by a number of Federal, Provincial and territorial laws. Three Canadian federal statutory laws; including the *Young Offenders Act*, the *Criminal Code* and the *Charter of Rights and Freedoms* are relevant to screening. These statutes provide for the protection of vulnerable people, privacy, freedom of information, and human rights. Some of the common law principles relevant to screening are duty of care, standard of care, negligence, and liability (occupier's, direct, vicarious).

In the last two decades, the law in Canada has provided more protection to vulnerable people through the Charter of Rights and Freedoms. Now there is a higher standard of care expected of someone in a position of trust. The Canadian Charter of Rights and Freedoms (www.pch.gc.ca/ddp-hrd/english/charter/contents.htm) provides protection for Canadians in a number of ways. The rights that are related to screening fall into two main categories:

1. Fundamental rights — protection for the freedom of conscience, religion, thought, belief, expression, assembly, and for the freedom of the press and other media.
2. Equality rights — discrimination is banned on the following grounds: race, national or ethnic origin, colour, religion, sex, age, and physical or mental disability.

While many fitness, recreation, sport, and community organizations may accept responsibility to protect the participants in their programs, they may feel overwhelmed by the need to screen every volunteer. Having a good screening policy implies a commitment to effective volunteer management. Volunteer management takes time and resources, both scarce commodities in the voluntary sector. Volunteer recruitment in many organizations is characterized by a desperate plea for volunteers, implying an open door to all. However, an open door policy provides the opportunity for perpetrators of abuse to infiltrate these organizations.

Clearly the onus is on the organization to screen individuals who work with children and other vulnerable populations. Volunteers who are never left alone or unsupervised differ from volunteers who are placed in significant positions of trust with participants. However, an important caveat must be stated here: THERE IS ALWAYS RISK! The premise of using a risk assessment approach to determine the amount of screening that will be done is based on the fact that voluntary organizations do not have the resources to screen everyone intensively. Even the most seemingly "safe" position, an usher at a hockey rink or a facility attendant at a community centre, can and has presented a risk. Organizations are accountable in a court of law.

Screening is an ongoing 10-step process designed to identify any person, volunteer or staff, who may harm children, youth, or other vulnerable persons. This chapter will provide an overview of volunteer screening, discuss why recreation and sport organizations should screen volunteers, and provide a step-by-step guide to the screening process.

Overview of Volunteer Screening

Screening is an ongoing process consisting of ten steps. Many, if not most, of the elements of screening are already in place in the majority of organizations but individuals are not aware that they are a part of the screening process. Screening begins long before anyone is interviewed for a volunteer position and ends only when the individual leaves the organization.

Volunteer Canada, the National voice for volunteerism in Canada, recommends the Safe Steps process for screening to assist organizations in the recruitment, selection and management of volunteers and staff (Volunteer Canada, 1998):

Safe Steps
1. Determining the risk,
2. Position design & description,
3. Recruitment process,
4. Application form,
5. Interviews,
6. Reference checks,
7. Police records checks,
8. Orientation and training,
9. Supervision / evaluation,
10. Participant follow-up.

Step 1 – Determining the Risk

It may seem tedious to determine the risk for every position; however, it is the key to an effective screening process. Being aware of the risks and avoiding them whenever possible is an essential component to effective

Table 3.1
Key Terminology

Duty of care
The obligation that one owes the other, especially the obligations to exercise reasonable care with respect to the interests of the other. This obligation includes protection from harm.

Orientation
Orientation is a period or process of adjustment. Providing information to a volunteer about the program they will be involved in, providing them with the rules and regulations and the code of conduct, are all part of the orientation process.

Participants
Many different words are used to name people who participate in programs or receive services from recreation and sport organizations. The word participant is used as the generic term and represents players, athletes, clients, users, et cetera.

Position of trust
1. Situations in which someone has a significant degree of:
   - Authority or decision-making power over another;
   - Unsupervised access to another person and to his/her property.
2. Situations where the success of the service depends on the development of a close, personal relationship between the individuals as in mentoring or friendly visiting programs.

Training
Training is a learning process, during which time an individual is taught specific skills that will assist them in performing their duties.

Volunteers
A volunteer is an individual:

- Who chooses to undertake a service or activity, someone who is not coerced or compelled to do this activity;
- Who does this activity in service to an individual or an organization, or to assist the community-at-large;
- Who does not receive a salary or wage for this service or activity.

The same principles apply to paid employees, interns, students on placement, and trainers.

Vulnerable person
One who has difficulty protecting him/herself from harm temporarily or permanently and is at risk because of age, disability, or handicap.

---

screening. Two leading American authorities on risk management for non-profit and charitable organizations put it this way:

> Risk management improves performance by acknowledging and controlling risk. It's about finding solutions, not just looking for trouble. At its heart, risk management not only reduces the likelihood of losses; it also maximizes the benefits of volunteer programs. The heart of risk management beats with three Cs":
>
> 1. Commitment to respecting the rights and safety of everyone the program touches.
> 2. Communicating that commitment to everyone.
> 3. Consistency in acting in accord with that commitment.
>
> Points of Light Foundation, 1994

Seeking to protect participants, volunteers, staff, and the community through screening measures is an exercise in risk management. The term "risk management" is simply a question of what could go wrong and how do we avoid it? Risk management involves looking at the possibilities of loss or injury that might arise in programs, activities or services and taking steps to stop, minimize, prevent, or eliminate them altogether. It is the nature of the position and its inherent level of risk that dictates the screening measures used. Volunteer positions vary with respect to degree of risk. The factors that help determine the level of risk in a position are participant, setting, position, supervision and nature of the relationship between the volunteer and the participant. Organizations must choose from a number of options in order to control the risks in a position. These risk management options include:

1. **Eliminate the risk.**

    Sometimes the risks are too great and the consequences are too serious to bear. In this case, the organization may decide to eliminate the activity altogether. For example, an organization providing day programming for seniors may decide that the level of risk (liability) is too high to continue taking the participants on trips in cars driven by volunteers. The organization may decide to eliminate the risk altogether by canceling such trips.

2. **Modify the activity.**

    There may be ways of changing some aspects of a position or activity so that it reduces the risk. This modification may involve changing how something is done, where, by whom, or it may mean that a particular element of an activity will be stopped. For example, when local teams canvass door-to-door during fundraising campaigns, the organization's policy may state that this activity will always be done in teams of at least two people. This reduces the risk that either the fundraisers or the homeowners will be harmed because there is a third party involved. It is also important to change the "teams" occasionally.

3. **Transfer liability.**

    In some circumstances, organizations may choose to have someone else (an individual, an organization) take on part of a task and assume the liability. This outside party is usually a company or an organization that can bear the risks because either it can afford to, or because it has a particular professional expertise not available within the original organization. For example, after having considered the risks and losses, an organization may decide to discontinue the practice of having parents driving groups of children to and from its activities. The organization may also have decided that the trips are essential, so they may look for someone else to take over that part of the activity, and to assume the risk at the same time. A bus or taxi service, for example, would offer the protection of significant insurance coverage for this activity.

4. **Assume the risk.**

    Having clearly identified the risks, assessed the probability of their occurrence, looked at the possible losses, and determined the consequences, organizations may decide that an activity or position is fundamental to their functioning and they will not give it up, they may decide to assume this risk. Elite cross-country skiers meet with a sport psychologist in groups to practice visualization for their races. However, since the team members are mostly at the same level, they also meet on an individual basis with the psychologist in order to develop their competitiveness with their own teammates. The athletes and coaches think that these meetings are critical to the performance of the athletes. The organization has decided to assume this risk and continue the practice.

5. **Assuming risk and minimizing the risk.**

    Having decided to assume the risk, the organization should nevertheless continue to seek ways of reducing or avoiding the risks and minimizing the possible losses. Purchasing insurance is one way organizations seek to do this while screening volunteers is another.

    Organizations can purchase insurance as part of their risk management process. Insurance can offer protection to volunteers, staff and board members through coverage including general third party liability and directors and officers insurance. Organizations must be aware that there are exceptions in every insurance policy and if found negligent, insurance may not cover the loss.

Summary of Key Concepts

- Analyzing the risk in a position is the first step in effective screening.
- Preventing problems before they occur is good risk management.
- Organizations can manage risk effectively.
- Analyzing risk for volunteer positions is dependent on the participant, the setting, the activity, the supervision, and the nature of the relationship.

Note: Large settlements awarded in cases such as Mount Cashel (residential school) and the Kingston choirmaster case will likely affect the availability of some forms of insurance. Some insurance companies have already excluded coverage for the sexual abuse of children.

The Mount Cashel case can be found on the www.lexum.umontreal.ca/csc-scc/ web site.

Step 2 – Position Design & Position Description

Position Design

By effectively designing positions the first level of screening takes place. Each position has a specific set of conditions and responsibilities and with these certain risks. The risk factors can be reduced by:

- First and most important – learn to think about risk realistically. Accept the fact that participants can be harmed while participating in your organization's programs;
- Establish behavioral standards or guidelines for your organization and communicate them to your volunteers and staff at scheduled orientation sessions. An example of a behavioral standard could be that an adult must never be alone with a child in a change room;
- Group the positions in your organization according to their level of risk:
  - **Low risk:** minimal or no contact with children and other vulnerable participants;
  - **Medium risk:** volunteers who work with children/vulnerable participants but are never alone with them;
  - **High risk:** volunteers who have the opportunity to be alone with children/vulnerable participants; volunteers who are in a position to exert influence over youth.
- Set the screening standard based on the risk factor (i.e., for low risk positions choose fewer, less intrusive measures, for high risk positions follow all of the 10 steps;
- Design positions that require people to work in pairs;
- Introduce an initial mentor phase where an experienced person works with new volunteers;
- If your volunteers are active in more than one position, make sure they are screened for the position with the highest level of risk. If volunteers change positions, make sure the extent of the screening used for the previous position is appropriate for the new one.

Position Description

A position description is a powerful and necessary tool. It is used to define a position and to set ground rules for volunteers and staff. Although writing position descriptions may be difficult in some cases, it is imperative to be able to describe the position and to define the inherent risk. Position descriptions should establish guidelines, protect volunteers by formalizing roles, and send a clear message that the organization is serious about providing safety for both their participants and volunteers. The following list identifies common elements in a position description:

- Title of position,
- Participant group (children, seniors, et cetera),
- Goals of position,
- Activities and tasks associated with position,
- Outline of responsibilities,
- Boundaries and limits to the position,
- Skills, experience and qualifications required,
- Personal traits and qualities needed and/or desired,
- Orientation and training available,
- Support, supervision, and evaluation provided,
- Mandatory activities (e.g. training, monthly meetings, travel),
- Working conditions (e.g. non-smoking environment),
- Benefits to the volunteer,
- Screening measures.

Include general dos and don'ts related to the position. For example, if a chauffeur for a hockey team is not supposed to enter an athlete's home when picking them up, make sure that condition is stated in the position description.

Summary of Key Concepts

- Comprehensive position design is the foundation for all other screening measures.
- Clear position descriptions send the message that your organization is serious about screening.
- The responsibilities listed for each position determines the position's level of risk.

Step 3 – Recruitment Process

Recruitment of volunteers is usually done less formally than the recruitment of employees. In fact, volunteer recruitment is often haphazard, as recreation and sport organizations encourage parents to move from watching their children participate to helping out with their activities. These personal ties between volunteers and the team or program can complicate the screening process.

The more informal the existing volunteer recruitment process is, the less comfortable recruiters are in applying formal steps. One of the ways to move from an informal to a formal recruitment process is to post notices or send home requests for volunteers accompanied by position descriptions and application forms.

It is important to achieve balance between formalizing the recruitment process and appearing desperate for volunteers. The worst recruitment notice, in terms of child safety and the integrity of the program, is something like "Help! We're desperate! Come and volunteer!" This sense of urgency does not always attract the type of volunteer the organization wants or needs.

Care must be taken during the recruitment process, especially for positions of trust with vulnerable participants. Ensure that your recruiting materials clearly outline that the organization takes its responsibilities for participants seriously, and screens all applicants thoroughly. Do not leave people with the impression that everyone who applies will be accepted. Be very clear that your organization is extremely careful about selecting volunteers and do not apologize for that fact.

Ensure that promotional materials, including position descriptions, are kept accurate and up-to-date. When recruiting through a local volunteer centre, keep volunteer centre staff informed about changes in position descriptions and of any special considerations that would affect the referral of volunteers. Send recruitment information to potential volunteers before you commit to an interview. Ensure that the documents include all the information available about the position in question, and about the organization's screening measures.

A formalized recruitment process is another way an organization can fulfill its duty of care. A documented process establishes the organization's credibility and due diligence regarding the safety of participants.

Summary of Key Concepts

- It is important to formalize the recruitment process.
- The organization should be open about its process and make it clear that not everyone is accepted for the position they apply for.
- Recruitment materials should indicate that your organization thoroughly screens applicants.

Step 4 – Application Form

An application form is the first screening tool that potential volunteers will encounter. Basic information – name, address, experience – while giving the organization permission to do reference checks and police records checks (if necessary) is collected. The reason for asking for references and the conditions for a police records check should be noted on this form.

Asking volunteers to complete an application form reinforces the seriousness of an organization's commitment to screening and provides a paper trail that will protect both the volunteer and the organization. Application forms must not ask for information about characteristics that are among the prohibited grounds of discrimination, such as age, gender, marital status, et

Table 3.2
Acceptable and Unacceptable Practices in Recruiting and Interviewing

Subject	Unacceptable practices	Acceptable practices	Comments
Name	• Asking for birth name of applicant • Asking for previous name when name was changed by court order.	• Asking for name under which applicant has been educated or employed.	
Address	• Asking for foreign addresses (which may indicate national origin).	• Asking for place and duration of current and previous address in Canada.	
Age	• Asking for birth certificate, baptismal record, or any other documents or information regarding age of applicant.	• Asking whether applicant has attained minimum age, or has exceeded maximum age, applying to employment by law.	Verification of age may be obtained after hiring.
Gender	• Asking about the gender of an applicant on the application form. • Use different or coded application forms for males and females.		Correspondence to applicants may be addressed to their home with or without the prefixes Mr., Mrs., Miss, Ms., e.g., "Dear Mary Smith."
Marital status	• Asking whether applicant is single, married, remarried, engaged, divorced, separated, widowed, or living common law. • Asking about the applicant's spouse, e.g., "Is spouse subject to transfer?" • Asking for number of children or other dependents. • Asking about child-care arrangements. • Asking about whether applicant is pregnant, on birth control, or has future childbearing plans.	• Asking if applicant is willing to travel or to be transferred to other areas of the province or country, if this requirement is job related.	Such information, if required for tax or insurance purposes, may be required after hiring.
National or ethnic origin	• Asking about birthplace. • Asking about nationality of parents, grandparents, relatives or spouse. • Asking about ethnic or national origin, e.g., requiring birth certificate, asking for mother tongue. • Asking whether applicant is native born or naturalized • Asking for date citizenship received. • Asking for proof of citizenship.	• Asking if the applicant is legally entitled to work in Canada.	An employer may ask for documentary proof of eligibility to work in Canada after hiring.

Table 3.2
Acceptable and Unacceptable Practices in Recruiting and Interviewing (continued)

Subject	Unacceptable practices	Acceptable practices	Comments
Medical information			A medical examination will necessarily reveal prohibited information about an applicant, such as his or her age, race, or sex. For this reason, employers should conduct medical examinations after the hiring decision is made. Employers may indicate on application forms that the job offer is conditional on the applicant's passing a medical examination.
Organization	• Asking applicant to list all clubs or organizations he or she belongs to.	• Asking for such a list with the proviso that applicant may decline to list clubs or organizations, which may indicate a prohibited ground of discrimination.	The request should only be made if membership in organization is necessary to determine job qualifications.
Optional inquiries	• Making any of the above prohibited inquiries, even if marked "optional" on the application form.		
Military	• Asking about military service.	• Asking about Canadian military service.	Asking about all military service is permissible if military experience relates to the job applied for.
Languages	• Asking about mother tongue or where language skills were obtained.	• Asking about which languages applicant speaks, reads, or writes, if job related.	Testing or scoring an applicant in English or French language proficiency is not approved unless English or French language skill is a requirement for the work to be performed.
Race or colour	• Asking anything which would indicate race, colour, or complexion, including colour of eyes, hair or skin.		
Photographs	• Asking for a photograph, or taking of photograph.		Photos may be required after hiring for identification purposes.
Religion	• Asking about religious affiliation. • Asking about willingness or availability to work on a specific religious holiday. • Asking about church attended, religious holidays, customs observed, or religious dress. • Asking for reference or recommendation from pastor, priest, minister, rabbi, or other religious leader.	• Asking about willingness to work a specified work schedule.	It is the duty of the employer to accommodate the religious observances of the applicant, it is reasonably possible to do so. After hiring, inquiry about religion to determine when leave of absence for religious observance is permitted.

Table 3.2
Acceptable and Unacceptable Practices in Recruiting and Interviewing (continued)

Subject	Unacceptable practices	Acceptable practices	Comments
Height and weight			Height and weight requirements may be discriminatory if they screen out disproportionate numbers of minority-group individuals or women and if they cannot be shown to be essential for the performance of the job.
Relatives	• Asking for relationship to applicant of next of kin to be notified in case of emergency.	• Asking for name and address of person to be notified in case of emergency.	
References	• Asking any questions of a person given as a reference that would not be allowable if asked directly of the applicant.		
Criminal	• Asking whether applicant has ever been convicted of an offence.	• Asking whether applicant has been convicted of an offence for which no pardon has been granted.	The Canadian Human Rights Act permits discrimination on a criminal conviction for which a pardon has not been granted. However, it discourages inquiries into unpardoned criminal convictions unless the particular conviction is relevant to job qualifications; e.g., a theft and fraud conviction is relevant to a job requiring honesty, but a conviction for marijuana possession is not.
Physical handicap	• Asking about all physical handicaps, limitations, or health problems which would tend to elicit handicaps or conditions not necessarily related to job performance.	• Asking whether applicant has any physical handicaps or health problems affecting the job applied for. • Inquiry as to any physical handicaps or limitations that the applicant wishes to be taken into consideration when determining job placement.	A physical handicap is relevant to the job when: (a) the handicap could be hazardous to the applicant, coworkers, clients, or the public; (b) the handicap could prevent the applicant from performing the duties of the job satisfactorily.

cetera. Please note that Federal and Provincial/State statutes are not identical in terms of these prohibited grounds.

If you require a police records check for the position a volunteer is applying for, the police will require a date of birth. This, of course, violates human rights. Therefore, police records check forms cannot be completed until the volunteer has been offered the position (with the condition that they can be eliminated after a police records check).

When creating application forms, organizations should ask themselves the following questions:

- Why are we asking for this information?
- Is this information necessary to establish the applicant's qualifications for this position?
- What effect will asking these questions have on the individual's prospects of being selected?
- Will the questions unduly or unlawfully prejudice his or her chances?
- Will any of the questions illicit information that falls within the prohibited grounds of discrimination?

Questions must be directly related to the volunteer position. Ensure that the questions being asked do not come as a surprise to applicants. They should have received information about the screening policies of the organization before being asked to fill in the application.

Human rights legislation distinguishes between what can be asked of people before they are selected, and what can be asked after they are selected. Organizations should check with the Human Rights Commission or Council in their respective Province/State for a list of the types of information that may be sought before and after someone is selected. Appendix "A" provides an example of acceptable and unacceptable practices for an application form, recruiting and/or interviewing procedures.

Many questions that are routinely asked on application forms are actually only required after the individual is selected in order to establish emergency contacts or to set up certain human resource procedures. For example, an employee's bank account number would be required for payroll purposes. This type of information should not be requested before an official job offer.

Summary of Key Concepts

- Ensure your application form only asks for information related to the requirements of the position.
- Information requests before selection are much more restricted than information requests allowed following an offer.
- Do not ask for information about characteristics among the prohibited grounds of discrimination, as set out by Federal and Provincial/State statutes.

Step 5 – Interviews

Interviews are an extremely important step in the screening process. The interview provides not only an opportunity to talk to the potential volunteer about their background, talents, skills, interests and availability, but also to explore any doubts your group may have about the suitability of the candidate. An interview also serves to express the expectations and to convey the norms/culture of your organization. In other words, an interview will help determine "the right fit" between the position and the applicant. You should be well prepared, in order to be thorough and make the best use of time, but an interview need not be long or difficult.

Most organizations rely on an informal and non-competitive interview structure for the selection of volunteers. An interview with a volunteer could be a 30-minute meeting where organizational standards, norms and expectations are discussed and the position description is reviewed. The purpose of the interview is to assess the suitability of the volunteer for a particular position. When planning an interview consider the following:

- Have at least two people conduct the interview;
- Explain the interview process to the applicant;
- Establish a safe environment for the applicant;
- Describe the position specifically, using the position description;
- Describe the screening policies/procedures required for the position;

- Document the applicant's responses to the questions and keep them on file;
- Look for attitudes towards children and vulnerable adults that do not fit with those of your organization;
- Ask all applicants the same questions to maintain consistency.

When selecting questions for an interview remember that the most revealing questions address situations that have already taken place. Past behavior is the best indicator of future performance. The selection of appropriate questions is very important in volunteer screening. Also, remember that interviews are subject to the same Human Rights laws as discussed in Step 4 – Application Form (see Table 3.2). Interview questions should encourage responses that allow you to judge:

- Relevant work related experiences;
- Relevant formal and informal education;
- Eagerness to work;
- Ability to work with others;
- Integrity;
- Supervision preferences;
- Initiative and judgement;

It is unusual to allow volunteers to run programs from their homes. However, if a volunteer and participant will spend time in a volunteer's home, an in-home interview is entirely appropriate. The applicant must consent to an in-home interview, but if he or she does not, this may be enough to reject the application. The purpose of the in-home interview is to determine if the home is a safe and appropriate place for the participant to be taken. If activities will take place in the home, you must ask for information about any other person who lives in the home or visits frequently.

Summary of Key Concepts

- To select the candidate most likely to succeed, the process must be completely objective.
- Like screening, the selection is based on the requirements of the position.
- Interviews are important ways to get to know the applicant better.

Step 6 – Reference Checks

A reference check may be the most effective screening step during the selection process. References will confirm the background and skills of the applicant and will provide an outside opinion on the suitability of the person for the position. It should not be assumed that applicants would only give the names of people who will speak well of them. It is a known fact that references are often not called. Tips for getting the most out of a reference check include:

- Outline the position description clearly to the person giving the reference. Ask about the applicant's skills and suitability to the tasks as defined.
- Identify the level of trust that will be developed between the children and the participant. (E.g. "Joe will be working closely with children and will be alone with them." Would you be comfortable with Joe having this kind of relationship with your child?")
- Avoid leading questions (e.g. "We really think Joe will make a great coach, don't you?").
- Leave space in the call for open comment (e.g. "Could you comment on Joe and how you think he would fit in this job?").
- Do more than one reference check. If the candidate has given names of people who might not be objective (family members) ask if it is okay to contact previous or current employers. Whenever possible get the name of someone who is familiar with the applicant's work with specific participant groups.

The following list is adapted from The Seven Rs of Volunteer Development: A YMCA Resource Kit (The YMCA of the USA, 1994):

- Do not proceed with reference checks until a signed release form is obtained. Make sure phone numbers for the references are listed.
- Do not make exceptions for anyone. If the position requires reference checks, follow through on each one.

- Do not accept one positive or negative reference without validation through other sources. Do not accept or reject the applicant based solely on one reference.
- Verify that the person to whom you are speaking is indeed the reference given on the applicant's form.
- After you mention the name of your candidate, listen carefully to the attitude, tone, and hesitancy of those you have called. If the person sounds upbeat and positive, it is likely that the candidate was a good employee/volunteer. If the person sounds guarded or hesitant, perhaps the candidate was a problem. Remember, however, that some problems arise because of the supervisor, not because of the employee. For this reason, it is important to get several references.
- Remember that you may be able to ask volunteers or other staff to help conduct the reference checks. These volunteers, of course, have to be trained using a specific format. A standardized reference check questionnaire ensures everyone is asked the same questions. When completed, it can be kept on file.

When checking references, keep in mind that the information you receive is personal information, which is controlled under the Personal Information and Electronic Documents Act. (www.privcom.gc.ca/english/02_06_02_e.htm)

According to this Act, organizations are required to meet a number of obligations when dealing with personal information such as the information received from a reference check. The following 10 principles outline the obligations of an organization:

1. Accountability,
2. Identifying purposes,
3. Consent,
4. Limiting collection,
5. Limiting use, disclose and retention,
6. Accuracy,
7. Safeguards,
8. Openness,
9. Individual access,
10. Challenging compliance.

Summary of Key Concepts

- A reference check is the most effective screening step during the selection process.
- To get the most out of a reference check, prepare a list of questions or a sample script beforehand.
- Develop organizational guidelines for reference checks.
- Obtain the volunteer's consent when their personal information is collected, used or disclosed.

Step 7 – Police Records Checks (PRC)

Police records checks are probably the most misunderstood element of screening. Too many people believe that doing a PRC means that the person has been screened. Nothing could be further from the truth. It is important to know if a potential volunteer has been convicted of a crime and the nature of the crime. If a conviction is an abuse or harassment offence, it can be more pertinent than a conviction for shoplifting, depending on the position that the volunteer will be filling.

What information do the police see when they enter a volunteer's name in their database?

Contrary to popular opinion, not all police forces check the same data sources. Local police units will consult their local records but may or may not consult the national database. In contrast, a national search done through the Canadian Police Information Centre (CPIC) produces federal level data but may not reveal pertinent local details. Local police forces will reveal convictions and charges, and information as plaintiff, victim, suspect, and witness. CPIC's database will reveal criminal charges and convictions, probation, and related court orders (i.e., possession of firearms, et cetera).

Prior to requesting a PRC, organizations must decide the type of information that will be required from the police. For example, if the position allows the volunteer access to the organization's finances but there is no risk of one-on-one contact with a participant, the police should be checking the data base for any convictions related to theft or fraud. If the police receive very specific information about the organization's needs, it is more likely that they will be able to provide the data needed.

Unfortunately many abusers and sex offenders have never been convicted of a crime. Furthermore, despite the excellent RCMP data system (CPIC) there are inherent problems with any list. The limitations of police records checks include:

- Recent convictions may not show due to inputting delays.
- There are lags in sending records from one country to another.
- The individual may be using an alias so only fingerprint checks will confirm their identity.
- Relying solely on police records checks is dangerous — organizations may believe that they have done enough and will not use any other screening measures. A false sense of security may be created.
- The individual may have obtained a "pardon" and therefore is no longer on the list.
- The information may not be available because the conviction occurred while the individual was a youth and is protected by the Young Offenders' Act.

Despite the built-in limitations of PRCs, they do serve a purpose, particularly in those cases (high-risk positions) where the organization is committed to a full and complete screening process. The PRC will also signal, in a very public way, that the organization is concerned about the safety of its participants. The following should be considered when requesting a PRC:

- The position application form, for high-risk positions, should state that the employee or volunteer would be asked to provide a PRC; the applicant should confirm acceptance of this. Just as stating your screening policy in your recruiting notices can be an effective deterrent, making all applicants aware that you conduct police records checks can ensure that some applicants screen themselves out.
- Use a release form, which states the agreement of the volunteer or employee to a PRC. The resulting information can be handled in one of two ways:
  1. The organization may ask the applicant to give permission to the police to release the result directly to the organization (the results will only indicate whether or not there has been a conviction).
  2. The organization may ask the applicant to take the form to the police, have the results released directly to the applicant and have the applicant bring the results back to the organization. This option puts more control into the hands of the applicant and allows him or her to decide whether or not to share the results.
- A written policy should be in place – that all current and prospective employees and volunteers are familiar with – that defines organizational policy on selecting individuals with criminal records.
- A number of police forces and municipalities now charge for doing PRCs. The organization will need a policy on whether these costs will be borne by individuals or the organization, depending on the position.

In some provinces/communities an organization signs a memorandum of understanding with their Provincial/State or local police force which specifies the roles of the police, the organization, and the individual being screened. An agreement about cost is also developed. The following paragraphs outline considerations for administrators when developing a screening policy, which includes police records checks.

Clear guidelines must be developed concerning how your organization will handle a volunteer whose PRC shows a previous conviction. For example, organizations must decide if for positions of trust where there is the opportunity for one-on-one contact with a participant, certain classes of convictions (e.g. fraud, violent crimes, and sex-related crimes) will automatically preclude a volunteer from filling that position.

Organizations must develop a policy regarding volunteers with convictions outside the specified classes (e.g. theft, possession of narcotics). There are a number of options including:

- Establishing a panel to assess individual cases which fall in the "gray area";
- Accepting volunteers with a criminal history, as long as they are not in positions of trust and dependent on the tasks required in the position they will be filling.

The decision your organization makes will depend on the activities you carry out, the participants you deal with as well as the organization's purpose, philosophy, and values.

When deciding whether to accept or reject an applicant, the organization will base its decision on the following:

- The nature of the program, services, and activities provided;
- The character and degree of vulnerability of the participant group served and the organization's duty of care to the participants, to the volunteers, and to the community;
- The relevant moral, ethical, legal and policy issues and principles;
- The potential risks involved in the position for which the individual is applying, based on the participant group being served, the nature of the position and its activities, the setting in which it takes place, the way in which it is supervised and the nature of the relationship being established.

Once organizations receive information about an applicant, whether from the applicant directly or from the police, the organization becomes responsible for that information and is then subject to many of the same legal requirements and regulations as other holders of personal information, in terms of confidentiality and access (see Step 6).

Organizations must also decide whether or not they will conduct police records checks more than once. Some organizations require that PRCs be done annually, or every two or three years. This requirement may act as a deterrent to some. However, the limitations on police record checks remain regardless of the number of checks conducted.

The bottom line is that police records checks can be an extremely important step in the screening process, however, they may not be appropriate for all positions. The only certainty is that they should never be the first, last, or only screening step used by an organization.

Summary of Key Concepts

- PRCs are only one step in the 10-step screening process.
- Be aware of the limitations of PRCs.
- PRCs are an important screening tool, particularly for high-risk positions.
- Organizations should consult with their local police force when establishing their policy.

Note: A number of cases of participant abuse reported over the last few years have been in organizations that have extensive pre-engagement screening. Sometimes, no matter how good the policies, procedures, and practices are, someone slips by. It is not enough to be vigilant at the outset only to stop screening the person once he or she is on board.

A new provision to the Criminal Records Act (March 2000), enables notations to be made in CPIC on records of pardoned persons in order to allow the disclosure of those records when individuals are screened for positions of trust with children or vulnerable adults. Bill C-7 is the amendment to the Act. For more details consult: www.parl.gc.ca/36/2/parlbus/chambus/house/bills/summaries/c7-e.htm

Step 8 – Orientation and Training

Orientation and training are an important part of the screening process. Screening continues through the early period of the volunteer's involvement and should be ongoing throughout the entire engagement. Ongoing vigilance on behalf of participants is a must. The responsibility does not end once the volunteer is in place.

A volunteer is considered to be on probation until the training period is complete. A three to six month probation period allows the organization and the individual the opportunity to ensure the volunteer position is the right choice. During the orientation and training period, an organization should achieve:

- Knowledge of the volunteer's approach, values and work style: role-playing may be used to explore some of these issues;
- Translation of organizational policy to the individual's role within the sport/recreation community: the policies need to be clearly understood by new volunteers, especially in areas that relate to participants who are vulnerable (e.g. dressing rooms, road trips);
- Development of interpersonal skills in areas where each individual will be working;
- A final decision of whether or not the person is appropriate.

It is perfectly acceptable to dismiss a volunteer during or after a probationary period. Any questionable actions should be noted and decisions made accordingly. Orientation and training sessions provide opportunities to test our observations of individuals, to see them under different circumstances. People who may be skilled manipulators in one-to-one interviews may demonstrate more questionable behavior in group settings.

Although training volunteers can be labour intensive, there are long-term benefits such as better-informed volunteers, effective job performance, increased job satisfaction, and the opportunity to continue with the screening process. Document the process for future reference and for verification of the standard of care provided in your screening process.

Orientation and training events should be mandatory. Refusal to attend, or constant excuses for not attending may be a warning signal. Orientation and training events provide an opportunity to pass on information (including manuals and handbooks), answer questions, as well as, providing time to follow up on the placement.

Summary of Key Concepts

- Responsibility does not end once the volunteer is in place – ongoing vigilance is a must.
- A probation period allows both the organization and the volunteer to learn more about each other.

- Host orientation and training sessions to provide new and existing volunteers with information on the organization's policies and procedures.
- Orientation and training sessions offer you the opportunity to observe volunteers in a social setting.

Step 9 – Supervision and Evaluation

Performance appraisals should be ongoing with formal evaluation occurring at least once a year. In order to give feedback, someone in the organization must be responsible for the supervision of the volunteer. The supervisor is responsible for on-the-job training and periodically reviewing the volunteer's performance. By instituting a formal supervision and evaluation process, the volunteer can be observed "on the job" and have their work monitored on an ongoing basis.

If supervision and evaluation is new to your volunteers, they may resist. Overcome this barrier by clarifying that the purpose of evaluation is:

- To ensure a standard level of practice;
- To improve the experiences of volunteers, staff, and participants in the programs;
- To enrich individuals' experience in their jobs;
- To protect all participants.

All supervision and evaluation processes should use the position description as a reference point. During the evaluation meeting:

- Go through the position description point by point;
- Ask the volunteer to comment on how they think they are doing in each area, and how they enjoy their work;
- Give feedback on their performance in each area;
- Keep comments positive but clearly state any concerns;
- Document the evaluation;

- Have the document signed by both the volunteer and evaluator;
- File the document.

There is nothing more difficult than letting someone go. By using a formal evaluation process and referring to the position description, the difficult decisions do not become personal. The amount of supervision and evaluation needed will depend on the level of risk in the position but all volunteers need to be periodically observed and given feedback. Any cause for concern requires immediate action. The following tips may be helpful when terminating a volunteer:

- Inform all personnel of the length of the probation period.
- Conduct a personal interview at the end of the probation period.
- Whenever possible, give the reasons for terminating the person's involvement.
- Unless you have clear and irrefutable proof that the individual intends to harm a participant, you should avoid mentioning this possibility for reasons of liability.

Organizations must have a *bona fide* reason to refuse or terminate a volunteer. Whereas discrimination normally has negative connotations, at times organizations must discriminate when looking for the volunteer or staff who best meets the requirements of the position. In this case legislation recognizes that there are circumstances when discrimination is both legitimate and legal.

Summary of Key Concepts

- Ensure frequent feedback during the first year.
- Assign someone in your organization the task of supervision and evaluation of your new volunteers.
- Base evaluation on the position description.
- The greater the risk in a position the more frequent and more intense the supervision and evaluation process should be.

Step 10 – Participant Follow-up

It is important to inform volunteers of the follow-up activities that may take place after they begin their volunteer work. Ensure that the volunteer is aware that any follow-up that happens is because of the level of risk in the position.

Regular ongoing contact with participants and family members can act as an effective deterrent to someone who might otherwise do harm and go undetected. It is vital that the organization let all volunteers know that regular supervision and evaluation, including contact with participants and families are part of the organization's risk management procedures and that there is nothing personal about it.

Participant follow-up is extremely important in high-risk volunteer positions. Checking in occasionally with your volunteers and program participants could provide you with information that is not communicated in formal interviews or evaluations. For example, if a volunteer and participant have developed a personal friendship and are socializing outside of the activities sanctioned by the organization, this might come up during an informal chat.

If a volunteer and a participant are usually alone together, it may be appropriate to conduct random spot checks by visiting the location where they are together. It should be made clear when the volunteer joins the organization that random spot checks are a possibility in high-risk positions. It should likewise be made clear to the participant that this is a risk management and screening measure that the organization intends to take for everyone's protection.

Summary of Key Concepts

- Make volunteers aware of follow-up activities that may occur.
- Stay in contact with participants and their families.
- Consider conducting spot checks on individuals working in high-risk positions with little or no supervision.

Conclusion

Although screening may be costly and time-consuming, it is an issue that organizations must address. Any organization working with vulnerable people must take on this responsibility.

Each team, each league, each provincial/state and national sports and recreation organization is different from the other. This difference is due to many factors: the province/state; the type of community (urban, rural, large, small, northern, southern); the nature of the activity (leisure, contact, individual, team, outdoor, indoor); the level of the activity; the age of the participant involved; the coaching styles used; the management culture; the socioeconomic level of participants. The context will affect the kind of screening policy adopted.

Steps can be taken to reduce your organization's workload while still ensuring the protection/safety of your participants. An orientation session on policies and expectations can serve a large number of low-risk volunteers who have limited access to participants. By introducing the concept of screening in this format, these volunteers will understand the policies that protect their participants and themselves without going through the individualized screening processes. This approach will serve two purposes. Initially, it will put the group on guard giving them the skills to watch for abusive and harassing behaviors, and secondly, it will put them at ease by helping them understand that the rules are not a "witch hunt" but a responsibility to protect all vulnerable participants. Medium and high-risk positions require a more in-depth screening process.

There are many practical strategies to meet the challenge of screening. Volunteer centers across Canada and the USA are able to provide local recreation and sport groups with training and consultation. Screening policies can be "custom made" for each organization.

Development of policies and procedures related to screening is not just to prevent legal liability but more importantly should be based on ethical and moral responsibilities to protect participants, volunteers, staff, and the general community from harm. It is particularly important to keep in touch with other organizations. By sharing the successes and failures of implementing a screening policy, with other organizations, eventually the process will become less daunting. Become an advocate of screening and become a resource to other organizations that are just beginning to learn about screening. Most importantly, continue to learn and grow as an organization.

Questions for Class Discussion

1. Discuss the legal principles that are relevant to volunteer screening.
2. List the ten steps to screening. Describe each step with the use of an example.
3. How can volunteer screening reduce the risk of liability in a sport organization?
4. Describe a situation where a volunteer in a sport organization would be in a "position of trust."
5. What can an organization do to decrease the risk in a volunteer position?
6. Discuss two methods that organizations can use to recruit volunteers.

Relevant Cases

There are two recent vicarious liability cases heard by the Supreme Court of Canada that dealt with the issue of unsanctioned inappropriate activities.

Bazley v. Curry (17 June 1999) — Children's Foundation

The Court found The Children's Foundation to be vicariously liable for the sexual abuse of a child by a counselor employed by the Foundation in a residential home for emotionally troubled children. The court determined that the terms of employment created the opportunity for intimate private control and a parental relationship and this fostered an environment that ultimately led to the sexual abuse.
www.droit.umontreal.ca/doc/csc-scc/en/html/bazley.en.html

Jacobi v. Griffiths (17 June 1999) — Boys' and Girls' Club

The Court ruled that the employer was not vicariously liable for the sexual abuse of children by the program director of a drop-in centre. It was determined that there was no link between the organization's recreational enterprise and the wrongs committed by the program director. The terms of employment did not introduce a level of intimacy from which the abuse flowed. www.droit.umontreal.ca/doc/csc-scc/en/html/jacobi.en.html

References

Canadian Association of Volunteer Bureaus and Centers. (1997). *What is Screening? Why Screen?* Ottawa, Ontario.

Canadian Association of Volunteer Bureaus and Centers. (1996). *The Screening Handbook: Protecting Clients, Staff and the Community*. Ottawa, Ontario: L. Street.

Canadian Association of Volunteer Bureaus and Centers. (1997). *Developing Effective Policy on Screening*. Ottawa, Ontario.

Canadian Hockey Association. (1998). *Speak Out!... Act Now! A Guide to Preventing and Responding to Abuse and Harassment for Sport Clubs and Associations.* Ottawa, Ontario.

Edmonton Public Schools. (1998). *Recruitment and Interviewing Guide.* Edmonton, Alberta.

Graff, Linda L. (1997). Risk Management. In G. Jonstone (Ed.), *Management of Volunteer Services in Canada: The Text.* (Ch. 5) Carp, Ontario: Jonstone Training and Consulting.

Graff, Linda L. (1997). Selection, Screening, and Placement. In G. Jonstone (Ed.), *Management of Volunteer Services in Canada: The Text.* (Ch. 9) Carp, Ontario: Jonstone Training and Consulting.

Graff, Linda L. (1997). *By Definition: Policies for Volunteer Programs.* Dundas, Ontario: Graff and Associates.

Lai, Mary L., Terry S. Chapman, Elmer L. Steinbock. (1992). *Am I Covered For...? A Comprehensive Guide to Insuring Your Non-Profit Organization* (2nd Ed.). San Jose, CA: Consortium for Human Services, Inc.

Minnesota Office on Volunteer Services. (1992). *Planning it Safe: How to Control Liability & Risk in Volunteer Programs.* St. Paul, MI: Minnesota Office on Volunteer Services.

NeighbourLink Canada. (1997). *Screening: NeighbourLink Volunteers Manual.* Toronto, Ontario. Whitmore, L.

Nonprofit Risk Management Center. (1995). *Child Abuse Prevention Primer for your Organization.* Washington, DC: Patterson, J., Tremper, C. & Rypkema, P.

Nonprofit Risk Management Center. (1994). *Staff Screening Tool Kit: Keeping the Bad Apples Out of Your Organization.* Washington, DC: Patterson, J., Tremper, C. & Rypkema, P.

Non-Profit Risk Management Center. (1993). *No Surprises: Controlling Risks in Volunteer Programs.* Washington, DC: Tremper, C. & Kostin, G.

Points of Light Foundation. (1994). A Look at the Heart of Risk Management.

Washington, DC: Tremper, Charles & Pam Rypkema.

The YMCA of the USA. (1994). *The Seven Rs of Volunteer Development: A YMCA Resource Kit.* Chicago: Wroblewski, Celeste J.

Volunteer Canada. (1996). *The Education Dossier.* Ottawa, Ontario.

Volunteer Canada. (1998). *Safe Steps: A Volunteer Screening Process for Recreation and Sport.* Ottawa, Ontario: Gallagher, B.

CHAPTER 4

LEGAL RESPONSIBILITIES OF THE MEET DIRECTOR

Dennis Fairall, Dick Moriarty, and Margery Holman

Athletes, coaches, administrators, officials, physicians, equipment manufacturers, operators of sports facilities and even unsuspecting sports fans share a common bond — the risk of sports litigation. A number of cases of varying types involving sports persist and large amounts of money in damages are being awarded to sports participants.

Accidents do not just happen. The majority of accidents and the resulting injuries have a clear cause and effect relationship between some preceding event, action or circumstance and the accident itself.

Accidents, resulting in death or permanent disability, appear to be increasing in the track and field arena. Athletes today are jumping higher, throwing further and pushing themselves to greater limits in running events. With these improvements in performance comes a greater risk for injury. A throwing implement has a greater chance of going astray as athletes attempt to throw farther. Athletes attempting to jump higher have a greater risk of injury if the equipment is not adequate or placed in the proper position. Athletes pushing themselves to the limit in the heat of the day during a track event have a greater risk of injury. Invariably, it is the responsibility of the Meet Director to ensure that all event areas are safe for the competitors, spectators and officials.

Numerous deaths and personal injuries during track and field competitions have been documented. Present literature indicates that most injuries and litigation resulting from injuries in track and field are sustained by participants and officials. On occasion, litigation occurs as a result of injuries to spectators. The literature also illustrates a sharing of liability for accidents between the Meet Director and the sponsor of the meet, owner of the facility and the sanctioning organization.

Virtually all competitions have, to some degree, a sanctioning organization and/or sponsor. The elementary school "field day" is sponsored by that individual school and the school has an obligation, through the meet director, to organize a safe event in a safe environment.

Secondary school, college and university competitions also are sponsored by the host school and indirectly endorsed by the school's Board as a program related activity conducted by its employees. Most non-school activities are sanctioned by the sport-specific governing body or an affiliate body, which also exercises their sanction in demanding particular requirements of the event director and the facility to obtain a sanction. Open invitationals often are organized by smaller, local organizations that assume sole responsibility for the event.

Most facilities are owned and operated by a municipality, a school board, a university or a college. The owner of a facility has a responsibility, along with the event director, to provide a safe competition site, reducing the risk of injury due to negligence.

Sport related lawsuits, involving injury or death, are becoming more and more prevalent. Every year thousands of school, regional, provincial, club-sponsored and corporate-sponsored athletic competitions are conducted. The competitions may vary in size from the fifty-participant school "field day" event with multi-sport competition, to a single game/match event. The range in number of competitors may vary from ten to two thousand. The training background of the participants may vary from those athletes who have not prepared at all for the event to those who have put in hours of planned training for the competition.

While there are numerous sport-specific rules and regulations regarding the conduct of an event from a technical aspect, few guidelines regarding safety and the legal responsibilities of meet organizers are available. For every competition, a designated individual must take the role of, and responsibilities associated with, the position of Meet Director. The individual assuming the role of Event Director is particularly vulnerable. It is the responsibility of the Event Director to provide as safe an environment as possible for all participants.

The Meet Director

The International Amateur Athletic Federation (IAAF) defines Meet Director (the Manager) as the individual responsible for the correct conduct of the meet (IAAF Handbook, 1988: 85). At the highest levels of competition the Meet Director acts on behalf of the organizing committee and delegates to, or shares much of the responsibility with, other management officials and the competition officials.

While many of the officials working a competition assume the responsibilities associated with their particular officiating duty, it is the Meet Director who is responsible to a multitude of people during a competition. Realizing that only a small percentage of competitions reach that highest level of organization, it is more appropriate to outline the duties, responsibilities and obligations of the Meet Director as most organizers know them.

Many Meet Directors tread on unfamiliar territory when organizing an event. Occasionally, as in the case of track and field or gymnastics, this responsibility entails many different sports within one setting. The fact that many different events occur simultaneously will elevate the risk of sustaining injury, and make the job of organizing a track and field meet very complex and potentially dangerous. Field days may include a number of different sports, indoor and/or outdoor, which heightens the responsibility of organizers to oversee the safety of many events. Tournaments may require the use of several facilities, which increases potential risk by adding transportation between sites and requiring additional monitoring of sites.

Complicating things even further is the fact that no other sporting event requires such a large number of participants and officials. Combine hurdlers, runners, javelin, discus and shot put throwers, long and triple jumpers and pole-vaulters into one setting competing at the same time and you have some obvious risks. When you add the forty to fifty officials, a number of overzealous coaches attempting to get as close to the action as possible, and some anxious parents trying to get a good picture of the event site, without careful planning and prudent organization, you may have an accident waiting to happen.

It is not an uncommon sight to see a javelin soar over another unsuspecting athlete's head as they hustle across the infield to get to the start of their race on time. Neither is it uncommon to hear "look out!" shouted aloud as a discus strays wild, nor is it unfamiliar to see a middle-distance runner struggling during a 5000-meter race scheduled during the heat of mid-day. Absence of marshals to prevent spectators from crossing the track and field event areas poses a further hazard.

The Meet Director assumes an immense role with responsibilities to the participants, the officials, the coaches and the spectators. It is important that the Meet Director understands the responsibilities and obligations of his/her role and exercises every precaution to eliminate the risk of injury to all parties. Regardless of the delegation of responsibility to assistants who will help with the event, it is the Meet Director who is responsible for the safe and proper operation of the competition. In the event of injury and the possible litigation that results, it is almost assured that the Meet Director will be named in the suit for damages.

Any organized structure of a track and field competition will outline the hierarchy of responsibility and it should reveal clearly that the Meet Director has responsibility to a large number of individuals — a responsibility that would evolve to a legal obligation should a lawsuit ensue because of an accident resulting in injury.

The structure also should present the sharing of responsibilities of the meet between the Meet Director, the sponsors, the sanctioning organization and the owner of the facility. Also it should illustrate clearly the many different classifications of individuals attending the meet to whom the Meet Director is responsible and owes a duty of care (See Figure 4.1).

Review of Cases

There have been cases cited that have resulted in awards for damages received at a track meet. A review of some of the actual cases may alert Meet Directors to some of the danger areas associated with the organizing of a track and field meet.

The case of *M. Poelker v. Warrensburg Latham Community School District No. 11*, 621 N.E. 2d 940 (Ill.App. 1993) illustrates the dangers involved in the throwing event area. During the warm-up prior to the start of the discus event, Ty Poelker, a member of the Warrensburg track and field team, was hit in the head by a discus thrown by a teammate. The warm-up prior to the competition was not supervised by the volunteer official assigned to officiate the event.

The court ruled in favour of the defendants as it determined that acceptable safety and supervision techniques were followed and that the injuries sustained by the plaintiff were not as a result of negligence. Although the court ruled in favour of the defendants, this case does illustrate the need for Meet Directors to include the warm-up period when assigning supervision or officiating duties to volunteers.

The case of *Sheppard v. Midway R-1 School Dist.*, 904 S.W. 2d 257 (Mo Ct.App. 1995) illustrates the need for proper facility preparation prior to hosting a track and field competition. In April of 1991, Terra Sheppard attended a track and field meet at Midway High School. During one of her attempts in the long jump, she was injured while landing in the long jump pit. The injury required surgery and resulted in a permanent disability in Terra's right knee.

Sheppard sued the school, claiming the pit was in an unreasonably dangerous condition because it was not properly prepared. She alleged that the pit did not have enough sand and was not properly raked between jumps during the operation of the event. The school contended that the pit was properly prepared and that the participant was injured due to an improper landing, a risk that is assumed by participants in the long jump event The case was sent back to the trial level for a new trial.

The case of *Johnson v. Municipal University of Omaha*, 184 Neb. 512, 169 N.W. 2d 286 (1969), illustrates the high safety standards that must be maintained at the pole vault area.

On May 12, 1967, Jack E. Johnson fell on a wooden box that had been placed beneath the pole vault standards. The action was for damages resulting from the injuries sustained, alleging negligence on the part of the University of Omaha in "placing hard, sharply protruding wooden boxes at a place which would unreasonably endanger such persons as the plaintiff; in failing to protect vaulters from hazard; and in failing to warn plaintiff of the presence of the boxes" (N.W. 2d, v. 169: 287).

The action was dismissed by the District Court, appealed by the plaintiff and later reversed and remanded for further proceedings, i.e., the case proceeded to trial.

The case of *Smith v. the University of Texas* (664 S.W. 2d 180 [Texas App. 1984]) involves serious injury sustained by a volunteer official at the 1980 NCAA Outdoor Track and Field Championships in Austin, Texas. James P. Smith was serving as a shot put official at the championship meet. Smith was under the impression that the warm-ups had concluded, as the supervisor was providing the participants with final instructions. While repairing a spot where a shot had landed, he was struck in the head by a shot and suffered serious injuries. Smith sued the University of Texas, the head track coach who was serving as Meet Director and the volunteer shot put supervisor. He alleged that they were negligent in the way they conducted the shot put event and in their failure to enact safety rules and regulations for the shot put event.

The court granted judgment in favour of the defendants, absolving those accused of negligence. The Texas Court of Appeals reversed this decision and remanded the case back for trial against the University, the chief official and head coach.

The University had admitted that both the track coach and shot put supervisor, on behalf of the University, were charged with seeing that safety guidelines concerning the shot put event were followed at the time of the incident (1984, *Sports and the Courts*, 5 (4): 7).

In the case *Harding v. New Rockford School District No. 1*, a member of a relay team was killed by a javelin at a track meet. Rochelle Harding, a member of the Tolna High School 4 x 100-meter relay team, ran across the infield to join her relay team members. A javelin was thrown and struck the runner in the chest, killing her.

Rochelle's mother sued the school district and the Kiwanis Club (the sponsor) for allegedly failing to properly administer the track meet. The court found the defendants not negligent in their duties performed operating the track meet.

While injury in the *Edmonson v. Board of Trustees for the Moose Jaw School District* (1920) 55 D.L.R., 563 was not sustained at an actual competition, it does illustrate the need to ensure the use of safe equipment in track and field. The plaintiff, an eight-year-old boy, was struck in the eye by a high jump crossbar while standing beside the high jump area. One of the jumpers knocked the "broken, sharply pointed" bar off, striking the plaintiff in the eye and destroying his sight. The jury found negligence on the part of the defendants for allowing the use of dangerous equipment.

While the *Neil Williams v. Road Race Sponsors* (1981) lawsuit is particular to a ten-kilometer road race, it does illustrate the need for Meet Directors to consider weather conditions in particular events. Williams sought $500,000 in damages for an allegedly sustained "thermal injury" from a July 4, 1977 road race in Atlanta, Georgia. Williams charged that race sponsors were negligent on several counts, including:

1. Failure to warn runners about specific injuries which could occur.
2. Failure to provide sufficient liquids and medical aid stations at proper intervals over the racecourse.
3. Failure to print warnings of hazards on application forms and pre-race advertisements or require medical certificates from entrants. (1980, *Sport and the Courts*, 1 (1): 39).

The plaintiff alleges he now limps, is unable to take part in "strenuous activity," received treatment for "renal failure" and suffered "possible brain damage" (Ibid.: 10).

Numerous claims for damages for injuries sustained at track and field meets have not reached the courts; however, many have resulted in settlements outside of court.

An unpublished case of an athlete seeking damages for injuries sustained as a result of improperly situated hurdles occurred in Ontario. The American athlete claimed damages for a broken ankle, which eliminated him from competing at the Olympic trials and the possibility of making the Olympic team. Following the completion of a women's hurdle race, meet officials moved all but "one" flight of hurdles to the "correct" men's hurdle markings. During the race the American hurdler crashed into the misplaced hurdle breaking his ankle forcing him to miss the U.S. Olympic trials.

A second unpublished and unresolved case involved a long jumper seeking damages for injuries sustained while competing at a meet in Ontario. The young athlete received a broken leg and claims the "landing pit" was not adequately prepared.

The foregoing cases, both on the track and in the field, illustrate a concern for the Meet Director of providing a duty of care by ensuring a safe facility and operating a "risk-free" meet. These cases also identify the many, many areas of concern when organizing a track and field competition.

The Meet Director, by the nature of the role and responsibilities associated with the position, is subject to legal liability under certain circumstances for injuries occurring during a competition. It is important for the Meet Director to understand the basic legal terms and responsibilities (outlined below) associated with the duties of Meet Director.

Tort Liability

Tort liability is defined as liability for personal injuries caused through the defendant's negligence or through intentional harm (Fahr, 1985).

From the court's perspective, proof of four elements must be ascertained for successful action in tort:

1. The defendant owed a duty to avoid unreasonable risks to others;

2. The defendant failed to observe that duty, failing to provide a reasonable standard of care;
3. The failure to observe that duty caused the damage which occurred; and,
4. That damage in fact occurred to the plaintiff, and the conduct of the defendant had a close causal connection to the injury, loss, or damage incurred (Fahr, 1985 and Ferris, 1977: 4).

Similar to physical education teachers in class, Meet Directors cannot "guarantee" that no injuries will occur at the meet, but the law requires them to act as a "reasonable person" would in similar circumstances. The reasonable person is one endowed with normal intellect, normal perception and normal experience (Fahr, 1985: 219).

The Meet Director, like the coach or physical education teacher, has a duty to protect. The Meet Director must recognize this element of negligence and is obligated to perform the following actions:

1. Anticipation of foreseeable risks.
2. Taking reasonable steps to prevent injury.
3. Providing a warning relative to risks that cannot be reduced or averted.
4. Providing aid to the injured.
5. Not increasing the severity of the injury.

In legal terms, the Meet Director becomes an occupier of a premise (i.e., track and field facility). Liability as an occupier generally falls on those who have sufficient possession and control of premises to give them a legal right to invite visitors to the premises (Barnes, 1981: 422). The occupier (Meet Director) is responsible for supervision and control of a facility and is under a duty to take reasonable care to see that the premises are safe.

The Occupiers' Liability Act in Ontario provides that occupiers include persons who are in physical possession of premises, who are responsible for, and have control over, the condition of the premises, the activities carried on therein, or the persons allowed to enter the premises. Premises in this Act represents both land and structures. The occupier of premises owes a duty to take reasonable care for the safety of persons and property coming onto the premises.

The Meet Director (legally named the occupier or operator) is under duty to five groups of individuals at a track and field competition: the competitors, the coaches, spectators, officials and the media. In the legal aspect, all of these individuals are "invitees," either expressed or implied.

It is the duty of the operator, under common law principle, "to see that reasonable care and skill has been used to make the invitees safe, against dangers which reasonably may be assured possible to happen" (Ibid., 426).

Spectators and Media

The occupier is bound only to keep the place in the same condition as other places of the kind and therefore finds a defense if proven compliance with standard safety precautions has been met at the competition site.

If a spectator chooses to place himself in a position where the risk of injury is higher than elsewhere, then he must accept the consequences, assuming there is no negligence on the occupier's part (Barnes, 1981: 427). Mere warning of the dangers and the risks involved are sometimes enough to relieve the defendant of liability.

Competitors, Coaches, and Officials

Competitors, coaches, and officials may all be considered participants and therefore fall under the "liability of operators to players" as far as duty is concerned for the Meet Director. A participant in a sporting event is deemed to accept certain necessary and expected risks that are incidental and inseparable from the sport. A participant (coach, athlete, or official) may bring an action in respect of injuries caused by unreasonable or improper behavior of the operator. Injury to a participant may arise from negligent organization or supervision of an event, or for unreasonable hazards in the condition or construction of the facility.

Meet Directors are similar to commercial operators organizing and supervising sports activities and are subject to various duties of care towards participants:

1. The duty to limit the number of participants in order to avoid crowding and collisions.
2. The duty to exercise efficient and competent supervision and control.
3. The duty to give instructions and warnings about ordinary and expected dangers.
4. The duty to exercise reasonable care in the selection of equipment.

The sports participant is considered to assume the ordinary risks associated with their sport or event, but is not precluded from suing in respect of damage caused through negligence in one of three forms: facilities and organizations, supervision, and medical care.

It is the responsibility of Meet Directors (organizers) to arrange for appropriate medical services.

> The persons and organization in charge of sports activities will have a duty to secure or provide reasonable medical assistance to injured participants or spectators as soon as possible under the circumstances. Whether the duty has been met in any given case normally will depend upon the quality of treatment, and the speed with which it is rendered. When satisfactory medical assistance is provided within a reasonable period of time, the duty will have been fulfilled (Barnes, 1979: 482).

Reducing the Risk

While many rules and regulations exist regarding the technical conduct of a competition, there are few written guidelines to ensure safety.

The International Amateur Athletic Federation (IAAF), the governing body for track and field, outlines facility standards for international competitions and facilities. Apart from these standards there are few guidelines for the majority of Meet Directors in Canada organizing a school or club meet at the local track or for those organizing competition in other sports. Only a few facilities in Canada meet the strict specifications for all events. Because the IAAF handbook is the only source available for reference for a track and field facility, most track and field Meet Directors and facility operators facing litigation are in a difficult position. For example, in the case of an injured long-jumper seeking award for damages sustained at a track and field meet, the defendant's lawyers can only refer to the IAAF handbook and its strict facility guideline requirements. Only a handful of facilities can boast of meeting the IAAF specifications for long jump, which includes a takeoff board 1.22 meters long, 198 mm to 202 mm wide, 100 mm deep, a minimum of 2.75 meters wide landing area with soft damp sand with the top surface level with the takeoff board.

The Ontario Track and Field Association's "Meet Director's Handbook," published in 1979, outlines the policies and procedures for the operation of a track and field meet. While the handbook does provide the Meet Director with excellent guidelines regarding most items pertaining to organizing a track and field meet, it does ignore many safety and legal factors. For example, nowhere is it even recommended that certain distance events (i.e., 5000 and 10,000 meters) not be contested during mid-day. The 1969 AAU outdoor track and field championships in Miami, Florida had the six-mile run scheduled for 5:30 p.m., under a blistering sun and intense heat. Despite protests from the meet organizers who contracted national television coverage and an anticipated crowd of 10,000 paid spectators, the event was rescheduled to 7:30 p.m. for the athletes' safety.

The handbook does not offer guidelines for eliminating risk in the most dangerous track and field event, the javelin. While there are guidelines for a discus cage, there is no recommendation of roping off the javelin area and providing adequate warning signs in the landing area.

Safety Factors in Track and Field Competitions

"Since the safety of the sports facility is essential to the participants' well being, injuries attributed to unsafe conditions often result in litigation" (Appenzeller, 1980: 259).

There are many areas of concern when organizing a track and field competition. The following test will

Table 4.1
General Risks of Track Events

General Considerations: Track Events

1. Track
2. Apparatus
3. Schedule of Events
4. Participant

— surface, hardness, curve radius, area beyond the finish line, lane widths
— hurdles, steeplechase
— limiting the number of events per participant, time intervals between popular "doubling" events, longer races should not be scheduled during the hottest time of day
— aware of the rules of competition
— properly trained both mentally and physically

Risk Recognition   Risk Management

Track Surface

Suitable track surfaces vary in material used; polyurethane, rubber, finely crushed cinder, stone or grass/dirt. The best tracks allow for water drainage and provide good traction even when wet.

Ensure track surface provides reasonable traction, particularly for races using the curve. Ensure track surface is level, free of dips, cracks, holes, and debris.

Track Hardness

The hardness of a track varies with the surface material and the base (e.g. wood, asphalt, concrete) upon which the surface is laid. Although a harder track may aid the participant in achieving better times in competition, it may also lead to soft tissue injuries if used too much in training day after day.

Ensure moderation in training on a hard track to reduce risk of injury.

Area Beyond the Finish Line

The finish line shold be situated on the track such that participants can safely decrease their speed by either continuing in a straight line or running around the curve.
In the finish of sprint races, request before the start of each race that all participants follow the same path after crossing the finish line (i.e., all continue straight ahead or all run around the curve).

When participants are requested to continue straight ahead after finishing a sprint race, ensure there is at least 10 meters of no obstructions and provide apparatus (e.g. foam landing pads) beyond to allow the participant to come to a halt without injury.

Curve Radius of Track

Curve radius varies from facility to facility as well as for the size of track (i.e., 200 meter to 400 meter). However, the smaller the radius, the more difficult it is for the participant when running at a fast pace around the curve and thus the greater stress on the participant to hold his/her line of direction.

For 200 meter tracks without banked curves, the radius should be at least 18 meters to the path of the runner in the innermost lane.

Table 4.1
General Risks of Track Events (continued)

Risk Recognition	Risk Management
Curve Radius of Track (continued)	If the curves are banked, the maximum andgle should not exceed 18º. A track with banked curves may allow a radius less than 18 meters byut the radius should not be less than 11 meters.
Lane Widths	Lane widths may vary depending on the size of the track as well as the age and ability level of the participant. International level requires a lane width of 122 cm −125 cm for outdoor tracks with a similar width for indoor sprint straightaway lanes while lanes on the oval of an indoor track may measure from 91 cm to 110 cm in width.
	Ensure that the lane width is sufficient for the level of the participants to prevent collisions when races are conducted in lanes.
Schedule of Events	The age and ability level of the participant should be considered when setting limitations on the number of events in which a participant may compete in one day. The following outlines some factors that may assist in the determination, if any, of the limitations; duration plus intensity level of each event in which the participant wishes to compete, the time interval between events in which the participant wishes to compete, fitness and motivation levels of the participant.
	Ensure that there is a reasonable time interval between events where it is likely a participant will be competing more than once in the same day. The longer the racing distance, the more time interval required to allow the participant a reasonable recovery before competing again. Very short sprint races may require only a 15 minute interval before the participant races again whereas a minimum of 90 minutes may be required between longer races. Spacing with reasonable time intervals running events that are more popular "doubling" events (e.g. 100m & 200m, 200m & 400m, 400m & 800m, 800m & 1500m, etc.) may reduce the risk of fatigue related injuries.

Table 4.2
Risks of Hurdle Races

Risk Management

Use appropriate size of hurdle and placement of successive hurdles relative to the age and ability level of the participant. For beginners and young participants, lightweight scissor hurdles are recommended with the crossbars arranged so that they can be easily dislodged. Modifications in the height and placement of successive hurdles should be considered for beginners (e.g. 50 meter race over 5 scissor hurdles each 60 cm in height with the first hurdle 11 meters from the start and 7 meters between successive hurdles).

Before the start of each race over hurdles, ensure that all hurdles are at the proper place on the track, at the proper height, and when using regulation hurdles, ensure that the base weights are set at the proper tip-over resistance level

Ht. of Hurdle Race	# of Hurdle	Start to Hurdles	Distance Between 1st Hurdle	Hurdles
80 m	76 cm	8	12.00 meters	8.00 meters
100 m	84 cm	10	13.00 meters	8.50 meters
110 m	99-107 cm	10	13.72 meters	9.14 meters
300 m	96-91 cm	7	50.00 meters	35.00 meters
400 m	76-91 cm	10	45.00 meters	35.00 meters

Regulation hurdles that are required for competitions at or above the secondary school level/club level, must meet the following specifications:

minimum hurdle weight: 10 kg
maximum width of crossbar: 120 cm
maximum length of base: 70 cm
force required to topple hurdle: 3.6 kg at any height

Table 4.3
Risks of Steeplechase

Risk Management

Ensure that the water area of the waterjump pit measures 366 cm in length, 366 cm in width, and is 70 cm deep for approximately 30 cm from the end closest to the hurdle before sloping upwards.

Ensure that the water is level with the ground from which the participant takes off.

Ensure that the hurdle at the waterjump is firmly fixed and strong enough to withstand the forces generated by the participants during each landing on and leap from the hurdle.

Ensure that the sloped floor of the waterjump pit where most particpants land is adequately padded with a material 366 cm wide, 2.5 cm thick, and extending 250 cm from the edge furthest from the hurdle down the slope toward the deepest part of the pit.

Before the start of each steeplechase race, ensure that all hurdles are approximately 80 meters apart (i.e. 4 hurdles & waterjump hurdle). If using hurdles less than regulation weight, secure each hurdle with the assistance of extra weight applied to the base.

Steeplechase Race	# of Hurdle Jumps	# of Water Jumps
3000 meters	28	7
2000 meters	18	5
1500 meters	12	3

Regulation hurdles that are required for competitions at or above the secondary school level/club level must meet the following specifications:

weight: 80 kg - 100 kg
height: 91.1 cm - 91.7 cm
length of base: 120 cm - 140 cm
width of top bar: a minimum of 396 cm

Table 4.4
Risks of High Jump

General Considerations: High Jump

1. Approach Area
   — reasonably level, free of dips, cracks, holes, debris
   — provides reasonable traction
2. Apparatus
   — proper use of appropriate uprights and crossbar
   — landing pit appropriate for the physical size and ability level of the participants
3. Participant
   — aware of the ideal takeoff area and landing technique
   — aware of the rules of competition

Risk Recognition | Risk Management

Indoors using a gym floor as an approach — Ensure participants wear shoes providing reasonable traction and when possible, enhance the traction of the take-off surface.

Outdoors using a grass, combination grass/synthetic approach — Locate the landing pit adjacent to the area with the greatest traction ensuring that the last 2-3 running steps are in that area.

Size of landing pit — Consider both the weight and ability level of the participant when determining size of pit.

Quality of landing pit — A properly constructed landing pit prevents an abrupt stopping of the participant and provides a safer, more gradual slowing of the body upon landing.

Using a multi-sectioned landing pit — When using landing pits that are multi-sectioned, securely fasten each section to the adjacent one, secure the solid top cover contact area pad to all sections and periodically inspect to prevent large gaps.

Improper use of uprights and/or crossbar — Placing the uprights appropriately and using a flexible, lightweight crossbar that bends when landed on enhances safety.

Participants not using safe takeoff/landing methods — Forward momentum of the approach run requires the participant to *take off near the end of the crossbar closest to the approach* in order to avoid missing the pit. Learning to land in the pit such that no small area of the body absorbs all the impact enhances a safer landing.

Table 4.5
Risks of Pole Vault

General Considerations: Pole Vault

1. Approach Area
   — level runway, free of dips, cracks, holes, debris and providing reasonable traction
   — vaulting box sunk level with takeoff area
2. Apparatus
   — landing pit appropriate size, construction, and properly placed
   — proper use of appropriate uprights and crossbar
3. Participant
   — trained in the proper technique of pole vaulting and using a proper pole
   — aware of the rules of competition

Risk Management

Risk Recognition

Indoors using a floor or elevated multi-sectioned runway for an approach

Esure participants wear shoes providing reasonable traction and when possible, enhance the traction of the take-off surface. When using a multi-sectioned elevated runway, ensure that each section is securely attached to the adjoining one and where possible, cover the runway with 10-15 meter long rolls of rubberized material that will cover the seams.

Construction of the vaulting box

Ensure that no part of the vaulting box protrudes above the level of the runway, which might impede a smooth sliding of the pole along the runway and into the box. Ensure that the box is securely anchored and reinforced in the runway.

Size of landing pit

Due to the inherent risks involved in pole vaulting even for highly experienced participants, the overall size of the landing pit is important. Of particular importance is the size of the front part of the pit closest to the takeoff area that envelops the vaulting box.

Quality of landing pit

A properly constructed landing pit prevents an abrupt stopping of the participant and provides a safer, more gradual slowing of the body upon landing. The front section of the pit that surrounds the vaulting box must be constructed such to allow the pole to bend fully yet be close enough to the back and sides of the box and *extend beyond the front of the box* to assist the landing of a stalled vault.

Placement of the landing pit

Stalled vaults where the participant has insufficient momentum to land in the main section of the pit are a common cause of injuries. The base of the front section of the pit that surrounds the vaulting box must be placed as close as possible to the back and sides of this section of the pit to interfere with the full bend of the pole. Where there is a gap of 15 cm or more between the base of this section of the pit and the vaulting box, it is recommended that a collar of form foam be placed in this area at least 5 cm high and the width of the gap.

Table 4.5
Risks of Pole Vault (continued)

Risk Recognition	Risk Management
Securing all sections of the landing pit	Pole vaulting landing pits usually have 5-6 units that must be properly joined together. The entended main landing area is comprised of 3 sections, the front unit surrounding the vault box may be for 2 sections, and all sections are covered by a one piece contact area pad. All units must be securely fastened to each other and periodically inspected to prevent large gaps.
Improper use of uprights and/or crossbar	Placing the uprights appropriately and using a flexible, lightweight corssbar that bends when landed on enhances safety.
Participants using either a defective or imporper vaulting pole	The participant should regularly inspect the vaulting pole for any signs of stress fractures and avoid using such poles. Reputable manufacturers of vaulting poles provide clear guidelines as to the appropriate rated pole a participant should use and warn against using a pole rated below the vaulter's body weight.
Participant not properly trained in the fundamentals of pole vault technique	Due to the inherent risks of this event, the participant must have a thorough understanding of and practice in the fundamental elements critical to successful vaulting. Attaining sufficient forward speed in the approach, maintaining that speed at takeoff, planting the pole with the top hand of the pole as high above the ground as possible at takeoff, and properly timing the initiation of the "rockback" all play critical roles in ensuring a successful vault and decreasing the chance of injury.

Table 4.6
Risks of Long Jump

General Considerations: Long Jump

1. Approach Area
   — level, free of dips, cracks, holes, debris and provides reasonable traction
   — cordoned to reduce the risk of collisions
2. Apparatus
   — take-off area is flush with the approach runway
   — landing pit appropriate for the physical size and ability level of the participant
3. Participant
   — using footwear that provides both reasonable traction and shock absorption qualities
   — aware of the rules of competition

Risk Recognition / Risk Management

Risk Recognition	Risk Management
Indoors using an elevated, multi-sectioned runway for an approach	Ensure that each section is securely attached to the adjoining one and where possible, cover the runway with 10 to 15 meters in length rolls of rubberized material that will cover the seams.
Outdoors using a grass or dirt approach	Locate the takeoff area where the traction is greatest.
Runway and Take-off Area	When using a take-off board that is sunk into the runway, ensure that the top surface of the board is level with the runway with no protrusions or dips.
Controlling access to Approach Area	Cordon the approach and take-off areas to deter individuals from crossing the runway when in use.
Size of the Landing Area	Consider both the weight and ability level of the participant when using a landing pit smaller than that specified in the rules.
Quality of the Landing	Ensure a softer landing by using a soft, damp sand with the pit deep enough to prevent the participant from touching the bottom of the pit when using pits framed with wood, concrete, etc. such as those for indoor competition. Ensure that the pit is level with the take-off area before each jump and that it is free of debris.

Table 4.7
Risks of Triple Jump

General Considerations: Triple Jump

1. Approach Area
2. Apparatus
3. Participant

— level, free of dips, cracks, holes, debris and provides reasonable traction
— provides a reasonable cushion to diminish the shock of each single foot landing
— cordoned to reduce the risk of collisions
— take-off area is flush with the approach runway
— take-off area located an appropriate distance from the front edge of the landing area
— using footwear that provides shock absorption qualities as well as traction
— aware of the rules of competition
— trained in the proper technique of the hop, step, and jump phases of the triple jump

Risk Management

Risk Recognition
Refer to Long Jump

Distance from take-off area to the beginning of the landing area

Consider the ability level of the participant when designating a take-off area so that the participant, in properly executing a triple jump, will land at least 1 meter beyond the front edge of the landing pit.

Size of the Landing Area

Consider both the weight and ability level of the participant when using a landing pit smaller than that specified in the rules. SEE LONG JUMP.

Hard Take-off ARea

Particularly where the landings occur for the hop and step phases, ensure that the runway has a cushioning quality to reduce the shock (e.g. a roll of rubberized material).

Participant's Footwear

Advise the participant to use footwear with a built-up heel and/or use shock absorption insoles/heel pads.

Table 4.8
Risks of Shot Put

General Considerations: Shot Put

1. Approach Area
   — level, free of debris, cracks, dips, and providing reasonable traction
   — proper construction
   — cordoned to reduce the risk of collisions
2. Apparatus
   — appropriate weight of shot for the strength and ability level of the participant
   — landing area level with the floor of the circle and cordoned
3. Participant
   — trained in the proper technique of putting the shot
   — aware of the rules of competition
4. Officials
   — aware of and enforcing the rules of competition
   — all judges attentive to the execution of each put of the shot

Risk Recognition / Risk Management

Risk Recognition	Risk Management
Floor Surface of Putting Circle	Ensure that the floor is firm and that there is reasonable traction. Avoid using a grass floor.
Unstable Stop Board	Ensure that the stopboard at the front of the putting circle is firmly fixed.
Proximity of bystanders	Ensure that all individuals, including the event judges are a safe distance from the putting circle, the flight path, and the landing area when a participant puts the shot. It may be necessary to cordon the entire area. Be particularly alert when participants use the spin/rotation technique in shot putting.
Size of the Shot	Consider both the strength and the ability level of the participant when selecting the weight of the shot to be used. Weights of shots tend to range from 2 kg for children to 7.26 kg for national/international men's competition.
Composition of the shot	With inexperienced shot putters and/or children, consider using light indoor shots with plastic or rubber covering as opposed to metal covered shots.
Participant not properly trained in the fundamentals of shot putting technique	Encourage the participant to use much of the body starting with the legs when putting the shot and to put the shot from the shoulder in accordance with the rules.
Retrieving the shot	Ensure that each shot that is put from the circle is carried back to the circle and not thrown back.

Legal Responsibilities of the Meet Director **67**

Table 4.9
Risks of Discus Throw

General Considerations: Discus Throw

1. Approach Area
 — level, free of debris, cracks, dips, and providing reasonable traction
 — proper construction
 — enclosed with an appropriate cage

2. Apparatus
 — appropriate weight of discus for the strength and ability level of the participant
 — landing area level with the floor of the circle and cordoned

3. Participant
 — trained in the proper technique of throwing the discuss
 — aware of the rules of competition

4. Officials
 — aware of and enforcing the rules of competition
 — all judges attentive to the execution of each throw of the discus

Risk Management

Risk Recognition

Floor surface of throwing circle
 Ensure that the floor is firm and that there is reasonable traction. Avoid using a grass floor.

Circle Enclosure
 Ensure that all throws are made within some suitable enclosure and that all bystanders including officials are outside the protective enclosure when a participant is ready to attempt a throw. Ensure that the enclosure is constructed of some type of loose hanging but strong mesh that will capture an errant discus and prevent it from rebounding back towards the participant.

Proximity of bystanders
 Ensure all individuals, including officials, are a safe distance outside the enclosure when a participant is in the circle ready to throw. Ensure all individuals are a safe distance from the flight path and landing area and that everyone is attentive to the execution of each throw of the discus. Use a signal (e.g. whistle or horn) to alert all that a throw is about to be made and cordon the boundaries of the landing area.

Participant not properly trained in the fundamentals of discus throwing technique
 Encourage an inexperienced thrower to first master throws from a standing position, then ffrom a partial turn beforeattempting throws from a full 1½ turn.

Retrieving the discus
 Ensure that each discus thrown from the circle is carried back to the circle and not thrown back.

Table 4.10
Risks of Javelin Throw

General Considerations: Javelin Throw

1. Approach Area
   — reasonably level, free of dips, cracks, holes, debris
   — provides reasonable traction
2. Apparatus
   — appropriate size javelin for the ability level of the participant
   — proper handling of the javelin *at all times*
   — landing area level with the approach area and cordoned
3. Participant
   — trained in the proper handling as well as the proper technique of throwing of the javelin
   — aware of the rules of competition
4. Officials
   — aware of and enforcing the rules of competition
   — all judges attentive to the execution of each throw of the javelin

Risk Recognition | Risk Management

Using a grass approach and release area | Locate the approach and release area where the traction is greatest. Ensure participants wear shoes prividing reasonable traction. If the level of competition precludes most competitors from wearing regulation javelin shoes, waive the international rule that the diameter of spikes cannot exceed 4 mm and allow cleated shoes to be worn.

Proximity of bystanders | Ensure that all individuals, including officials, are a safe distance from the runway when a participant is about to begin an attempt. Ensure all individuals are a safe distance from the flight path and landing area and that everyone is attentive to the execution of each throw of the javelin. Use a signal (e.g. whistle or horn) to alert all that a throw is about to be made and cordon the boundaries of the landing area.

Participant not properly trained in the proper handling as well as the proper technique of throwing the javelin | Encourage the participant always to carry an uncased javelin with the shaft and ends perpendicular to the ground. Encourage the participant to initiate the throw with the legs, hips, tand trunk followed by a release of the javelin well above shoulder level.

Retrieving the javelin | Ensure that each javelin that is thrown from the runway is properly carried back to the runway and not thrown back.

Table 4.11
Risks of Hammer Throw

General Considerations: Hammer Throw

1. Approach Area	— level, free of debris, cracks, dips, and providing reasonable traction — proper construction — enclosed with an appropriate cage
2. Apparatus	— proper construction of hammer — appropriate dimensions and weight for the strength and ability level of the participant — landing area level with the floor of the circle and cordoned
3. Participant	— trained in the proper technique of throwing the hammer — aware of the rules of competition
4. Officials	— aware of and enforcing the rules of the competition — all judges attentive to the execution of each throw of the hammer

Risk Recognition / Risk Management

Risk Recognition	Risk Management
Floor surface of throwing circle	Ensure that the floor is firm and that there is reasonable traction
Cage	Ensure that all throws are made within a cage securely fixed to the ground and meeting the guidelines outlined in the rules.
Proximity of bystanders	Ensure that all individuals are a safe distance from the flight path and landing area and that everyone is attentive to the execution of each throw of the hammer. Use a signal (e.g. whistle or horn) to alert all that a throw is about to be made and cordon the boundaries of the landing area.
Participant not full trained in the fundamentals of hammer throwing technique	Encourage an inexperienced thrower to first master throws from a partial turn, then progressively add turns as skill level improves
Retrieving the hammer	Ensure that each hammer thrown from the circle is carried back to the circle and not thrown back.

Legal Responsibilities of the Meet Director **69**

provide guidelines for track and field Meet Directors for safety at competitions. The Meet Director should examine eight factors or areas when organizing the track and field meet:

1. The **physical layout** of the facility;
2. **Equipment safety;**
3. **Scheduling** of the events during the meet;
4. The condition of the **surfaces** at the facility on the day of the meet;
5. **Spectator safety** during the meet;
6. **Officiating**, including number of officials, their experience and qualifications;
7. **Medical and first aid** available during the meet; and,
8. **Sanction and insure the meet**.

If each factor is considered carefully by the Meet Director, and steps for safety taken in each area, the risk of injury and possible liability will be reduced. The Meet Director must "examine the overall structure of a meet and inspect every event area for the slightest defect" (Marra, 1986: 21).

Physical Layout of Facility

The first consideration when organizing a track and field meet should be the physical capabilities of the facility to be used for the competition. As previously discussed, it is the duty of the Meet Director to limit the number of participants in order to avoid crowding and the possible accidents resulting from crowding. An eight-lane track has greater physical capabilities than a six-lane track. The size of the track and the time allowed for the completion of the meet will dictate the number of competitors that should be allowed to participate in the meet.

Other factors involving the physical layout and condition of the facility must be considered by the Meet Director before finalizing the plans for the meet. If the discus competition is scheduled, the facility must have a properly constructed and safe discus cage. Without a cage, which is required under the Ontario, Canadian and International rulebooks, the Meet Director's chance of being held liable for an injury at the discus event is greatly increased.

Many near misses have been witnessed at the most potentially dangerous area at a track and field meet, the javelin event. Consideration must be given to the longest and widest possible throw and the area roped or fenced off, combined with ample signs warning coaches, athletes, officials and spectators of the danger.

The actual physical condition of the track must be examined by the Meet Director well in advance of the meet. A competition must not be held at a potentially dangerous facility. It is the Meet Director's responsibility to ask for repairs to be made to the facility prior to the meet if he or she is unsatisfied with the condition of the facility following inspection. If repairs cannot be made, there are only two legally responsible actions; cancel the competition, or move to another site.

Other areas to be inspected during the early visit should include the condition of the runways for the jumping events, the takeoff boards for the long and triple jumps and the presence of correct hurdle markings. The hurdle marks must be accurate for the various distances to be contested, as improperly spaced hurdles can lead to serious injury. The cost of stenciling in clear markings and the time spent meeting with the hurdle crew prior to the meet is infinitely small compared with the cost of human pain and financial drain resulting from negligent injury and a lawsuit.

Finally, the capabilities of the facility to handle spectators and restrict their movement into the competition areas must be considered. The Meet Director owes "duty of care" first and foremost to paying spectators, but also is responsible for any spectator at the meet. Every effort must be made to restrict the spectator from entering the competition area, which may lead to injury to the spectator or to a participant. A fence separating competitors and officials from spectators and coaches is a worthwhile investment.

Equipment Safety

With the inception of the back layout high jump technique and ever increasing heights attained by both high jumpers and pole-vaulters, proper landing pits are essential. The days of foam chunks in large nets are gone.

It is important to use landing pits with the proper dimensions — length, width and depth. The use of less than adequate pole vault and high hump landing pits may lead to extensive injuries. Additionally, it is important to make use of the top cover for both events, eliminating the possibility of falling through the crevices between the "modules" of the pits. The landing pits themselves must be placed tightly beside each other and the connecting buckles secured before the top cover is placed in position.

As illustrated earlier in a case, a splintered crossbar can cause serious injury and crossbars must be inspected for defects prior to the meet. The high hump and pole vault standards also must be inspected for any potentially dangerous defects.

The hurdles must be thoroughly inspected to ensure that there are no protruding pieces of metal or wood which may cause serious injury to a competitor. The hurdles also should be counted to determine if enough safe hurdles are available and also checked to see if they can be lowered or raised easily and locked in at the various heights required for the meet. In the event of the use of international specification hurdles, the weights must be inspected to ensure that they can be moved easily to correspond with the various hurdle heights.

Scheduling

The schedule of events should be established only following a trip to the competition site. Careful consideration must be given to the physical layout of the facility and the climatic conditions expected during the competition.

The physical layout of many facilities prohibits the scheduling of certain events at the same time. Many facilities contest both the javelin and discus events on the infield of the track. It would be extremely dangerous to schedule both of these throwing events at the same time at a facility with that physical layout. Although international rules require both the javelin and discus events to be contested within the arena, it is advisable for Meet Directors to schedule these events either outside the track area, or during a time when no tack events are being contested.

A carefully planned schedule of events can decrease the potential for injury in the field events and also can produce a safer environment on the track. The anticipated temperature of the season should be considered when scheduling the middle and long distance events. As discussed earlier, common sense prevailed at the 1969 United States (AAU) Outdoor Championships where the six-mile run was moved back two hours due to intense heat at the scheduled time of the event. Meet Directors can avoid last minute changes and the accompanying confusion by scheduling the longer races in the early morning or evening sessions of the meet. Consideration also should be given to postponing or rescheduling events that become dangerous in the presence of rain (e.g., pole vault). The pressures or inconvenience to competitors, coaches, parents, spectators and media are nothing compared to a debilitating injury, loss of life, or the trauma of a lawsuit. The rules of safety must supersede the rules of the sanctioning body of the meet.

Surfaces

While a preliminary inspection two or three months prior to the meet will allow time for major facility revisions or repairs, an inspection on meet day must be made prior to the start of the meet. All running surfaces, the track and the runways should be inspected for foreign objects or any other dangers. This pre-meet inspection can eliminate some unnecessary risks created by broken glass or other items thrown on the track.

Spectator Safety

If the facility is not constructed to restrict spectator movement into the areas of competition, temporary roping or fencing must be placed to keep the spectators out of danger and from possibly affecting the normal operation of the meet. Officials should be used to ensure that spectators remain in the spectator area and warning signs placed at the entrances to the competition area. Remember that young children cannot read or are oblivious to printed warnings, making it imperative that officials be on hand for crowd control.

Officiating

A set of trained, qualified and prudent officials not only will allow the meet to run smoothly, but also will decrease the risk of injury. It is important that the rules and regulations governing the meet, including the unwritten rules of safety, be strictly enforced by the officials at each event.

The rules of competition must be explained to the participants, assistant and minor officials at each event by each respective head official. For example, in the throwing events, the participants should not retrieve their own implement from the throwing area and must remain behind the throwing circle or runway when not competing. It is recommended that one official at each throwing event be responsible for ensuring that no implement is thrown by a competitor when the officials are not ready or the landing area is not clear. This official should have no other capacity at the event other than to ensure safety.

It is important to have experienced or knowledgeable officials in charge of the potentially most dangerous events such as pole vault, the throwing events, high jump and the hurdles. The chief and the hurdle crew must be aware of the correct spacing, the track markings and the heights of the various hurdle events to be contested during the meet.

The Meet Director or the chair of the officials must meet with the key or chief officials and emphasize the safety precautions that must be followed at their particular event. The following tables (Vigars, 1995) outline the "risk recognition" and "risk management" for the various events that are contested during a track and field competition.

Medical and First Aid

It is imperative that arrangements be made to provide first aid or medical treatment at the track and field competition. Consideration must be given to the number and age of the participants, the events and their associated danger. As stated earlier, it is the duty of the meet organizers to provide reasonable medical assistance to injured participants or spectators as soon as possible under the circumstances. Therefore arrangements must be made for appropriate medical or first aid personnel to be in attendance at the meet. The additional cost of this service is necessary for the safe operation of the meet. The presence of "St. John's First Aid" personnel, for example, may weigh heavily in court in the event of injury resulting in a lawsuit.

Sanction and Insure the Meet

If the competition is organized by a school or university, the institution normally is considered the meet's sponsor or sanctioning organization. If the competition is hosted or organized by an individual, club or corporation, it must apply for a sanction from the Ontario Track and Field Association (in Ontario). Any sanctioned meet is covered by Ontario Track and Field Association (OTFA) insurance for all members — officials, athletes, coaches and the organizing committee (Smith, 1988).

It is the Meet Director's responsibility to ensure that the aforementioned concerns are considered and a safe competition is offered at a safe facility. In addition to this, a call to a local insurance company can be made and comprehensive coverage for the day(s) of the competition may be obtained for protection of the Meet Director and officials.

Conclusion

The track and field Meet Director assumes a great deal of responsibility with the title and a legal duty to provide the participants with safety. The review of cases in track and field illustrates some of the varying areas of a track and field meet where injury may occur.

It is important to educate those involved in organizing a track and field meet on their legal responsibilities. The review of literature and personal interviews with those associated with meet directing reveal that little guidance is offered with regards to organizing a safe track and field meet. Therefore, the Meet Director is advised to be attentive to the environment for the purpose of identifying safety needs, and to concentrate on establishing an efficient system of supervision, facility maintenance and scheduling.

Questions for Class Discussion

1. Document cases of sport injuries in your community in school sport, amateur or professional athletics or parks and recreation departments.
2. Track and Field is one of the most difficult of sports events to organize due to the number of competitors,

officials and spectators. In view of the large number involved, why is the Meet Director vulnerable to a lawsuit? Why does the "buck" stop with the Meet Director?
3. Go to the law library and find some of the cases listed in this Chapter. For each summarize on the following format:
   a) Case name,
   b) Deciding court,
   c) Date of decision,
   d) Plaintiff's name,
   e) Defendant's name,
   f) Facts of the case,
   g) Legal issues,
   h) Decision or holding,
   i) Reasoning or rationale of the Court, and,
   j) Students' reaction.
4. What are the responsibilities of the Meet Director in terms of negligence tort and occupier's liability to each of the following: competitors, coaches, officials, spectators, media?
5. Assign different students to examine each of the seven major concerns of the Meet Director:
   a) Physical layout,
   b) Equipment safety,
   c) Scheduling of events,
   d) Condition of surfaces,
   e) Spectator safety,
   f) Officiating, and,
   g) Medical and First Aid.
   h) Attend a meet and evaluate on each of these factors.
   i) Find actual Canadian or American cases which involved these factors.
6. Have someone read the Chapters on insurance and suggest what types of coverage would be appropriate.

References

Appenzeller, Herb. (1970). *From the gym to the jury*. Charlottesville, Virginia: The Michie Company.

Appenzeller, Herb and Appenzeller, Thomas. (1980). *Sport and the courts*. Charlottesville, Virginia: The Michie Company.

Appenzeller, Herb and Ross, C. Thomas. (1980). *Sports and the courts — physical education and Sports Quarterly*. Winston-Salem, North Carolina: Sports and the Courts, Inc.

Barnes, J. (1981). *Sports and the law in Canada*. Ottawa, Canada: Carleton University.

Doughtery, Neil J. (1987). *Principles of safety in physical education and sport*. Reston, Virginia: The American Alliance for Health, Physical Education, Recreation and Dance.

Fahr, Samuel M. (February, 1985). Legal liability for athletic injuries, *Iowa AHPERD Journal*, 219-223.

Ferris, B.F. (1977) and Peters, B.A. (March, 1977). Legal aspects of physical education: A need for professional standards of conduct. *CAHPER 43*: 3-8.

International Amateur Athletic Federation. (1988). *IAFF Handbook*.

Koehler, Robert W. (1978). *Law, sport activity and risk management*. Champaign, Illinois: Stipes Publishing Company.

Marra, Harry W. and Elia, John P. (March, 1986). Safety Factors in Track and Field, *Athletic Journal*, 65: 20-23.

Nygaard, Gary and Boone, Thomas H. (1985). *Coaches guide to sport law*. Champaign, Illinois: Human Kinetics Publishers, Inc.

OTFA (1979). *Track and field meet director's handbook*. Toronto, Ontario: Ontario Track and Field Association.

Prpich, Margery; Brown, Ray and Moriarty, Dick. (1982). *Sport activity and the law*. Windsor, Ontario: University of Windsor SIR/CAR.

Ross, C. Thomas, J.D. (1994). *Sport and the Courts — Physical Education and Sports Law Newsletter*, 15(4). Winston-Salem, North Carolina: Sports and the Courts, Inc.

Ross, C. and Thomas, J.D. (1994). *Sport and the Courts — Physical Education and Sports Law Newsletter*, 17(4). Winston-Salem, North Carolina: Sports and the Courts, Inc.

Smith, Cecil. (1988). [Personal Interview].

Vigars, Robert J. (1995). *Track and field curriculum for physical education*. London, Canada: The University of Western Ontario.

CHAPTER 5

RISK MANAGEMENT FOR TRIATHLON DIRECTORS

Tony Nurse and Margery Holman

Introduction

The Event

The evolution of Triathlon as an independent event, incorporating multiple activities, has captured the interest of a new generation of competitors. Looking for novel ways to incorporate athletic prowess into a competitive realm, females and males in a variety of age groups have been attracted to the challenges of triathlon. While many of the same risk management strategies for track and field, swimming cycling, and other single site events apply to Triathlon, there are management features in events such as Triathlon that are unique and require special attention to ensure that the safety of all involved is optimized.

The sport of Triathlon has evolved over many years and has become an increasingly high participative sport. The Triathlon itself is comprised of swim, bike and run sections that occur consecutively. Since the 1989 founding of the International Triathlon Union (ITU) in Avignon, France, the multi-sport disciplines within the ITU family have undergone significant changes and substantial growth. Under the leadership of President Les McDonald, ITU has developed into an efficient and flexible organization to govern the sport. Triathlon was admitted to the 2000 Sydney Olympic Games as a full medal sport. Evolving from the core of Triathlon (1.5k swim, 40k bike, 10k run), ITU has developed popular new disciplines including Long Distance Triathlon, Duathlon (run, bike, run), Long Distance Duathlon, Winter Triathlon (cross country ski, bike and run), Indoor Triathlon (pool swim, velodrome bike and track run) and Aquathlon (run, swim, run) (ITU, 1999b).

The technical aspects of the sport are evolving and ITU works hard to keep pace with the demands of modernization while maintaining safety and fairness for all competitors. ITU events are spectator friendly, often drawing crowds of more than 25,000 fans (ITU, 1999b). The drama of Triathlon races involves the strategy of the game, in addition to the swimming, bicycling and running segments, which produces dramatic and exciting television programs. With the combination of urban and rural settings, the typography of courses varies from flat to mountainous terrains. Some swims are in lakes, while others in rivers or oceans. Each provides a different athletic challenge and visual backdrop, as well as different risk concerns for the event manager.

Organizational Structure

ITU now has more than 110 National Federations on five continents. Each continental association conducts a championship for its members. The multi-event nature of the sport presents a unique challenge with rules and regulations that encompass several disciplines.

Triathlon Canada is a recognized member of the International Olympic Committee and has a mandate to promote, foster, organize and develop the sport of Triathlon in Canada. It is responsible for establishing rules, regulations, dates, criteria for selecting coaches and athletes, encouraging participation for both elite athletes and the general public. There are currently nine provincial Triathlon federations.

The Ontario Association of Triathletes (OAT) is the official governing body for multi-sport events in Ontario. It is a voting member of Triathlon Canada, which governs the sports of Triathlon and Duathlon nationally and which, in turn, is a member of the International Triathlon Union, which governs the sports of Triathlon and Duathlon internationally. OAT is a non-profit organization, run by a volunteer Board of Directors. In 1989, OAT became the official governing body for multi-sport events in Ontario. The OAT is responsible for sanctioning all triathlon events that occur in Ontario. Sanctioning is a process where a permit is issued by an authority, in this case the OAT. The aims of sanctioning are to assist the Race Director in staging safe and fair events that are equitable for all competitors. It also includes assisting the Race Director, local councils and the Police to minimize the risk of injury to the competitors and the public, or damage to their property and to ensure a safe and fair competition event (Triathlon Ontario, 1999).

Since triathlons have become an increasingly popular sport, those who are involved with the organization and facilitation must be concerned with various aspects in relation to participant safety. One method that is effective and important to help regulate the safety concerns for both participants and spectators is to develop a comprehensive risk management plan.

Managing the Risk

Risk management for Triathlon has many similar characteristics to other sport programs and events. Risk management is a total program that analyzes where and why accidents may occur and how the hazards might be controlled (Forsyth & Moriarty, 1994). An effective program is one that will determine what calculated risks are acceptable. In arriving at this determination, it is a common legal principle that a person who is responsible for an activity is expected to provide an activity that is as safe as possible (Watson, 1996). According to Peterson (1989), a pro-active approach to managing risk will reduce the likelihood of accidents occurring, a lawsuit being filed or a plaintiff being successful.

In order to help understand a risk management program, Kaiser (1986) developed a model to identify a cycle through which a risk management program should progress. There are five components to this model, including program feasibility, risk identification, risk treatment, risk evaluation and risk implementation. (See Chapter 2 on Risk Management.)

The Triathlon Director has a vast amount of responsibility, including such areas as course layout, and management of the actual event, its participants and the spectators. In addition, the immense spatial boundaries of a Triathlon course prohibit the Director from personally monitoring all areas. There must be a well-trained staff with whom the Director maintains a high level of communication with respect to delegated responsibilities and expectations. A disciplined team approach to event management will reduce the potential for injury to both participants and spectators.

Use of Waivers

It is important for Triathlon Directors to implement the use of waivers in their risk management programs. Sport organizations use waivers to document that participation is voluntary and that the risks are acknowledged and assumed by the participant. The main purpose of the waiver is to release the sponsoring organization from responsibility for an injury that may occur (Appenzeller, 1998). Although it has commonly been referred to as a waiver in the past, there has been a shift toward labeling it as a release as it releases the organization from responsibility. In the event of a lawsuit, the waiver, or release, will be used to request summary judgment, a decision by the judge that the participants have accepted responsibility for a possible injury (Clarke, 1998). The validity of release forms in the courts varies according to quality of the document, laws of the state or province, and previous case law. Anderson (1995), in an examination of waiver law and issues concerning development of a waiver, states:

It is important to understand that the extent to which liability can be waived is determined by the laws of the state where the event is being held. Although there are some basic principles that apply across the country, there are nuances in the various laws and legal advice should be obtained in order to construct a valid waiver. It should be understood that there are some instances where a pre-injury release will not relieve the sponsor of legal responsibility. For example, no state will release a party from liability for criminal behavior and releases are considered void where they are entered into under fraud or duress. A release will not absolve a party from wanton or gross negligence or in cases where they would be held strictly liable. Strict liability is imposed in cases where the injured party has no control over the event or instrumentality that causes the injury. For example, most manufacturers are strictly liable for injuries caused by a defect in the manufacturing process. Courts may also invalidate a waiver for injuries resulting from activities that have hidden or extreme dangers or where severe injury has occurred (p.1).

The use of a waiver can be examined in a recent case involving a Virginia Triathlon that centered on the acceptance of a waiver form. In *Hiett v. Lake Barcroft Community Association, Inc.*, 244 Va.191, 418 S E 2d 894 (Va. Jun 05, 1992) (NO. 911395), cited in Anderson (1995), the Virginia Supreme Court ruled that a waiver was unacceptable for the defense of negligent actions in this particular case. During a Triathlon the plaintiff was rendered a quadriplegic when he struck his head on his entry into Lake Barcroft. Similar to the rest of the participants, Mr. Hiett had signed a release prior to the competition in which he agreed not to claim damages against the association for injuries suffered from participation in the event. The Virginia Supreme Court ruled the waiver invalid, stating that a waiver, used for release from negligence that results in an injury to a person, is against public policy (Anderson, 1995).

Development of the Waiver/Release

According to Anderson (1995) the law imposes the burden on the party drafting the release to prove that the individual who signed the release knew, or should have known, what they were doing when he or she signed the release. Therefore, the release should contain clear and succinct language so that the individual signing the document understands that its purpose is to relieve the sponsoring organization from liability. The release language should not be hidden in a lengthy document that addresses a number of other matters. It should be printed in large, not small, type, in a visible format, not on the back of an equipment rental agreement. The person signing the release must be the participant and no one else should be permitted to sign on the participant's behalf. Words like "release" or "disclaimer" or "waiver" should be prominently featured in the title of the release. Persons executing the release must be directed to read the release, provided sufficient time to read it, and then asked if they understand its consequences (Anderson, 1995; Clarke, 1998; Neville & Moriarty, 1994).

The release should specifically describe the event, and its time and place. Even if the type of risk is apparent, it should be clearly stated so that the participant is aware of, and acknowledges the risk. Also, the waiver should state that the party signing the document is releasing the organizing association from liability resulting from injury due to simple negligence. All releases should be kept in a secure place and retained until the statute of limitations has expired (Anderson, 1995).

Neville and Moriarty (1994) make reference to the means by which a waiver may be deemed invalid by the courts, six of which are as follows:

1. They are contrary to public policy;
2. They have ambiguous language;
3. They are signed by minors;
4. They cover reckless/wanton negligence;
5. They are caught by mutual mistake theory; or,
6. They contain misrepresentations or disparity in bargaining.

Triathlon Directors need to understand the importance of waiver release forms during the development of Triathlon races and implement them according to their needs. They need to adhere to specific guidelines and procedures to ensure the greatest likelihood that these will hold up in court. They should establish examine existing procedures and checklists in order to identify the content essential to the development of the most effective waiver.

Cases Relevant to Triathlon Directors

Banfield v. Songea, 589 So. 2d 441 (1991).

Case Summary: Susan Banfield was a participant in a Triathlon when she was struck by a car and seriously injured. She argued that the promoters and sponsors (Louis Songea, Bon's Barricades, Mike's Cyclery, Anheuser Busch, Quaker Oats, International Swimming Hall of Fame, Triathlon Federation, Mike Eaccarino, CAT Sports, City of Fort Lauderdale) were negligent in their duties to ensure a safe bicycle course and that they failed to control traffic around the course. Susan had signed a waiver prior to the race and chose to enter the event voluntary. The original decision ruled in favour of the Sponsors and Promoters due to Susan's acceptance of the terms and conditions presented in the waiver.

Legal Issues and Court Decision: This case is based on whether or not a waiver can exonerate the sponsors and promoters of an event from liability. In this case, the defendants were not held liable for the accident. The court cited a variety of cases where a waiver form eliminated the liability for race organizers and promoters. In *Theis v J & J Racing Promotion*, 571 So. 2d 92 (Fla. 2d DCA 1990), a participant was unable to claim damages from the organizers after they were injured from a runaway wheel. A second case, *Okura v United States Cycling Federation*, 186 Cal. App. 3d 1462 (1986), it was ruled that a waiver contained within the entry form was valid and enforceable because the racer's participation was voluntary. A waiver that identifies parties is sufficient to absolve those parties from liability as a matter of law. This is supported by two additional cases, *Etiole Int'l. v Miami Elevator Co.*, 573 So. 2d 921 (1990) & *Sheen v. Lyon*, 485 So. 2d 422 (1986). Banfield's additional argument was that the waiver should be ruled invalid because it is against the public policy of the state of Florida to allow sponsors and promoters to release themselves from liability. Banfield attempted to illustrate that the organizers and promoters displayed a prejudice to the dominant public interest but the courts felt otherwise and subsequently found all of the defendant's innocent. The ruling explained that a contract should not be declared void unless it is clearly injurious to the public good. The courts also felt the need to refuse to strike down contracts unless it is clearly shown that there is prejudice to the dominant public interest sufficient to overthrow the public policy of the right to freedom of contract between parties.

Characteristics of a Triathlon

When attempting to develop a safe environment for athletes it is important to examine all areas concerning the staging of triathlons. These areas do not stop at the athletes' or spectator safety but involve underlying issues such as drafting rules, employment of qualified officials and proper established procedures for dealing with appeals. Triathlon Directors must take into account all aspects involved with the organizing of triathlons in order to eliminate and/or reduce the possible risk and conflict that may arise. Four of the more important areas concern the actual race and involve the transition area in addition to the run, bike and swim sections.

Triathlon Definitions

Wave Start: The Triathlon swim section involves a variety of groups that begin a specific times (e.g., Men between 20-29 begin a the same time). This is referred to as a wave.

Elite: These are athletes who have achieved specific times and compete against other elite athletes.

Age Grouper: These are those participants not classified as elite who compete against others in a similar age group (e.g., Male 20-24).

Drafting: Drafting is when a participant rides within 5 meters of someone's back wheel and does not overtake them or rides next to someone within 2 meters.

Bicycle Dismount/Mount: This is just outside the transition area where a competitor must get on or off their bike by a specific line. Returning from the bike section a participant must be off their bike by a certain line.

Safety Concerns for the Swim Section:

When developing the swim portion of a Triathlon it is essential for directors to explore and examine all of the aspects regarding the water area, including the transition space used to both enter and exit the swimming site of the race. The International Triathlon Union has developed a comprehensive package that outlines the various safety concerns that must be addressed. Although these guidelines have been developed for international events, most of the safety features and rules can be applied to local triathlons.

Swim Start

It is important for Directors to provide a starting area that offers equal positioning for all competitors. The swim start will be a minimum of 50 meters wide for elite waves and a minimum of 30 meters wide for age group waves. This will allow sufficient room for all competitors. It is important to note that there is contact between the swimmers during this portion of the race. The swim starting area will be defined by hard crowd control fencing (minimum 1 meter tall) providing the competitors with a buffer from media and spectators. Media will be provided an observation zone of at least 20 square meters along the length of the swim start that will be secured from spectators by hard fencing and managed by security personnel. The swim start will occur at the shoreline or, in deep water, by diving from pontoon or dock. In no instance will competitors start from dry land and run into the water. For dive starts, the starter will hold competitors until the competitors are judged to be prepared to start. In the event of a false start, the starter will signal swim start officials to drop a false start rope across the course to stop the swimmers and return them to the starting area for a re-start (ITU, 1999a).

For deep-water starts, the competitors will be constrained by a swimming pool anti-wave swim lane floating on the water surface and tightly secured at both ends. A minimum of four swim start officials on paddleboards will raise the swim lane at the starting sound, signifying the start and eliminating the possibility of a false start. For shoreline starts, the competitors will stand behind a start line 10 centimeters wide painted on a carpet that is 40 meters long. Competitors' toes will be behind the line until the starter's signal.

Competitors will be allowed to warm-up in the designated warm-up area, but will not be allowed to warm-up on the swim course. Competitors must be out of the water a minimum of ten minutes prior to the announced starting time. For safety purposes, competitors must wear their official swim caps during the warm-up period, while in the swim start area and during the swim portion of the competition.

Lead Craft

There will be a lead kayak or canoe for the elite men, elite women, junior women and junior men categories. A flag must be extended at least two meters above the craft in order to identify it. It will have radio contact/communication with the race announcer on shore (ITU, 1999a).

Wave Start Requirements

In each wave, a maximum number of 75 elite athletes can participate. For age groupers, 150 is the maximum number of participants. Each wave will have different colored swim caps. A competitor's race number will be marked on both sides of the cap. Age group competitors will have only one body marking – a letter indicating their age group category, i.e., A for 20 to 24 year old women (ITU, 1999a).

Wave Start Specifications

The regulations call for the women's and men's races for elite and junior athletes to be completely separated with a minimum of 30 minutes between the finish of one and the start of the next. There is to be no overlap on any portion of the course. All wave starts will be given the final swim instructions prior to the start of their wave (ITU, 1999a). While these regulations are applied to the International Triathlon Union series, most local Triathlon races such as the President's Choice Triathlon series, do not consistently have separate elite males and females.

Water Safety Support

There will be a minimum of 2 motorized boats positioned equal distance throughout the length of the course and a minimum of 15 certified lifeguards (on surfboards, kayaks, rowboats or canoes) staggered throughout the course. Each boat must be equipped with communication to shore officials and to race headquarters (ITU, 1999a). Lifeguards should be qualified, trained and accountable in all phases of the aquatic risk management plan. They must understand all operations manuals specific to the event as well as lifeguard safety procedures. It is critical that they remain alert to the potential of danger at all times.

Power Boats

Powerboats must be prevented from crossing any section of the swim course. Provision must be made for a beaching point where powerboats can off-load any casualties without crossing the swim course. Exhaust fumes must not affect air quality around competitors. Recreational powerboats must be prevented from coming within 50 meters of the course (ITU, 1999).

Course Design

The swim course should be reasonably protected from potentially adverse weather conditions. The start and finish areas must be firm, clean, clearly marked and free from hazards. The course must be designed so that safety monitor positions and mobile evacuation units can be stationed and operate from all sides of the course. The swim course will be one directional, or an out and back. If it is an out and back course, there will be a separation lane of at least 100 meters between the out and back swimmers. If rectangular or triangular in shape, it will have the following dimensions for one lap swims: the first turn may be no less than 400 meters from the start (this rule may be amended in the case of a lap course for the elite wave); and, the second turn will be at least 100 meters from the first turn. The turns will never be more than ninety degrees.

Course Markings

A swim lane rope must mark the entire course. In addition, the following markings apply:

1. Turn buoys will be at least 2.5 meters high and will be a distinctive colour;
2. There will be intermittent buoys every 100 meters;
3. Crossovers are forbidden;
4. Buoys will always be on the left or right side, but never a slalom combination;
5. The colour of the buoys will be easily distinguishable from the swim cap colour; and,
6. All turn buoys will be monitored by three officials to prevent any cutting of the turns.

Water Temperature

Water temperature must be taken one day prior to race day and one hour prior to the start of the event on race morning. It must be taken in the middle of the course at a depth of 60 centimeters.

A Case Relevant to Safe Swimming

Triathlon Directors must understand the importance of providing safe swimming conditions for the participants if they want to avoid a case of negligence. The following case contains details that are applicable to the Triathlon environment.

Moddejonge v. Huron (County) Board of Education [1972], 2 O.R. 437 (H.C.)

Case Summary: This incident occurred during a field trip where the defendant, John McCauley, the coordinator of the outdoor educational program at a local high school, supervised a field trip that was organized by the school and sponsored by the Board. During the field trip, a group of students persuaded McCauley, who did not know how to swim, to take them swimming at a conservation area. McCauley informed David McClure, another teacher on the excursion, of their plans and no objection was taken. In the water there was a shallow area with a sharp drop off to a deep area. McCauley explained to the children about the drop off and warned them not to enter that part of the water. The children were swimming when a gust of wind pushed them into the deeper water. Geraldine Moddejonge swam out to rescue the struggling girls and, during the attempt, both she and a student peer, Janet Guenther, drowned.

Legal Issues and Court Decisions: A question of whether there was a breach of duty alleged to be owed to the children by the defendants to take reasonable care of them was present. The liability of an employee of the Board of Education acting as a supervisor was also in question. The courts ruled that McCauley was liable for the death of Janet Guenther and Geraldine Moddejonge because he did not protect the girls against the foreseeable risks of the drop-off area. McCauley was also responsible for the death of Geraldine because his negligence had created the danger to Janet whom Geraldine had reasonably sought to rescue. The case against teacher McClure was dismissed. However, since coordinator McCauley was acting under the scope of his employment the school board was also held responsible. The decision was based on a ruling by Lord Esher on the case of *Williams v. Eady* (1893), 10 T.L.R. 41.

> ... as to the law on the subject there can be no doubt; and it was correctly laid down by the learned Judge, that the schoolmaster was bound to take such care of his boys as a careful father would take care of his boys, and there could not be a better definition of the duty of schoolmaster.

The judge argued that McCauley should have guarded the children from the risk. In the case involving the rescuing girl, the plaintiff was held liable according to a ruling in the case of *Wagner v. Int'l R. Co.* (1921), 232 N.Y. 176.

> ... the risk of rescue, if only it be not wanton, is born of the occasion. The emergency begets the man. The wrongdoer may not have foreseen the coming of a deliverer. He is accountable as if he had.

The judge held McCauley accountable for the death of the rescuing girl because he was negligent on the initial act that caused the secondary act to occur. The court awarded $2,800 in damages to John Moddejonge and Carl Guenther, the fathers of the two girls.

This case provides important information for sport administrators and ultimately Triathlon directors. It is essential to understand the layout of the swimming course before the event ensues. The necessary procedures such as the appropriate number of lifeguards and boats can be adjusted to contend with varying degrees of dangers for parts of the course. Trained, qualified and attentive lifeguards are needed for the safe operation of a Triathlon swim course. This decision was expected because John McCauley owed the children the duty of care and this, coupled with his inability to swim, should have made him avoid the situation altogether.

Safety Concerns for the Bike Section

Roads

All roads should be closed to vehicular traffic. The road surface must be hard and smooth with no holes. For local Triathlon, some portions of the roads are closed while others are open to the public and monitored by police and marshals. The road, especially corners, must be swept free of debris ITU, 1999a).

There will be no out and back courses unless there is at least a one meter buffer lane, or a grass or concrete meridian, which separates the out-going and in-coming cyclists. There will be no crossovers during the bike segment. The cycle course will not overlap with the run course or with spectator space unless a three-meter safety zone is created with hard barriers, except on elite and junior courses with the approval of the Triathlon Director. The road leading into transition and out of transition will be secured with hard fencing. Fencing will extend for 400 meters at both the exit and entrance of transition. It should avoid railroad tracks, bridges with gates, drawbridges, et cetera (ITU, 1999a).

Safety Precautions

1. All corners and areas of high spectator involvement must be completely secured with hard fencing.
2. Railroad tracks will be covered with thick rubber matting.
3. There will be straw bales, or similar safety devices, on sharp turns and corners.
4. Police or race marshals will be at every access road, intersection, and turn on the course.
5. All participants are required to wear certified helmets (ITU, 1999a).

Spectators

Spectators should be discouraged and physically prevented, where necessary, from entering the course and/or interfering with the competition especially at the beginning and end of the bike segment. The risk management plan can significantly aid crowd control efforts and help prevent accidents and losses (Miller, 1993). The ITU specifies certain crowd control measures such as perimeter fencing and sectioned off participants' area. Triathlon Directors must understand the importance of crowd control in establishing safe courses for the participants. Without vigilance, there is an increased chance of litigation.

A Case Relevant to Safe Biking

Johnson & Johnson v Steffen et al. 685 N.E. 2d 1117 (1997)

Case Summary: Otis Johnson, a police officer, was assigned to work and control traffic at an intersection during the Budlight triathlon. There were six lanes to the road with two lanes sectioned off and used for the bike section. Johnson was directing a car not to move when a cyclist collided with him. The original case found that the police officer fell into a category specified by the Fireman's Rule that prevented him from taking legal action.

Legal Issues and Court Decision: The basis of this case centers around the Fireman's Rule which states that a landowner owed no duty to a firefighter responding to a fire on the landowner's property except that of abstaining from any wrongful act which may result in injury. This rule was established from the case of *Woodruff v Bowen*, 136 Ind. 431 (1893) and later expanded and included professionals such as police officers. The rule stated that professionals whose occupations by their nature expose them to particular risks, may not hold another individual negligent for creating the situation in which they respond in their professional capacity. This rule was the main legal issue surrounding the case.

The original case found that defendants did not have a responsibility to the police officer. The appeal court reversed the decision and felt that the Fireman's Rule could not bar Johnson's claim. In the case of *Koehn v Devereaux*, 495 N.E. 2d 211 (1986) it was found that police officers could be included in the Fireman's Rule. The Supreme Court reversed an earlier decision regarding the case of *Heck v Robey*, 630 N.E. 2d 1361 (1994) and explained that the rule characterized the duty owed by a landowner to those coming onto the premises under a public duty during emergencies. The Supreme Court examined the courts decision in the Heck case closely on three theoretical principals, the defense of incurred risk, premise liability and public policy concerns. In reference to this case the court rejected incurred risks and public policy as justifications for the Fireman's Rule. The courts declined to accept a public policy position that would relieve the defendant of responsibility based on the plaintiff's occupation. Essentially, if a police officer is injured as a result of negligence, the rule can not protect the defendant because the officer was doing his job. Ultimately, the court found that the Fireman's Rule does not apply to prevent Johnson's claim and the trial court was wrong in their decision. The decision was reversed.

This was an interesting case that had a split decision with the judges. Two of the judges agreed that the Fireman's Rule should not prevent the claim against the defendants. The other judge stated that Johnson failed to provide evidence that the defendant engaged in positive wrongful acts. This case is important for Triathlon Directors because, as they recruit volunteers and staff, they need to understand the rules of law that can apply. Perhaps race directors need their employees and volunteers to sign waivers to reduce the potential of litigation. This case sets a specific precedent for those involved with the operation of triathlons and helps to illustrate the increased amount of litigation present in society.

Safety Concerns for the Run Section

Roads

As with the bike section, all lanes should be closed to vehicular traffic and the road surface must be hard, smooth surfaces, free from obstacles and hazards. There will be no crossovers between cyclists and runners or runners and runners. A clearly identified lead official on a bicycle will stay a minimum of 30 meters ahead of the Host Broadcaster Television camera bike with the lead competitor. All turns where cutting the course is possible must be controlled by race officials. Police or "trained" race officials will be at every access road, intersection, and turn. All corners and areas of high spectator involvement must be completely secured with hard fencing. The area leading to the finish line, and the exit from transition will be secured with hard fencing, at least 400 meters (ITU, 1999a).

Concern for Triathlon Directors

In the event of an injury that occurs as a result of a collision between a motor vehicle and a participant, the Triathlon Director can be named in the suit and potentially be held accountable for negligence. It is important for the Triathlon Director and an associate race director to take the proper caution to prevent such occurrences. An added concern is introduced for events that extend past dusk and finish in darkness. Diminished visibility further puts participants at risk, requiring related precautions.

Safety Concerns for the Transition Area

Layout

The surface must be hard, flat, and smooth. The area must be completely secured by hard fencing and security marshals. Lanes within the transition must be at least 5 meters wide, with a minimum space per competitor of 1.5 meters for elite and junior competitors, and .75 meters for age group competitors. The cycle and run course will never cross. The Official ITU Television Host Broadcaster and the Official ITU Photographer will be the only media allowed inside the Transition Area. If in the opinion of the Triathlon Director, either of these media is compromising the safety or fairness of the competition, they will be removed from the Transition Area.

The Bicycle Mount Zone will be a secure, bright colored carpet which covers the width of the road, and which is 5 meters deep. The edges of the carpet must be secure to the pavement to avoid slippage. Competitors must mount their bicycles while on the carpet.

The surface of the ground from the swim finish to the Transition Area must not be such that it could cause injury to competitors; otherwise, it must be covered with a non-slip material.

The area must be completely secured by hard fencing and security personnel to patrol the area. Media and spectators must not have access to the area between the swim finish and the Transition Area.

Bike Racks

Bicycle rack rows must be placed so that when bicycles are on the racks there is a lane for bicycles to travel into and out of the transition area. Bicycles and running gear must be placed in numerical order on the bike racks.

Medical Requirements

There is a duty to provide health care facilities and services for all athletes during competitions. This includes a wide range of services including experienced and competent staff, first-aid equipment, access to ambulance services and general activities associated with providing safer health conditions for the participants. One important and applicable component for a Triathlon Director is to ensure that athletes are treated properly by the staff. Although certification in first aid offered by national organizations is not a guarantee against a negligence suit, it can demonstrate that a staff member was qualified (Gray, 1993). This proper training is vital to understanding when, and when not, to provide particular treatments for a participant. For example, if an immobilizing injury occurs and a participant is mistakenly moved causing further injury, the Triathlon Director and others associated with the incident, may be named in legal action for negligence. In *Welch v. Dunsmuir* (1958) a high school athlete sustained an injury. After the coach tested the player using a grip test, he determined that the student could be moved. During the transport of the player by eight of his teammates, the injured athlete sustained a spinal cord injury and was consequently paralyzed. The court found negligence was the cause of the paralysis (Gray, 1993). Triathlon Directors must provide properly trained individuals who understand their responsibilities. If they are unaware of what must be done, then the proper staff must be contacted and procedures must be administered correctly. It is important to examine the various factors associated with health and medical safety as they relate to the sport of triathlons.

The medical/first aid area and drink facilities must be in clear view, with easy access of transition area. These medical care guidelines are for the care of competitors at ITU competitions and are based upon the experiences of caring for tens of thousands of competitors and spectators in multi-sport endurance events throughout the world. There is no consideration more important than the safety and care of the competitors.

Doctors and Authority: Two doctors must be present and on duty for the entire event. One doctor should be located centrally and the other mobile. Two paramedics per 200 competitors is the minimum suggested. Physicians have authority to withdraw a competitor at any point for safety or health reasons.

Finish Line and Transition: Paramedics and stretchers must be in attendance adjacent to the transition area and at the finish line area. Medical personnel at the rate of one per 100 competitors will be at the finish area to spot stressed competitors and escort them to the medical tent.

Facilities: Two medical tents or buildings or covered areas with walls to prevent media access must be established in a quiet place near the finish line, one for recovery and the other for the treatment of dehydration, hypo/hyperthermia and other medical problems. The placement of the tent takes precedence over other considerations. A separate tent or building must be available at the end of the swim leg. The treatment tent or building will be large enough to contain cots for five percent of the competitors and include an area for communications and supplies.

Hospitals and Ambulances: The nearest hospital, and preferably two, will be informed well in advance of the competition and advised of the possible emergency admissions from the race, including the type of injuries or problems to expect. A follow-up report should be obtained regarding each admission.

Heat Concerns: A risk management plan should take into account the factors relating to heat stroke and exhaustion. According to Bernard (1996) preventing heat illness will depend on managing the risk associated with it. The ability to tolerate heat stress varies with each participant. Staff and volunteers should be trained to look for signs of heat stroke and attend to the participants. It is also important for staff to reinforce re-hydration concepts and ensure that the participants have access to fluids (Wright, personal communication, 2000).

Conclusion

Risk management has been, and will continue to be, an important issue for Triathlon Directors as well as those involved with hosting a competition. There are a number of concerns that need to be addressed in order to accommodate and protect both the participants and spectators. As the sport of triathlon continues to grow, the need for new safety and security measures will be continuously evolving as well. The sport of triathlon has progressed rapidly and only through effective risk management planning and the dedication of the staff, will the safety of those involved be met. The International Triathlon Union has provided guidelines for event managers. These, combined with an evaluation of local needs, provide a good starting point to host a safe competition and avoid litigation.

Questions for Class Discussion

1. Discuss the value of a risk management plan for Triathlon.
   a. Identify the components of the Triathlon that require attention be given to risk management strategies.
   b. Which areas of a Triathlon require that special attention be given to manage/eliminate the risk that may exist?
   c. Develop some hypothetical cases that might emerge from a Triathlon that was poorly planned and administered. Discuss the ways in which such cases might be avoided.
2. Develop a waiver that might be effectively used by a Triathlon Director as part of a risk management plan.

References

American College of Sports Medicine. (1992). *ACSM's health/fitness facility standards and guidelines*. Author.

Appenzeller, H. (1998). *Risk management in sport*. Durham, NC: Carolina Academia Press.

Anderson, J (1995). *The effectiveness of liability waivers*. [on-line] www.haspc.com.

Bernard, T. (1996). Risk management for preventing heat illness in athletes. *Athletic Therapy Today, 6*, p. 19-21.

Clarke, K. (1998). On issues and strategies. In H. Appenzeller (Ed.), *Risk management in sport* (pp. 11-22). Durham, NC: Carolina Academia Press.

Fairall, D., D. Moriarty, & M. Holman. (1994). Legal responsibility of the meet director. In Moriarty, Holman, Brown, Moriarty (Eds.), *Canadian/American sport, fitness and the law* (pp. 73-87). Toronto: Canadian Scholars' Press.

Ferris, B. & B. Peters. (1977). Legal aspects of physical education: A need for professional standard of conduct. *Canadian Association for Health, Physical Education, Recreation and Dance, 43*, pp. 3-8.

Forsyth, J. & D. Moriarty. (1994). Risk management: The Road to prevention. In Moriarty, Holman, Brown, Moriarty (Eds.), *Canadian/American sport, fitness and the law* (pp. 109-127). Toronto: Canadian Scholars' Press.

Gray, G. (1993). Providing adequate medical care to program participants. *Journal of Physical Education, Recreation and Dance, 65*, 56-57.

Hanna, G. (1986). *Legal liability in outdoor education/recreation*. Edmonton AB: University of Alberta Press.

International Triathlon Union. (1999a). *Operations manual*. [on-line] www.worldsport.com.

International Triathlon Union. (1999b). *International Triathlon union multi-sport for the new millennium*. [on-line] www.worldsport.com.

Miller, L. (1993). Crowd control. *Journal of Physical Education, Recreation and Dance, 64*, 31-32.

Neville, N. & D. Moriarty. (1994). Waivers in fitness and sport: Are they worthwhile? In Moriarty, Holman, Brown, Moriarty (Eds.), *Canadian/American sport, fitness and the law* (pp. 131-154). Toronto: Canadian Scholars' Press.

Peterson, J. (1987). *Risk management for park, recreation and leisure services*. Champaign, IL: Management Learning Laboratories.

Siegenthaler, K. (1996). Supervising activities for safety. *Journal of Physical Education, Recreation and Dance, 67*, 29-36.

Triathlon Canada. (1999a). *Organizational facts*. [on-line] www.triathloncanada.com.

Triathlon Canada. (1999b). *Competition rules*. [on-line] www.triathloncanada.com.

Triathlon Canada. (1999). *Ontario Association of Triathletes*. [on-line] www.triathloncanada.com.

Watson, R. (1996). Risk management: A plan for safer activities. *Canadian Association for Health, Physical Education, Recreation and Dance, 6*, pp. 13-17.

Welch (Anthony L.), a Minor, Through His Guardian Ad Litem, Gladys A. Welch, Plaintiff and Respondent v. Dunsmuir Joint Union High School District, a Political Subdivision, Defendant and Appellant, 326 P.2d 633 (Cal.App. 1958).

Wong, G. (2000). *Legal issues in intramural & recreational sport*. Paper presented at the National Intramural and Recreational Sport Association Conference, Rhode Island, USA.

Wright, G. (2000). *Personal communication.*

CHAPTER 6

PERSONAL TRAINING: LEGAL LIABILITY AND RISK MANAGEMENT

Carrie Czichrak Lancaster

Participation in sport and fitness activities continues to be a popular past-time activity for much of Canadian society. As technology and automation continue to pervade our everyday lives, many individuals seek ways to increase their amount of physical activity, relieve stress, and interact socially with other individuals. Sport, fitness, and recreation programs offer a variety of activities such as a leisurely stroll in a park, a competitive volleyball game, group fitness classes, rock climbing, and downhill skiing. Each activity is designed to provide unique experiences to those who choose to participate. The health and fitness industry is a sub-field within the larger sporting world that has increased in popularity as individuals have become more aware of the benefits of physical activity towards a healthy lifestyle (Bell, 1995). Personal training professionals provide a unique service to individuals that include fitness and health assessment, program design, exercise consultation, motivation, and general fitness education (Cotton, 1996). Individuals who participate in physical activity under the instruction and supervision of a personal trainer engage in activities to optimize cardiovascular fitness, muscular fitness, and flexibility.

The purpose of this chapter is to increase the awareness and knowledge of legal issues specifically related to the area of personal training. The chapter is divided into sections.

The first section examines the personal trainer and the roles and responsibilities of this specialized profession. The second section provides a basic understanding of the term legal liability and its application to the personal trainer. In the third section, the four conditions of negligence are reviewed, and then each condition as it pertains to personal training is discussed. Relevant cases are presented to provide examples of negligence claims. The final section applies the five steps of risk management and relevant defenses to a lawsuit to the profession of personal trainer. The special case of at-home training will be addressed as an example of implementing a risk management strategy.

Personal Training

The area of health and fitness may include a variety of services provided by professionals such as personal trainers, fitness instructors, physiotherapists, massage therapists, nutritionists, and recreational programmers. As previously noted, individuals in Canadian society have increased their awareness and emphasis on health and fitness. Both physically active and non-active individuals are cognizant of the benefits of exercise. General benefits of exercise, coupled with healthy nutrition and lifestyle choices, include improved cardiovascular function, improved body composition, decreased resting heart rate, lowered blood pressure, increased ease of performing activities of daily living, and improved self-esteem (Cotton,

1996). The result of an increased awareness and emphasis on health and fitness has led the fitness industry to become a two billion dollar a year business (Bell, 1995). Current trends suggest continued growth, particularly in the area of personal training (Maggio, 2000).

According to the American Council on Exercise (ACE), personal trainers are professionals within the health and fitness industry who are (Cotton, 1996, p. 455):

- Competent to assess a client's health/medical/fitness status effectively,
- Design safe and effective physical activity programs utilizing goal setting, exercise science principles, and safety guidelines,
- Implement the exercise program safely and effectively, modifying the program as necessary in order to achieve reasonable goals, and
- Adhere to all codes, laws and procedures applicable within the recognized scope of practice for personal trainers.

The roles and responsibilities of the personal trainer are extensive, and therefore specialized knowledge and experience of exercise physiology and biomechanics is expected by the client. The service the personal trainer is providing is based on the expectation that he or she knows more about health and fitness than the average citizen. Despite this expectation, the guidelines by the Minister of National Health and Welfare (1980) stated that no academic qualifications or certifications are required. Some administrators of fitness centers have chosen to require certification in cardiopulmonary resuscitation (CPR), standard first aid, experience in exercise training (Maggio, 2000), and possibly personal training specialist certification from organizations such as ACE, Can-Fit Pro, or Canadian Personal Training Network (CPTN).

The conditions and environment in which a personal trainer works may vary. A personal trainer may work as an employee in a fitness club, or as an independent business person as the sole proprietor of the business, a partner in a business, or as a member of a legal corporation (Cotton, 1996). Each condition of employment has its own roles and legal responsibilities. The environment in which a personal trainer works may also vary according to the job requirement. Within a fitness club, the personal trainer may be responsible for general supervision of a group individuals exercising at the facility. One-on-one training sessions require the personal trainer to focus his or her attention and expertise on the client. These sessions typically last one hour and involve a personalized exercise program, technique instruction, and client monitoring. Personal training sessions increasingly occur outside the confines of the fitness club and may entail a run outside, road biking, or exercise training within the client's residence (Maggio, 2000). Training within the client's residence will be discussed at length later in the chapter.

Having stated the roles and responsibilities of a personal trainer, there are certain actions that are outside the scope of practice of this profession. Often-times a client will ask a personal trainer about the latest dietary supplement, to diagnose acute pain in a part of their body, how a client's friend should be training, or even what to do in a troubled personal relationship. Personal trainers are not licensed or qualified dietitians, physicians, chiropractors, marriage counselors, or social workers. It is important for the personal trainer to identify the scope of practice to the client, and refer that individual to the appropriate healthcare professional (Cotton, 1996). A personal trainer may also choose to network actively with other heath and fitness professionals to develop partnerships that may benefit a client in his or her goal of health and fitness.

Although the demographic composition of clientele with which a personal trainer may work will vary from fitness club to fitness club, there are certain populations that frequently hire a personal trainer. According to Maggio (2000), there are three main categories of clients: teens aged 13 to 16, young athletes aged 21 to 30, and adults aged 30 to 55. Each category poses unique legal risks because of the physiological, developmental, and social differences. The youngest age group consists of individuals who are not legally adults and would require parental/guardian consent to engage in fitness training. In addition, these individuals are still growing physically and extreme care must be provided to ensure training does not negatively effect the normal growth of the individual. Due to the unique legal issues related to training and instructing minors, this age group will not be addressed in the present discussion. Young athletes aged 21-30 are the most prevalent age group in the fitness industry because these individuals have the time, disposable income, and motivation to join, while remaining relatively injury and problem-free.

Adults over 30 are a unique category since they may be motivated to participate in fitness and training because of health problems that are restricting everyday activities, or because health studies have indicated exercise is linked to living longer (Maguire, 1999). These individuals may require more specialized education to account for their medical needs (i.e., low-back pain, arthritis, heart disease). Some studies have suggested that participants aged 55 and older is the fastest growing population of health-club members (Maguire, 1999). Personal trainers should be aware of the specific health and fitness needs of each age category, and adjust the exercise program to meet those needs.

Legal Liability

The term legal liability denotes some legal obligation or responsibility in the broadest sense. According to Black (1990, p. 914), liability is, "the condition of being actually or potentially subject to an obligation; condition of being responsible for a possible or actual loss, penalty, expense, or burden; condition which creates a duty to perform an act immediately or in the future." Individuals are legally responsible for their actions and omissions regardless of potential or actual loss. Sport managers are no longer allowed the luxury of considering their actions and the actions of their employees and athletes to exist outside the boundaries of the law. As society has become more litigious, lawsuits have increased within the realm of sport (Young, 1998). As sport managers are becoming more aware of the legal issues applicable to sport, conscientious managers are learning more about the legal process and how to manage the risk of a potential lawsuit.

Legal liability is a broad term that can be subdivided into two main branches. Criminal law, the first branch of legal liability, concerns wrongs committed against the state, as representative of the community at large (Moriarty, Holman, Brown, & Moriarty, 1994). The branch of criminal law can be further subdivided into property and persons. The second branch of legal liability is civil law. This area of law concerns the rights and duties of private parties as individual entities (Moriarty, et al., 1994), and can be further subdivided into contract law and tort law. A tort is a civil wrong committed against a private party for which the offender may be liable in damages. The most common cases of legal liability (Figure 6.1) arise in the area of negligence, under tort law (Adapted from Kaiser, 1986):

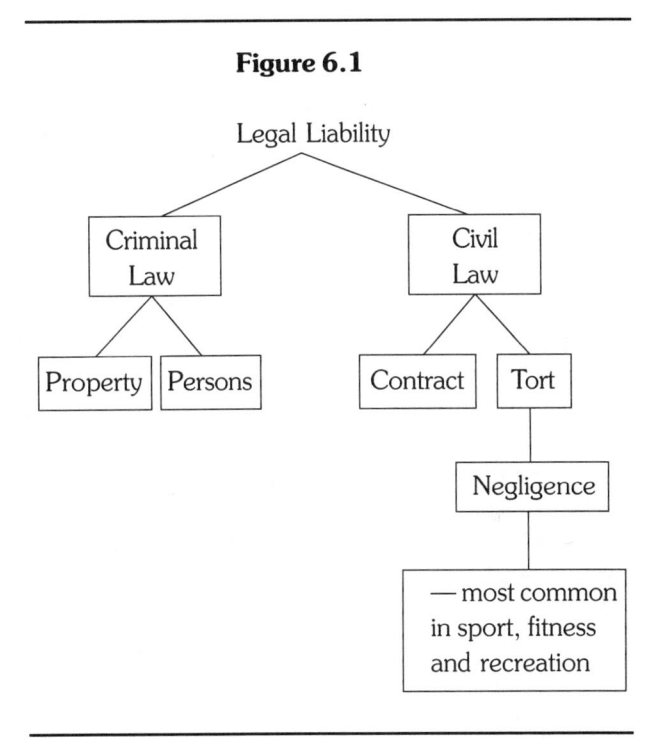

Figure 6.1

Legal Liability
├── Criminal Law
│   ├── Property
│   └── Persons
└── Civil Law
    ├── Contract
    └── Tort
        └── Negligence
            — most common in sport, fitness and recreation

Personal trainers have unique issues to consider when assessing their own legal liability towards a client. When considering the activity of weight lifting, participants often learn informally from other participants within the fitness facility (Baley & Mathews, 1998). Tips for training and technique may also originate from magazines and other forms of media, such as television, infomercials, the Internet, and books. Although these sources may provide valuable information to the client, personal trainers are educated in the area of exercise training and should have the knowledge to discern between an exercise fad that may cause harm to the client and legitimate exercise protocol. The personal trainer is legally responsibility for potential injury, loss, or damages incurred by the client, in association with exercise training. As previously noted, most cases arise in the area of negligence.

Negligence

Negligent conduct is an action or omission that falls below the established standard. In general, the established standards of an individual are compared to that of a prudent person. The court uses the fictional, prudent, reasonable person to assist in the evaluation of negligence (Allen, 1988a). Conduct is considered negligent if it creates unreasonable risk of harm, however, many physical activities pursued in sport depend on an amount of risk and uncertainty. The courts attempt to balance the danger of risk as created against that of the social value of the activity (Allen, 1988a).

The simple equation of PL=OC as presented by Allen (1988a), may be examined to further explain the relationship between risk and social value. P represents the probability that the risk of harm will occur, and L represents the severity of the loss if the injury results. Together, these elements determine the danger created by the defendant's conduct. O represents the purpose or object of the act in question, and C represents the cost or burden to the actor to eliminate the hazard. The object of the activity multiplied by the cost determines the burden to the defendant. If the risk is greater than the social value or burden (PL>OC), then the defendant is liable for the conduct. If the risk is less than the social value or burden (PL<OC), then the defendant is blameless for the conduct. For example, a personal trainer may decide to instruct a client to perform dead lifts, which can be considered a higher risk activity than hamstring curls on a stationary machine. The value of the client training his or her hamstring muscles in a functional activity may be greater than the associated risk.

There are four conditions that must all be present to determine liability for negligent conduct. The four conditions are (Kaiser, 1986; Moriarty, 1994):

1. A duty of care must be owed by the defendant to the plaintiff according to the established standard of care.
2. A failure of the defendant to conform to the standard of care (breach of duty).
3. Actual injury or loss is suffered by the plaintiff.
4. A causal connection must be found between the defendant's conduct and the resulting injury of the plaintiff.

The defendant is the person against whom a civil action is brought (i.e., personal trainer). The plaintiff is the person who initiates the civil action (i.e., injured client). Each condition is examined in detail with respect to the profession of personal training.

Duty of Care

A personal trainer must ensure reasonable safety to the client as a condition of the trainer's legal obligation. The Occupiers' Liability Act clearly defines the common law that is concerned with tort responsibility of those who control land or premises to those who enter the premises (Law Reform Commission of British Columbia, 1994). The occupier is the individual in control of the premises, and is not dependent on the ownership of the premises. A personal trainer has immediate supervision and control of the premises and retains the power to admit and exclude the entry of others is therefore assigned the status of occupier. The personal trainer may or may not actually own the fitness facility.

There are three categories of entrants according to occupiers' liability: trespassers, licensees, and invitees. Each category has a different standard of care. The trespasser is an individual who enters the premises without the permission of the occupier. A licensee is an individual who enters the occupiers' premise with permission but who is not there for any business purpose (i.e., social guest). Of particular interest to the health and fitness industry is the invitee, a lawful visitor who enters the premises for a specific purpose or economic relationship (Allen, 1988b). A client who enters the fitness facility for the purpose of receiving personalized exercise training in exchange for an established monetary sum is considered an invitee, and as such is entitled to expect the occupier to use reasonable care to prevent damage from unusual danger. Unusual danger is a relative term dependent on the kind of premise. The invitee must also exercise his or her own reasonable care for safety. The personal trainer is then legally required to ensure the safety of the client from any unusual dangers, through actions such as written and verbal warning of an out-of-order machine.

In an attempt to protect themselves from litigation, personal trainers and other professionals in the field of sport and fitness may implement the use of a waiver. There are several different forms of a waiver that need to be distinguished:

Waiver: intentionally or voluntarily relinquishing a legal right (Moriarty, et al., 1994, p. 455)

Liability waiver: an agreement between the participant and the recreation agency where in the participant promises not to sue the agency for any injury he or she might sustain because of the agency's negligence (Kaiser, 1984, p. 54)

Exculpatory clause: a clause in favour of an agency in an agreement which excuses him or her from all responsibility for any loss so long as he or she acts in good faith (Moriarty, et al., 1994)

In the case of a personal trainer, a waiver is often incorporated into the fitness club membership agreement. For a waiver to be upheld in a court of law, the waiver must be determined to be valid.

There are several issues to consider when assessing the validity of a waiver. Firstly, the case must be examined to determine if the subject or incident may have some bearing on public policy. Agencies that provide public services are not able to contract away their liability; however, private businesses are able to enter into waiver contracts and have them upheld by a court (Jackson, 1994; Neville & Moriarty, 1994). Since the service provided by a personal trainer is not essential, or of great importance as to be considered a necessity for some members of the public, the use of a waiver does not violate public policy (Bell, 1995). The case of *Shields v. Sta-fit*, 79 Wash. App. 584 (1995) directly addressed the issue of public policy and a health club. Paul Shields contended that the membership agreement, which included an exculpatory clause indicating the release of Sta-Fit and its employees from any negligence or fault, should not be upheld. Shields was injured when a Sta-Fit personal trainer instructed him to remove his support belt while performing squats. Exculpatory clauses are valid unless they violate a public policy interest of the state. As noted by the Court, there are instances when public policy concerns outweigh the freedom to contract. Although membership to a health and fitness club is beneficial, it is not an indispensable necessity as a matter of public policy. The trial court's summary was affirmed and the appeal was dismissed.

The language in which a waiver is written must be clear, explicit, unequivocal, and specific to the activity in which the individual is intending to participate (Bell, 1995; Jackson, 1994; Neville & Moriarty, 1994). The case of *Winkler v. Kirkwood* 816 S.W. 2d 111 (1991) clearly exemplifies the application of this condition to the health and fitness industry. Mr. Winkler suffered a fatal heart attack following an exercise workout at the Kirkwood Atrium Office Park. The widow and children of Winkler submitted an appeal after not being awarded wrongful death and survival claims against Kirkwood. The membership agreement had a medical release that discharged any and all claims against Kirkwood for injuries suffered by the client while participating in any program. Winkler's family contends that Winkler was fraudulently induced to sign the release because the brochure indicated the client would receive an "exercise prescription" from "Dr. Sam." The exculpatory language in the release clearly stated the staff are not licensed physicians and the client's signature would evidence the understanding and agreement of the waiver. The court ruled that the membership agreement release be upheld and that the evidence did not establish that Winkler was fraudulently induced to sign. Summary judgment in favour of Kirkwood was decided.

The validity of a waiver may also be determined according to the age of the individual who is signing. A minor is not legally able to waive his or her own rights, and a parent cannot waive the rights of his or her child (Neville & Moriarty, 1994). This condition should be carefully considered if a personal trainer or fitness facility allows minors to join as members to the fitness facility.

The type of negligence that created the injury or damage will determine if the defendant will be held liable for negligent conduct (Kaiser, 1986; Neville & Moriarty, 1994). The three types of negligence are: slight, gross, and willful. Slight negligence is the failure to exercise great care or absence of degree of care by extraordinary prudence. Gross negligence is the failure to use even slight care or omission to use ordinary care. Willful, wanton, or reckless negligence is an intentional act of an unreasonable character; obvious disregard of safety (Kaiser, 1986). In the case of slight negligence and resulting injury, a waiver will be deemed valid. Conversely, in cases of gross or willful negligence, the defendant will be held negligent (Neville & Moriarty, 1994).

Breach of Duty

The second condition of negligence is verifying the defendant failed to conform to the established standard of care. There are four areas within which to test for a breach of duty: a) reasonable person test, b) professional standards, c) supervision and instruction, and d) equipment and facilities (Goodman & McGregor, 1997).

Reasonable Person Test

The reasonable person test is a measure against the standard of care required of a reasonable professional. In the profession of personal training, the conduct of the defendant is compared against that of a reasonable, prudent professional.

Professional Standards

The area of professional standards is closely linked to the reasonable person test. It is the comparison of the conduct of the defendant to recognized and accepted practices in the relevant industry. Therefore a personal trainer must be aware of the common practices of other professionals in his or her field of exercise training. Two cases, *Penner v. Theobald* and *Zaba v. Saskatchewan Institute of Applied Science and Technology*, concern the issue of professional standards in the health and fitness industry.

The first case, *Penner v. Theobald* (1962), 40 W.W.R. 216 (Man. C.A.) This case was the first action dealing with negligence on the part of a chiropractor since the passing of the Chiropractic Act in 1954. The plaintiff, Penner, suffered intermittent bouts of lower back pain for approximately ten years when he consulted a chiropractor, the defendant, who performed an examination and an adjustment. The plaintiff felt pain later that day and returned to the chiropractor the following day to receive another adjustment. Pain in the plaintiff's back became so intense that the chiropractor performed the adjustment in the plaintiff's home. The following morning, the plaintiff experienced pain and numbness so he went to the hospital, later undergoing surgery for a ruptured disc. The plaintiff claimed his injury was due to poor diagnosis, ensuing injury, and negligence in further treatment. The court considered the principle regarding the standard of care required for a chiropractor to be the same as that of a medical practitioner when concerning negligence. The chiropractor must exercise the degree of skill, knowledge and care expected of a normal, prudent chiropractor. The defendant was held liable for negligence, and the ensuing appeal was dismissed.

In *Zaba v. Saskatchewan Institute of Applied Science and Technology* (1997), 152 Sask.R. 245 (Sask. C.A.) The case of Morgan Zaba versus The Saskatchewan Institute of Applied Science and Technology and Shirley Christbason was an appeal filed by the defendants to the Saskatchewan Court of Appeal on May 30, 1997. The plaintiff, a student nurse enrolled in the Certified Nursing Assistant Program, injured his back while performing a patient lift as assigned by the defendant instructor. The injury was deemed foreseeable, however, the plaintiff was contributorily negligent in failing to advise the instructor of his previous back injury. Key legal issues included standard of care for a professional and a breach of that duty. The plaintiff was awarded and found to be 70% contributorily negligent. The defendants appealed based on whether the negligence of the defendants caused the damage to the respondent. Saskatchewan Court of Appeal stated that one cannot conclude the injury would not have happened but for the negligence of the appellants and the appeal was affirmed. This case is important to the health and fitness industry in that is raised the issue of a higher standard of care for a professional, which a personal trainer would be considered to be. A personal trainer will be held to provide a higher standard of care to a client, as was reflected in the case in point.

Supervision and Instruction

Personal trainers must adequately supervise and properly instruct the client or his or her conduct may be deemed a breach of duty. Supervision of a client may alter depending on the level of risk of the activity, the environment, the readiness of the client, and the condition of employment. As the risk of an activity increases, the level of direct supervision should also increase. For example, an unassisted squat with very heavy weight requires direct and close supervision from the personal trainer, whereas a seated hamstring stretch would require less supervision. The environment may also dictate the level of supervision. A crowded fitness facility differs from an empty fitness studio, which differs from extreme weather conditions during an outdoor training session. Readiness of a client entails the physical and psychological awareness and preparation for physical activity, in addition to the actual degree of knowledge in exercise training possessed by the client. The condition of employment may preclude the amount of supervision afforded to a client. If the personal trainer is employed as a floor supervisor, that individual must oversee the activities of all the participants in the facility. A trainer may also be hired to provide exercise programming and instruction for a small group, usually two to five clients. In the situation of one-on-one personal training, the trainer should provide the client with his or her undivided attention and supervision, as is expected in the terms of employment.

An important component of the personal trainer's duty is to instruct the client on proper and appropriate exercise training techniques and protocols (Cotton, 1996). The case of *Corrigan v. Musclemakers Inc.*, 258 A.D. 2d 861, 686 N.Y.S. 2d 143 (1999) demonstrates the possible repercussions for inadequate instruction and supervision. The case of Norma Corrigan versus Musclemakers Inc., doing business as Gold's Gym, was an appeal following an order that announced Musclemakers Inc. liable for plaintiff's injuries as a result of a breach of duty. The plaintiff, Corrigan, had purchased an annual membership to the defendant's health and fitness facility which included three, one-hour individual sessions with a personal trainer. During the first personal training session, the plaintiff was instructed to use a treadmill while the personal trainer left her unsupervised and not instructed as to the operation of the exercise machine. The plaintiff was unable to maintain the programmed speed of the treadmill and fell off, resulting in a broken ankle. The defendant appealed the order on the grounds that an athletic activity lowers the standard of care under the doctrine of primary assumption of risk. The assumption of risk doctrine resides on three elements: the nature of the risk is intrinsic to the activity, voluntary and knowing consent to the exposure of risk, and understanding, appreciation, and knowledge of danger (Scheele, 1997). The court order was affirmed, with costs. The court reasoned that the use of a treadmill within a fitness facility was not a sporting event wherein a lesser standard of care should be applied. In addition to this line of reasoning, the court stated the inherent risk associated with the use of a treadmill was not obvious, particularly for a novice, sedentary client, as was the plaintiff. This case clearly defines the standard of care associated with a professional personal trainer, and the possible liability resulting from a breach of duty concerning inadequate supervision and instruction.

Equipment and Facilities

Properly maintained and used equipment and facilities are required components of the reasonable and prudent personal trainer. In the event that equipment or facilities are not safe, adequate warning or elimination of the hazards needs to be employed. *Nelson v. Sheraton*, unpublished opinion, W.A. (1997) is an interesting case concerning the maintenance of exercise equipment. In 1991, Rodnie Nelson was a paying guest at a Sheraton hotel where a weight room and exercise room was available. Nelson was exercising on the butterfly weight-training machine when one of the cables broke and struck the plaintiff in the head, knocking him unconscious. The plaintiff brought a lawsuit against Sheraton Operating Corporation, and the manufacturer of the equipment, Marcy Gym Equipment, on the basis of negligence. The frayed and damaged cable was not produced before the court. The trial court dismissed Nelson's claim of evidence, following which Nelson appealed claiming the doctrine of *res ipsa loquitor*, because genuine issues of fact existed that Sheraton should have foreseen injury, and because the trail court did not give Nelson the benefit of the spoliation of evidence. In addition to this appeal was a cross-motion for summary judgment against Sheraton and Marcy concerning spoliation of evidence. The present court agreed that Nelson was not entitled to the benefit of the doctrine of *res ipsa loquitor*. The court reversed in part because Sheraton would have discovered unreasonable risk of harm due to the frayed cable and therefore did not uphold a reasonable standard of care. Key issues raised in this case concern proper maintenance of equipment and facilities at a health and fitness facility. It is the responsibility of the fitness club to eliminate unsafe conditions that may result in injury to invitees.

In a related case, *Garrison v. Combined Fitness Centre*, 201 Ill. App. 3d 581 (1990), the plaintiff was injured when a weighted bar slipped off the stands of the bench press. The plaintiff, Garrison, contended the bench press provided by the health club facility was not adequate or safe for its intended use. Combined Fitness Centre had an exculpatory clause contained within the membership agreement relieving it of all liability for injury arising out of the use of its facilities and equipment. The summary judgment granted to Combined Fitness Centre was affirmed. As an aside, the court noted that an exculpatory clause might not always relieve a defendant from liability arising from its provision of defective equipment.

Actual Injury or Loss

The third condition of negligence is to prove an actual injury was suffered by the plaintiff. Injury may be physical or psychological, but the damages must be verifiable. Examples of injuries suffered by the client of a personal trainer could be broken bones, cuts or abrasions, sprains and strains, and heart attacks.

Causal Connection

A proximate connection must be demonstrated between the plaintiff's injury and the defendant's behavior. This may be referred to as the "but for" rule. According to Moriarty, et al. (1994, p. 437), " in order to establish liability in a negligence action, it must be shown that the negligent conduct was a "cause-in-fact" of the injury or damage about which the plaintiff complains." In a situation where a client was previously injured or had experienced pain prior to the situation in question, causal connection may be very important in determining negligence.

Risk Management

The goal of risk management is to provide a safe environment for participants and employees. Conscientiously designed and implemented risk management strategies reduce the likelihood of claims and lawsuits, and may reduce the severity of a lawsuit that is filed (Mull, Bayless, Ross, & Jamieson, 1997). According to Forsyth and Moriarty (1994, p. 110), risk management "is a total program that analyzes where and why accidents may occur and how the hazards might be controlled." There are five general steps to minimize risk associated with the role of the personal trainer (National Fitness Leadership Advisory Committee, 1990). The steps are:

1. Identification of risks,
2. Analysis of risks,
3. Development of policies and procedures,
4. Implementation,
5. Evaluation.

Identification of Risks

The first step in a risk management strategy is to identify all the inherent and possible risks associated with the activity. As previously noted, the majority of liability cases in the health and fitness industry arise in area of negligence. In broad terms, identification of risk may occur by reviewing the four conditions of negligence. More specifically, the personal trainer and the health and fitness club should review the Occupiers' Liability Act, the membership agreement presently utilized, established professional standards, supervision, instruction, facilities, and equipment. A list of potential risks associated with each position may be developed.

As noted within the ACE Certification Manual, personal trainers may work with clients with health challenges only after the individuals have been cleared by their personal physician. Examples of health challenges that a personal trainer may encounter include coronary artery disease, hypertension, stroke, peripheral vascular disease, diabetes, asthma, cancer, osteoporosis, low-back pain, arthritis, older adults, and pregnancy.

Analysis of Risks

After having thoroughly identified the risks associated with personal training at a fitness facility, the list of risks may be daunting. The role of the personal trainer is to analyze the identified risks and determine the appropriate response to each one. The elimination of all activities that have inherent risk is neither realistic nor necessary. Participants of sport and fitness activities are motivated by the existence of risk, whether real or perceived. Real risk would be present in an outdoor climbing excursion wherein the participants voluntarily chose not to use climbing ropes. Perceived risk is present in an indoor climbing facility wherein the participants use the climbing apparatus and safety features. Participants may experience a brief and controlled fall off the climbing wall, but the safety devices and backup procedures minimize the actual risk of injury.

Forsyth and Moriarty (1994, p. 114) provide a simple grid (Figure 6.2) to aid in the analysis of risks.

Table 6.1
Risk Analysis

High Real Risk Present	Avoid	Transfer
	Reduce	Retain
Low	Low ⟵⟶ High	
	Participant Readiness	

Avoidance of high-risk activity is an appropriate decision if the participant is not ready for the activity. The personal trainer makes a conscious decision to avoid the specific risk present at that time. Transference of risk may occur if the participants are ready, through the use of education, instruction, and supervision, to partake in a high-risk activity. The participants then assume the risks inherent in the specific activity. The use of additional safety devices or procedures may reduce the risks of potential accidents. The personal trainer may intentionally retain an activity when the real risk of injury is low, and the participant readiness is high (Forsyth & Moriarty, 1994).

Development of Policies and Procedures

After the personal trainer has identified and analyzed the risks associated with exercise training, he or she must decide on the appropriate actions to eliminate or minimize risk. The development of policies and procedures within a fitness facility may be time consuming, but the benefits of a detailed policy manual will become invaluable to reduce the likelihood and severity of liability for a personal trainer. Upon entrance to a fitness facility, the client's readiness for participation should be determined. A pre-exercise consultation and orientation session may be designed as a first step in preparation to participation (Maggio, 2000). Following the consultation, a needs assessment can be conducted to include documentation of the client's health history, exercise questionnaire, nutrition questionnaire, a membership agreement which includes an assumption of risk form and detailed description of the rules, policies, etiquette and possible risks upon participation at the facility (Pond, 1999). The Physical Activity Readiness Questionnaire (PAR-Q) is a standard form used by fitness facilities in Canada that indicates the readiness of the client to participate in physical activity. In addition to the needs assessment, the personal trainer may implement a fitness test administered prior to the initial training session, which may include measurements such as blood pressure, body fat, resting heart rate, girth measurements, and flexibility (Maggio, 2000).

Facility and staff preparedness must also be developed. Clearly posted rules, policies, regulations, and any safety warnings are related to facility preparedness. Facility inspections should occur regularly using a safety checklist. The hiring of staff may be conditional on their having current First Aid, CPR, and Personal Trainer certifications. Those individuals who are hired should experience an orientation session and possible in-house training. All employees need to be knowledgeable and practiced in the facility emergency action plan. This plan should include detailed procedures for injury identification, treatment, and follow-up. Emergency action plan procedures should include written documentation of the incident, treatment administered, and names of witnesses (Pond, 1999; Cotton, 1996).

Due to the rise in litigation in the sport and fitness field, purchasing insurance is an important aspect of risk management strategy. An insurance policy is a contract designed to protect the personal trainer and his or her assets from litigation (Cotton, 1996). The fitness facility may possess insurance, however, it is up to the personal trainer if he or she decides to purchase individual insurance (Maggio, 2000). Vicarious liability is imposed on a person who wasn't personally negligent, but is held liable because of the relationship with the individual who committed the negligent act (Goodman & McGregor, 1997). This is sometimes referred to as *respondeat superior*, as in the case of a personal trainer coordinator, or a fitness establishment being named vicariously liable for the negligent conduct of a personal trainer. The case of *Renco v. The Fitness Institute Ltd.* (1996), 25 O.R. (3d) 88 (Ont. C.A.) concerns the issue of a fitness club's insurance policy.

In 1986, Linda Renco attended an aerobic class at the Fitness Institute facilities. During the aerobics class, the instructor, Jeanette Lanovaz, took hold of Renco's leg and manipulated it, causing injury. Renco filed a lawsuit based on negligence and was awarded damages. The case in point is a contest between Fitness Institute Ltd. and the third party, Allstate Insurance Company of Canada, regarding who is required to pay for damages. The key issue was the interpretation of the language within the exclusionary clause in the insurance policy. The exclusionary clause clearly stated that it did not apply to bodily injury arising from "error or omission by the insured," in this case, Fitness Institute. The key issue determining the final decision was that the injury to Renco did occur from an error or omission in the exercise instruction, therefore the insurance company is excluded from coverage. The ruling of the court was important in raising the issue of exclusions in insurance policies that may result in the cost of damages to be paid by the health club despite efforts to employ insurance coverage as a strategy for risk management. In respect to a personal trainer, the individual needs to be cognizant of exclusions in insurance policies.

Implementation

Detailed and thorough development of risk management policies and procedures is inadequate if not implemented. Clear understanding of the policies and procedures by the employees may increase the likelihood of them being implemented. Other techniques to implement policies and procedures may include employee training sessions, in-house testing and certification, and encouragement from facility management.

Evaluation

Periodic review of the risk management strategies of a fitness facility is an important and often overlooked step. Evaluation should occur on a regular basis. It may be performed by one of the employees of the fitness facility, and/or by an outside specialist who is familiar with the legal issues associated with the sport and fitness field (Forsyth & Moriarty, 1994). The evaluation procedure should ideally involve all five steps of risk management.

Conscientious risk management strategies will not eliminate all incidents resulting in injury to clients. In some cases, the injured party will decide to file a lawsuit against the personal trainer and his or her fitness establishment. There are a number of negligence defenses that apply to a lawsuit filed against a personal trainer (Holman, Bullock, & Norwood, 1994; Kaiser, 1986). Figure 6.3 shows a list of negligence defenses with a brief description of each:

"At Home" Personal Training

As a conclusion to the discussion of risk management strategies, a special case is examined in terms of legal liability and the personal trainer. The area of personal training has experienced an evolution from informal instruction, to training sessions within the fitness facility, to that of at-home personal training. The future for personal training will expand into homes, organizations, and communities (Maggio, 2000). At-home training sessions involve an agreement between the personal trainer and the client for the exercise training to occur within the client's residence. By incorporating the key terms and issues of negligence discussed in section IV, one can determine the proper steps to minimize risk for at-home training.

Figure 6.2
Negligence Defenses

X **Assumption of risk:**	injured knowingly took on inherent danger (Scheele, 1997)
X **Comparative negligence:**	liability is assessed between plaintiff and defendant according to the comparative fault of each party (Moriarty, et al., 1994)
X **Contributory negligence:**	the injured was partly responsible for his or her own injury (Scheele, 1997)
X **Exculpatory agreement:**	written documents outlining the conditions of participation (Scheele, 1997)
X **Immunity:**	status of exemption from lawsuits or other legal obligations (Moriarty, et al., 1994)
X **No breach of duty:**	the defendant's conduct met the required standard of care
X **No duty of care:**	the personal trainer did not have a duty of care towards the injury party
X **No injury suffered:**	an absence of legitimate damage
X **No proximate causation:**	the injury did not occur but for the negligence of the defendant
X **Statute of limitations:**	a law that states the maximum time period a claim may be filed (Moriarty, et al., 1994)
X **Waiver:**	intentionally or voluntarily relinquishing a legal right (Moriarty, et al., 1994)

The first step in risk management is to identify the relevant risks associated with at-home personal training. At first glance, the issues of safe and adequate equipment and sufficient space arise (Maggio, 2000). If the equipment that is present within the client's home is unsafe, improperly maintained, not used for its intended purpose, or simply inadequate for the desired training protocols, the equipment itself could pose a risk of harm to both the client and the trainer. The personal trainer may decide to bring his or her own equipment from the fitness facility, but this may also prove to be a possible risk due to the frequent transportation of the equipment.

Upon closer examination, other issues arise that may be potential risks for liability. Since the personal trainer is entering the client's residence for business purposes, the application of the Occupiers' Liability Act is reversed to protect the personal trainer as an invitee from unreasonable risk. Written documents such as waivers, membership agreements, and exculpatory clauses may need to be re-drafted to pertain to the specific conditions of at-home training. The roles, responsibilities, and conduct of the trainer may be held to a higher standard because of the private, unsupervised environment in which the sessions occur. There is the possibility of unprofessional conduct occurring on the part of the personal trainer. The personal trainer is in a position of power and may be liable for conduct deemed as harassment or abuse by the client. The conduct of the client may also be deemed inappropriate by the personal trainer. A client may view their position as one in which they have power over, an admiration for, or other emotional attachment to, the personal trainer. These assumed statuses have the potential to spawn harassing behavior in a variety of forms.

The next step is to analyze the risks according to the risk management strategy grid. Depending on the condition of the equipment, the personal trainer may decide to avoid the use of the client-owned equipment, and retain the use of the fitness facility's equipment with planned consideration of the risks of wear and tear from frequent transportation. The use of clearly worded, unambiguous waivers may be useful to transfer the risk associated with the application of Occupiers' Liability Act and the assumption of risk to participate. An insurance policy may transfer the responsibility of paying for damages as a result of a negligence lawsuit to that of the insurance carrier. The risk of unprofessional conduct in the client-trainer relationship may be reduced through random checks by supervisors, or the use of communication and documentation of the times and activities engaged in during the training sessions.

The development of policies and procedures is an important step to minimize the risk of legal liability. The personal trainer and his or her facility management team may decide to develop a policy manual specifically designed to address the unique conditions and risks of at-home training. The manual should include copies of waivers, insurance policies, emergency action plan procedures, detailed description of appropriate conduct, and safety checklists.

Implementation of the risk management strategies should decrease the likelihood of an incident, as well as decrease the severity of the incident. Personal trainers should have a through understanding of the requirements demanded by the fitness facility, and knowledge of the established standard of care of other personal training professionals. Evaluation of the risk management strategies should be reviewed on a regular basis. Upon initiating an at-home training service, the personal trainer together with the facility management team should consider more frequent evaluation of the procedures. Any changes or omissions should be documented and followed with proper implementation.

Conclusion

Goodman & McGregor (1997) observed that we live in a litigious society, and this has become increasingly prevalent in the health and fitness industry. Personal training professionals provide a unique service to individuals that include fitness and health assessment, program design, exercise consultation, motivation, and general fitness education (Cotton, 1996). Personal trainers must become aware of the key terms and issues related to their profession. The most common cases of legal liability arise in the area of negligence, under tort law (Kaiser, 1986). An understanding of the four conditions of negligence and its application to the fitness industry is an important step to minimize risk. The five steps of risk management are useful to assess and implement risk management strategies. Although the five steps provide a guideline, each fitness facility and personal trainer must consider the unique situation of their facility and clients in order to manage risk properly. As stated by Mull, et al. (1997, p. 282): "The prudent recreational sport manager who complies with [risk management strategies] and keeps written record of periodic inspections and repairs will be able to provide an excellent defense against potential legal actions." Injuries will occur, but it is the prudent personal training professional who can minimize the risk of exercise training and continue to enjoy the benefits of this growing profession.

Questions For Class Discussion

1. Identify the unique features of a profession as a personal trainer that need to be considered in a risk management plan:
   a) In a fitness centre.
   b) For an "at home" service.
2. Apply Allen's danger of risk model to the decision of whether or not to provide 'at home' personal training services.
3. Discuss the use of a waiver for the clients of a personal trainer in a fitness centre and in an 'at home' fitness program.
4. Discuss how the cases cited in this chapter inform the personal trainer as an entrepreneur.

References

Allen, A. M. (1988a). Negligence: The standard of care. In A. M. Allen, *Canadian tort law* (pp. 105-145). Toronto, ON: Butterworths.

Allen, A. M. (1988b). Occupiers' liability. In A. M. Allen, *Canadian tort law* (pp. 599-610). Toronto, ON: Butterworths.

Baley, J. A., & Mathews, D. L. (1998). *Law and liability in athletics, physical education, and recreation*. Dubuque, Iowa: Wm. C. Brown Publishers.

Black, H. C. (1990). *Black's law dictionary* (6th ed.). St. Paul, MN: West Publishing Co.

Bell, L. P. (1995). The heavy weight of the health club waiver. *Thurgood Marshall Law Review, 21* (1), 229-247.

Cotton, R. T. (Ed.) (1996). *Personal trainer manual*. San Diego, CA: American Council on Exercise.

Forsyth, J. & Moriarty, D. (1994). Risk management: The road to prevention. In D. Moriarty, M. Holman, R. Brown, & M. Moriarty (Eds.), *Canadian/American sport, fitness, and the law* (pp. 109-130). Toronto, ON: Canadian Scholars' Press Inc.

Goodman, S. F., & McGregor, I. (1997). *Legal liability & risk management* (2nd ed.). Toronto, ON: Risk Management Associates.

Holman, M., Bullock, L., & Norwood, D. (1994). The role of the teacher and coach. In D. Moriarty, M. Holman, R. Brown, & M. Moriarty (Eds.), *Canadian/American sport, fitness, and the law* (pp. 43-72). Toronto, ON: Canadian Scholars' Press Inc.

Jackson, J. J. (1994). Exculpatory clauses and dangerous sports. Paper presented at the Proceedings for the 10th Commonwealth & International Scientific Congress: Access to Active Living.

Kaiser, R. (1984). Program liability waivers — Do they protect the agency and the staff? *Journal of Physical Education, Recreation and Dance, 55* (6), 54-56.

Kaiser, R. A. (1986). *Liability & law in recreation, parks, & sports*. Englewood Cliffs, NJ: Prentice-Hall.

Law Reform Commission of British Columbia (1994). *Report on recreational injuries: Liability and waivers in commercial leisure activities* (LRC: 140). British Columbia: Author.

Maggio, R. (2000, February 24). Personal interview by Carrie Czichrak.

Maguire, T. (1999). Pre-boom a boon to gyms. *American Demographics, 21* (1), 17-18.

Minister of National Health and Welfare (1980). *Guidelines for fitness centres and health clubs*. Ottawa, ON: Minister of Supply and Services Canada.

Moriarty, D. (1994). Physical activity and legal liability. In D. Moriarty, M. Holman, R. Brown, & M. Moriarty (Eds.), *Canadian/American sport, fitness, and the law* (pp. 15-42). Toronto, ON: Canadian Scholars' Press Inc.

Moriarty, D., Holman, M., Brown, R., & Moriarty, M. (1994). *Canadian/American sport, fitness, and the law*. Toronto, ON: Canadian Scholars' Press Inc.

Mull, R. F., Bayless, K. G., Ross, C. M., & Jamieson, L. M. (1997). *Recreational sport management* (3rd ed.). Champaign, IL: Human Kinetics.

Mullin, B. J., Hardy, S., & Sutton, W. A. (1993). *Sports marketing*. Champaign, IL: Human Kinetics.

National Fitness Leadership Advisory Committee (1990). *Legal liability considerations for the fitness leader*. Government of Canada: Author.

Neville, N., & Moriarty, D. (1994). Waivers in fitness and sport: Are they worthwhile? In D. Moriarty, M. Holman, R. Brown, & M. Moriarty (Eds.), *Canadian/American sport, fitness, and the law* (pp. 131-154). Toronto, ON: Canadian Scholars' Press Inc.

Pond, J. (1999). Preventing negligence. *Fitness Management, 15* (10), 38-39.

Scheele, K. K. (1997). *Administrator liability for negligent employment practices: Issues for campus recreation*. (Doctoral dissertation, University of Nebraska, 1997). *Dissertation Abstracts International, 58* (05), 1531.

Young, S. J. (1998). *Perceived liability and risk management trends and issues impacting the delivery of recreational sports programs in the 21st century*. (Doctoral dissertation, Indiana University, 1998). *Dissertation Abstracts International, 60* (02), 548.

CHAPTER 7

THE RIGHTS OF ATHLETES, COACHES, AND PARTICIPANTS IN SPORT

Hilary A. Findlay and Rachel Corbett

Introduction

There are many sources of law that apply to sport organizations, athletes, coaches and other participants in the sport setting. Both statute law and case law have a bearing on how sport organizations, and individuals participating in sport, should conduct themselves. For example:

- Most sport organizations are incorporated under provincial or federal legislation pertaining to societies or corporations, and this legislation stipulates how a sport organization must conduct certain business affairs;
- In terms of safety and injury prevention, sport organizations must meet an objective standard of care that is determined by the common law principles of negligence and by statutes relating to occupier's liability;
- In some cases, although not all, the actions of sport organizations must meet the requirements of human rights legislation for equal access to facilities, programs and services without discrimination;[1]
- Sport organizations must adhere to an array of other statutes relating to specific obligations such as product liability, occupational health and safety, environmental protection, workers compensation, employment standards, income tax, societies and business corporations, and the Criminal Code, among others;
- Lastly, sport organizations have an obligation to meet the requirements of procedural fairness in all of their decisions and actions as they relate to members.

It is this latter obligation, the "duty to be fair," that is the focus of this chapter.

The vast majority of Canadian sport organizations are "private tribunals" – that is, they are autonomous, self-governing, private organizations that have the power to write rules, make decisions and take actions that affect their members, participants and constituents. A body of law called "administrative law" prescribes the rules by which tribunals must operate in Canadian society and allows for legal remedies when these rules are not followed and someone is harmed as a result.

To understand the sport organization's legal duties and obligations, one must understand two important principles that apply to tribunals – the first is the notion of *contract* and the second is notion of *natural justice,* now virtually synonymous in Canada with *procedural fairness.*[2] These principles were first highlighted in the 1952 landmark case, *Lee v. Showmen's Guild of Great Britain* (see case summary in this chapter). Although this case had nothing to do with sport, it has been referred to by almost every athlete and amateur sport organization that has found itself in court over a decision-making dispute.

Contract

As private tribunals, sport organizations are self-governing and derive their authority from their constitution, bylaws, policies, procedures and rules. Taken together, these are the "governing documents" of the organization and form a contract between the organization and its members. This contract provides the sport organization with the legal authority to establish the rights, privileges and obligations of membership. As in any contract, the parties to the contract are expected to adhere to its terms and provisions, and failure to do so may result in a breach of the contract. In serious matters, such a breach of contract may give rise to disputes for which there may be legal remedies.

When an individual joins a sport organization, he or she accepts the inherent authority of the sport organization and the terms of the contract expressed in the organization's governing documents. In most cases, athletes, coaches, and officials are members of their respective sport organization and thus are parties to a contractual relationship with the sport organization. This contract works to the benefit of both parties by establishing and clarifying their respective rights and obligations. Occasionally, however, the contract may work to the detriment of the parties if the policies that make up the contract are poorly designed, vague, contradictory or ill-suited to the organization's needs, resources or realities.

A sport organization's governing documents are critical as they provide the foundation of the organization's structure and authority and contain all of the rules by which the organization and its members govern themselves. Typically, sport organizations pay too little attention to their governing documents and only realize their importance when the deficiencies in these documents land them squarely in the middle of a dispute with a member, such as an athlete. For many sport organizations, "it is a sobering lesson to learn that policy is what's written on the paper and not what's in the mind of the drafters of the policy, or in the collective memory of the organization" (Corbett and Findlay, p. 14).

If an organization and its members agree that they do not like the terms of their contractual relationship, then they can take steps to change the governing documents using conventional policy-making channels. If a group of members, such as athletes, takes the view that they do not like the terms of their contractual relationship with the sport organization, then they can take steps to influence the leaders and decision-makers of the organization using conventional democratic procedures.

A group of members, or one member alone, cannot unilaterally rewrite the terms of the contract with the sport organization, and a court cannot do this either. The courts are very reluctant to interfere with the internal matters of private tribunals, and will not rewrite the governing documents and policies of private organizations. However, an individual, such as an athlete, may apply to the court and the court may intervene if these policies are ignored, not followed, improperly interpreted or wrongly applied. These issues are discussed more fully later in this chapter.

In addition to the contractual relationship described above, there may also be explicit contracts between an organization and its members. All high performance athletes who are members of national teams in Canada enter into binding contracts with their national sport organization. The early rationale for these contracts was to set out the requirements and expectations of athletes who received financial assistance through Sport Canada's Athlete Assistance Program.

Today, these contracts typically include commercial and dispute resolution provisions in addition to specifying the respective responsibilities and entitlements of the athlete and the national sport organization. The rights and obligations in an athlete contract do not replace the rights and obligations that exist in the contractual relationship between the athlete and the sport organization, but rather incorporate, confirm and clarify them.

Procedural Fairness

The second fundamental legal principle highlighted by the Lee case is that private tribunals are subject to the rules of procedural fairness. In other words, a sport organization must be fair in how it exercises its powers and makes decisions. The organization that fails to be fair will ultimately find itself in the middle of a nasty dispute, and may ultimately find itself in a courtroom.

All of us generally have a good sense of what is fair and what is unfair. In law, *procedural fairness* (or the "duty to act fairly") has a specific meaning. Being fair means following a minimum of two basic rules:

- The decision-maker has a duty to give persons affected by the decision a reasonable opportunity to present their case (commonly referred to as the "right to a hearing"); and
- The decision-maker has a duty to listen fairly to both sides and to reach a decision untainted by bias (commonly referred to as the "rule against bias")

These two rules of procedural fairness are discussed below.

Right to a Hearing

It is a long established rule of law that before an adverse decision can be made against a person, that person has a right to know the case against him or her and to be given a reasonable opportunity to respond on his or her own behalf. There are two obvious purposes for this rule: firstly, the person adversely affected by the decision has an opportunity to defend his or her interests or assert a claim and secondly, by allowing the person to have input, the decision-maker is better able to make a rational and informed decision.

Although all organizations have a duty to be fair and to follow these rules, the procedural safeguards that are required to satisfy the right to a hearing will vary with the circumstances. Such safeguards may be described as falling along a spectrum from simple and flexible at one end to complex and formal at the other. For example, in some circumstances an opportunity to make written submissions may be appropriate whereas fairness in other circumstances may require that the person be given the opportunity to make oral representations.

Even within these two types of hearing (written submission and oral presentation), there are ranges of formality and complexity. For example, written submissions can be as simple as a letter or series of letters stating one's position or as complex as a written application supported by documentary evidence and expert reports. Similarly, oral representations can be as simple as an interview or group discussion with the decision-maker(s) or as complex as a court-like proceeding with examination and cross-examination of witnesses. A hearing can also be a combination of written submissions and oral presentations wherein the decision-maker reviews documents and written arguments and then convenes a conference to ask questions and clarify any uncertain matters.

Disclosure

The rule of the "right to a hearing" has one additional element. In order for a person potentially affected by a decision to make a full and meaningful response, that person must know the details of the case to be met. Thus, in addition to an affected person having the right to be heard, he or she must also be afforded the right to be informed. Just as procedural fairness occurs along a spectrum, what is required by the right to be informed will vary with the circumstances. In some cases it is sufficient to provide the affected person with a précis or summary of the details of the case[3] and in other cases the person may have a right to review original documents and cross-examine witnesses. Again, fairness will dictate the nature and extent of the disclosure but to the greatest extent possible, disclosure should be as complete as possible.

In any given case, the information upon which a decision will be based may come from many sources. Some sources produce more reliable information than others do. It is critical that the parties affected by a decision have an opportunity to confirm, correct or contradict any information contrary to their interests. This can only happen if the information is disclosed to them.

Sport organizations often promise confidentiality to individuals providing information about another individual, particularly if such information is negative in nature. For example, athletes are sometimes reluctant to provide a negative performance review of a coach for fear it may harm their future relationship with the coach and opportunities within the sport. Individuals wishing to lodge a complaint of harassment are often reluctant to do so if their identity is revealed, out of fear of retaliation. Similarly, those providing information are often reluctant to do so unless it can be done anonymously. It is the very rare case where information should be withheld from an affected party. The details and completeness of the disclosure will depend on the complexity and seriousness of the case. At times, a summary of factual information may be sufficient, but where credibility is an issue, the identity of the source of the information and context in which the information was given may be necessary in order to allow the affected party to fully and completely respond.

Guidelines for Determining Appropriate Procedures

There are a number of guidelines that can assist in determining what process and what extent of disclosure will meet the required threshold of the duty of fairness, given all the circumstances of the situation. These guidelines include:

Granting versus Withdrawing Privileges

As a general rule, decisions relating to withdrawing rights or privileges *already conferred* require greater procedural safeguards than decisions relating to withholding rights or privileges *not yet granted*, where such rights or privileges are equivalent. In other words, decisions about athlete conduct or discipline often require more stringent procedural safeguards than decisions about athlete eligibility or selection.

Effect of the Decision

The guideline just described must be applied in conjunction with a second guideline, which is that procedural safeguards should be in direct proportion to the potential *consequences* of the decision — in other words, to what is at stake. For the gifted amateur athlete, a great deal may be at stake. A sport organization differs from many voluntary organizations in that membership is compulsory (not voluntary) for any individual contemplating athletic pursuits within that particular sport discipline. The failure to award membership, or once awarded, the loss of membership, precludes such pursuits entirely. Therefore, denying or revoking membership to an amateur athlete requires strict procedural safeguards.

Denial of competitive opportunities to athletes, particularly elite athletes, may also have the effect of denying other more significant opportunities, including future income, employment and scholarship opportunities. Denial of these opportunities also demands careful attention to procedural safeguards.

Nature of the Decision

The choice of procedure also depends upon the extent to which a decision is final and binding on a person. Procedural safeguards are generally higher with respect to a final decision than they are with respect to an interim decision. Also, although expediency is not an excuse to override the principles of fairness, it may be a consideration in determining the nature of the process. Thus, issues arising during the course of a tournament or competition may be dealt with differently than those arising outside of competition, so long as the fundamental principles, or rules of fairness, are respected.

Where an appeal is not available procedural safeguards must be more strictly observed because there is no opportunity for procedural errors to be corrected. For example, where a decision-maker of last resort makes a procedural error during the course of the hearing, it may be possible to correct or cure the default as part of the decision-making process. But if the error is not corrected, then the only other recourse is litigation in the courts. If the decision being made is not absolutely final and there are opportunities for further appeal, it is not so critical that procedural errors be promptly corrected as there are subsequent opportunities to correct them.

Rule against Bias

The second rule of procedural fairness relates to the impartiality, or bias, of those making decisions. There are two types of bias:

- The first is *actual bias*, wherein a decision-maker is predisposed to deciding a matter in

one particular way over any other. The decision-maker is said to have a "closed mind" and is unwilling or unable to take into consideration any other perspective.
- The second type of bias is *apprehended bias,* that is, one has a reasonable belief or apprehension the decision-maker is, or will be, biased. This type of bias is much more common than the first type.

Clearly, where a decision-maker has a direct material interest in the outcome of a decision, bias may be established and the decision-maker may be disqualified. However, situations involving allegations of bias are rarely so clear cut or concrete. Typically, bias arises from the state of mind of the decision-maker. While a previous or existing friendship, business relationship, or family relationship might be perceived as biasing a decision-maker, it is important to note that it is not the relationship itself that creates the bias, or the apprehension of bias, but rather the extent to which the relationship influences or is perceived to influence the decision-maker. This is often difficult to prove.

For bias to be found, the relationship must be direct, consequential and influential. The test used by the courts in these cases is whether "a reasonable person, knowing the facts concerning the person [i.e., the decision-maker] would suspect that the person would be influenced, albeit unintentionally, by improper considerations to favour one side in the matter to be decided" (Blake, p. 92). In other words, the test is an objective test: it is not what the person raising the allegations believes but rather what a reasonable and objective third party would believe, given all of the circumstances.

Relationships and elements that may result in bias or a reasonable apprehension of bias can be grouped into six broad categories (Kligman, 1998):

Personal Relational Bias

This would include personal relationships that might suggest favoritism such as friendship, kinship or a coach-athlete relationship. It also includes personal relationships that might invoke animosity or prejudice such as personality conflicts, a history of strained relations or involvement in a previous dispute. The cases of *Garrett v. Canadian Weightlifting Federation* and *Depiero v. Canadian Amateur Diving Association et al.* are cases where personal relational bias influenced a sport organization's decision. (See case summaries of both in this chapter.)

Non-personal Relational Bias

This category typically relates to a commercial or business relationship between a decision-maker and a party that might result in bias either in favour of or against a party. This might include an employee-employer relationship, competitors, or even one party's membership in a particular organization or interest group.

Informational Bias

This category involves situations in which the allegation of bias is made because a decision-maker learns details about a person or a relevant issue as a result of some prior involvement, perhaps through a previous dispute proceeding. This typically arises where a decision-maker has participated in an earlier hearing that involved the same person or issues.

Attitudinal Bias

This category of bias relates to whether a view or a position taken by a decision-maker in the past, although not specifically directed to the matter under consideration, suggests a predisposition on the part of the decision-maker towards one side or the other. This is a tricky issue. As noted by one court, "A person serving in an adjudicative role must have an open mind, but not necessarily a blank or void one."[4] Clearly, decision-making bodies can make policies and general statements regarding various issues and how they intend to deal with them. But they cannot be so entrenched in a position so as to have a "closed mind."

Institutional Bias

This category of bias refers to the manner in which the organizational structure of an organization creates or builds in a bias or apprehension of bias. A classic case of such bias arises where a Board of Directors is authorized to make a certain decision and any appeal of such a decision is to be heard by the Executive Committee. In most sport organizations, the Executive is a sub-group of the Board and thus is in the position of hearing an appeal from its own decision. This is a clear example of actual bias. In this situation it can be reasonably expected that the original decision-makers will be predisposed to up-hold their original decision.

Another aspect of institutional bias is the degree of independence of the decision-maker, or the degree to which those appointing the decision-maker have a stake in the matter being heard. This occurs often in sport situations because directors of sport organizations are often parents of athletes. The case of *Kulesza v. Canadian Amateur Synchronized Swimming Association Inc. et al*, summarized in this chapter, is an example of a case where an athlete alleged bias because an employee who was making selection decisions held her job as Technical Director at the pleasure of the Board, which included among its membership the parent of one of the other athletes. This allegation failed as the athlete was unable to provide evidence of any influence arising from institutional bias.

Operational Bias

This category of bias arises from the manner in which a hearing is conducted. More specifically, operational bias may be alleged where the procedure adopted by the decision-maker has created a situation of unfairness for one of the parties.

Where a decision-maker communicates with one of the parties in the absence of another, a reasonable apprehension of bias or preference to that party may arise. Any information discussed or exchanged with one party should be discussed or exchanged with all parties, so that all parties have the opportunity to address the decision-maker on the issues in dispute. While casual contact between a decision-maker and a party may be logistically unavoidable, the nature of the contact should not relate to the subject matter of the hearing.

Operational bias may also be alleged where the decision-maker becomes involved in the proceeding to such an extent as to appear to be an advocate for one side or another. Similarly, a decision-maker who takes an overly adversarial position in the conduct of the hearing may give rise to a claim of bias.

Administrative Appeals

At law, sport organizations have no legal obligation to offer individuals an appeal of their decisions. As an athlete cannot seek recourse in the courts until he or she has exhausted internal remedies, it makes good sense to make internal remedies available. This is simply good risk management and good governance.

There are two exceptions to the general rule that an individual must first exhaust internal remedies before taking a matter to court: first, where time does not allow an internal appeal and there is insufficient flexibility in the appeal procedures to accommodate time considerations and second, where it is clear the athlete will simply not get a fair hearing from the organization. The onus is therefore on organizations to put fair appeal procedures in place and furthermore, to ensure that they are flexible enough to accommodate the short timelines that are typically associated with disputes relating to sport competitions and selection issues.

Scope of the Appeal

What decisions may be appealed? This is up to the sport organization to decide — provided, of course, that the matter under appeal lies within the powers that are vested in the organization through its bylaws and other governing documents. In other words, an organization cannot hear appeals on decisions over which it has no jurisdiction. It is important to distinguish between those matters for which a sport organization makes *recommendations* and those matters for which it makes *decisions*. For example, a sport organization *recommends* athletes for carding and *recommends* athletes for selection to national teams competing in international multi-sport games. If a sport organization does not recommend an athlete for carding or selection, the athlete's recourse for appeal is to the sport organization. However, final *decisions* on carding are made by Sport Canada and final *decisions* for selection to international games are made by the Canadian Olympic Association or the Commonwealth Games Association of Canada. If the final decision on carding or selection has already been made, then the athlete's recourse of appeal is to these bodies, not to their sport organization.

Within its scope of powers, a sport organization may adopt either a narrow or a broad approach on appeals. A narrow approach would only allow appeals on decisions where the rules of procedural fairness require the greatest procedural safeguards. Thus, only decisions that result in the revoking of certain rights or privileges, such as discipline matters, would be open to appeal. A broad approach would allow appeals on decisions made by any committee or by the board of directors of the organization. This would mean that decisions about selection, eligibility, and certain personnel matters, in addition to discipline, could be appealed.

Keeping in mind that an important purpose of administrative appeals is to resolve disputes internally, the broad approach is highly recommended. This doesn't mean that the organization will be inundated with appeals, because not all decisions being challenged will reach the threshold for an actual appeal hearing. Thus, while the *scope* of appeal may be broad, the permissible *grounds* for an appeal may be more limited, thus restricting the number of appeals.

Grounds for the Appeal

When may decisions be appealed — that is, on what basis may a decision be challenged? The organization's appeal policy should clearly set out the "grounds" on which a decision may be appealed. Typically the grounds of appeal relate to issues of proper authority and issues of procedural fairness, as discussed in the first part of this chapter.

Such grounds of appeal presume that decisions will be based upon policy and that such policies reflect the will of the membership and have been properly approved and implemented. Underlying this approach is the presumption that decisions should not be appealed just because someone is dissatisfied with the outcome. To allow this would undermine the decision-making authority of individuals and committees properly entrusted with making decisions in the first place.

The practice of limiting grounds of appeal also assumes that the policies of the organization are clearly written and reflect a rational, workable and fair approach to the subject matter in question – whether that be selection, discipline or some other issue relating to the allocation of rights and obligations in sport. No individual should be able to appeal the substantive aspects of any policy that is properly made by an organization. The normal and democratic method of making policy is the appropriate avenue for reviewing the substance of an organization's policy.

A selection dispute before the 1996 Olympics nicely illustrates this distinction between procedure and substance. Leading up to the Atlanta Olympics, Judo Canada put in place a fairly complex point system for selection based upon international matches. Part of the process anticipated that there could be a tie in accumulated points in any weight division and thus, not one, but three tie-breaking procedures were incorporated. However, the association never tested the third tie breaking procedure to make sure it worked as anticipated.

As it happened, it was necessary to invoke the third tie-breaking procedure which itself then gave rise to a certain controversial, albeit unanticipated dilemma. Essentially, byes were not counted in the final point total. The higher ranked athlete in a tournament would typically receive more byes. The two athletes in question ended up accumulating the same number of points from the tournaments in which they each competed (that is, they achieved the same end placing in each tournament). The athletes achieved these results competing in different tournaments from one another although of a relatively similar degree of difficulty. The athletes were ranked differently going into their own respective tournaments resulting in a different number of byes for each. Under the third tie-breaking procedure, the difference between their final point total was the difference in the number of byes each had.

The Association was bound by its policy and applied the tie-breaking provision as written, even though it didn't work as anticipated; however, the athlete adversely affected by the process appealed. The initial appeal panel found the tie-breaking policy to be unfair and essentially rewrote the tie-breaking process. The matter then went to independent arbitration where the appeal decision was overturned. The following rather extensive quote from the arbitration decision[5] illustrates the rationale of the arbitration panel:

> What the [Appeal Panel] did, in effect, was to substitute its own decision as to who was the

better athlete and accordingly manipulated the rules of the Handbook by reversing the order of the criteria to arrive at that conclusion. This is clearly inappropriate especially in a case such as this, where the tie-breaking formula contained criteria that were clear, concise, objective and non-discretionary. It is not within the jurisdiction of the [Appeal Panel] to intervene into the affairs of Judo Canada and re-write their selection rules based on what the [Appeal Panel] thinks is fair, or what it thinks the criteria should be in order to select the best possible athlete. The tie-breaking formula involved, in essence, the mechanical application of the criteria set out in the Handbook: adding up points, identifying the highest category of tournament and counting the number of wins. There was absolutely no room for the abuse of discretion, subjective evaluation or ambiguity. In such circumstances, it is not for the [Appeal Panel] to become involved in whether the selection criteria enable Judo Canada to identify the best possible athlete. It is up to the experts in the sport organization, which, in this case, was the Technical Committee...

The tie-breaking formula was set out in the Handbook so that all athletes knew well ahead of time what the "rules of the game" were in the event of a tie... Decisions with respect to clear and concise criteria cannot be appealed simply because an athlete does not like the outcome and feels they are a better overall athlete than the person who won the tie-breaker. [To do this] would be grossly unfair.

This decision highlights several important points. First, it recognizes the value of clear, objective criteria known by athletes well ahead of time. In so doing it sets out those aspects of organizations' policies and procedures that typically cause problems and lead to appeals – the abuse of discretion, subjective evaluation and ambiguity in policies and procedures. But the decision also goes on to emphasize that review panels should not rewrite the policies of organizations. Just as our courts do not have jurisdiction to rewrite legislation, policy is the sole prerogative of the duly elected, duly appointed, and properly authorized committees and boards of the organization.

We have described situations where appeals are not appropriate and should not be heard. In what situations are there legitimate grounds for an appeal? Such situations are described below.

Appeals Based on Lack of Authority

Those individuals and groups making decisions must be properly authorized to do so. This refers not only to the identities of those making decisions, but also to the policies, procedures and rules pursuant to which such decisions are made.

In *Kane v. Canadian Ladies Golf Association* (see case summary in this chapter) the Chair of the National Teams Committee had no authority to change selection criteria, and also did not follow the properly authorized procedure in applying the existing criteria. In *Lassen v. Yukon Weightlifting Association* (see case summary in this chapter) the association lacked the authority to discipline a member by means of suspension of membership. In another decision, *Omaha v. British Columbia Broomball Society*,[6] three athletes were suspended from the association for roughhousing on a bus returning from a competition. As in the Lassen case, the Society had no code of conduct or discipline policy and its bylaws clearly stated that members could *only* be suspended for non-payment of membership fees. Thus there was no authority to suspend the athletes for misconduct.

Appeals Based on Failure to Follow Policies

As described in the opening of this chapter, the policies and procedures of an organization form a contractual relationship with athletes, and with other members. Without the consent of the other party, significant deviations from such policies and procedures represent a breach of that contract.

In the case of *Kelly v. Canadian Amateur Speed Skating Association* (see case summary in this chapter) in addition to finding that there had been a breach of the individual Athlete Agreement, the court also struck down the appeal decision that the Association had made (a decision to reject Kelly's appeal of the decision to not select him to the national team) because the executive had not followed the Association's own appeal policy. This raises an interesting side issue: what if an organization is asked for an appeal but does not have such a policy or the policy is ambiguous or inappropriate?

This was the case in *Fernandes et al. v. Sport North Federation et al.* (see case summary in this chapter) where the Sport North Federation had no set procedures for appealing an issue on eligibility for the Arctic Winter Games. The court found that if there is no set procedure and an ad-hoc procedure is followed, the rules of natural justice, or procedural fairness, are implied terms of such a procedure. The court looked at whether the procedures used were in accordance with natural justice (*Fernandes*, p. 123):

> The basic requirements are notice, opportunity to make representations, and an unbiased tribunal. But, as numerous tribunals have held, the content of the principle of natural justice is flexible and depends on the circumstances in which the question arises. I must consider the peculiar circumstances of this case. The ultimate question is whether the procedures adopted were fair in all the circumstances.

Appeals Based on Abuse of Discretion

This ground for appeal is similar to the previous category, and typically arises in the context of team selection. "Discretion" means giving the selector, who is often a coach, an opportunity to exercise judgment and make a subjective choice in coming to a decision. Discretion is not absolute but exists in degrees. Viewing it on a continuum, at one end the selector is given no discretion, because selection is based entirely on objective criteria such as physical performance or rank. There is nothing to evaluate and there are no choices to be made. At the other end of the continuum, the selector may be given complete discretion to consider any factors the selector considers relevant.

Between these two extremes there are a range of situations where the selector has varying degrees of discretion. In other words, discretion is controlled to a greater of lesser extent by the organization's policies. Where the selector goes beyond the discretion that is granted, then he or she is said to have "abused their discretion" – in other words, they have gone outside the parameters prescribed or authorized by the organization.

In a recent appeal over selection to the Canadian team competing at the 1999 Pan-American Games, a number of athletes argued that the coach, who was duly authorized to make selection decisions, had abused his discretion when he ignored one of the selection criteria incorporated into the selection process[7]. In its selection policy, the association had set out nine criteria for the coach to consider: however, it had given the coach absolute discretion as to how he wished to weigh or rank the criteria. In other words, the coach could put whatever emphasis he felt appropriate on each criterion (although proportionally the same for each athlete) but he had to at least consider each criterion. The coach acknowledged he felt one criterion to be irrelevant and had not considered it. The athletes were thus successful in their appeal.

In another appeal,[8] the selectors were found to have prejudged certain athletes and applied the selection criteria in an uneven and ad-hoc manner, if they applied them at all. The Appeal Panel characterized the selection process as being entirely subjective, almost a "we know one when we see one" approach to team selection. It went on to say (p. 18):

> Such subjective approaches to team selection are inevitably followed by allegations of bias, unfairness and impropriety... Some criteria must be used to ensure that any personal biases are eliminated, and some method of scrutinizing the selection process should be in place to ensure that even the subjective elements are fairly and properly applied.

While there needs to be some flexibility in the selection process to deal with unexpected circumstances and the selectors should be afforded some degree of judgment, there is a danger that completely unfettered discretion can lead to arbitrary decisions. And if it doesn't lead to actual arbitrariness, it certainly can give the perception of arbitrariness. Arbitrary decisions are not fair decisions and are, without exception, open to review.

Arbitrariness can be controlled by controlling discretion, using objective criteria, defining subjective criteria as much as possible, using more than one selector and providing reasons for selection, among other measures.

Appeals Based on other Grounds

Further grounds for appeal include a decision-maker failing to consider relevant information or placing weight on irrelevant information; exercising discretion for an improper purpose or in bad faith; or arriving at a decision that was wholly unreasonable. Unreasonableness in this case does not relate to a state-of-mind or an intention to be unfair, but rather to the end-result of the decision.

In the cases of *Meli v. Canadian Kodokan Black Belt Association*[9] and *Blaney v. Canadian Kodokan Black Belt Association*[10] a court found it unreasonable to require athletes, already selected on their merits, to attend with virtually no notice a three-week training camp which would result in lost income in one case and loss of a job in the other. A similar example of unreasonableness in a discipline matter might be exacting a punitive sanction far in disproportion to the nature of the misconduct.

Judicial Review

A member of an organization, including an athlete, is never barred from taking a matter to the courts. However, what the courts can or will do is very limited. As noted previously, courts are reluctant to interfere in private matters, and it is well established that a party must first exhaust their internal remedies before seeking an external remedy. This principle has been affirmed time and time again in the Canadian sport community.[11]

Judicial review is not an appeal. The courts will not review the merits of a matter, nor will they review the *substantial* fairness of a matter. The courts defer entirely to the expertise within the private organization and, as shown in the Kane case, will not substitute their own decisions for those decisions more properly made by those with the necessary expertise. Courts will only review a procedural error. As well, the courts will not intervene where an organization has acted properly according to its policies and rules, no matter how unfair the outcome may seem. (See, for example, the case summary of *Stachiw v. Saskatoon Softball Umpires Association* in this chapter.)

In *McCaig et al. v. The Canadian Yachting Association et al.*,[12] two athletes argued they were denied the opportunity to fully compete for selection to the 1996 Canadian Olympic Sailing Team. The selection procedure involved three regattas; however, weather conditions forced the cancellation of the third regatta shortly after its commencement. The selection process made no contingency provision for cancellation due to weather and the Association argued there were no suitable alternate regattas available prior to the selection deadline. Selection to the team was thus made on the basis of the two completed regattas. The court in its decision stated:

> There was no provision in the agreement that provided for an alternative if, without fault on the part of either party, the event could not be completed.
>
> If the relief sought by the applicants were to be granted, it would, by necessary implication, require the court to write into the agreement a clause that does not exist. Apart from a claim for rectification, I know of no basis upon which a court can rewrite a contract by inserting a fresh clause into the agreement, no matter how desirable it might be.

Dispute Management

The most effective way for dealing with disputes in sport organizations is to prevent them from occurring in the first place. This can often be achieved by planning ahead and ensuring that governing documents and key policies are sound and that elected boards, committees, volunteers and staff implement policies properly.

When a dispute does arise in the sport setting, common ways to address the dispute include:

- Relying upon the internal appeal policies of the organization to hear the respective sides of the dispute and to make a decision as to which side will prevail;

- Where internal appeal policies are lacking, looking to policies of the parent sport organization, including provincial or national sport governing bodies, where appropriate;
- Where the dispute cannot be resolved by the sport organization itself, seeking assistance of government representatives or elected officials who have influence through their funding policies;
- Where political routes fail, gaining public support through coverage in the media; or
- As a last resort, seeking recourse to the courts.

Some additional options for resolving conflict that are often more appropriate and desirable than those listed above include various techniques of alternative dispute resolution, or ADR. In the sport community, the following three techniques of alternative dispute resolution are the most common and are being used more and more frequently by athletes, coaches and others:

Negotiation

This is a process where two parties in dispute work together without outside help to reach a mutually agreeable settlement.

Mediation

This is a process where an independent, neutral third person helps parties in a dispute reach a mutually agreeable settlement by facilitating negotiations between them. Mediation can be a powerful technique for dealing with conduct and discipline matters.

Arbitration

This is a process where the parties refer their dispute to a mutually acceptable, knowledgeable, independent person to determine a settlement. The parties usually agree beforehand to be bound by the arbitrator's decision. Binding arbitration is often the best option for resolving selection disputes, where compromise solutions or "win-win" outcomes are not suitable options.

In almost all cases, the above techniques are simpler, less costly, less adversarial and more timely than legal action in the court system. In many cases, they are also preferable to taking a dispute to the media or to government. As well, disputes are messy and referring a dispute to an outsider may mean that positive internal relationships and clear communication channels are preserved.

Dispute resolution within an organization can be enhanced by putting in place the proper policies to keep a dispute from getting out of hand, going public or ending up in court. These policy tools are:

- Bylaws that gives the board explicit power to implement policies for dispute resolution and a statement that all disputes will be dealt with accordingly;
- Unambiguous, clearly written policies to guide all decision-making about granting and revoking of rights and privileges of sport (that is, policies for eligibility, selection, conduct, discipline, harassment and conflict of interest);
- An appeal policy to review decision-making where and when procedural errors may have occurred;
- A policy that indicates that at any time any dispute may be referred to mediation, where suitable for the issue in dispute and where the disputing parties consent (keep in mind that mediation isn't a solution to every problem, as some disputes, such as selection, simply do not lend themselves to a mediated resolution);
- A policy which states that beyond the appeal level, all disputes will be referred to independent, binding arbitration; and
- A provision in policy that prohibits any member from pursuing a dispute in court until all other internal and independent remedies, as set out above, have been exhausted. This may also be called a "privative clause" and even though a person always has the right to take a matter to court when a procedural error has occurred, such a clause will restrict the basis on which a court challenge may be made.

Conclusion

In recent years we have witnessed an increase in litigation in amateur sport. Much of this litigation has occurred in the area of "athletes rights" – that is, the rights of participants in the sport experience to equitable opportunities and fair decision-making procedures and remedies. The willingness of today's amateur athletes, at all levels of the sport system, to resort to the extreme measure of litigation is likely the result of several factors, including:

- Athletes having a greater understanding and awareness of their rights;
- Athletes having more to lose financially by not protecting their rights (future sponsorship income, future scholarship opportunities, future employment income and opportunities);
- Strong public support, and growing political support for a sport system that is more "athlete-friendly"; and
- An overall societal trend towards greater litigation.

Many Canadian amateur sport organizations have taken steps to improve their governing policies and to incorporate fair procedures and alternate dispute resolution techniques into their decision-making systems. However, it is still generally the case that athletes remain in a disadvantaged position and are the weaker party when it comes to disputes with sports administrators. Although the funding policies of most governments require that sport organizations allow athletes to hold positions on boards and committees that make decisions affecting athletes, it is evident that many active athletes, through no fault of their own, do not have the knowledge, skills or time to be effective in policy-making or decision-making roles.

As well, the organizational structure of an average national sport governing body does not include athletes as "members" of the organization: rather, the actual members are local, regional, provincial and territorial sport bodies and these entities are represented at the national level by sport administrators and volunteers. As a result, athletes are often "disenfranchised," do not have a powerful membership voice and are unable to influence their organizations through conventional policy-making channels.

In light of the imbalance of power between organizations and athletes, the growing acceptance in sport of alternate dispute resolution techniques is a positive development.[13] Mediation and arbitration techniques are advantageous because they are quicker and less costly than litigation – but more importantly, they can be readily accessed by all parties. Managed properly, these techniques can also go a long way to correcting the inherent imbalance of power between disputing parties so that disputes are heard more openly and resolved more equitably.

Questions For Class Discussion

1. In many cases the membership structure of national sport organizations (NSOs) is composed of provincial sport organizations, which typically are incorporated entities. In this type of structure, organizations are recognized members as opposed to a structure where individuals are members.
   a) What are some of the legal implications of this form of membership?
   b) How might an NSO whose members are corporate entities (that is, provincial sport organizations) gain and maintain authority over program participants?
2. An individual member of a club wishes to bring a harassment complaint. In the process, the member wants his/her name kept confidential because he/she is afraid of possible retaliation.
   a) How might this relate to the issue of disclosure and the right to a hearing?
   b) How might a sport organization handle the trade-off between the rights of the complainant and the rights of the respondent?
3. In the case of a doping infraction by an athlete at the Olympic Games, a number of different organizations may have jurisdiction over the athlete, and the doping situation, at any one time. These organizations include the athlete's national sport organization, the international sport federation, the International Olympic Association and the athlete's national Olympic association.

Discuss the scope of jurisdiction each organization might have and how they would interact:
a) National sport organization
b) International sport federation
c) International Olympic Association
d) Athlete's national Olympic association

4. Often, sport organizations run internal hearings to decide disciplinary matters. Usually, the sport organization appoints the members of the hearing panel. This sometimes raises a concern about bias, both actual and perceived. For example, the individual who is the subject of the hearing might perceive that the hearing panel will be predisposed towards favoring the organization.
   a) Discuss the different sources of bias and determine how these sources might apply to the situation described above.
   b) What strategies might the sport organization use to reduce or eliminate such concerns about bias?

5. In a team sport situation, selection of team members is complex and somewhat subjective, because selecting the most skilled and physically talented players might not produce the best "team."
   a) Discuss the pros and cons of using objective selection criteria, subjective selection criteria, or a combination of the two.
   b) How might an organization that wishes to incorporate at least some subjective criteria into its team selection process make such criteria more defensible from a procedural and legal point of view?

6. A sport organization initiates an investigation into a disciplinary matter. The investigator is given the authority to recommend whether the matter should go to a hearing or be dismissed. In this case the investigator recommends the matter go to a formal hearing.
   a) Discuss whether or not there is a different standard of fairness that applies to the investigation as compared to the hearing.
   b) It has been said that the concept of procedural fairness is a flexible concept, and that procedural safeguards may vary with the circumstances. What factors might be considered in determining appropriate procedural measures?

Relevant Cases

Lee v. Showmen's Guild of Great Britain

(1952) 1 All E.R. 1175

This 1950s landmark case from England established two very important legal principles for private organizations. Although the case had nothing to do with sport, it has been quoted by almost every athlete and amateur sport organization that has ever gone to court over a decision-making dispute.

Very briefly the facts of the case are that Lee was a seller of pots and pans in a flea market and the Showmen's Guild was the voluntary association that operated the flea market. Lee was a member of the Guild and in fact, was required to be a member if he wanted to sell his pots and pans. One day Lee got into a scuffle with another vendor in the market over who was going to have the prime corner spot – upon receiving a complaint from the other vendor who alleged that Lee was the instigator of the scuffle, the Guild suspended him.

Lee was eventually successful in his court challenge to be reinstated as a member of the Guild, but more importantly, the court made two statements that have a direct bearing on how sport organizations must govern themselves:

- Firstly, the court said that the jurisdiction of a domestic (or private) tribunal is founded on a contract which it has with its members, and
- Secondly, the court said that domestic tribunals are subject to the rules of natural justice in how they deal with their members.

Kelly v. Canadian Amateur Speed Skating Association

Unreported decision, February 1995. Ontario Ct. Gen. Div. (Ottawa)

Kelly was a speed skater and a member of the Canadian Amateur Speed Skating Association (CASSA). Like many high performance athletes, Kelly had entered into an athlete agreement with CASSA. This agreement formed a part of CASSA's governing documents, and stated that CASSA must publish selection criteria for national teams at least three months before the selection date. The agreement further stated that the selection process must conform to the generally accepted principles of natural justice as well as substantive and procedural fairness.

The original selection process specified that the top four skaters at the Canadian Championships would be named to the national team competing at the 1995 World Sprint Championships. One week before the Canadian Championships, CASSA unilaterally changed the selection criteria to specify that only the top two skaters would be chosen at the Canadian Championships (an event taking place outdoors in uncertain weather conditions) and the remaining two would be chosen following a subsequent World Cup meet (an event taking place indoors in controlled conditions). The coaches were in favour of this change, as were all of the athletes vying for a spot of the team, with the exception of Kelly.

Kelly finished fourth at the Canadian Championships. It had been part of his training plan to qualify in the third or fourth position and then to "peak" at the World Spring Championships some seven weeks later. Under the original selection process, he would have been named to the national team competing at the World Sprint Championship. Under the revised criteria, he was not.

Kelly immediately filed a notice of appeal. His appeal was rejected on the grounds that the changes to the selection criteria were reasonable and justifiable. Kelly then filed an action with the court for judicial review. The court found that the basis of the relationship between Kelly and CASSA was contractual. The athlete agreement set out terms and conditions of this contract that CASSA had clearly breached. Specifically, CASSA had changed the selection process without giving the athletes three months notice. The court thus ruled that the revised selection criteria were void, and as such Kelly had qualified for the national team and was entitled to represent Canada at the World Sprint Championships.

Kane v. Canadian Ladies Golf Association

Unreported decision, September 1992. P.E.I. Trial Division (Charlottetown)

Kane was a highly ranked amateur golfer and a member of the Canadian Ladies Golf Association (CLGA) in 1992. She was vying for one of three spots on the Canadian Ladies World Amateur Golf Team which was to compete at the World Amateur Championships in Vancouver.

Prior to 1992, the approved policy of CLGA had been to select teams solely on the basis of differential average scores in designated national and international tournaments over the previous two years. On the basis of differential average scores, Kane had ranked among the top four golfers in the country in the five years leading up to the World Amateur Championships in 1992, including ranking second in the country in 1991 and 1992.

In February of 1992 the Director of the Teams Committee issued a written memo that altered the original selection criteria by adding a number of subjective elements, including *exceptional performances in provincial and national championships, international experience* and *results from past performances*. On the basis of these revised criteria, Kane was selected as an alternate member, and not as a playing member, of the Canadian Ladies World Amateur Golf Team.

Kane challenged the revised criteria in court, arguing that the CLGA had failed to follow its own rules by relying upon a selection process that was not properly approved. The court agreed, finding no evidence that either the Executive Committee of the CLGA or the Teams Committee had approved the revised criteria. Furthermore, the court observed that even if the revised criteria had been properly approved by either committee, they were not properly implemented. Specifically, the selections were to be made by the Executive with input from the Teams Director and the National Coach, which did not happen, and there was also inconsistency in the time-span over which the differential scores were considered for different players.

Kane also asked the court to declare a new Canadian team for the World Ladies Amateur Golf Tournament. The court declined to do this, instead referring the matter back to CLGA to make the decision according to its own properly authorized rules and procedures. Due to the shortness of time between the court hearing and the Vancouver event, CLGA had no choice but to revert to the previous practice of selecting teams based upon two years of differential average scores, which resulted in restoring Kane to the team.

Depiero v. Canadian Amateur Diving Association
(1985) A.C.W.S. (2d) 331

A diving meet in Brantford, Ontario was the final selection event to name three female divers to the Ontario team competing at the 1985 Canada Games in Saint John, New Brunswick. Two of the three divers had already been selected on the basis of previous competitions, one of whom was Depiero's sister.

Going into the final dive of the competition, Depiero was in first place and her selection to the team seemed certain. Depiero and her sister were coached by the same coach, and he directed that Depiero's sister pass on her final dive so as not to jeopardize Depiero's position. The meet concluded, Depiero remained in first place, and thus was selected to the Ontario team.

The Canadian Amateur Diving Association (CADA) determined that the coach's actions violated the rules of fair competition. The Board of Directors declared the results of the event invalid, disciplined the coach and named a third diver to the team in place of Depiero.

Depiero appealed this decision and the matter went before an Event Jury of Appeal that was organized by CADA in accordance with its bylaws. This Jury upheld Depiero's selection to the team but made recommendations for changing the rules of competition to prevent a similar situation from arising in the future.

The Board of Directors of CADA held a meeting and rejected the decision of the Event Jury of Appeal and voted to remove Depiero from the team

Depiero took the matter to court and asked the court to order CADA and the Ontario Ministry of Tourism and Recreation to revise the team roster to include Depiero instead of the third diver. The court granted the order, noting that CADA's bylaws and rules did not authorize the Board of Directors to overturn a decision of an Event Jury of Appeal, and even if they did, the actions of the Board were unfair.

In particular, one of the Board members who participated in the decision had a clear conflict of interest, as he was the coach of the third diver. Depiero was being punished by the Board for actions which were not hers but rather were the coach's. As well, Depiero had no notice of the meeting of the Board at which the decision to drop her from the team was made, and was allowed no opportunity to make representations on her own behalf.

Stachiw v. Saskatoon Softball Umpires Association et al.
(1985) 5 W.W.R. 651 (Sask Q.B.)

Stachiw was a softball umpire and a member of the Saskatoon Softball Umpires Association (SSUA). The Executive of the Association received information that Stachiw had been drinking beer at a game that he was umpiring, a practice prohibited by SSUA's rules. The Executive suspended Stachiw and gave Stachiw notice of the hearing at which he could speak to the suspension and, if he wished, refute the allegations that he was drinking beer.

Stachiw did not attend the hearing and SSUA confirmed his suspension for one year. The constitution of SSUA provided that the Executive could suspend a member for just cause provided that the member be given an opportunity to appeal the suspension.

Stachiw appealed his suspension and denied drinking the beer. The Executive heard evidence from a number of witnesses, including those who changed their testimony about the beer drinking and denied that they saw Stachiw drinking beer. However, the Executive also heard evidence that this recanting of testimony had been done under some duress. At the end of the day, the Executive considered all of the relevant evidence and denied Stachiw's appeal, thus upholding his one-year suspension.

Stachiw appealed to the court. The court ruled that he was bound by the rules of SSUA and that he had been given a reasonable opportunity to refute the allegations made against him. Unless fraud could be proven, the court would not interfere to reverse a decision of an elected Executive acting properly and within the scope of its powers as set out in the constitution and policies of the SSUA.

Garrett v. Canadian Weightlifting Federation
Unreported decision, January 1990. Alta. Q.B. (Edmonton)

Garrett was an accomplished weightlifter and a member of the Canadian Weightlifting Federation (CWF). Garrett had been advised in writing of his selection to the Canadian team competing at the 1990 Commonwealth Games in Auckland, New Zealand. Garrett attended the team's final training camp in Vancouver, but two days into this camp was advised by the national team Coach (who was also the President of the CWF) that he was being removed from the team and being replaced by a reserve athlete, one whom Garrett had bettered throughout the year-long selection process.

Garrett was sent home from the training camp. When they learned of the coach's decision to replace Garrett with a reserve, the remaining directors of the CWF met by conference call and determined that the Coach's actions were unauthorized and invalid. The CWF ordered the Coach to reinstate Garrett to the team, but the Coach disregarded this order and took the reserve athlete to Auckland.

Garrett went to court seeking an order to reinstate him to the team. Due to the shortness of time and the great urgency, the court granted the order, having found that the decision to remove Garrett from the team was made arbitrarily and without proper authority. The court also noted that the decision was influenced by bias because the national Coach was also the personal coach of the reserve athlete who was placed on the team in Garrett's place.

In spite of the Court order, Garrett was not able to compete at Auckland because by the time the order was made, the national weightlifting team had already been constituted by the Commonwealth Games Association of Canada (CGAC), on the basis of recommendations from each national sport organization. CGAC had not been named in the order and was not subject to the order, and in this case chose not to follow the order of the court regarding the make-up of the team.

Kulesza v. Canadian Amateur Synchronized Swimming Association Inc.

Unreported decision, June 1996. Ont. Ct. Gen. Div. (Ottawa)

Kulesza was a synchronized swimmer competing for a spot on the Canadian synchronized swimming team competing in the 1996 Olympics in Atlanta. As a member of the national team program of the Canadian Amateur Synchronized Swimming Association (Synchro Canada), Kulesza had entered into an athlete agreement the previous year which had specified the selection process, selection criteria and the identity of the selectors for the 1996 Olympic team.

Synchro Canada selected its Olympic team based upon a process and criteria set out well in advance. Kulesza was selected as a travelling alternate to the team. Kulesza launched an internal appeal of the selection decision, alleging bias on the part of selectors. Specifically, she alleged that three of the judges involved in the selection decision coached some of the individual athletes vying for selection, and were paid for their services and thus had a professional and financial association with Synchro Canada. The three judges in question were the Head Olympic Coach, the Assistant Olympic Coach and the National Team Director.

Before the appeal could be heard, Kulesza appeared in court seeking an injunction stopping the team from competing in the Olympics and declaring the team selection null and void. She asked the court to order a new selection before a panel of three independent judges including Olympic Games judges from 1988, 1992 and 1996.

The court did not grant the order. The court found no evidence that there was bias in the selection and in fact, took the view that it was entirely appropriate and sensible that coaches within Synchro Canada, who were familiar with the athletes, should make the selections. The court also observed that the Head Coach was the personal coach of Kulesza, a fact that greatly undermined Kulesza's complaint about bias of the selectors.

The court also observed that Kulesza's court action was not timely. She should have complained about the selection procedures and the identity of the selectors at the time she agreed to the terms of the athlete agreement the previous year. By entering into this contract, she waived her right to object to the selection process. She also failed to exhaust her internal remedies by abandoning her internal appeal. The court concluded that "it should be loathe to substitute its opinion on the selection process in the stead of those so clearly knowledgeable in the field."

Lassen v. Yukon Weightlifting Association

Unreported decision, May 1995. Yukon S.C. (Whitehorse)

Teenager Lassen was an accomplished junior weightlifter and a member of the Yukon Weightlifting Association (YWA). Following her silver medal performance at the Canada Games in 1995, she qualified for both the 1995 National Weightlifting Championships in Montreal and the 1995 Junior World Weightlifting Championships in Poland.

Shortly before the Montreal event, the YWA and the Canadian Weightlifting Federation got into a dispute over the national body's decision to not fund a team to attend the World Championships, and the choice of the Coach who would accompany those team members who could finance the trip themselves. The YWA advised Lassen that she could not attend the Worlds, even though funding was not an issue as Lassen's family had planned to pay for her trip.

A short while later Lassen was advised by the YWA that she could not attend the National Championships either, although airline tickets had already been purchased and arrangements made. When Lassen's parents asked YWA for an explanation of these decisions, the YWA responded by suspending Lassen's membership indefinitely, citing as reasons interference by her parents in the YWA's affairs, Lassen's lack of commitment to her sport and lack of maturity to compete at the national and world level.

Due to the shortness of time Lassen had no choice but to pursue the matter in court. The court found that the decision to suspend Lassen's membership was not authorized, as YWA lacked the authority in its bylaws or other governing documents to suspend or revoke any individual's membership. Lack of authority notwithstanding, the court also found the manner in which Lassen had been treated to be unfair. The YWA's dispute with the national body did not involve Lassen personally and she should not have been punished for matters clearly beyond her control. There was no factual basis to support YWA's claims that Lassen lacked commitment and maturity – in fact, evidence pointed to just the opposite. Procedurally, Lassen had not been given notice of the suspension of her membership, was not informed of the reasons for the suspension, was not given an opportunity to present her case, and was denied an appeal.

The court ordered that Lassen be reinstated as a member of YWA and that the YWA and the Canadian Weightlifting Federation allow her to compete at both the National Championships and the World Championships.

Trumbley v. Saskatchewan Amateur Hockey Association
(1986) 49 Sask.R. 296 (Sask. C.A.)

This case involved a coach, Trumbley, who was a member of the Saskatchewan Amateur Hockey Association (SAHA). Trumbley was suspended for coaching a midget team in a tournament that was not sanctioned by SAHA or by the Canadian Amateur Hockey Association. The constitution of SAHA permitted suspension of members for participation in unsanctioned tournaments. Prior to the tournament in question, Trumbley and his team were informed by SAHA that the tournament was not sanctioned and that they would face suspensions if they participated.

After being suspended, Trumbley submitted notice of his intention to appeal SAHA's decision. Shortly after, he withdrew his appeal and instead brought court action against SAHA. The Saskatchewan Non-Profit Corporations Act contains an unusual provision relating to discipline by private associations of their members, and allows an aggrieved member to apply to the court to issue an order when the member has been treated unfairly. Trumbley argued that SAHA's constitution and policies violated this statutory provision and that the decision to suspend him was unfair. The trial court agreed and overturned Trumbley's suspension.

SAHA appealed the trial court's decision and on appeal the court held that Trumbley could not seek judicial review of SAHA's decision until he had exhausted all other available remedies. SAHA had offered Trumbley and appeal, and in the court's view there was nothing to suggest that he would not have received a fair hearing by the appeals committee. As well, the court noted that the appeal could have been conducted in a timely manner as Trumbley had been suspended in the summer and the new hockey season was not yet underway. Finally, the court stated that the internal appeal hearing was clearly preferable to court action in terms of convenience, timeliness and cost to the parties.

Fernandes v. Sport North Federation
(1996) N.W.T.R. 118. (NWT S.C.)

This case involved a dispute about the eligibility of two figure skaters who had qualified for the NWT team competing at the 1996 Arctic Winter Games. There was some concern about their residency (and thus their eligibility to compete) and the Sport North Federation resorted to its usual practice of asking the Technical Committee of the host organization for a ruling.

The Committee ruled they were NWT residents and thus eligible. The governing body for figure skating in the NWT became concerned because if the skaters were later found to be ineligible, it could jeopardize the entire team. This body asked Sport North Federation to review the skaters' eligibility, which they did using ad-hoc procedures, ultimately determining that the skaters were not eligible.

The skaters went to court, arguing that the initial decision of the Technical Committee should stand. In particular, they claimed that Sport North Federation had no formal procedures for reviewing eligibility and no appeal mechanism, and that the usual practice of sending the matter to the Technical Committee should be relied upon in their case.

The court found that the process used by Sport North Federation, while ad-hoc and improvisational, was not inherently unfair in the circumstances. The basic requirements of fairness had been met because the skaters were given notice and were allowed to make representations before unbiased decision-makers. As well, Sport North Federation had not acted arbitrarily, in bad faith or otherwise outside its jurisdiction.

The court also pointed out that Sport North Federation might wish to correct and formalize its procedures, so as to avoid similar problems in the future.

Endnotes

1. The *Canadian Charter of Rights and Freedoms*, while an important source of human rights, has little impact on the sport community in Canada. This is because the *Charter* applies to "government action" and nearly all sport activities in Canada are organized by private and autonomous sport organizations, not by governments. Human rights in Canada are also protected in a variety of federal, provincial and territorial statutes that prohibit discrimination in the provision of goods, services, facilities and accommodations to the general public. In the past, many courts took the view that Canadian sport organizations did not provide services to the general public and thus were not required to comply with human rights legislation. More recently the courts have taken a more inclusive view of the term "public" by looking at the nature and quality of the relationship between the organization and the users of its services rather than simply the quantity of users. This has had the effect of bringing more so-called "private" organizations into the scope of human rights legislation. For a full discussion, see *Mediated Agreement Between David Morrison, the City of Coquitlam and the Deputy Chief Commissioner* (1999), available from the Centre for Sport and Law's web site at www.sportlaw.ca.

2. In the past, a distinction was made between judicial and quasi-judicial decisions and administrative decisions. The first category of decisions was subject to the rules of "natural justice" while the second category was not. Making this distinction was tricky and often resulted in unfairness. The law has now evolved to impose a "duty of fairness" on those making administrative decisions, and this duty has replaced the rules of natural justice. As noted by Blake (p. 13): *"The distinction is now meaningless: every tribunal making decisions that could adversely affect individual rights or interests must proceed fairly."*

3. At a minimum this would include disclosure of any information that will be taken into account in making the decision. However, it is prudent to disclose to all parties any information that is provided to the decision-maker, regardless of whether the decision-maker relies upon that information in making his or her decision.

4. *Thompson v. Chiropractors' Association (Saskatchewan)* (1966), 36 Admin. L.R. (2d) 273 (Sask. Q.B.)

5. Arbitration Decision, Judo Canada. June 21, 1996, p. 7.

6. (1981), 13 A.C.W.S. (2d) 373 (B.C.S.C.)

7. Internal and confidential appeal decision, National Sport Governing Body, August 1999.

8. Internal and confidential appeal decision, Bobsleigh Canada, August, 1999.

9. Unreported decision. July 1987. Alta. Q.B.(Lethbridge)

10. Unreported decision. July 1987. Alta. Q.B.(Lethbridge)

11 *Kulesza v. Canadian Amateur Synchronized Swimming Association Inc. et al.* (1996) Unreported decision, Ont. Ct. Gen. Div. (Ottawa), *Smith v. International Triathlon Union* (1999) Unreported decision, B.C.S.C. (Vancouver), *Gray v. Canadian Track and Field Association* (1986), 39 A.C.W.S. (2d) 483 (Ont. H.C.), re *Dickie et al. and British Columbia Lacrosse Association et al.* (1984), 28 A.C.W.S. (2d) 178 (B.C.S.C.), *Trumbley v. Saskatchewan Amateur Hockey Association* (1986) 49 Sask.R. 296 (Sask. C.A.)

12 Unreported decision, April 1996. Man. Q.B. (Winnipeg). Simonsen, J., p. 6.

13 In January 2000, the Secretary of State for Amateur Sport announced a Ministerial Work Group to develop a National Dispute Resolution System for Amateur Sport in Canada. A voluntary program has existed in Canada since 1995, and the Working Group will be looking at ways to improve this program, to make participation mandatory and to extend it to the provinces and territories.

References

Blake, Sara. *Administrative Law in Canada.* Toronto: Butterworths, 1992.

Corbett, Rachel and Hilary A. Findlay (1998). *Your Risk Management Program: A Handbook for Sport Organizations.* Centre for Sport and Law.

Kligman, Robert D. *Bias.* Toronto: Butterworths, 1998.

CHAPTER 8

NATURAL JUSTICE AND SPORT: ATHLETES' RIGHTS, DRUG TESTING, AND AGENTS

Edward W. Ducharme

Introduction

The distinguished literary critic, I. A. Richards, is one of a number of renowned educators to lament the fact that teachers' classroom strategies too frequently bear little or no resemblance to a particular theory or "philosophy" of education. Richards was an English professor at Cambridge University, and in *Speculative Instruments* (1955) he challenged teachers all across the educational spectrum to say what they stood for:

> The teacher ... at whatever level, is oddly reluctant to discuss his principles. Whether they could be granted, were they available for inspection, must be doubted until they are set forth.

I share Richards' conviction that, as a rule, teachers have been reluctant to discuss the principles upon which their pedagogical practices rest. As educators we need constantly to ask, what are our principles, and what are the consequences of our attachment to them? I propose to set out briefly some principles to which I subscribe related to natural justice and sport.

Natural Justice and Fairness in Sport

Sports governing bodies exercising authority over athletes, either by virtue of powers granted by statute or by virtue of internal rules constituting, in effect, the legal system for a particular sport, must afford athlete members the procedural protections of natural justice when these athletes are subject to such disciplinary sanctions as suspension or expulsion. The requirements of natural justice, referred to popularly in the United States as "due process," turn on three fundamental principles: the right to notice of the charge; the right to be heard; and the right to an unbiased adjudication.

Were I to become involved in a disciplinary proceeding involving an athlete, I would subject the matter to the following analysis:

1. What governing association or body is it that presumes to exercise the disciplinary power?
2. From what enabling statute, if any, does the governing association derive its disciplinary power?
3. If a statute is applicable, does the language of the statute expressly empower the governing association or body to exercise a disciplinary power?

4. Does the statute contain a "privative clause," that is, a clause purporting to exclude judicial review of the decision made by the governing association or body?[1]
5. Has the governing association or body afforded the athlete in question some or all of the following:
    a) The right of adequate notice of a hearing;
    b) The right of a hearing;
    c) The right of adequate notice of the case to be met;
    d) The right to make full and proper defense before the decision-maker, a right which, depending upon the circumstances, may very well entail the right to be represented by counsel and to examine and cross-examine witnesses?
6. Has the governing association or body in the exercise of its disciplinary authority over the athlete abrogated his or her constitutional rights as guaranteed by the *Canadian Charter of Rights and Freedoms* (the "*Charter*")?[2]
7. Has the governing association or body in the exercise of its disciplinary authority over the athlete violated the common law[3] of Canada generally and, in particular, the rules of natural justice?

Not too long ago in Canadian law the rules of natural justice were thought to apply only to those bodies exercising authority under statute and only when those bodies were engaged in "judicial" or "quasi-judicial" as opposed to "administrative" functions. If the precise nature of the power or function being exercised by the governing body was one that a court would deal with, the function was said to be judicial or "quasi-judicial" (whatever that means), and the rules of natural justice were held to apply. But the difficulty in defining the precise nature of the power or function exercised led invariably to court battles and to a morass of contradictory, irreconcilable decisions. The result was that one could not reliably predict when or on what grounds courts would exercise their discretion to interfere with the powers exercised by the administrative tribunals or agencies.

Now, thankfully, courts tend to be less concerned about distinguishing between such terms as "judicial" and "quasi-judicial," and more concerned about whether or not the decision-maker acted reasonably and responsibly in all the circumstances. The court asks of an administrative tribunal with the power to enforce discipline: has the governing body imposed its discipline consistent with a standard of reasonableness and fairness? With this trend in mind, I adopt as a starting point the principle that athletes subjected to discipline, particularly in cases involving expulsion or suspension, are entitled, at a minimum, to the protections afforded by the rules of natural justice; they should immediately and vigorously challenge the right of any governing body to discipline in the absence of those fundamental procedural protections. In disciplinary cases, the violation of the athlete's right to natural justice makes the decision void (Wade and Forsyth, p. 465).

In adopting the principle that rules of natural justice apply or ought to apply presumptively in all disciplinary cases involving athletes, I am aware, of course, that arguments have been made and will continue to be made that in some circumstances the rules of natural justice may not apply or may have to be modified. Bruce Kidd and Mary Eberts provide the following example (p. 29):

> In a world championship or major competition, it may be necessary to make a disciplinary decision very quickly. The number of officials available to make the decision may be limited. These factors must be taken into account when we examine the extent of "natural justice" and "fairness" in disciplinary cases in the sports governing bodies.

Decisions required to be taken in haste may occur, but those circumstances will be rare and, even then, the rules of natural justice should be adjusted to the circumstances and applied as fairly as possible, never wholly abrogated.

The applicability of the rules of natural justice may be somewhat different in the context of professional sport, especially where the governing authority is a privately owned sports franchise and especially where the governing authority, the owner of the sports franchise and the athlete have a relationship governed by a contract, specifically a collective bargaining agreement. In the context of the collective bargaining agreement, the athlete is a member of a bargaining unit. As such, his workplace rights, obligations, and remedies are held by his collective bargaining agent, the Players' Association. It speaks on the athlete's behalf as regards the terms that must appear in every player's contract. Those standard terms, arrived at through the process of collective bargaining between union and management, may then be supplemented by further terms specific to the individual player and negotiated either by the player himself or his agent. But what happens when the union is silent when the player's workplace rights are jeopardized? Sometimes athletes' rights are abused in this context, and with thundering consequences.

A case in point is that of Bob Probert, the tough left-winger now of the Chicago Black Hawks and formerly of the Detroit Red Wings. In the early morning hours of March 2, 1989, when Probert played for the Red Wings, he was arrested at the U.S. border in Detroit and charged with unlawfully importing into the U.S. Customs territory of the United States 14.3 grams of cocaine. At the time of his arrest, he was 23 and by all accounts the fiercest fighter in the game.

On March 4, 1989, two days after his arrest, Probert was expelled from the National Hockey League by its President, John Ziegler. Prior to the expulsion, neither Ziegler nor any other official of the NHL spoke to Probert or to anyone representing him regarding the events surrounding his arrest. (I should point out here, in passing, that about eight months after his arrest Probert pleaded guilty to the offence of importing cocaine for his personal use and was sentenced to ninety days in a U.S. federal penitentiary. Neither the guilty plea nor the ensuing sentence is relevant, however, to the point I am seeking to illustrate.)

When Ziegler expelled Probert, he acted pursuant to subsection 17.3 (a) of the NHL by-laws that provide, in part, as follows:

> If, in the opinion of the President, based upon such information and reports as he may deem sufficient, any act or conduct of any ... player ... has been dishonorable, prejudicial to or against the welfare of the League or the game of hockey, he may expel or suspend such a person.

The effect of section 17 is to empower the NHL President to expel or suspend as he sees fit without having even to speak to the athlete or his representative. The provision is clearly contrary to the guarantee of equal protection and due process enshrined in the fourteenth amendment to the American Constitution. But this unfettered power to expel and suspend is probably unassailable on constitutional grounds because according to American constitutional law the right to equal protection operates only in situations where the person or body exercising authority is connected in some tangible way with the government.

From the player's perspective, the way to respond to the flagrant violations of due process in cases such as Probert's is to mount a challenge against the NHL President's sweeping discretionary powers through the NHL Players' Association (the "NHLPA"). In Probert's case, the NHLPA, led by the now disgraced Alan Eagleson, did nothing. Having the status of a trade union, the NHLPA bargains collectively with the owners on behalf of its members and is in a good position to insist at the negotiating table that subsection 17.3 (a) of the by-laws be revised to provide for due process. When Probert was arrested, then summarily expelled by Ziegler, the league did not have a comprehensive disciplinary policy and program dealing with such issues as alcohol and drug addiction. Its "policy," with which Eagleson agreed, was that drugs were not a major problem in the NHL, but that if anyone became involved with them and was caught he would be subject to immediate, automatic expulsion at the absolute discretion of the League President. By contrast, the National Basketball Association, the National Football League, and Major League Baseball had long before fashioned drug policies in concert with their respective Players Associations and incorporated them into the collective bargaining agreements.

Finally, in the fall of 1996, the NHL and the National Hockey League Players' Association announced the establishment of a program to address drug and alcohol abuse, HIV, and related health matters for players. The plan was and still is to incorporate the policy into the NHL/NHLPA Collective Bargaining Agreement, when the parties finally get around to re-negotiating that Agreement. At the moment, the substance abuse policy is attached as an appendix to the Collective Bargaining Agreement. It provides supervision and discipline in up to four stages, as follows:

Stage One — First in-patient treatment; no penalty.

Stage Two — For violation of Stage-One treatment plan, suspension without pay during active phase of treatment and then eligible for reinstatement.

Stage Three —For violation of Stage-Two treatment plan, suspension without pay for at least six months and then eligible for reinstatement.

Stage Four — For violation of Stage-Three treatment plan, suspension without pay for at least one year. Reinstatement not assured.

Until the creation and implementation of this policy, it was open to the NHL and to individual teams to treat athletes with substance abuse problems according to whim rather than according to consistent, fair processes and procedures. The old view was in fact a curious mixture of willful blindness and naiveté: few hockey players ever experimented with drugs, but those who did and were caught were subject to immediate expulsion without further consideration. The NHL's substance abuse program formally acknowledges, at long last, that professional hockey players are, like the rest of us, flawed and thus occasionally require emotional and educational support and care to control addictive or anti-social behavior.

Athletes' Rights and Mandatory Drug Testing

In the absence of a collective agreement entered into in good faith by the parties to the collective agreement and setting out a comprehensive policy and program on drug abuse, including penalties, mandatory drug testing (MDT) is unlawful, either:

(a) Because it violates the athlete's constitutional rights under section 7 and section 8 of the *Charter*[4] (in the United States, essentially these same rights are guaranteed by the fourth, fifth and fourteenth amendments to the U.S. Constitution); or

(b) Because it violates one or more Human Rights statutes which operate in every province and in the federal jurisdiction as well.

Professor Trossman's article on mandatory drug testing in Canada is an intelligent, thoughtful analysis of the section 7 and section 8 *Charter* issues as they relate to MDT and, to my knowledge, an accurate survey of the law. I need not restate his analysis, except to say that *Charter* arguments raised by athletes relating to invasion of privacy (section 7) and unlawful search and seizure (section 8) are likely to succeed only in cases where the governing authority insisting on the MDT is a governmental agency or an agency or meaningfully connected to the government. The reason for this limitation is that subsection 32(1) of the *Charter* states that the *Charter* applies:

32. (1)(a) to the Parliament and government of Canada ...; and
(b) To the legislature and government of each province.

Thus, says Trossman, section 32 would likely operate to exclude privately owned sport franchises from *Charter* constraints because they are neither legislators nor government and are not meaningfully connected to government. On the other hand, publicly owned sports franchises (such as the Saskatchewan Roughriders of the CFL) and governmental bodies such as the Ontario Racing Commission probably would qualify as "government" within the meaning of s. 32, making their actions subject to *Charter* scrutiny (pp. 197-201).

In cases where the *Charter* does not apply, a particular Human Rights statute may well be applicable. In Ontario, for example, the *Human Rights Code*[5] provides at subsection 5(1):

5. (1) Every person has a right to equal treatment with respect to employment without discrimination because of ... handicap.

Trossman asks (p. 216):

How does a proscription against discrimination on the basis of handicap affect MDT programs for athletes? The Ontario Human Rights Commission, which administers the *Code*, recently explained the relevance of this provision in its release entitled *Policy on Drug and Alcohol Testing*. There are two senses in which the handicap provision is relevant. First, "where an individual's use of drugs or alcohol has reached the stage where it constitutes an illness," then the individual may actually be handicapped. Thus, actual substance dependency that could be termed an illness qualifies as a handicap.

The other scenario is where the employer *believes* that a drug dependency exists, whether or not this is, in fact, true. As the commission states, "an employer may interpret a positive test of a casual drug user to mean that the individual has a drug dependency." In fact, a casual drug user is not, in ordinary parlance, handicapped. But, where the employer incorrectly concludes that a drug dependency exists, and discriminates on that basis, this will constitute discrimination on the basis of a handicap for the purposes of the *Code*.

The only way that private owners of sports franchises could defend against a charge of discrimination in these circumstances would be to argue, by reference to s.10 (1) of the *Code*, that not being handicapped is a *bona fide* occupational qualification. But there is no guarantee that this argument would be successful. Many athletes have admitted to habitual use of marijuana, cocaine and other harmful narcotics with no noticeable diminution in their performance levels. Drug dependency, in other words, is not necessarily correlative with inability to perform. This is especially true in cases where the dependency is on so-called performance-enhancing drugs such as anabolic steroids. Ben Johnson's reliance upon stanozololol, an anabolic steroid, obviously *enhanced* his performance in the 100-meter sprint at the 1988 Olympic Games in Seoul. However, even if a team or organization were to establish successfully that not being handicapped was a *bona fide* occupational qualification, the team or organization would still be under a duty to accommodate such athletes, a duty which might very well include assisting them in their rehabilitation.

The apparently widespread use of drugs among professional and amateur athletes and in our society generally is deplorable, of course, but it does not follow that individual constitutional rights such as those enshrined in sections 7 and 8 of the *Charter* may be justifiably violated on the ground that athletes are role models and that as role models they must be held to a higher standard of personal conduct. No constitutional rights are too precious to be bargained away in exchange for public confidence in the integrity of athletes. Section 1 of the *Charter* provides as follows:

> 1. The *Canadian Charter of Rights and Freedoms* guarantees the rights and freedoms set out in it subject only to such reasonable limits prescribed by law as can be demonstrably justified in a free and democratic society.

Public perceptions of the integrity of sporting functions or of the athletes participating in them come nowhere close to satisfying the implied balance of interest test specified in section 1 of the *Charter*. There is no real evidence that MDT has resulted in a decrease of drug abuse. Society in general and the sports world particularly must be challenged to find better and more lawful means than MDT to combat the scourge of drug abuse.

The Role of Agents

Ideally, sports agents should be lawyers, or at any rate professionals with knowledge or experience in a myriad of issues bearing on constitutional, contract, business, tax and agency law, some or all of which at some point touch the life of the athlete. Sports agents perform an amalgam of services for their clients and assume differing relationships with them, some being more impersonal and formal than others. But all of them require, at the very least, minimal competence in reading and interpreting a standard form contract and collective bargaining agreements, and even this modest skill is likely to be realized most frequently in a person possessing a legal education.

The case of the journeyman hockey player, John Tonelli, illustrates how even a Standard Player's Contract can become for an athlete and his agent as well as the employer a quagmire of rankling and confusion.[6] In September of 1974, the then seventeen-year-old Tonelli entered into a Standard Form Agreement with the Toronto Marlboros of the Ontario Hockey Association Junior "A" League. Before signing the contract, which was to run for three years, Tonelli engaged the services of an agent and acted on the agent's advice. One year later, on the day following his eighteenth birthday, Tonelli repudiated the contract and immediately signed a three-year contract with the Houston Aeros of the now defunct World Hockey Association (WHA).

The Marlboros countered by launching an action in the Supreme Court of Ontario against Tonelli, his agent, the Aeros and the WHA for damages for breach of contract and for conspiracy to induce breach of contract. The Marlboros alleged, among other things, that the agent acting on Tonelli's behalf when he entered into the Marlboros contract deliberately caused the contract to be breached by persuading Houston to offer employment to Tonelli and by counseling Tonelli to accept the offer. After five years of litigation, Tonelli and his agent escaped liability when a three-member panel of the Ontario Court of Appeal found by a 2:1 majority that, on the whole, the contract between Tonelli and the Marlboros was not beneficial to the player and thus voidable at his option.

In law, the Tonelli case now stands for the proposition that a contract of service is enforceable against an infant (a person under eighteen years of age) only if it was for his benefit when made, the onus being on the adult party to establish the benefit. One member of the judicial panel, Mr. Justice Zuber, found in his dissenting judgment that the contract was beneficial to the player, but Justices Arnup and Blair disagreed and dismissed the action against Tonelli, the agent, and the other defendants.

It is unclear from the three reported judgements in the Tonelli case whether or not the agent advising the player knew at the time of the signing of the Marlboros contract that it was likely to be construed by a court as onerous and one-sided and therefore voidable at Tonelli's option. Tonelli's lawyers certainly understood the legal principles applicable to infants' contracts and advocated them successfully through a series of undoubtedly costly legal proceedings. Elemental principles of contract and agency law inevitably operate in the player/agent relationship: an agent uninformed in these areas fails in his or her obligation to deliver professional, competent services.

In most jurisdictions across North America anyone who wants to be an agent can be, provided only that she or he finds at least one athlete who consents to be represented. No formal education or training is required, nor any system of registration, certification or licensure. Not surprisingly, agents are a very diverse group indeed; they are accountants, former teachers and coaches, family friends and relatives, management entrepreneurs, many of them lured by the celebrity status of the athletes and the glittering expectations of big business. In light of lawyers' reputed fondness for fame and money, it is perhaps surprising that so few of them also act as sports agents. Statistics indicate that only about five percent of sports agents are lawyers (Meehan, 1987). Yet, so long as agents are allowed to practice without qualification or regulation, the lawyer is, on balance, the athlete's best option, if only because lawyers are required as a condition of practice to uphold the *Rules of Professional Conduct* prescribed and enforced by the profession's governing body, the Law Society, in the province(s) in which they are permitted to practice.

In Ontario, for example, the *Rules of Professional Conduct* are as prescribed by The Law Society of Upper Canada. The Law Society's duty is to regulate the province's 30,000 lawyers in the public interest. Its *Rules* are a comprehensive code, setting concrete, unambiguous standards respecting integrity and honesty as well as competence and quality of service. Lawyers who violate the *Rules* are subject to a wide range of disciplinary actions, including disbarment. The newly revised *Rules* contain this definition of a "competent lawyer":

2.01 (1) In this rule, "competent lawyer" means a lawyer who has and applies relevant skills, attributes, and values in a manner appropriate to each matter undertaken on behalf of a client including:
  (a) Knowing general legal principles and procedures, and the substantive law and procedure for the areas of law in which the lawyer practices;
  (b) Investigating facts, identifying issues, ascertaining client objectives, considering possible options, and developing and

advising the client on appropriate courses of action;
(c) Implementing, as each matter requires, the chosen course of action through the application of appropriate skills including:
　(i) Legal research,
　(ii) Analysis,
　(iii) Application of the law to the relevant facts,
　(iv) Writing and drafting,
　(v) Negotiation,
　(vi) Alternative dispute resolution,
　(vii) Advocacy, and
　(viii) Problem solving ability;
(i) Communicating at all stages of a matter in a timely and effective manner that is appropriate to the age and abilities of the client;
(j) Performing all functions, conscientiously, diligently, and in a timely and cost effective manner;
(k) Applying intellectual capacity, judgement, and deliberation to all functions;
(l) Complying in letter and in spirit with the *Rules of Professional Conduct*;
(m) Recognizing limitations in one's ability to handle a matter, or some aspect of it, and taking steps accordingly to ensure the client is appropriately served;
(n) Managing one's practice effectively;
(o) Pursuing appropriate professional development to maintain and enhance legal knowledge and skills; and
(p) Adapting to changing professional requirements, standards, techniques, and practices.

Agents who are not lawyers are under no such similar obligation to deliver competent services to their clients.

The lawyers' *Rules* also require that lawyers maintain trust accounts and fully disclose their fees and disbursements that must be at once fair and reasonable. Lawyers must also decline to offer advice or to act in any case when there is likely to be a conflict of interest and they must hold in strict confidence all information concerning the business and affairs of the client acquired in the course of the professional relationship. Failure to discharge these solemn obligations to clients can have catastrophic consequences. Lawyers can be sued for professional negligence or, worse, they can be summoned before the Law Society's Discipline Committee and subjected to such sanctions as reprimand, suspension, or disbarment.

The professional standards demanded of lawyers are no guarantee of minimal competence, but in the present circumstances in which young, inexperienced athletes are often prey to unqualified, unscrupulous hucksters, the best advice one can give them on retaining agents is to be cautious, to treat all advances with healthy skepticism, then, following a period of quiet reflection, to seek out the dispassionate counsel of an experienced lawyer for a least a second opinion.

Questions for Class Discussion

1. What do you understand by the terms "natural justice" and "due process"? Why or how are these concepts essential in the context of sport?
2. Debate this proposition: Decisions made by governing bodies in sports and athletics are different from those made in everyday business and commerce; therefore, the protections of natural justice (or due process) and procedural fairness cannot and should not be equally available to athletes as to individuals who are not athletes.
3. Many professional athletic leagues and U.S. college conferences now have random drug testing programs that are designed to discourage the likelihood of drug use by team members. The NCAA testing program, for example, tests college football players and track and field athletes randomly throughout the year, and other sports are tested in-

season during NCAA competition.
   a) Has random drug testing worked in the sense of minimizing drug use among athletes?
   b) Is every form of mandatory drug testing (MDT) unconstitutional? When or under what circumstances, if any, would MDT not violate sections 7 and 8 of the *Canadian Charter of Rights and Freedoms*?
3. How might subsection 5(1) of the Ontario *Human Rights Code* operate to assist an athlete with a drug problem?
4. What qualifications must you have upon graduation to act as a sports agent? Should agents be certified or licensed? If so, by whom?
5. Athletes, especially professional athletes, are often the object of hero-worship. Should this be? If athletes are not to be viewed as heroes, then what about as role models for our youth? If they are role models, should they be held to a higher standard than others in society?
6. Allan Eagleson was for many years the Executive Director of the National Hockey League Players' Association. He was also a lawyer and an agent, representing such players as Bobby Orr. What lessons can be drawn from Eagleson's fall from grace about agents and their obligations to clients?

Endnotes

1. For centuries now in England, Canada and the United States, the decisions of lower or inferior courts and administrative tribunals have been subject to review by higher or superior courts. In Ontario, when someone unhappy with a decision of an administrative tribunal seeks to have that decision reviewed and overturned by a court, he or she makes an application to the court (in Ontario, the Superior Court of Justice: Divisional Court) for judicial review of the decision in question. In Canada and England, when legislative bodies establish an administrative tribunal, it is a common practice of the legislature to include within the statute from which the tribunal derives its authority a privative clause. The intended purpose of the privative clause is to deprive the courts of their traditional supervisory function. The idea is to bring finality to the decision making of the tribunal, so that the tribunal need not worry about courts constantly reviewing and interfering with its actions.

   Privative clauses are of many types and have many different meanings and effects. A so-called "full" privative clause purports to declare not only that the decisions of the tribunal are final but also that they are not subject to review by any court under any circumstances. While the avowed purpose of all privative clauses is to achieve finality for the actions or decisions of the tribunal, in practice no tribunal enjoys an intrinsically unreviewable discretion to act as it pleases. However courts tend to be more deferential to those bodies with full privative clauses in their enabling statutes, reviewing and interfering with only those decisions that the court finds "patently unreasonable."

2. Part I of the *Constitution Act, 1982*, being Schedule B of the *Canada Act, 1982* (U.K.), 1982, c.11.

3. The term "common law" originally meant the law common to the whole of England upon which, of course, much Canadian law is based. Its more usual meaning today is, in the words of Granville Williams, "the law that is not the result of legislation, that is, the law created by the custom of the people and decisions of the judges." See Granville Williams, *Learning the Law* (London: Stevens & Sons Ltd.), 1969, p. 25. The common law is thus to be distinguished from statutory law, the laws made by governments and expressed in statutes.

4. Sections 7 and 8 of the *Charter* are as follows:
   s.7: Everyone has the right to life, liberty and security of the person and the right not be deprived thereof except in accordance with the principles of fundamental justice.
   s.8: Everyone has the right to be secure against unreasonable search or seizure.

5. R.S.O. 1990, c.H. 19.

6. *Toronto Marlboro Major Junior "A" Hockey Club et al. v. Tonelli et al.* (1979), 23 O.R. (2d) 193 (Ont.C.A.); (1978), 18 O.R. (2d) 21 (H.C.J.); (1975), 11 O.R. (2d) 664 (H.C.J.).

References

Kidd, Bruce, and Mary Eberts, *Athletes' Rights in Canada* (Toronto: Ministry of Tourism and Recreation, 1982).

Meehan, Donald E., *"Agents -- Should They Be Carrying the Ball?"* paper presented to Canadian Bar Association — Ontario, Toronto, Ontario, January 16, 1987.

Richards, I. A. *Speculative Instruments* (London: Routledge and Kegan Paul, 1955).

Trossman, Jeff, *"Mandatory Drug Testing in Sports: The Law in Canada"* (1989), 47 Toronto L. Rev. 191

Wade and Forsyth, *Administrative Law*, 7th ed. (Oxford: Clarendon Press, 1994).

CHAPTER 9

MANDATORY DRUG TESTING IN ATHLETICS

Charles Palmer

The Problem

Athletes abuse drugs for two fundamentally different reasons. Some athletes, like other members of our society, use cocaine, marijuana, and alcohol to alter their moods. Other athletes use performance enhancing, ergogenic drugs to better compete.

The problem of performance enhancing (ergogenic) drugs presents different public policy questions from the abuse of mood altering drugs. Athletes run faster, jump higher and perform better, or at least they think they do, when using these drugs. There are rewards and glory for undetected use of performance enhancing drugs. Sport is a competition of athletic performance. The premise is that a combination of innate ability and training causes superior performance. Ergogenic drugs change that premise so that an athlete can win with superior ability, superior training, and/or superior drugs. This new element is overwhelming. Not only may an athlete be rewarded for the use of undetected drugs, many athletes feel that they are compelled to use such drugs in order to keep up with their competition. Thus, Canadian athletes complain because the Canadian Athlete Assistance Program measures an athlete's performance against that of the best athletes in the world. If the best athletes in the world use performance-enhancing drugs because their countries are either lax in enforcement of laws prohibiting those drugs or encourage the use of such drugs, the Canadian athletes may feel compelled to use such drugs.

Anabolic, Androgenic Steroids

The primary performance-enhancing drugs used in sports today are anabolic androgenic steroids. Anabolic means muscle-building, androgenic means masculinizing, and steroids are hormones. These drugs are made by slightly modifying the male hormone, testosterone, so that it can be absorbed by the body and not rapidly degraded by the liver. Anabolic androgenic steroids cause an increase in muscle mass only when given to athletes who train intensively and maintain a high-protein diet.

The performance-enhancing ability of steroids is controversial. It has been shown that moderate doses of anabolic androgenic steroids increase the amount of weight that may be lifted in a single repetition. However, many athletes use larger doses of steroids that are certainly harmful to their health. Scientists are ethically restrained from testing at these larger, commonly used dosages. Even without scientific tests, one can conclude that the known effect of steroids on muscle mass and the increase in human aggressiveness caused by steroids show that these drugs can be performance enhancing. Even if steroids are not performance enhancing, it is important to note that they are perceived to be in the athletic community.

Two-thirds of the positive drug testing disqualifications have been for steroids. Not only are Olympic athletes taking steroids, it also appears that our youth are following their lead. A study of steroid use published in the Journal of the American Medical Association indicated that 6.6 percent of twelfth grade students use or have used steroids. Another study showed use of steroids by 11 percent of eleventh grade students in an Arkansas town. Dr. Robert Huizenga, a former team physician for the Los Angeles Raiders, estimated that a million people use steroids, most of whom are young. He concluded by saying, "I think we have a real time bomb on our hands."

There is no controversy about the harmful effects of steroid use. The detrimental effects of steroids on the liver, the cardiovascular system, the reproductive system, and the user's mental health have all been established.

Amphetamines

Steroids are not the only performance-enhancing drugs. A study of runners, swimmers, and throwers showed a small but noticeable improvement in athletic performance after using amphetamines. These drugs delay the point of fatigue and also facilitate prolonged attention.

Amphetamines are also commonly used in our society as psychoactive, recreational drugs. An Institute of Social Research study on stimulant abuse showed that the percentage of high school seniors who had taken stimulants within the last year was over 9 percent.

Not only are amphetamines performance-enhancing, they also cause serious behavioral and personality changes. They can be addicting. Unlike steroids, amphetamines must be present in the body to stimulate athletic performance. Testing for amphetamines at the time of the athletic event is necessary to detect these drugs.

Diuretics

There are other drugs that are used by athletes. Diuretics are relatively common drugs used in sports such as wrestling, to "make weight." By promoting urine formation, diuretics reduce the concentration of prohibited substances for detection through urinalysis. Although diuretics have beneficial effects, and are medically prescribed for hypertension and congestive heart failure, self-medication by athletes for the competitive purposes must be prohibited. Any drug-testing program should monitor for diuretics.

Human Growth Hormones

Human growth hormones are a relatively recent fad in athletic drug abuse. These drugs are genetically engineered substitutes or supplements for naturally produced growth hormones. Human growth hormones cannot be detected by the technology available in today's drug testing.

Dietary Supplements

Dietary supplements are the new problem in sports. Mark McGwire's use of these supplements in 1998 while chasing the home-run title drew public attention to creatine and androstenedione. Neither of these substances is illegal or controlled by the United States Food and Drug Administration (FDA). In fact, creatine has been advertised in nationally televised baseball games. Creatine sales have increased from $30 million in 1995 to $180 million in 1998. Creatine is an amino acid produced naturally in the body. It is thought to increase energy supplies to the muscles during short duration exercise. It is also expensive, running $20 to $100 per month. One athletic trainer in Riverside, California said, "it works" and often provides an edge to economically advantaged student athletes.

The health risks of creatine are not clear. Dr. Barry Goldberg, Director of Sports Medicine at Yale University says that creatine may have long-term negative effects. "It is being absorbed by muscle cells, and some of those cells are in the cardiac muscle." In addition, the little medical research that has been done shows the effect only of prescribed uses of creatine, but many athletes take considerably more than that level.

Androstenedione (commonly called andro) is an anabolic steroid with many of the harmful side effects of steroids mentioned above. Its sales have increased from $5 million to $100 million annually.

Creatine and androstenedione present special problems for drug testing. First, they must be prohibited. Since these drugs are legal dietary supplements, they are not regulated in the United States by the FDA. Some authority, probably the school and the league, must legally ban these dietary supplements. Second, as a matter of fairness and due process, the athletes should be told that these substances are prohibited. This would be a good opportunity for education about the health effects of dietary supplements and the other drugs discussed in this chapter. Third, school authorities will have to discuss the testing for these substances with the laboratories that test the urine. Since these drugs are not otherwise illegal, the laboratories will not be testing for these substances. Androstenedione will probably present many of the same drug testing problems presented by steroids.

Cocaine and Marijuana

The testing of athletes for the use of cocaine and marijuana will always be controversial. These drugs do not appear to have any performance-enhancing attributes. Systematic medical testing of cocaine is obviously not possible, but anecdotal evidence indicates that cocaine abuse interferes with athletic performance. Both Tim Raines of baseball's Montreal Expos and Lonnie Smith of the Atlanta Braves reported that cocaine abuse interfered with their ability to play baseball.

Marijuana negatively affects essential athletic skills such as hand-eye coordination, perceptual accuracy, reaction time, and tracking accuracy. Athletes thus have a reason to avoid cocaine and marijuana abuse. It appears that they do avoid these drugs. A study of varsity athletes at eleven NCAA colleges found that athletes were substantially less likely to use marijuana and cocaine than the general population of college students.

Testing athletes for marijuana and cocaine abuse is generally justified, if at all, for two reasons. First, athletes are leaders and idols who many people emulate. Discouraging drug abuse in this class of leaders may have an impact upon drug abuse in general. However, we do not drug test all of our leaders. Prime ministers, presidents, members of parliament, and other community leaders are not subject to drug testing.

Secondly, athletes participate in activities that are dangerous if the participant is impaired by drug abuse. The United States Supreme Court considered this an important factor in approving drug testing of athletes in *Veronia School District v. Acton*, 515 U.S. 646, 115 S.Ct. 2386, 132 L. Ed. 2d 564 (1995). However, it must be remembered that urinalysis does not determine the extent or time of drug abuse. Urinalysis only tests whether the subject has used drugs in the past. Although cocaine and marijuana abuse may be dangerous prior to certain types of athletic competition, urinalysis does not determine how dangerous.

Preventing Drug Abuse in Sports

The existence of fair and equal athletic competition is, undoubtedly, threatened by steroids and performance-enhancing drugs. Not only do these performance-enhancers represent cheating but also the widespread interest and support for athletic competition will be undermined if it is thought to encourage harmful drug abuse. The first defense against drug abuse is education. However, the ability of education to slow steroid abuse is questionable. Any discussion of steroid use must include not only the long-term harmful effects of steroids but also the short-term performance-enhancing effects as well as the ethical implications of their proliferation. Many athletes are willing to accept harmful long-term health effects in return for immediate athletic success. A group of athletes at the Los Angeles Olympic Games were asked if they would be willing to take a special pill that would guarantee them an Olympic gold medal even if they knew this pill would kill them within a year. Over 50 percent of the athletes surveyed said "yes." While education is essential in changing values in athletic competition, it is not going to solve the problem in the short run.

Athletics will also be affected by society's fight against mood altering drugs. Athletic competition is not a required part of high school or college courses. School officials who see athletes as role models in their schools may condition participation in athletics on the athlete's drug free status. Drug testing may often be imposed on this part of the student body simply because they are visible and more easily tested.

In the Short Run – Drug Testing

In the short run, drug testing will be used to deter the use of drugs. Drug testing by urinalysis has been the preferred method of detecting illegal drug use in sports. Urine testing has been used because it is easier, less expensive, and less invasive of personal privacy than obtaining other body substances. Urinalysis was first used in sports in 1965 to detect the presence of drugs in three cyclists at the Tour of Britain cycle races. It was first used in the Olympics in Munich in 1972. Its most famous use was in the 1988 Olympic Games when Canadian Ben Johnson tested positive for drug abuse after winning the gold medal in the 100-meter sprint. While urinalysis has the potential to identify drug users, it also has substantial difficulties. It is highly invasive of individual privacy. Urinating is one of the most private acts in our culture. Public urination is illegal in most jurisdictions. Society pays a high price when the government intrudes upon this very private act.

Urinalysis has other drawbacks. Although the gas chromatography-mass spectrometry testing technology is accurate, scientific testing methods depend upon human administration that is always fallible. The chain of custody of the urine specimen from the donor to the laboratory will always be subject to error. The possibility that the urine donor will tamper with the specimen by taking masking drugs or by adulterating the urine sample is always possible. Finally, one must consider the effects of a positive drug test on the person being tested. The information should be used to provide drug counseling, but will there also be unauthorized disclosure of positive results to people who have no need to know?

When drug testing occurs in the public sector, the law will require that it be reasonable. Determining whether the advantages of a particular drug testing program outweigh the disadvantages requires a balancing of the tester's interest in the search, or who they represent, against the interests of the individual being tested. The tester's interest can be divided into two parts: the harm the tester is trying to prevent and the probability that the harm will occur or be detected. The severity of the harm depends upon the particular drug being used (see above) and the value judgment of society about the abuse of that drug. The probability of harm (drug abuse) is more problematic.

The United States Supreme Court faced the issue of drug testing of athletes in public schools in *Veronia School District v. Acton* 515U.S.646 (1995). This case, once again, held that the ultimate test of the constitutionality of a government search is its "reasonableness" (p. 651). This process involves the balancing of the intrusion of the individual's privacy against the promotion of legitimate governmental interests (p. 651). The balancing done in *Veronia Schools* is helpful in analyzing how a school should structure a drug-testing program.

The *Veronia* case reveals a great deal about the nature of the government interest necessary to justify random drug testing.

1. The term "compelling state interest" does not establish a "minimum quantum of governmental concern" (p. 659). In fact, there is "no minimum quantum of governmental concern." There only has to be an amount of government interest sufficient to justify the particular search in question.
2. The government does not have to show any abuse of performance enhancing drugs among athletes.
3. The government does not have to show that drug abuse is greater among athletes than among other students. In *Veronia* the district court found that certain athletes may have been injured as a result of drug abuse but there was no showing that athletes were more likely to use drugs than other students.
4. The government does have to show some increased use of illegal or prohibited drugs in the student body. Since this evidence of drug abuse will be used to justify drug testing, it will probably be anecdotal evidence of drug use or possession in school.

In *Veronia* the teachers and administrators had observed "a sharp increase in drug use" (p.647). With some testimony of illegal drug use, the Supreme Court seems to be willing to supply the rest of the findings necessary to show important governmental interest. The Court in *Veronia* found that: (1) athletes were leaders and role models; (2) drug use increases the risk of injury in sports; and, (3) the addictive effects of drugs are more severe for children. Thus, it appears that if a school district can show definite drug use in the student body of a school, the court is armed with enough other permissible factual inferences to support a finding of a government interest sufficient to justify random drug testing.

The Veronia School District drug testing policy, because it has been reviewed and approved by the United

States Supreme Court, will probably become the model for drug testing policies, at least in the United States. It is worthwhile, then, to review the Veronia policy and its implications.

1. The Policy applied to all student athletes. It was a random drug-testing program. When particular students or particular student groups are tested, the drug testing loses its random nature. If students are not selected at random but picked out for particular reasons then individualized suspicion will be necessary.
2. Students athletes and their parents were required to sign a consent form for urine testing before participating in interscholastic sports.
3. All athletes were tested at the start of their season and 10% of the athletes were selected on a completely random basis for testing each week. Again, it is important that the athletes to be tested are selected on a random basis. A student with two adults selected the names to be tested by blind draw.
4. The student to be tested filled out a specimen control form that had an assigned number, which was presumably placed, on the specimen bottle. This is obviously a critical part of the process. The integrity of the process depends upon filling out this information correctly. It may be prudent to require the supervising adult to verify this information and its accuracy with the student.
5. The student to be tested went into an empty locker room with an adult monitor of the same sex. Boys and girls were treated differently at this point. Some parents may object to this. Girls went into an enclosed bathroom stall where they could be heard but not seen. Boys went to a urinal, facing away from the monitor, and produced the sample. The student then handed the sample to the monitor who checked it for temperature and then transferred the specimen to a vial.

    The production of the urine specimen is obviously the point of maximum invasion of privacy. This is also the point where the student who knows that he or she has recently used prohibited drugs will be tempted to cheat. The policy of the Veronia Schools does not require exposure of the students' private parts to the monitor. This lessens intrusion on privacy but also provides an opportunity for cheating. Military regulations generally require the monitor to observe urine flow into the specimen bottle. Each school should consider the mechanics of urine collection but the system used by the Veronia Schools provides the advantage of having been specifically approved by the United States Supreme Court.

6. Each sample was tested for amphetamines, cocaine, and marijuana. Some were also tested for LSD. However, most importantly, the identity of a student did not affect which drugs would be tested. Any variance from these standardized testing procedures will run the risk of a court saying this is not random testing but testing based upon suspicion which would require probable cause.
7. The drug-testing laboratory for the Veronia Schools was 99.94% accurate. The accuracy of the laboratory will not only be scrutinized by the court but also the parents and students to be tested. Accuracy is essential.
8. The Veronia School District also required strict procedures for the chain of custody. This may require a professional testing service to administer the test. Coaches and teachers charged with this responsibility for the first time, during the athletic season when they have many other responsibilities, and often without specific training about how to administer the test are bound to make mistakes. More experienced, professional testers will almost certainly do a better, more accurate job.
9. The test results were only released to the superintendent, principals, vice-principals, and the athletic directors. The fewer the better. The more people who have access to the test results, the greater the invasion of privacy.
10. If the first test was positive for prohibited drugs, then a second test was administered.

This was the procedure for the Veronia Schools and approved by the Supreme Court. However, the second test may undermine the whole testing process. Cocaine clears the system fairly quickly. By the time the first sample is tested and the results returned to the school authorities, the original cocaine will almost certainly be flushed from the student's body. The second test will catch continuing cocaine abuse but the student who presumably understood that they have been caught the first time, and will soon be tested a second time, will probably not use cocaine again. Nothing about the reasoning in *Veronia School District v. Acton* would require this second test. It is a cautious rule but may undermine the whole procedural effectiveness.

11. If the second test was positive, then the student's parents were notified and a meeting took place among the student, parent, and the school official. Administrative, but not punitive, measures were then taken. The student was required to participate in an assistance program or be suspended from athletic competition for the remainder of the current season and the next season. Subsequent positive tests were dealt with more severely.

    The administrative, remedial response to positive drug tests is essential to the legal analysis of the case. The United States Supreme Court has distinguished between (a) non-punitive, remedial, administrative searches and (b) punitive, criminal law searches. The analysis in the *Veronia School District* case was based upon the search being an administrative, remedial search.

12. One aspect of the search in *Veronia School District* definitely gave the Supreme Court second thoughts. At some point during the drug testing process, the tester must determine what prescription drugs are being taken by the subject. The subject may have a prescription for drugs that may look like prohibited substances on drug tests. The tester can ask the subject about prescription drugs before the test as the *Veronia School District* did. This requires the subject of the testing to disclose this information before receiving a positive test and having a motive to fabricate this information. On the other hand, this procedure requires the school to gather confidential, health care information about every student athlete, a large invasion of privacy. The Supreme Court in *Veronia School District v. Acton* (p. 659) speculated that the School district may have allowed the subject of the testing to provide the information in a sealed envelope delivered to the testing laboratory. The school could also gather the prescription information after the first positive test but before the second test in the Veronia School District two-test procedure. The school could also gather the prescription information after the laboratory results in a single test procedure.

    The process of mandating teachers to gather prescription information from every student on their team in anticipation of drug testing should be discouraged. School districts should minimize the invasion of privacy in drug testing and should, therefore, develop a procedure that will keep this prescription information confidential.

The reception of athletic drug testing in United States state courts has been different to that of the federal courts. Some of the state courts, in interpreting their laws and state constitutions, have determined that the intrusiveness of drug testing outweighs the benefits. They have required some evidence that athletes (the targeted class) had previously used drugs. Thus, the New Jersey Supreme Court found that analyzing urine for controlled substances was unreasonable because "[t]he raw numbers and percentages of students referred to student counseling as compared with the total student body is not reasonably related in scope to the circumstances which justified the interference, urinalysis, in the first place." *Odenheim v. Carlstadt-East Rutherford Regional School District 211*, N.J. Super. 54, 510 A.2d 709, 713 (1985).

There seems to be two conflicting lines of cases in drug testing. The United States Supreme Court have approved drug testing even without evidence of previous drug abuse in the targeted class of athletes to be tested. The state courts have looked to the targeted class of athletes to be tested to see whether there is evidence of previous drug use. If not, the state courts have generally not approved drug testing.

There is another fundamental difference about drug testing in sports. According to Dubin, *Commission of Inquiry into the Use of Drugs and Banned Practices Intended to Increase Athletic Performance,* "[t]he overwhelming majority of athletes not only agree to be tested but consider testing to be protection against unfair competition by others and proof that they themselves obey the rules." In the Canadian criminal case dealing with drug testing, *Re Dion and the Queen,* 30 C.C.C. (3d) 108 (1986), the Canadian Supreme Court looked into "to what extent does [drug testing] limit that exercise of the right by a citizen who does not commit the evil that is sought to be avoided?" The athlete who is clean must submit to the embarrassment and the assault on the athlete's integrity caused by mandatory drug testing. On the other hand, the clean athlete is benefited from the knowledge that his or her competitors have also been tested for drugs. The athlete will not have to take drugs in order to compete.

Drug testing in the private sector is not restrained by the United States Constitution or the Canadian Charter of Rights and Freedoms. Although particular aspects of drug testing may still be regulated by state, province or federal laws, the primary control of drug testing will come from union-negotiated collective bargaining agreements. One must also consider tort law and its relation to drug testing. Causes of action for negligence, defamation, invasion of privacy, and intentional infliction of emotional distress, as well as the contract action for wrongful discharge are important.

Conclusion

Mandatory drug testing will always be controversial. It should be. The invasion of personal privacy should never be undertaken lightly. Nevertheless, we cannot ignore the threat of drugs in sports. It is always easier to resolve these difficult competing interests with dogmatic positions either totally prohibiting drug testing or allowing it in all situations. Although these positions provide a clear resolution of the controversy, they avoid the courts' responsibility to weigh the competing interests in each situation or case. The controversy regarding drug testing will have to be resolved in that manner, i.e., on a case-by-case analysis of each situation.

Questions for Class Discussion

1. When, if ever, should athletes who have no previous history of drug abuse be tested for drugs?
2. Why would a drug-testing program require direct observation of urination? Is that a good idea? Does direct observation of urination affect the legality of the drug-testing program?
3. Would a drug-testing program for anabolic steroids be easier to justify that a testing program for marijuana? Explain.
4. If it is determined that anabolic, androgenic steroids do not enhance sports performance, would testing for these substances then be unreasonable?
5. Would the obtaining and testing of blood for the presence of drugs be less or more intrusive of privacy than the obtaining and testing of urine? How would this affect the legality of drug testing?
6. Do you agree with the United States Supreme Court that the testing procedure in the Veronia School District was reasonable?

References

Alzado, Lyle. (1991, July). I'm sick and I'm scared. *Sports Illustrated.* 23.

Anderson, William et al. (1991). A national survey of alcohol and drug use by college athletes. *Physicians and Sports Medicine, 19*(2), 101.

American College of Sports Medicine (1987). The use of anabolic-androgenic steroids in sports. *Medicine, Science, Sports Exercise, 19,* 534.

Beckett, A.H. & Cowan, D.A. (1979). Misuse of drugs in sports. *British Journal of Sports Medicine, 12,* 185.

Blakeslee, S. (1988, July 13). Drug cheaters are growing smarter. *New York Times*, p. A23

Buckley, William E. (1988). Estimated prevalence of anabolic steroid use among male high school seniors. *Journal of the American Medical Association, 260*, 3442.

Canadian Bar Association (1987). *Report on mandatory drug testing* (July). Ottawa: Author.

Chass, M. (1985, August 20). Cocaine disrupts baseball from field to front office. *New York Times*.

Colwell, W. B. (1999, March). Beyond Veronia: When has a school district drug testing policy gone too far? 131 Ed. Law Rep 547

Dubin, Honourable Charles L. (1991). *Commission of inquiry into the use of drugs and banned practices intended to increase athletic performance*. Ottawa: Ministry of Supply and Services Canada.

Gibeaut, J. (1998, May). Seeking substances 84 *May A.B.A.J.* 42

Harvard Law Review. (1999, January). Constitutional Law — Fourth Amendment — Seventh circuit holds that random suspicionless drug testing of participants in extracurricular activities does not violate the Fourth Amendment - *Todd v. Rush County Schools* 133 F 3d 984 (7th Cri.), Cert. Denied, 119S.Ct68 (1998) 112 Harv. L. Rev. 713

Johnson, M. (1989, June). Anabolic steroid use by male adolescents. *Pediatrics, 83*(6), 921.

Johnson, W. D. & Moore, K. (1988, October 3). The loser. *Sports Illustrated*, 20.

Palmer, C. A. (1992, Spring). Drugs vs. privacy: The new game in sports. *Marquette Sports Law Journal, 2*(2), 175.

Shepherd, Jr., R. E. (1998). School searches after T.L.O. and Veronia School District 15GP Solo & Small Firm Law. 34 and 13SUM Crim. Just 45.

Smith, G. M. & Beecher, H. K. (1959). Amphetamine sulfate and athletic performance: Objective effects. *Journal of the American Medical Association, 170*, 542.

Trossman, J. (1988, Fall). Mandatory drug testing in sports: The law in Canada. *University of Toronto Law Review, 14*, 191.

Wadler, G. & Hainline, B. (1989). *Drugs and the Athlete*.

University of Michigan Institute for Social Research (Jan. 24, 1991). *Monitoring the Future: A Continuing Study of the Lifestyles and Values of Youth*.

CHAPTER 10

GENDER EQUITY IN SPORT BY LEGISLATION AND LITIGATION

Margery Holman

Sport is a reflection of society and, in many respects, society is a reflection of sport. This opens the door for each to be influenced by the other. Because of the high profile given to sport in North American society, gains made within the various sport structures created in education and the community will impact upon the image of society. However, sport has been slow to respond to changes in equity realized in other segments of society. This is partly due to the influence of a professional athletic model that is structured on an androcentric, capitalist, patriarchal model. This model is resistant to change, particularly resistant to the infusion of females.

One mechanism for overcoming this resistance is the law. Until recently, sport has been viewed as a sub-culture existing above or outside of society and the laws that govern. Sport has functioned as its own judge and jury, with norms and values that are acceptably different from those imposed upon society as a whole. An example of this is the tolerance and self-regulation that sport maintains for the violence in sports such as hockey and soccer, where behaviors are often exhibited that could lead to assault charges in a non-sport milieu.

In spite of modest gains by females in sport and physical activity, equity remains somewhat distant. Participation rates are consistently higher for males than females; leadership roles, such as coaching, officiating and administration, continue to be dominated by males; females are at greater risk of sexual harassment and sexual imposition than males; professional or other career opportunities are greater for males than for females; and, media recognition continues to be greater for males than for females.

This chapter will provide a brief history of legislative influence on the traditional decision making and actions within a sport environment. It will update the growth of female sport participation rates as well as the social climate that erects barriers to full and equal participation of females in sport. In the process, it will provide case examples that have employed legislation and litigation for the purpose of achieving gender equity in sport.[1]

Understanding Equity and the Law

Law

In the comparison of the Canadian and American sport systems, the historical development of opportunities for women have been very different. The educational system provides an example of this difference. Traditionally the Canadian system has incorporated school sport programs as co-curricular and vital to the overall experience of student life for both females and males. In contrast, the American system, with the exclusion of NCAA Division III schools, has viewed sport as ancillary to the core curriculum. This has resulted in a quasi-professional approach dependent upon extrinsic values and rewards, a capitalistic approach that has proved to better serve male athletic endeavors. These differences have influenced the legal response to strategies for the achievement of gender equity in sport.

Equity and Canadian Law

Canadian law, applied to gender equity in sport, falls within legislation that applies to all segments of society. Federally, the Canadian Charter of Rights and Freedoms and the Canadian Human Rights Act, and provincially, the Human Rights legislation specific to each province or territory within Canada address equity. This legislation demonstrates a short history of support for equal treatment of individuals based upon sex. For example, in 1962, the enactment of the Ontario Human Rights Code provided the first comprehensive step in protection against discrimination. In 1982, the Canadian Charter of Rights provided legislation at a federal level to parallel the objectives of earlier provincial legislation.

Canadian Charter of Rights and Freedoms

The Canadian Charter of Rights and Freedoms was incorporated into the Constitution of Canada in 1982. This legislation provides a source of protection from discrimination in sport, including gender discrimination. The significant sections of the charter are as follows:

> Section 1: The *Canadian Charter of Rights and Freedoms* guarantees the rights and freedoms set out in it subject only to such reasonable limits prescribed by law as can be demonstrably justified in a free and democratic society.

This section determines that there are limits on the rights of individuals. However, it declares that when limits are applied they must be "reasonable, prescribed by law, demonstrably justified, and in keeping with the standards of a free and democratic society" (Canadian Council on Social Development, 1987, p.10). By proving that one or a combination of these criteria apply an action may be justified. Complainants must influence the interpretation of these criteria to argue their particular disadvantage.

> Section 15. (1): Every individual is equal before and under the law and has the right to the equal protection and equal benefit of the law without discrimination and, in particular, without discrimination based on race, national or ethnic origin, colour, religion, sex, age or mental or physical disability.
>
> Section 15 (2): Subsection (1) does not preclude any law, program or activity that has as its object the amelioration of conditions of disadvantaged individuals or groups including those that are disadvantaged because of race, national or ethnic origin, colour, religion, sex, age or mental or physical disability.

This section may be the most relevant clause in the Constitution to deal with equality rights. It is the protection that individuals be treated equally by laws or government programs, it allows an option by which systemic discrimination can be addressed, and it validates affirmative action as a strategy for redressing conditions of the disadvantaged.

> Section 28: Notwithstanding anything in this Charter, the rights and freedoms referred to in it are guaranteed equally to male and female persons.

This section clearly states that the rights and freedoms included in the Charter of all individuals, both females and males, are protected by the Charter.

> Section 32(1): This Charter applies a) to the Parliament and government of Canada in respect of all matters within the authority of Parliament ... b) to the legislature and government of each province in respect of all matters within the authority of the legislature of each province.

Charter legislation rarely applies to situations that fall outside the jurisdiction of government authority. This creates a limitation in its value for ensuring equal treatment in the public sector that may be minimal in most instances and may have detrimental implications for sport equity.

Challenging the Ontario Human Rights Code

The belief that sport was a special environment to be treated differently than society as a whole was reflected in the legislative content of the Ontario Code. The original document included a now well-known clause within Section 19(2), which provided that:

> ... the right under Section 1 of the Code to equal treatment without discrimination is not infringed where membership in an athletic organization or participation in an athletic activity is restricted to persons of the same sex.

A landmark case challenged this exemption for athletic organizations from the Ontario Human Rights Code. In *Blainey v. Ontario Hockey Association* (1986),[2] Justine Blainey, a 12-year-old hockey player, earned a position during tryouts for the Etobicoke Canucks but was denied the opportunity to play. The Metropolitan Toronto Hockey League, a member of the parent body Ontario Hockey Association (OHA), ruled against Blainey's eligibility to play on the boys' team based upon their restricted integration policy.

This policy allows a female to play on a male team only when there are no all-female teams available within the geographical area. Although there was an all-female team in the area administered by the Ontario Women's Hockey Association (OWHA), Justine preferred an all-male team because the boys' teams got more practice time at better hours, the competition was better, and the rules permitted body checking. In addition, she wished to play on the same team with her brother, David. Justine was an excellent defensive hockey player, who was sought after by one "A" level team and two "AA" level teams.

During the pleading of this case, the usual arguments were presented:

1. Justine Blainey had the right to play under Section A of the Human Rights Code and Section 15(1) of the Charter of Rights and Freedoms.
2. Justine Blainey had the ability to play in the Metro Toronto Hockey League, permission was not being sought to try out and she already had been selected by coaches of three teams.
3. Justine Blainey had signed a letter of commitment and it was the MTHL who was refusing a card on the basis of Rule 250 of the OHA, which prohibits mixed teams except where the restricted integration rule came into effect.
4. Sport administration in Canada and the national Canadian Amateur Hockey Association (CAHA), provincial OHA and their agents (MTHL) were wrongly denying her an opportunity to participate in hockey.

On behalf of the OWHA/OHA/MTHL, and other defendants, the following arguments were put forward:

1. The Ontario Women's Hockey Association (OWHA) was responsible for providing hockey competition for women and they strongly opposed the transfer of Justine Blainey to a boys' team, as they felt it would be destructive to women's programs.
2. It was maintained that a woman was not capable of playing hockey in the MTHL, which to a certain extent contradicted their first argument.
3. It was maintained that the Ontario Women's Hockey Association provided superior training to the Metro Toronto Hockey League.
4. They maintained that weaker effeminate boys would flood into women's programs if girls were allowed to play in boys' leagues.
5. They felt that boys would not accept a girl participating in a boys' league and that this would lead to a decline in morale.
6. They cited problems in terms of injury, dressing rooms and loss of volunteers.
7. They argued that women are weaker than men.

Both the complainant and the respondent agreed on several major points: they both wanted equity; they both agreed that females had not had equal opportunity in the past; and, they both wanted to encourage females and female programs in the sport area.

In the end, the decision of the Supreme Court of Ontario was in favour of the complainant, Justine Blainey. Anna Fraser, Blainey's lawyer, maintains that the decision turned on two major points, medical evidence and the implementation of Section 15(1) equality rights of the Charter of Rights and Freedoms. The Ontario Human Rights commission awarded Justine Blainey $3,000 in December 1987 for mental anguish and lost opportunity. A further outcome of this case has been the promotion of affirmative action within sport. A Human Rights Board stated that, while boys' hockey can accommodate qualified female players without damaging their programs, girls' hockey needs a special status to compensate for past inequities.

> The evidence clearly establishes that, as a group, females in this province do not have the same opportunities as males to play organized competitive hockey. Female hockey must continually struggle against the view that hockey is a male only sport. It must also struggle for access to ice time ... OWHA teams can continue to refuse to admit males (Canadian Human Rights Advocate, 1988).

This allows the OWHA to qualify as a special program under Section 13(1) of the Ontario Human Rights Code, which states:

> A right under Part I is not infringed by the implementation of a special program designed to relieve hardship or economic disadvantage or to assist disadvantaged persons or groups to achieve or attempt to achieve equal opportunity or that is likely to contribute to the elimination of the infringement of rights under Part I.

Equity and American Law

The major impetus for increased opportunity in sport and physical activity for American girls and women has come through the educational system. American legislation affecting females in educational sport was introduced in 1972 with the passing of Title IX of the Educational Amendment Act. This states that:

> No person in the United States shall, on the basis of sex, be excluded from participation in, be denied the benefits of, or be subjected to discrimination under any education program or activity receiving Federal financial assistance.

This legislation is further reinforced by the Equal Protection Clause of the fourteenth Amendment, which states that:

> Equality of rights under the law shall not be denied or abridged by the United States or any state on account of sex.

As Title IX legislation was being considered, an organization called the Association for Intercollegiate Athletics for Women (AIAW) was founded with the purpose of governing interuniversity sport for women. In spite of a growing membership, an increase in the number of females competing and an increase in the number of female championships, the National Collegiate Athletic Association (NCAA) began to sponsor national championships for women. Unable to compete with the resources of the NCAA, the AIAW began to loose members to the NCAA. In one last effort to protect their status, the AIAW filed suit against the NCAA, citing antitrust violations. "The D.C. Circuit Court of Appeals, however, rejected AIAW's allegations of the NCAA being a monopoly and violating the Sherman Antitrust Act" (Miguel, 1994, p. 281). By 1984, the AIAW ceased to exist.

Concurrently, the debate over the jurisdiction of Title IX legislation began (Wilde, 1994). Resistance from the NCAA to legislation that required gender equity in athletics was demonstrated in the attempts made to declare themselves exempt from the legislation. Athletic departments claimed a programmatic approach, declaring that Title IX applied only to those programs that received direct federal funding. Since most athletic departments did not, they deemed themselves exempt from compliance with Title IX regulations. In contrast, advocates for gender equity in sport interpreted Title IX with an institutional approach, requiring that all programs comply with the legislation when their institution was in receipt of federal funds.

This issue had to be resolved within the courts. In 1984, a Supreme Court judgment in *Grove City v. Bell*[3] determined that Title IX applied only to those programs that received direct federal funds. This essentially liberated most athletic departments from any responsibility to comply with the regulations outlined in Title IX. This decision threatened any growth in women's programs that had been experienced since the enactment of Title IX.

Immediately, action was taken to introduce amendments that would reverse the *Grove City v. Bell* decision and apply Title IX legislation from an institutional approach. In 1987, Congress was successful enacting the Civil Rights Restoration Act,[4] overriding a veto by President Ronald Regan. This restored the power of Title IX that required athletic departments to comply with legislation prohibiting gender discrimination.

In spite of the Civil Rights Restoration Act, implementation of Title IX has been heavily debated. Through its evolution to date, a three-pronged test has been developed to determine whether or not an athletic department is in compliance. Proportionality has become the cornerstone of this test. The three-prong test questions:

1. Whether the ratio of male and female intercollegiate athletes is substantially proportionate to the ratio of male and female students enrolled in the institution;
2. Where women have been and are under represented among college athletes, whether the school can show a history and continuing practice of expanding programs and opportunities for women to participate which is responsive to the developing interests and abilities of women; and,
3. Where women are under represented and the institution cannot show a history of program expansion, whether the school can demonstrate that the interests and abilities of women have been fully and effectively accommodated by the current athletic program.

A 1992 case, *Franklin v. Gwinnett County Public Schools*,[5] is a landmark case because it was "the first Title IX case where the court explicitly stated that compensatory damages constitute an available remedy for victims of gender discrimination having claims grounded in Title IX" (Miguel, 1994, p. 282). This case involved a high school female who was sexually harassed and assaulted by her coach and teacher. Franklin brought a case under Title IX which was dismissed by the District Court on the grounds that Title IX does not authorize award of damages, which was affirmed by the Court of Appeals (*Sport and the Courts, 13*(1): 7). The Supreme Court, however, granted *certiorari* to review the case.

The Court noted that all appropriate remedies were available unless expressly indicated otherwise and pointed out that at the time Title IX was passed (1972), denial of a remedy was an exception. The school board arguments that (1) award of damages would violate separation of powers, (2) awards were denied for unintentional violations and this should extend to intentional violations, and (3) award by precedent should include back pay only, were countered by the Court which maintained that (1) award of appropriate relief would not involve increase of judicial power and indeed would be a safeguard against abuse of legislative and executive power, (2) those entities receiving federal funds are responsible for intended violations and (3) limiting to back pay would leave Franklin without relief, since she was a student. The Court of Appeal judgment of the case was reversed and the case was returned to the lower court for assessment of damages.

More recently, the salaries of coaches of women's teams and response to retaliation for advocacy of equity for women's programs have become matters for litigation. Both Title VII of the Civil Rights Act of 1964 and the Equal Pay Act (EPA) of 1963 have become tools, along with Title IX, by which decisions have been delivered. "Title VII of the Civil Rights Act of 1964 prohibits employers from refusing to hire or discharge or otherwise discriminate against any individual with respect to compensation, terms, conditions or privileges of employment because of the person's sex (42 United States Code Annotated 703[a]). Employers are forbidden to classify applicants or employees in any way that would tend to deprive the individual of employment opportunities because of their sex (42 United States Code Annotated 703 [b]). Under the Equal Pay Act (EPA), an employer is prohibited from paying an employee in the same establishment at a lessor rate than that at which he/she pays employees of the opposite sex where the work is equal (Clement, 1998, p. 136).

Organizational Policy

An organization or institution can express their commitment to gender equity through the incorporation of policy that guides decision making. Such a policy contributes to the provision of fair access to programs and associated benefits.

Canadian University Athletics

On the Canadian university scene, a pattern has evolved that reflects trends seen elsewhere. The Canadian Interuniversity Athletic Union (CIAU) expressed concern for limited female involvement in Canadian interuniversity sport, particularly at an administrative level (CIAU, 1992). In June 1980, the CIAU supported the following motion:

> Whereas the CIAU is committed to the development and promotion of interuniversity sport, and WHEREAS there is evidence to suggest that the absence of representatives from decision making bodies has a detrimental effect on the programs and policies of those groups not represented, and WHEREAS the CIAU Board of Directors has instructed the Constitution Committee to consider legislation to encourage greater female representation at the annual general meetings of the CIAU, BE IT RESOLVED that an Ad Hoc committee of the CIAU be struck to prepare a comparative report on Canadian Women's Intercollegiate programs (CIAU AGM Minutes, 1980).

The results of this ongoing study (1982, 1986, 1990, 1992) revealed that the opportunities for males were greater at every organizational level — athlete, coach, assistant coach, athletic therapist, sport information director, administrator, and program. Following the 1986 report, in an attempt to increase the ratio of female to male administrators and voting delegates at the annual general meeting, the CIAU membership passed the motion that:

> Members shall appoint one or two persons as delegates to meetings of the General Assembly; if two persons are appointed as delegates, one shall be male and one shall be female.

Ontario University Athletics

In Ontario, the Council of Ontario Universities (COU) comprised of university presidents, commissioned a report on interuniversity athletics known as the Rickerd Report. From the recommendations put forward in this report, the COU established a commission entitled "Ontario Commission on Interuniversity Athletics." This commission would oversee critical issues in the Ontario Women's Intercollegiate Athletic Association and the Ontario Universities Athletic Association (see Note). The Commission developed a position paper on "Gender Equality in Interuniversity Athletics" that outlined a number of recommendations.

1. That each member institution review the opportunities for female student athletes on its campus, and develop a five-year plan to ensure gender equality in interuniversity athletics by 1993;
2. That each member institution develop an affirmative action program aimed at increasing the percentage of female coaches of women's teams;
3. That each member institution forward copies of its gender equality plan and affirmative action program to the Commission by June 3, 1988; and
4. That the interuniversity leagues, the OUAA and OWIAA, work together to develop a plan so that the small minority of institutions already participating in the maximum number of sorts offered by the two leagues may be able to achieve equality by 1993 and that they forward a copy of this plan to the Commission by June 3, 1988.

Initiatives were also taken on individual campuses over the years. For example, the University of Windsor's Department of Athletics and Recreational Services passed the motions that:

1. In the appointment of coaches for women's interuniversity teams, every effort be made for the recruitment and hiring of a female coach; and,
2. In the appointment of assistant coaches every effort be made for the recruitment and hiring of a female for any women's interuniversity teams having a male as head coach.

Overall, there has been some progress in providing opportunities for girls and women. However, equity is far from being achieved. While a policy is a critical first step in the process, there must be ongoing monitoring, evaluation and revision to ensure that decision-makers are held accountable and progress continues. Policy failure is often a predecessor to legal action.

Participation

The university systems in both Canada and the United States have been a focal point for monitoring the participation rates of females as athletes, coaches and administrators. In both cases, the opportunities for females as athletes has increased, and particularly so for females in American universities. Prior to the enactment of Title IX, there were approximately 2.5 sports offered for females (Wilde, 1994). Statistics reveal that " ... in 1977-78, the academic year just before the Title IX mandatory compliance date, the number of sports offered women was 5.61 per school. In 1988 the number had grown to 7.31 and in 1996 to 7.53 ... In 1998, the number of teams per school is 7.71 ... " (Acosta and Carpenter, 1998, p. 3). This increase has translated into females representing approximately one third of university athletes. The participation rate of females in Canadian institutions is similar. However, not all programs yet meet the requirements of Title IX in the United States or legislative expectations in Canada.

Celebration of the gains that girls and women have made to date includes recognition of role of the legal process. Many of the gains had to be fought for through the courts. Cases have identified the diversity of the challenges that advocates of female programs have faced.

Legitimacy of Dropping a Team

The federal district court heard arguments in *Favia v. Indiana University of Pennsylvania* (1993).[6] In this case, the athletic department decided to terminate funding for men's soccer and tennis and women's gymnastics and field hockey due to budgetary restraints. Each of these teams would be allowed to continue on a club basis. The court ruled in favour of the plaintiffs after applying the three-prong test. The court found that the athletic opportunities offered to women was disproportionate to the representation of female students enrolled at IUP, that IUP did not show a history of expanding its women's programs and that program growth did not reflect the increasing interest of the female student population (Miguel, 1994; Wilde, 1994).

Attempts to reach compliance with Title IX legislation has resulted in the implementation of different strategies. One of these is to reduce male participation to reach equity goals instead of increasing female participation. This is the basis of the complaint in *Harper v. Board of Regents, Illinois State University*.[7] Students at the university filed suit against the university, challenging its elimination of the men's intercollegiate soccer and wrestling programs. The plaintiffs prevailed when the courts held that the justification of proportionality was allowable and that the minor reduction of male participation was insignificant.

Appeal for Program Growth

In a prominent case seeking more equitable status with the men's program, Colgate University,[8] on September 28, 1992, was found to be in violation of Title IX with respect to their women's ice hockey team. This team existed with club status and had, on occasion, requested varsity status and was turned down. It was found in the court hearing that Colgate denied the women's ice hockey players equal opportunities and ordered Colgate to grant the team varsity status and to provide the associated support. Colgate University sponsors a men's varsity hockey team.

In their defense, Colgate argued that the entire program should be examined to determine whether or not discrimination occurred, rather than looking at a specific sport. The court rejected this argument, claiming that the purpose of Title IX is to protect individuals as well as a group of individuals.

Further, Colgate proposed the following reasons for denying varsity status to the women's ice hockey team:

1. Women's ice hockey rarely is played at the secondary school level;
2. The NCAA does not sponsor a women's ice hockey championship;
3. There are few teams sponsored by other colleges, thus limiting available competition;
4. Hockey is expensive;
5. There is a lack of general student interest;
6. There is a lack of ability among the women's club team players.

The court ruled that funding concerns were the primary reason for denying varsity status and did not accept this as a justification for their decision. Colgate University was required to provide the team with equipment and supplies, practice time, a schedule of games, travel and per diem allowance, coaching, academic tutoring, locker rooms, medical services, housing and dining services and publicity (Wong and Barr, 1992, p. 14).

A component of equal status within athletic programs includes allocation of scholarship money. In 1997, the National Women's Law Center filed a complaint against Duke and Wake Forest Universities. The suit claimed that there was a large disparity between the scholarship money awarded to female and male athletes with the percentage of money allocated to women being far less than the percentage of females participating in the athletic programs. The complaint was settled by the Office of Civil Rights (OCR) with the presentation of a five year plan, addition of some scholarships and plans to add scholarships during the next three years (From the Gym to the Courts, 1998).

Female Eligibility on Male Teams

The changing role of women in society began to effect change in sport. It is noted that:

[c]ourt decisions and legislation have reinforced the equal treatment between women and men.

Most important have been the expanding judicial interpretation of the intent of the Equal Protection Clause of the fourteenth Amendment, and Title IX of the Educational Amendments of 1972 (Alexander and Alexander, 1984:195).

Both pieces of legislation prohibit discrimination based on sex. In *Brenden v. Independent School District*[9] (1973):

The Minnesota State athletic rule was challenged because it forbade girls' participation in the boys' interscholastic athletic program either as a member of a boys' team or as a member of a girls' team competing against boys (Alexander and Alexander 1984:198).

The court ruled in favour of Peggy Brenden, stating that being denied the right to participate on the boys' interscholastic tennis team was a violation of Ms. Brenden's constitutional rights under the Fourteenth Amendment. Further, the school was required to change its existing eligibility rules.

In another early case, where separate versus integrated programs are at issue, a suit, *O'Connor v. Board of Education of School District*[10] (1981 & 1982), was filed when 11-year-old Karen O'Connor was denied the opportunity to try out for the boys' sixth grade basketball team. A girls' team did exist, but it was argued that Karen's development was beyond the girls' team, and her future would be damaged without higher caliber competition. Initially the court ruled in favour of Karen's right to develop, but this decision was reversed in an appeal. In this case, it appears that the decision supports the concept that the goal of Title IX is to equate opportunity in general, not to assure relief in each individual case.

In Ontario, in addition to the Blainey case previously cited, *Ontario Rural Softball Association v. Banner* (1979) and *Gail Cummings v. Ontario Minor Hockey Association* (1979) sought the right to improve their athletic opportunities through the courts. In the former, Debbie Bazso was a ten-year-old softball player for the Waterford Squirts All-Star Softball team. Although she played throughout the regular season, she was declared ineligible when the team earned a berth in the Ontario

Rural Softball Association tournament, since ORSA did not allow mixed competition. The Board of Enquiry of the Ontario Human Rights Commission supported Debbie Bazso's case, but an appeal was upheld by virtue of the aforementioned Section 19(2) of the Ontario Human Rights Code.

Gail Cummings was a ten-year-old hockey goalie who was registered with the Huntsville Minor Hockey League and ultimately selected as one of the goalies for the All Star Atom team. Since participation as an all star required registration with the Ontario Minor Hockey Association, Gail Cummings was rejected on the basis that the OMHA directive was to promote and govern hockey for boys. When taken to the Board of Enquiry of the Human Rights Commission the case ultimately was dismissed. However, much debate centered on Section 19(2) of the Human Rights Code. As a result, the legitimacy of this clause was examined which led to its ultimate removal from the Code. While these cases were lost, they were instrumental in change that opened opportunities for girls.

In a recent case heard for *Mercer v. Duke University*[11] a student alleged discrimination in violation of Title IX for refusing her membership on the football team. In this particular case, the court ruled that the defendant university had no obligation to allow the female place kicker a position on the team. The contact sport exception permitted the university to deny female participation in this case.

The physicality of male contact sports appears to influence the decisions made by the courts. Wrestling provides another example. The courts ruled for the defendants in *Barnett v. Texas Wrestling Association*.[12] The plaintiffs, female students who were denied permission to participate in wrestling matches against boys had attempted to challenge that decision by claiming sex discrimination in education. The court's decision adds strength to the argument for separate programs based upon the sex of the participants, particularly in contact sports.

Sex, Sexuality, and Discrimination

"To discriminate means to act on the basis of differences between individuals or groups of individuals, or to make a distinction between how individuals are treated" (CAAWS, 1994, p. 6). There are a number of ways in which individuals experience discrimination based upon sex and sexuality. Some of these may occur in employment practices and climate issues.

Sexual Harassment and Sexuality

The relationship between a coach and an athlete is unique. It is comprised of trust, close interaction, accessibility, prestige and a power differential. Often the age difference between a coach and an athlete is small or, the athlete has legally reached age of consent. The question of whether or not there is a statutory obligation to limit personal relations remains unanswered while failure to do so may contribute to accusations of exploitation and sexual harassment. However, sexual harassment is not limited to the relationship of coach-athlete. It can occur between colleagues or peers. Incidents may involve either opposite or same sex harassment.

In *Franklin v. Gwinnett,*[13] monetary compensation was awarded for the first time in a complaint of sexual harassment under Title IX. Prior to this case, awards for damages in Title IX complaints were given in the form of increased opportunities within athletic programs.

Organizations must be aware of their responsibilities in harassment cases. In *Faragher v. City of Boca Raton,*[14] a city lifeguard sued, claiming sexual harassment on the part of supervisors. In this particular case, the court held the employer responsible for vicarious liability. The city was found to have failed in its responsibility to provide reasonable care for the prevention of harassing behaviors.

The procedures by which organizations investigate complaints of sexual harassment are critical for providing a reasonable environment for its constituents as well as for developing a sound defense in the case of litigation. The case of *Ericson v. Syracuse University*[15] demonstrates this point. Former members of the university's women's tennis team brought suit against the university and its officials alleging that they had been sexually harassed by their former coach over an extended period of time. Their claim stated that the university knew about the harassment and, while they had investigated the charges, the investigation was a fraud that concealed the misconduct on the part of the coach. A failure to manage the complaint adequately became a contributory factor in moving the dispute to litigation.

While most complaints of sexual harassment involve a female complainant and a male defendant, there are exceptions to this pattern. In *H.M. v. Jefferson County Board of Education*[16] a male student claimed discrimination, alleging that he had experienced same-sex harassment from a teacher and a coach. The defendant's motion to dismiss was not upheld when the courts found that the complaint could be heard under Title IX.

Wendy Weaver filed suit against the Nebo School District for violation of rights. She claimed that school officials denied her the right to talk about her sexual orientation with students and staff and fired her for her sexual orientation. The court ruled in her favour, awarding $1,500 in damages and ordering the school district to offer Weaver the coaching position while also lifting the gag order (Appenzeller, 1998c).

Employment Practices

Debbie Masten was a basketball coach at Truman State University for seventeen years until she was fired in 1997. She unsuccessfully argued with the athletic administration that the women's team should have more equitable treatment, making comparisons with the men's basketball team on coaches salary, travel, accommodations, practice and game times, access to the weight room and locker room facilities. The complaint, settled out of court, awarded Ms Masten $175,000 with the condition that she not apply for a position at the school for five years. In addition, the settlement ordered a gender equity compliance audit to be completed by a gender compliance officer familiar with Title IX regulations, maintenance of NCAA II status (as opposed to dropping to NCAA III), and maintenance of the sports budget or the number of athletes on any team for five years (Appenzeller, 1998b).

As in the Masten case, there are others who feel that their right to free speech is infringed by retaliatory actions on the part of the athletic department or by the fear of such retaliation. While some may be silenced by this fear, Vicki Dugan, softball coach at Oregon State University for six years, was not. Ms. Dugan filed a discrimination suit against the university and its athletic director when she was replaced by a male coach. Ms. Dugan had complained about salary inequities, poor facilities for her softball program, and budget restrictions that prevented her from hiring assistant coaches and providing adequate scholarship support to athletes. The plaintiff prevailed and was awarded $1.28 million. The university was responsible for economic damages, compensatory damages, and damages under the Equal Pay Act while the athletic director was responsible for compensatory damages ($60,000) and punitive damages ($125,000) (Appenzeller, 1998a).

The case of *Perdue v. City University of New York*[17] provides a summary of the criteria that can be successfully applied to claims of discrimination. A female, who served as former women's basketball coach and administrator, submitted her claim under Title VII and the Equal Pay Act (EPA). The courts held that:

1. Evidence was sufficient to support determination that employee's work was equal to that of men's basketball coach and men's sports administrator, as required to support employee's EPA claim
2. Evidence was sufficient to support determination that EPA violation was willful, as would entitle employee to liquidated damages under the Act
3. Evidence was sufficient to support intentional discrimination claim under Title VII
4. Jury's award of $85,000 compensatory damages was not excessive

This case highlights the importance of comparative analysis between the women's and men's programs and the demands made of each as well as the need to determine intention.

Organizations must also be conscious of the rights of individuals to challenge the allocations of resources as well as other decisions that may have an adverse effect of certain member constituents. In *Lowrey v. Texas A&M University System*[18] a female complainant had served her institution as women's basketball coach, physical education teacher and Women's Athletic Coordinator. She failed in a bid to become Athletic Director and was subsequently removed from the position of coordinator.

Lowrey claimed that these decisions were acts of retaliation in violation of Title IX. The courts held that the coach's removal from the position of Women's Athletic Coordinator qualified as an adverse employment action supporting the claim of retaliation. It was further noted that comments related to gender issues on campus were of public interest and could not be subject to retaliation.

Litigation as a means by which to achieve equity based on sex is a relatively new phenomenon. There has been a longer history for female participants to turn to the courts for resolution of their complaints. However, more recent court challenges extend beyond the participant to coaches, officials and administrators who have failed to find satisfaction within their sport organizations for disputes on a variety of issues. It is unlikely that this trend will reverse until greater parity between the women's and men's programs, and those who are responsible for their management, is achieved.

Questions for Class Discussion

1. Legislation for equity within educational programs, including sport, differ in Canada and the United States.
   a) Explain the difference.
   b) What is the intent of Title IX?
   c) What is the three-prong test of Title IX?
   d) Discuss cases that have been supported by Title IX legislation.
   e) What are the Canadian laws that would be used in a case seeking gender equity?
   f) Why did the Blainey case succeed when others before it had failed?
   g) Discuss the mutual influence that legal action has on Canadian and American sport cultures.
2. As sport managers, discuss the ways in which you can reduce the likelihood of litigation grounded in gender equity.

Endnotes

1. Gender equity in sport means "eliminating discriminatory practices which are barriers to full participation in sport programs, leadership and employment." (CAAWS, 1994, p.4)
2. *Blainey, Justine v. Ontario Minor Hockey Association et al.* (1986), 54 O.R. Ct. App. (2d) 513-544. Other related cases include *Cummings v. Ontario Minor Hockey Association* (1988), 33 C.C.L.T., 73 (2d) D.L.R. 446-50 (S.C.R.) and *Human Rights Commission (Ont.) v. Ontario Rural Softball Assoc.* (1978), 90 D.L.R. (3d)
3. *Grove City College v. Bell*, 1045 S.Ct. 1211 (1984).
4. Id., citing *AIAW v. NCAA, 735 F.2d 577, 580 (D.C.Cir. 1984)*
5. *Franklin v. Gwinnett County Public Schools*, 112 S. Ct. 1028 (1992).
6. *Favia v. Indiana University of Pennsylvania*, 7 F3d 332 (3rd Cir. 1993).
7. *Harper v. Board of Regents*, Illinois State University, 35 F.Supp.2d 1118 (C.D.Ill. 1999).
8. *Cook v. Colgate University*, 992 F. 2d 17 (2nd Cir. 1993)
9. *Brenden v. Independent School District* 742, 342 F. Supp 1224 (D. Minn. 1972) aff'd 477 F. 2d. 1292 (8th Cir. 1973).
10. *O'Connor v. Board of Education of School District* 23, 645 F. 2d 578 (7th Cir. 1981); 545 F. Supp. 336 (1982) (N.Y.S. 2d 329).
11. *Mercer v. Duke University*, 32 F.Supp.2d 836 (M.D.N.C. 1998).
12. *Barnett v. Texas Wrestling Association*. 16 F.2d 690 (N.D. Tex. 1998).
13. *Franklin v. Gwinnett County Public Schools*, 112 S.Ct. 1028, 117 L.Ed.2d 208, (1991).
14. *Faragher v. City of Boca Raton*, 118 S.Ct. 2275 (1998).
15. *Ericson v. Syracuse University*, 35 F.Supp.2d 326 (S.D.N.Y. 1999).
16. *H.M. v. Jefferson County Board of Education*, 719 So.wd 793 (Ala. 1998).
17. *Perdue v. City University of New York*, 13 F.Supp. 326 (E.D.N.Y. 1998).
18. *Lowrey v. Texas A&M University System*, 11 F.Supp.2d 895 (S.D.Tex. 1998).

References

Acosta, R. Vivian & Carpenter, Linda Jean. (1998). *Women in intercollegiate sport: A longitudinal study — twenty-one year update 1977-1998*. Brooklyn: Department of Physical Education and Exercise Science.

Appenzeller, Herb (ed.). (1998a). Former coach awarded $1.28 million in discrimination suit. *From The Gym to The Jury, 9*(3), p. 1.

Appenzeller, Herb (ed.). (1998b). Title IX case settled: Coach receives $175,000. *From The Gym to The Jury, 10*(3), p. 8.

Appenzeller, Herb (ed.). (1998c). Judge rules in favor of lesbian coach. *From The Gym to The Jury, 10*(3), p. 11.

Canada. (1986). *The Charter of Rights and Freedoms: A guide for Canadians*. Ottawa, Ontario: Canadian Unity Information Office.

Canada. (1986). *Sport Canada Policy on Women in Sport*. Canada: Minister of Supply and Services.

Clement, A. (1998). *Law in sport and physical activity*. Tallahassee, FL: Sport and Law Press, Inc.

Corbett, R. (1994). *Harassment in sport: A guide to policies, procedures and resources*. Ottawa: CAAWS.

Corbett, R. and H. Finlay. (1994). *An introduction to the law, sport and gender equity in Canada*. Ottawa: CAAWS.

Fitness and Amateur Sport Women's Program and the Canadian Interuniversity Athletic Union. (1992). *A comparative study: Relative opportunities for women in the CIAU*. Ottawa: Fitness and Amateur Sport Women's Program.

Kirke, G. I. (1997). *Players first: A report prepared for the Canadian hockey league*. Scarborough, ON: Canadian Hockey League.

Leatherman, C. (1988, March 23). Reagan vetoes bill expanding scope of anti-bias laws. *The Chronicle of Higher Education*.

Leatherman, C. (1988, March 30). Congress overrides President's veto of civil-rights bill, countering high court's "Grove City" decision. *The Chronicle of Higher Education*.

Miguel, T. M. (1994). Title IX and gender equity in intercollegiate athletics: Case analyses, legal implications, and the movement toward compliance. *Marquette Sports Law Journal, 1*, 279-302.

Moriarty, D. and Holman M. (1988, March). Comparing Canadian-American sports/fitness policy and the law. *First Annual Conference on Sport, Physical Education, Recreation and Law Proceedings*. Jekyll Island, Georgia.

Nelson, M. B. (1991). *Are we winning yet? How women are changing sports and sports are changing women*. New York: Random House.

Nelson, M. B. (1994). *The stronger women get, the more men love football*. New York: Harcourt Brace and Company.

Philadelphia. (1988, June 22). In lawsuit accord, Temple University to boost women's sports aid. *The Chronicle of Higher Education*.

Sage, G. H. (1990). *Power and ideology in American sport*. Champaign, Illinois: Human Kinetics Books.

Sopinka, J. (1984). *Can I play too? The report of the Task Force on Equal Opportunity In Athletics*: Volume I. Toronto, Ontario: Ministry of Labour.

Sopinka, J. (1984). *Can I play too? The report of the Task Force on Equal Opportunity In Athletics*: Volume II. Toronto, Ontario: Ministry of Labour.

Wilde, T. J. (1994). Gender equity in athletics: Coming of age in the 90s. *Marquette Sports Law Journal, 4*, 217-258.

Wong, G. M. and Barr, C. A. (1992, December). Bad judgment on Title IX. *Athletic Business*, p. 14.

CHAPTER 11

AIDS, SPORTS, THE LAW, AND EDUCATION

Helen Pratt Mickens

On November 7, 1991, Earvin "Magic" Johnson made an announcement that stunned the world. He announced that he was retiring from a brilliant career with the Los Angeles Lakers basketball team because he had contracted HIV (Human Immunodeficiency Virus), the virus that leads to AIDS.

For many people, Magic Johnson's announcement made it clear that AIDS and sport share important relationships. They both involve people. Both have a far-reaching impact on society as well as on individuals. Finally, as Earvin Johnson's announcement illustrated, sport is able to draw attention to the seriousness of the AIDS epidemic in the modern world.

Prior to Earvin Johnson's announcement of his infection with HIV, other celebrities had been reported to be infected with, or to have died from, AIDS. None, however, had personified youthful vigor, athletic prowess, stamina and a positive attitude the way Magic did. It had become clear that even money, fame and athletic skill were not protection against the deadly virus. If Magic Johnson could get HIV, anyone could.

What We Need to Know

This article is intended to share information about HIV and AIDS. It is also intended to stimulate thought and discussion about the relationship of AIDS to sport and explore individual and organizational responsibility in this matter.

Because many sports involve contact between persons, the issue of transmission through sports contact will be discussed. That is an obvious point of discussion. Less obvious issues in AIDS and sports include:

1. The right of privacy, the right of an infected person to keep his or her health information confidential;
2. A school, institution, health organization or coach's position in disclosing a sports participant's positive HIV status;
3. An infected person's continued participation in sports activities;
4. Sports hygiene and AIDS; and
5. Counseling and education of athletes and sports professionals about AIDS.

What is HIV? What is AIDS?

The Human Immunodeficiency Virus, or HIV, is a virus that can live in the human body for years without apparent symptoms. Infection with HIV can make it impossible for the body to fight off disease or infection when the virus moves into cells and damages the immune system. Infection can eventually lead to death.

AIDS is spread by contact with infected body fluids. Most people infected with HIV got their virus by having sex with a person who was infected or by sharing needles with an infected person. Prior to the availability of tests for HIV in the blood supply, some people were infected through exposure to infected blood products.

The American Red Cross and the United States Center for Disease Control report:

> Unlike many other viruses HIV does not spread by travelling through the air. Even though HIV is sometimes found in saliva, the virus is not spread by saliva. HIV is very fragile and dies quickly outside the body. Also, skin without cuts or sores helps prevent germs — including HIV from infecting us. For these and other reasons, HIV cannot be spread by shaking hands, hugging, coughing, sneezing, a kiss, or from swimming pools, toilet seats, straws, spoons or cups, food, insects including mosquitoes [or] animals.

AIDS was believed to be a disease of homosexual men when it first came to worldwide attention. Recent statistics, however, have taught us that female as well as male sexual partners of persons with HIV, persons who use intravenous drugs without medical supervision and share blood-contaminated needles, babies born to parents with AIDS, and persons who have received contaminated blood products all risk contracting the AIDS virus (Daniels, 1985). Since 1985, a blood test has been available for the presence of antibodies produced to fight off the AIDS virus (Dornette, 1992, p. 328; Daniels, 1985, p. 57). Testing, along with intensive screening of donors, has kept the incidence of blood transfusion related infection from HIV at very low levels since the beginning of testing procedures.

In a comprehensive look at the Canadian response to AIDS in laws and policy, citing statistics from L. E. Rozovsky's *AIDS and Canadian Law*; and *AIDS In Canada — Quarterly Surveillance Update* from Health Canada, Ralf Jurgens reports (p. 65):

> As of March 1997, Health Canada (the Canadian ministry of health) had received reports of 14,836 cases of AIDS: 14,677 adults and 159 pediatric cases. A total of 10,837 deaths had been reported. In 73% of cases, the mode of infection was attributed to homosexual or bisexual activity; in 4.1% to injection drug use; in 4.3% to both of the above risk factors; in 9.8% to heterosexual activity; in 3.5% to treatment with infected blood or infected blood products; in 0.8% to perinatal transmission; and in the remaining 4.2% of cases no risk factor was identified. (citing **AIDS In Canada — Quarterly Surveillance Update**, Health Canada, May, 1997.) It is estimated that between 30,000 and 50,000 people in Canada are HIV positive.

The number of new cases of AIDS continued to grow each year until 1996. It is now expected to fall due to availability of new drugs. Nevertheless, it has been estimated that there will be another 15,000 cases of AIDS in the next five years. In 1992, the annual number of deaths from AIDS surpassed 1,000 for the first time, and AIDS has been the leading cause of death among males aged 25 to 44 in large metropolitan centers.

Today we face the fact that some of the mysteries of HIV and AIDS have been revealed but many more remain. In the meantime, the number of people infected with HIV and with full-blown AIDS continues to increase. Sports, law, education and many other segments of society must wrestle with issues that result from the pandemic of AIDS.

Is There a Relationship Between Sports & AIDS?

"There is no documented instance of transmission of the HIV virus through participation in sport" (Global Programme on AIDS). The World Health Organization, the International Federation of Sports Medicine as well as representatives of the Medical Commission of the International Olympic Committee, the International Federation for Wrestling, and the International Rugby Football Board conclude that the very low risk of transmission of HIV through direct contact with an athlete must be considered and discussed. Sport educators and participants must practice appropriate procedures in sports or situations where bleeding occurs." Perhaps just as significantly, the *Consensus Statement From Consultation on AIDS and Sports* noted the special opportunity of those involved in organized sports to transmit information about AIDS (Global).

Well-Known Athletes and AIDS

In addition to Magic Johnson's announcement that he had contracted HIV, other well known sports figures have either announced their infection with HIV or have been reported to be dying or have died from the disease. It was reported by the Associated Press that Jerry Smith of the Washington Redskins football team was the first professional athlete known to have died of AIDS. He died at the age of 43, on October 15, 1986.

In April, 1989 *The New York Times* ran a story on Esteban de Jesus, former world lightweight boxing champion who at the time was dying of AIDS after testing positive for HIV in 1985. The boxer, de Jesus, was infected by sharing needles for the injection of illegal drugs. He died May 11, 1989. We will discuss athletes, AIDS and intravenous drugs later in this chapter.

After being pressured by the media, the American tennis star Arthur Ashe announced that he had contracted HIV (the virus that leads to AIDS) from a blood transfusion he received during heart surgery in 1983. This was prior to the time that the American blood supply was screened for the virus (Rhoden, 1992).

Although there have been rumors or conjecture that persons were infected with HIV by contact with an infected persons' blood by means other than by sharing intravenous needles or by passing of bodily fluids during sex,[1] the likelihood of athlete-to-athlete or athlete-to-trainer infection is extremely low.[2] This is especially true where appropriate hygiene procedures are followed. These will be discussed later in the chapter.

Discrimination: How Does The Law Relate to AIDS Issues and Sports?

In a book entitled *Confronting AIDS: On the Campus and In the Classroom: A Guide For Higher Education*, Jackie R. McClain and Tom E. Matteoli assert that an important aspect of the issue of AIDS on campus is the role of laws *prohibiting* discrimination based on a person's handicap or disability, which in some jurisdictions includes positive HIV status (p. 74; Wolohan, 1997).

Local, provincial, state and federal legislation such as the United States Rehabilitation Act of 1973[3] or the Americans with Disabilities Act[4] address the discrimination issue. They impose a legal obligation on higher education institutions, including their sports departments, to treat persons infected with HIV like other people in their programs. McClain and Matteoli "recommend that institutions avoid questions regarding HIV status and HIV testing for all three groups [students, employees, and patients] except when needed as a diagnostic tool in patient care" (p. 83). They "further advise that the concepts of nondiscrimination and accommodation should be incorporated into various institutional policies for dealing with HIV positive individuals and that aggressive training programs be developed to educate faculty, staff, patients, and students about HIV infections, how the infection is transmitted, and when and how to exercise protective measures" (p. 83).

Other Legal Issues

Issues in addition to the legal or perhaps moral prohibition of discrimination against persons with AIDS are tort issues and employee torts.

Tort Issues

Possession of information about a person's HIV status raises the possibility of a person or institution's exposure to liability for defamation. According to Black's Law Dictionary (6th ed., 1990), defamation is the holding up of a person to ridicule, scorn, or contempt in the community (p. 417). Included in the concept of defamation are both libel, defamation through print communications (p. 915), and slander. Slander is defamation through the spoken word (p. 1388).

Liability for libel and slander could arise when a teacher, coach, other staff person, or even a fellow athlete believes he or she has knowledge of another athlete's positive HIV status and communicates that information to others with the result of scorn or ridicule from the community. "Because of the strong social stigma and extreme fear associated with AIDS, there can be little doubt that some harm may be experienced by an individual whose HIV positive status becomes known. For this reason, many individuals who are HIV positive have chosen to keep this fact confidential" (McClain and Matteoli, 1989, p. 84).

Of course, the fact that an assertion is true may work to defeat a claim of libel or slander but other issues of release of confidential information about a person's HIV status remain. State or provincial law may preclude or restrict publishing (orally as well as in writing) a person's HIV status.[5] Breach of a fiduciary duty and breach of confidentiality may be an issue.[6]

There may be exceptions to laws concerning disclosure of confidential information about a person's HIV status. Where a law prohibits disclosure of a person's HIV status, but, where that information and the person's identity are a matter of public record, such as the case of a person charged with the crime of criminal transmission of the HIV virus, the confidentiality law may not prohibit disclosure of the person's identity.[7]

In addition to claims for violation of a statute[8] prohibiting disclosure of information about a person's HIV status,[9] other claims may be raised. These may include intentional or negligent infliction of emotional distress, invasion of privacy, public disclosure of private facts, and violation of a person's constitutional right to privacy.[10] Just as physicians may be restricted by law in what they may disclose about a person's HIV status, a trainer, coach or sports instructor may also be subject to restrictions (Price, 1990).

Those involved in organized sports must consider not only how they will communicate or not communicate an athlete's HIV status, but also who else will have access to the information, how and where it will be stored, and how confidentiality will be safeguarded. McClain and Matteoli recommend that administrators develop policies about HIV records (p. 85):

> Administrators at institutions of higher education should take care to assure that members of the institutional community understand that this information should be treated confidentially.

Administrators should also define where such information may appropriately be maintained within institutional written records and should assure that safeguards regarding access of such records are in place.

Employee Torts

Another issue that must be considered under potential AIDS-related liability is the duty of an employer to provide a safe workplace environment. Persons whose health and safety must be considered are persons such as trainers, coaches and medical personnel (AIDS and the Law; Jurgens, 1988, p. 63). Just as there is an extremely low risk of athletes contracting HIV from other athletes, there is also a low risk of infection for trainers and coaches. That small risk can be further minimized by appropriate hygiene procedures. We will discuss hygiene procedures later in this chapter.

AIDS, Sport, and Drug Testing

Testing of athletes for the presence of illegal or banned drugs has been an issue in amateur and professional sports for many years. Issues relating to drug testing include whether such testing violates an athlete's constitutional rights (Rose; Scanlon; Covell and Gibbs; DiMaggio).

The cost of testing athletes for HIV, at a time when sports organizations are looking at ways to hold down costs, is another issue in the drug testing of athletes (Rose and Girard). Also at issue is whether a testing program should be mandatory or voluntary, and whether the athletes' consent is required (Duda; Johnson and Ritter; Ranney; Rovere, Haupt and Yates; Shaller).

AIDS experts tend to come down against mandatory testing for the virus. This view is based on the comparatively small numbers of persons who would be found to be positive for HIV in relationship to the cost of such programs. Experts also feel that it is important that counseling always be a part of any testing program. Recommendations from the National Commission on AIDS state[11]:

HIV antibody testing must be accompanied by pre- and post-test counseling. People with both positive and negative results should receive counseling. For those engaging in high-risk behaviors, whether infected or not, counseling must be viewed as a sustained process ...

Despite the potential therapeutic benefit of HIV antibody testing, there exists an array of educational and counseling interventions that can proceed independent of testing.

There is general agreement that education about AIDS, about behaviors that put a person at risk for exposure to HIV, and appropriate sport hygiene are important parts of any sport program.

Even before Magic Johnson announced that he was infected with HIV in November, 1991, an International Olympic Committee panel recommended to the Olympic Committee Sports Medicine Council that they "reject routine AIDS testing of athletes as costly, unnecessary and an invasion of privacy" (Sternberg, 1991, p. C3).

The Sports Risk

The risk to an athlete of contracting AIDS through participation in sport has been described as "infinitesimally small."[12] The World Health Organization, in speaking of the possibility of HIV infection through sport participation said:

> No evidence exists for a risk of transmission of the human immunodeficiency virus (HIV) when infected persons engaging in sports have no bleeding wounds or other skin lesions. There is no documented instance of HIV infection acquired through participation in sports. However, there is a possible very low risk of HIV transmission when one athlete who is infected has a bleeding wound or a skin lesion with exudate and another athlete has a skin lesion or exposed mucous membrane that could possibly serve as a port of entry for the virus.[13]

The virus that leads to AIDS lives in human cells and body fluids such as blood, semen and vaginal secretions. Although the virus may be present in minute amounts in other bodily fluids such as saliva or urine, "[a]vailable evidence, however, has only implicated blood, semen, vaginal secretions and possibly breast milk in the transmission of HIV."[14]

All the experts agree that the AIDS virus is very fragile outside the human body and is vulnerable to exposure and destruction. "Because of its chemical composition, the virus is susceptible to certain agents or procedures, including alcohol, bleach, household detergents, ultraviolet light and air drying."[15] This means that the AIDS virus cannot be transmitted through swimming pool water or on surfaces in locker rooms (Landry, 1989). Ruth Hamel, in *The Physician and Sports Medicine* reports that "[t]he virus can live for only a short time outside the body, and it cannot be transmitted by breathing, touching, or other casual contact. Still, the theoretical risk remains, and sports teams and physicians are now grappling with what precautions are needed to deal with it" (p. 140).

Recognizing that the risk of acquiring HIV through sports activity is very low, but that there is a theoretical risk of transmission from one person's bleeding wound to abraded or open skin or exposed mucous membranes of another person (Goldsmith, 1992, p. 1311), what kinds of precautions should be taken and by whom should they be taken?

Athletes: Anti-HIV/AIDS Hygiene

Although there is very little risk of HIV transmission through sport contact, it is necessary to address the theoretical exposure and hygiene issues. Dr. Lawrence Rink, M.D., designated physician for the United States track team at the 1992 Summer Olympics in Barcelona, Spain, is quoted as having evaluated the extremely low risk of AIDS transmission and the theoretical risk in combative sports. "We felt that if indeed you could transmit the virus during sports activity — and theoretically it's possible although the chances are extremely improbable — participants in three sports would be at greater risk than others. These sports (all in Olympic competition) are tae kwon do, boxing, and wrestling" (Goldsmith, 1992).

Dr. Gregory Landry, in his booklet *AIDS in Sport*, gives advice to athletes in this age of AIDS (p. 23):

> Because blood can transmit AIDS and other infections, follow these guidelines to minimize your exposure to possible infections:
> - Cover open skin wounds such as scrapes and abrasions before practice and competition.
> - Stop the competition as soon as possible after bleeding begins. At that time, control bleeding, and clean up any blood that may have dropped on the floor or mat.
> - If you are exposed to the blood of another athlete, wash the blood off as soon as possible with soap and water.
> - Avoid sharing a towel with other athletes — it may be contaminated with blood.
> - Properly dispose of soiled towels. Ask the coach where to store towels that are used to wipe up blood.
> - When you launder your own clothes and towels that have been exposed to blood, use detergent and hot water.
> - If you are asked to clean blood from a surface, use a solution of one part household bleach to 10 parts water.

Should an HIV Infected Person Participate in Sport?

The question of an infected person's continued participation in sport activities involves two sub-issues. One issue has to do with the health of the infected person. The other issue has to do with the health of teammates, opponents, and sport personnel such as trainers and coaches. We will discuss these two issues separately.

The Health of the Infected Athlete

We began this chapter by talking about the startling retirement from basketball by Earvin "Magic" Johnson of the Los Angeles Lakers and his revelation that he was infected with HIV. Months later, Johnson again shocked the world when he announced his intention to participate in the 1992 Olympic Games in Barcelona, Spain, as a member of the United States' Olympic Basketball Team. There were many questions about his decision. Would he be well enough to participate? Would his participation in basketball, at a level of competition that is known to be aggressive and hard-hitting, have a detrimental short-term or long-term effect on his health? Would the physical activity required for training for the Olympics and then the competition itself accelerate a decline in his health?

Johnson participated in the 1992 Olympics. He made a significant contribution to the gold-medal-winning performance of the United States "Dream Team." He appeared to suffer no ill health effects. After the Olympics, the next step in Johnson's saga was his announcement that he planned to return to play for the Los Angeles Lakers in regular season play.

What do we know about the effect of HIV or AIDS on athletes? The answer is that not a great deal is known at this time. It is believed that with appropriate attention to an athlete's health and habits, with proper diet, adequate rest, avoidance of over-exertion and injury, an athlete can participate in sport activities as long as the athlete and the sport and health professionals agree that it is not detrimental to the athletes' health.

Ruth Hamel reports that "no studies have assessed the effect of strenuous exercise on an HIV-positive athlete. [However, Arthur] LaPerriere's research indicates that moderate aerobic exercise increases the number of helper T cells and boosts the immune system's ability to fight other viruses. But, [LaPerriere] says, very strenuous exercise has been shown to suppress the immune system ... This is even found in immune systems 'of healthy, elite athletes who are not HIV positive.' [LaPerriere] says, `[W]hen I consult with (HIV positive) patients who want to adapt an exercise program for themselves, exhaustive exercise is certainly not something I recommend'" (p. 45).

A school's exclusion of a player from sports based upon the school's belief that it is in the student's best interest has given rise to litigation.[16]

What About the Other Players?

We return to Earvin Johnson's story. He retired from professional basketball only to return months later to participate in Olympic competition. That participation was not without controversy. A physician for the Australian basketball team made statements to the effect that Johnson should be excluded from play because of his positive HIV status. Olympic officials and Australian team officials quickly distanced themselves from that position (Goldsmith, 1992, p. 1314).

After his much-publicized return to full-time professional basketball for the 1992-93 season Earvin Johnson felt compelled to finally retire, for the second time, from basketball on November 2, 1992. He blamed this second retirement not on his positive HIV status but on other players' reactions to it. In a preseason game, Johnson had received a scratch on his arm. That scratch received a great deal of media attention. This incident occurred after a period when Johnson had become the subject of off-the-court discussions by players and the media concerning some players' anxieties or fears about playing in a game with an HIV positive person. Johnson saw his HIV infection changing the nature of basketball in the National Basketball Association. He felt forced to leave. The pressure to leave basketball was not, apparently, because of his health or ability to perform but because of outside pressures.

Health care professionals agree that continued participation in sports by an HIV positive athlete is a decision for an athlete to make in conjunction with his or her health advisors. However, that decision brings in outside factors such as other athletes' and fans' opinions. Because of the importance of the assistance and support of coaches and trainers, we must examine sports workers' relationships with the HIV infected athlete.

Trainers, Coaches, and the HIV-Infected Athlete

Recommendations for Minimizing Exposure to HIV-Infected Blood

Experts in the study of AIDS agree that AIDS is an extremely difficult disease to get if one does not engage in what are considered high risk behaviors, such as sex without a condom with someone who has the disease, or sharing contaminated, intravenous needles. Recommendations for trainers and coaches for minimizing exposure to HIV infected blood are similar to those recommendations for health care workers. Dr. Gregory L. Landry, in his publication for the American Coaching Effectiveness Program[17] advises coaches to observe the procedures outlined in Table 11.1.

A History of Hygiene Precautions

Barrier precautions such as rubber gloves have been used by trainers and coaches even prior to the high visibility of the AIDS in sports issue. Notably, boxing has been an area of athletics where rubber gloves have been mandated in many states for a number of years. The New Jersey State Athletic Control Board began requiring all cornermen to wear rubber gloves in 1986 (Gauthier, 1987, p. 51). Barrier protection was not always a rule aimed at AIDS prevention (Gauthier, 1987, p. 54):

> Fred H. Lampson, athletic commissioner of Kentucky, which recently adopted the use of rubber gloves in the ring, claimed that "the rule protects the boxers, the cornermen, and the referees against infectious diseases, not necessarily AIDS." Lampson explained that the rule was written so as not to imply that anyone in the boxing ring had AIDS. He said that during the course of a match it is common for cornermen and referees to handle mouthpieces that may have been contaminated with blood or saliva. "Suppose somebody in the ring had the flu," said Lampson. "We insist that the mouthpieces

Table 11.1 – Minimizing Exposure to HIV-Infected Blood

Using Barrier Precautions: Wear rubber gloves whenever touching open skin, blood, body fluids, or mucous membranes. Change gloves after contact with each athlete. You may wear a mask or protective eyewear if the care you are giving is likely to produce droplets of blood or body fluids. These barriers will prevent exposure of the mucous membranes of the mouth, nose, or eyes to the blood or body fluid.

Washing Hands: Wash your hands with soap and water immediately after exposure to blood or body fluids even if you used gloves.

Cleaning Surfaces: Any surface (e.g., counter, floor, pool deck, wrestling mat) must be thoroughly washed after blood has come in contact with it. Use a household bleach solution of 1 part bleach to 10 parts water as a cleaner.

Disposing of Sharp Objects: You will not be involved in the use of hypodermic needles. However, you may need to dispose of scalpel blades or callus cutters. Place all sharp implements being discarded into a red container specifically designed for disposal of the implements.

Avoiding Contamination: Do not allow athletes to share towels contaminated with blood or bloody body fluids. Provide a receptacle lined with a plastic bag to isolate contaminated items before laundering.

Disposing of Soiled Linens: Discard towels and clothing contaminated with blood or bloody fluids in a receptacle designed for that purpose. These materials should be double-bagged and handled as infective material by laundry personnel. The items should be washed in detergent with hot water.

Covering Wounds: Be sure that all athletes' wounds are well covered before practice or competition. Not only will the bandage protect the injured site, but it will also decrease the probability of others coming in contact with the athletes' blood.

Providing CPR: Although saliva has a very low risk of AIDS virus transmission, the use of breathing bags and masks allow additional protection in that CPR (cardiopulmonary resuscitation) can be performed effectively without mouth-to-mouth contact.

Providing Care When You Have an Open Wound: If you have an open wound, especially on the hands, avoid providing first aid care of injuries involving bleeding and body fluids until your wound is healed. If you must care for an athlete, wear gloves.

---

be handled with rubber gloves. An ounce of prevention is worth it."

Some sports and organizations are ahead of others in addressing AIDS issues in sports. Because of very close physical contact in wrestling and the risk of transmission of other infections, that sport has long had rules about athletes competing with skin lesions or open wounds NCAA News, 1991, p. 4).

The National Basketball Association (NBA) has a program of disease prevention education and information that includes information on HIV and AIDS for players in the league's 27 teams (Goldsmith, 1992, p. 1311).

The National Football League, National Hockey League, Major League Baseball, the National Collegiate Athletic Association and the National Federation of State High School Associations met in February, 1992, to discuss the NBA's list of recommendations. The NBA recommendations were based on the *Consensus Statement from Consultation on AIDS and Sports*

The major professional, collegiate, and high school athletic organizations have all urged teams to make information and counseling available to athletes and others. Some organizations have included opportunities for voluntary and confidential AIDS testing, as well as related counseling as part of their programs (Goldsmith, 1992).

What Is the Role of Sports Organizers and Institutions?

Without a doubt, organized sports' greatest contribution to combating the spread of the deadly disease AIDS is educational and informational.

> When all is said and done, it seems, more needs to be said and done. In the United States today, nearly 11 years into the age of AIDS, the watchwords are still education and information. People, including people who play and coach and manage athletics, need to better understand what HIV infection is and how it can and cannot be caught (Goldsmith, 1992, p. 1314).

After his November, 1991 announcement of his HIV infection, Earvin Johnson:

> has been both praised for his forthrightness and excoriated for the promiscuity he detailed. The public is still struggling with labels, like hero and victim, to describe him. But Johnson is not a hero because he contracted a virus, nor is he less of a victim because of the way he was exposed to it. The heroic part for Magic can begin now, in the manner in which he brings public awareness to a worldwide scourge (McCallum, 1991, p. 29).

As much as Earvin Johnson or other celebrities can do to focus public attention on AIDS in the 1990s, and the relationship of AIDS to sports and athletes, much more can be done at a local level.

Education and Policy Formation

Colleges and universities must respond to the AIDS epidemic with educational programs (McClain and Matteoli, 1989, p. 150). Lack of knowledge about HIV and AIDS can lead to prejudice and discrimination based on ignorance. Health and sport officials find that once athletes or organizers know the facts about infection and transmission, they are more comfortable in dealing with AIDS and sport issues.

We have seen that although there is a theoretical possibility of transmission of HIV during sports activity, the possibility is extremely small. We previously mentioned the "riskiest sports, [which] are the bloodiest: boxing, wrestling and tae kwon do. Of moderate risk are: basketball, field hockey, ice hockey, judo, soccer and team handball. The lowest risk sports involve little physical contact, such as baseball, gymnastics and tennis" (Hamel, 1992, p. 142). The real dilemma in the sport world is the same as it is in the rest of society. People, largely young people, continue to engage in activities that subject them to the risk of HIV infection.

Athletes Contracting AIDS Outside of Sports

Leonard H. Calabrese, head of the Section of Clinical Immunology in the Department of Rheumatic and Immunologic Disease at the Cleveland Clinic Foundation says, "[t]here will be many athletes who develop AIDS in the next decade but it's the best bet you ever made that not a single one of them will ever get it playing sports" (Hamel, 1992, p. 146).

The use of anabolic steroids through intravenous injection puts athletes at risk of contracting the AIDS virus. In 1989, the Journal of the American Medical Association reported the case of a 26-year-old bodybuilder, married for five years, who shared a hypodermic needle and syringe with another bodybuilder. They used the needle to take black market anabolic androgenic steroids in cycles. The other bodybuilder was diagnosed with and died from AIDS. The subject bodybuilder was tested and he too was infected with the AIDS virus (Scott and Scott, 1989, p. 207-208).

It is imperative that sport professionals take advantage of their unique position as educators and health advisors to inform sport participants about HIV and AIDS. Lack of information or misinformation can be deadly. Sex with more than one partner, a practice more accepted by many in society today than in the past (not only athletes) can lead to HIV infection. Abstinence or monogamy, or, in the alternative, sex with the conscientious and correct use of a condom each time must be emphasized. The danger of sharing needles for injection of anything must be made very clear.

The American College Association Task Force on the Acquired Immunodeficiency Syndrome (AIDS) urges institutional policies and programs which emphasize avoidance of specific high-risk behaviors (Strohm, 1991). High-risk behaviors include sharing needles to inject illicit drugs and engaging in sex without consistent use of a condom and spermicides containing monoxynol-9. The Task Force also recommends campus wide educational programs for faculty and staff as well as students to "increase awareness and provide education to prevent further spread of the virus." Another key objective would be to prevent "discrimination against people who have, or are perceived to have, HIV infection [which] is unwarranted, hurtful, and wrong" (Strohm, 1991, p. 214).

The Job Ahead

Earvin "Magic" Johnson drew the world's attention to athletes who have the AIDS virus. There was no allegation that Johnson acquired the virus in any sport-related activity. It was not the health effects of this potentially lethal virus, but the reaction of some players that forced Johnson to leave professional basketball.

Johnson's tragedy is his own. It is shared by many others. Family, friends, fellow players and fans suffer. Those persons with whom Johnson engaged in the unsafe sex as well as those persons' loved ones suffer. It is important that sports use Johnson's tragedy as an educational tool and vehicle.

A person does not have to be a drug addict or a sports celebrity who lives in the fast lane to become infected with HIV. AIDS is a scourge that unfortunately is a part of life and interaction at the beginning of the 21st century. Fortunately, however, AIDS is a preventable disease.

Questions for Class Discussion

1. If student athletes have been told the difficulty they would have in contracting the HIV virus that leads to AIDS from casual or sports contact, how would they react to the information that a teammate was infected with the HIV virus?
   a) Would the student athletes' reactions vary depending on the team's sport?
   b) What other factors might affect teammates' reactions to the information that one of their own was HIV positive?
2. Do coaches, teachers, and trainers have an impact on players' activities away from their sport activity and training rooms?
   a) Should trainers and coaches be concerned with athletes' outside activities that may affect a player's health?
   b) Are there measures or sanctions that a coach or teacher could use that would affect players activities outside the sport activity?
   c) If you answered "yes" to 2b, *should* these measures or sanctions be used if the coach or teacher suspects activity that could be potentially harmful to an athlete's health?
3. When young athletes hear of famous athletes or celebrities who are HIV positive, have developed AIDS, or have died from AIDS, do the young athletes equate the celebrity's risky behaviors (sharing infected intravenous needles, sex with potentially infected partner without protection of a condom) that led to the celebrity's infection with HIV and choices in the young athletes' own lives?
   a) What would it take to reach a young athlete effectively to influence his or her activities which put them at risk for contracting AIDS?

Endnotes

1. *British doctors report man got AIDS virus from fight*, **The Detroit News and Free Press**, Jan. 25, 1992, at 2A (referring to a letter to the medical journal, *Lancet*, where British doctors diagnosed HIV in a wedding guest who was not believed to have engaged in any other behavior at high risk for exposure to HIV [intravenous drug use, sex with persons at a greater risk of infection with the disease]. The wedding guest, however, had engaged in a very bloody fistfight with an intruder at the wedding, who died of AIDS prior to the diagnosis in the guest).
2. Hamel, 1992, p. 140 notes that the rumor of an Italian soccer player's on-field infection was generally dismissed by experts who said the risk of getting HIV through sports participation is almost nonexistent.
3. *See* 29 U.S.C.A. § 793 *et seq.* (West 1993).
4. *See* 42 U.S.C.A. § 12101 (West 1993).
5. *See* Ordway v. County of Suffolk, 583 N.Y.S. 2d 1014, 1017 (1992) (where a doctor who operated on a patient later found to be HIV positive claims he lives in fear of contracting AIDS and that the County should have informed him of the patient's HIV status. In granting the defendant county summary judgment, the court spoke of the duty of maintaining confidential information:

    Defendant's duty is defined by N.Y. Public Health Law Art. 27-F which imposed severe restrictions on the dissemination of a person's Status vis-a-vis HIV infection. In enacting this statute the Legislature stated that it ." ... recognizes that maximum confidentiality protection for information related to human immunodeficiency virus (HIV) infection and acquired immune deficiency syndrome is an essential public health measure ... strong confidentiality protections can limit the risk of discrimination and the harm to an individual's interest in privacy that unauthorized disclosure can cause ... " (McKinney's N.Y.C.R.R. Title 10, Subchpt. G, Part 63, Sec 63.5 (b) (J) prohibits the disclosure of HIV related information solely to carry-out "infection control precautions." *Id.* at 1017.
6. John Doe v. Jane Roe, 588 N.Y.S. 2d 236 (1992).
7. In re Application of Multi media KSDK, Inc., 221 Ill App 3d 199, 581 N.E. 2d 911 (1991).
8. *See e.g.,* Benjamin R. v. Orkin Exterminating Co. Inc., 390 S.E. 2d 814 (1990) (for AIDS as a handicap under the West Virginia Human Rights Act).
9. *See Douglas C. Petri v. Bank of New York Co., Inc.,* 153 Misc. 2d 426, 582 N.Y.S. 2d 608 (1992) (for a claim under the New York Human Rights Law for discrimination due to the perception that the claimant had AIDS, and AIDS as a disability under the New York statute).
10. *Hillman v. Columbia County,* 474 N.W. 2d 913 (1991).
11. *Report of the Working Group on Social/Human Issues to the National Commission on AIDS*, Wash. D.C. (Apr. 1991), p. vi.
12. *See* Hamel, 1992, p. 139, quoting David. E. Rogers, M.D., Vice Chairman of the National Commission on AIDS in Washington, D.C., and professor of medicine at Cornell University Medical College in New York City.
13. Global programme on AIDS.
14. Policy No. 20: *AIDS and Intercollegiate Athletics, The NCAA News, Nov. 18, 1991,* p. 5.
15. *Ibid.*
16. *See e.g.,* Application of John Colombo, Jr. v. Sewanhaka Central High School District No. 2, 87 Misc. 2d 48, 383 N.Y.S. 2d 518 (1976) challenging a school's directive prohibiting a student with a hearing deficit from participating in contact sports such as football, lacrosse or soccer. The directive was based upon the school medical officer's belief that the student's hearing impairment leaves the student at an increased risk of bodily harm in contact sports. In examining the basis for the school's exclusion of the student the court concluded that the action was not arbitrary and capricious. The court stated that in light of courts' reluctance to interfere with an administrative body's determination in situations like this which are based on a school doctor's judgement and published guidelines of the American Medical Association, the school's directive would be allowed to stand.
17. *Landry, 1989, pp.* 20-21. Dr. Landry notes that his precautions were adapted from guidelines provided by the U.S. Public Health Service, Centers for Disease Control.

References

Black's Law Dictionary 417 (6th ed. 1990).

Celebrities who have died, *Lansing St. J.,* Apr. 9, 1992.

Covell, Kerrie S., and Annette Gibbs, Drug Testing and the College Athlete, 23 *Creighton L. Rev.* 1 (1989)

Daniels, Dr. Victor G., *AIDS: The Acquired Immune Deficiency Syndrome.* MTP Press Ltd. eds., Lancaster, England, 1985 (*see generally* chapter 2).

DiMaggio, Anthony, Suffering in Silence: Should They Be Cheered or Feared? (Mandatory Testing of Athletes as a Health and Safety Issue), 8 *Seton Hall Journal of Sport Laws* 663 (1998).

Dornette, William H.L.; Blood Products and Tissue Transplants, *AIDS and the Law.* Wiley Law Publications, 2d ed., 1992.

Duda, Marty, Drug Testing Challenges College and Pro Athletes, *The Physician and Sports Medicine,* Nov. 1984, p. 109.

Gauthier, Michele, Sports Health Workers Respond to AIDS, *The Physician and Sports Medicine,* Nov. 1987, pp. 51, 54.

Global programme on AIDS, Consensus Statement from Consultation on AIDS and Sports. Geneva, Switzerland, Jan. 16, 1989.

Goldsmith, Marsha F. When Sports and HIV Share the Bill, Smart Money Goes On Common Sense, *JAMA,* Mar. 11, 1992.

Hamel, Ruth, AIDS: Assessing the Risk Among Athletes, *The Physician and Sports Medicine,* Feb. 1992.

Johnson, Alex, and James Ritter, *The Legality of Testing Student-Athletes For Drugs and The Unique Issue of Consent,* 66 *Or. L. Rev.* 895 (1987).

Jurgens, Dr. Ralf, "Canadian HIV/AIDS Policy and Law: Least Intrusive, Most Effective," in *Legal Responses to AIDS in Comparative Prospective,* Stanislow Frankowski, ed. Kluwer Law International, 1998.

Landry, Gregory L. M.D., *AIDS in Sport.* Leisure Press, Champaign, Ill. 1989.

McCallum, Jack, Magic Johnson, AIDS and Sports, *Sports Illustrated,* Nov. 25, 1991, p. 29.

McClain, Jackie R., and Tom E. Matteoli, *Confronting AIDS: on the Campus and in the Classroom: A Guide for Higher Education.* College and University Personnel Association, 1989.

NCAA News, Coaches, Others Fear AIDS' Impact, Dec. 2, 1991, p. 4. (An article focusing on the debate about mandatory testing of athletes for HIV and the possible negative and positive effects of such testing requirements.).

N.Y.Times, This Foe's Tougher Than Duran, Apr. 22, 1989, pp. 30, 49.

Price, David P.T., Between Scylla and Charybdis: Charting a Course to Reconcile the Duty of Confidentiality and the Duty to Warn in the AIDS Context, 94 *Dick. L. Rev.* 435 (1990).

Ranney, James T., The Constitutionality of Drug Testing of College-Athletics: A Brandeis Brief for a Narrowly Intrusive Approach, 16 *Journal of College and University Law* 397 (1990).

Red Cross, H*IV Infection and AIDS; the facts.* The American National Red Cross 1989.

Rhoden, William C., An Emotional Ashe Says That He Has Aids, *N. Y. Times,* Apr. 9, 1992, p. B15, col. 1.

Rose, Allison, Mandatory Drug Testing of College Athletes: Are Athletes Being Denied Their Constitutional Rights?, 16 *Pepp. L. Rev.* 45, (1988).

Rose, Laurence M., and Timothy H. Girard, Drug Testing in Professional and College Sports, 36 *Kan. L. Rev.* 787 (1988).

Rovere, George D., M.D., and Herbert A. Haupt, M.D. and C. Steven Yates, ATC, Drug Testing in a University Athletic Program: Protocol and Implementation, *The Physician and Sports Medicine,* Apr. 1986, at 69-75.

Scanlon, John A. Jr., Playing the Drug Testing Game: College Athletes, Regulatory Institutions, and the Structures of Constitutional Argument, 62 *Ind. L. J.* 864 (1986-1987).

Scott, Michael J., M.D., and Michael J. Scott, Jr., D.O., HIV Infection Associated With Injection of Anabolic Steroids, *JAMA,* July 14, 1989.

Shaller, William Lynch, Drug Testing and the Evolution of Federal and State Regulation of Intercollegiate Athletics: A Chill Wind Blows, 18 *Journal of College and University Law* 131 (1991).

Sternberg, Steve, AIDS Testing Considered for Athletes, *Atlanta Journal Constitution,* May 11, 1991, at C3.

Strohm, Leslie Chambers, ed., *AIDS on Campus: A Legal Compendium,* National Association of College and University Attorneys, Wash., D.C., 1991.

Wolohan, John T., An Ethical and Legal Dilemma; Participation in Sports by HIV infected Athletes, 7 *Marquette Sports Law Journal* 373 (Spring, 1997).

CHAPTER 12

LEGAL INTERVENTION IN SPORT FOR PEOPLE WITH DISABILITIES

Jennifer Larson

Kenny Doyle requires leg braces and crutches to walk. His upper body strength is formidable, muscles built from years of moving his body around using only his arms and torso. Kenny has used his strength to his advantage, becoming a successful powerlifter and competing in both able-bodied and disabled events. He has achieved a great deal of success in the bench press, an event ideally suited to his abilities as it does not require standing.

At the age of seventeen, Kenny qualified for the 1992 Bench Press World Championships in Finland. He did not think of telling anyone at the event about his disability. After all, he had been competing in non-disabled events frequently and no one had paid any attention to it before. Kenny was anticipating his first lift of 157.5 kg. When his name was called he began to make his way to the lifting platform using his braces and crutches. Suddenly, a judge stopped him and informed him that the International Powerlifting Federation did not allow leg braces in IPF-sanctioned bench-press meets and he had three minutes to remove them. This normally took at least ten minutes when a crowd of 3,000 spectators was not watching. As a result, Kenny missed his first lift. He cannot move without his leg braces and crutches, so his coach assisted him to the platform. The judges stopped him again and informed him that coaches could not assist lifters onto the lifting platform. Another rule. The time limit for Kenny's second lift expired. On his third lift, his teammates, coaches and the spectators were forced to witness Kenny crawling from the warm-up area to the lifting platform and dragging himself up on to the bench. This time, he made it within the time limit and completed his first lift weight (Gregson, p. 40). Just another day in the life of a disabled athlete in a non-disabled world.

Kenny Walker is a defensive tackle in the Canadian Football League. Despite the fact that he cannot hear, he was a successful student-athlete. At his high school, he received individualized attention and supplemental services to assist him both on and off the field. His teammates were supportive and helped him understand the coach's instructions. He was an All-American nominee for football and played successfully for the University of Nebraska before joining the Denver Broncos of the National Football League (Dougherty et al., 1994, p. 75).

These two stories are indicative of the broad spectrum of treatment of people with disabilities in sport. Kenny Doyle's experience provides an example of the indignities many athletes with disabilities have endured and continue to endure when faced with organizations and officials who use rules to keep them from participating alongside their able-bodied counterparts. However, his story is not indicative of the experiences of all people with disabilities in sport. Kenny Walker was lucky enough to be nurtured in an environment that supported his athletic needs. In reality, the experiences of most disabled people in sport and recreation fall somewhere between the two stories. Generally, most

163

sport organizations, recreation programs, facilities and schools are welcoming to people with disabilities and are willing to make the modifications required for them to participate. Those that are not so accommodating are the reason that discrimination forms the bulk of legal challenges in the area of disabilities and sport. The underlying issue in most disability sport cases has been access, or lack thereof, to sport and competition opportunities.

Currently, there are an estimated 1.5 million Ontarians (Raina, 1999, p. 1) and 43 million Americans[1] with a disability. Through accident, injury or birth, these ranks grow daily. In the past, the challenge of living with a disability has been compounded by systemic discrimination in all areas of society and people with disabilities have had few legal avenues through which to effect change of these practices.

This chapter will trace the development of legislation impacting the participation in sport of people with disabilities in Canada and the United States in two areas; accessibility and risk management. In addition, it will provide an overview of disabled sport in Canada. At the end of this chapter, students should be able to:

1. Define disabilities under the law.
2. Understand the impact of the Charter of Rights and Freedoms and the Ontario Human Rights Code on sport and physical activity for people with disabilities in Ontario and Canada.
3. Understand the effect of the Rehabilitation Act of 1973, the Americans with Disabilities Act of 1990 and the Individuals with Disabilities Education Act of 1997 on sport and recreation for people with disabilities in the United States.
4. Know the facts and decisions of the following cases: *Youth Bowling Council v. McLeod*, *Southeastern Community College v. Davis* and *Pottgen v. Missouri State High School Activities Association*.
5. Demonstrate a greater understanding of the opportunities for people with disabilities to participate in the Canadian sport system.

Each piece of legislation will be reviewed in terms of its impact on, and implications for, people with disabilities and sport.

Canadian Legislation

Charter of Rights and Freedoms—Overview

Canada is unique in that it is the only democracy thus far to enshrine the rights of people with disabilities into the constitution (Lepofsky, 1993). This was accomplished in 1982 with the passing of the Canada Act containing the Charter of Rights and Freedoms. People with mental and physical disabilities are among the minority groups whose rights are protected under Section 15(1) of the Charter.

> Every individual is equal before and under the law and has the right to equal protection and equal benefit of the law without discrimination, and, in particular, without discrimination based on race, national or ethnic origin, colour, religion, sex, age or *mental or physical disability*.[2] (Emphasis added)

The move to include people with mental and physical disabilities in the Charter began in 1975, with the passing of the United Nations Declaration of the Rights of Disabled Persons.[3] As a member nation, Canada was expected to live up to the provisions of the Declaration. They included, among other things, the right to participate in social and recreational activities.[4] During this time, the civil rights awareness that had such a large impact in the United States was moving north of the border. Many provinces were enacting or expanding Human Rights Charters to include people with disabilities in a limited way (Lepofsky, 1993, p. 133).

The United Nations declared 1981 to be the International Year of the Disabled. During this time, legislation was being proposed to replace the Canadian Bill of Rights of 1960[5] with the Charter. However, there was no reference to people with disabilities among the minority groups included in the proposed Charter (Lepofsky, 1993, p. 133). The government felt that the cost of extending rights to people with disabilities would be too high and it would be too difficult to find a suitable definition of the term "disability." They also proffered the weak excuse that the rights of people with disabilities were already covered by statutory human rights codes, although several of the codes in existence did not extend any protections to people with disabilities at that time. After extensive pressure from advocacy groups, the Charter was passed into law in 1982, *with* the inclusion of people with mental and physical disabilities.

In replacing the Bill of Rights, the Charter removed a human rights code that had a negligible impact on civil liberty protection for people with disabilities (Lepofsky, 1993, p.131). The Bill of Rights only applied to areas of federal jurisdiction, had many restrictions and was limited in scope. The courts narrowly applied it because it was only a statute, not part of the constitution, and thus provided little in the way of human rights protection. Unlike the Bill of Rights, the Charter is a constitutional guarantee of fundamental rights for individuals subject to the limits of a free and democratic society.[6] The sections of the Charter with the greatest impact for sport and people with disabilities are the previously noted section 15(1), and section 15(2).

Section 15(2) provides that any program that is intended to improve the condition of the identified disadvantaged groups is not discriminatory under the Charter.[7] This section provides protection for sport organizations or groups for disabled athletes (e.g. Ontario Special Olympics, Ontario Wheelchair Sports Association). Most of these organizations developed from of a lack of opportunities for people with disabilities in mainstream programs. Although these organizations give a preference to people with disabilities, the Charter protects them because they are assisting a traditionally disadvantaged group.

Ontario Human Rights Code—Overview

The second major piece of legislation impacting on the rights of people with disabilities in Ontario is the Ontario Human Rights Code.[8] In practical terms, the Ontario Human Rights Code prevents discrimination on the basis of disability, in the private, commercial or public sector.[9] Section 10 of the Code defines disability to include physical, mental or learning disabilities.[10]

To illustrate how severe the problem of discrimination against people with disabilities is, it is helpful to note that since the enactment of the Code, forty percent of complaints to the Ontario Human Rights Commission have been related to disability discrimination (Swanson, p. 2). However, few of these challenges have come in the area of sport.

Although the right of people with disabilities to be protected from discrimination is enshrined in the Code, rights are not infringed if disability renders a person "incapable of performing or fulfilling the essential duties or requirements attending the exercise of the right.[11] " In other words, a person with a disability must be able to fulfill the requirements of a program despite their disability. The challenge of this requirement is in determining which duties or requirements are essential, and which can be modified to make the participation of a person with a disability possible.

This provision was challenged in *Youth Bowling Council v. McLeod*.[12] At age eleven, Tammy McLeod, an athlete with cerebral palsy, was a regular bowler in a league with the Youth Bowling Council (YBC) of Ontario. Although McLeod's disability prevented her from being able to grasp and release a bowling ball from her wheelchair, she was able to bowl successfully with the use of a ramp designed by her father. In 1985, McLeod qualified to attend the Four Steps to Stardom Tournament. The YBC did not permit McLeod to compete in the event because she used a ramp to deliver the ball. It was felt that the ramp provided McLeod with an unfair advantage over the other bowlers. Tammy challenged the decision of the YBC through Section 1 of the Ontario Human Rights Code. The case went to appeal four times and, after a nine-year battle, McLeod won the right to compete. It was held that the Youth Bowling Council had a duty to accommodate McLeod's disability up to the point of undue hardship. In the opinion of the court, allowing McLeod to play using a bowling ramp did not constitute undue hardship and that grasping and releasing a bowling ball without mechanical assistance was not an essential requirement of participating in a bowling tournament. The court found in McLeod's favour partially due to the fact that bowling is an individual sport and it was determined that use of the ramp did not adversely affect other players. In fact, the other players were very supportive of McLeod and included her fully in all aspects of club play and competitions.

As no other cases involving disabled athletes have come under the Ontario Human Rights Commission, the McLeod case is a landmark case for athletes with disabilities. The decision of the court in this case has many implications for sport, recreation and fitness organizations. It is no longer acceptable for a sport organization to use the rules of a sport to prevent the people with disabilities from participating. Rather, the onus is on the sport organization to devise alternatives to meet the needs of disabled participants.

Ontarians with Disabilities Act—Overview

Although the Charter of Rights and Freedoms and Ontario Human Rights Code heralded an age of sweeping changes in human rights and unprecedented protection of the rights of people with disabilities, there is still a need for legislation specifically designed to meet the needs of people with disabilities in Ontario. Under Premier Bob Rae, the New Democratic Party was the first government in Canada to propose legislation for people with disabilities. However, with an election called, the Ontarians with Disabilities Act died before it could be passed (Raina, p. 1). During the 1998 parliamentary session, the Government of Ontario under Premier Mike Harris proposed a new Ontarians with Disabilities Act. Only three pages in length, the Act was roundly denounced by advocacy groups as weak and ineffective and died on the first reading. The Act applied only to government agencies and did not contain any requirements, enforcement methods or sanctioning for noncompliant agencies. The provincial government has since committed to a broader and more in depth consultation process and the bill is currently being redesigned.

Ontario Disability Support Program Act

In the past, people with disabilities who required assistance in activities of daily living like bathing, dressing or buying groceries were forced to rely on inadequate homecare programs or family and friends to meet their daily needs. The homecare system was overworked and understaffed, with the end result that people with disabilities were not in control of their own care. Instead of being able to decide for themselves when they would like to wake up, dress and eat, a person with a disability in a homecare program would be at the mercy of staff schedules and the needs of other people with disabilities in their geographic area. Certainly this type of care had a negative impact on the ability of a person with a disability to participate in recreation or sport programs. These programs were seen as non-essential when compared to medical or personal care needs and thus were given a low priority.

The Ontario government took strides to put people with disabilities in control of their own care in 1997 with the passage of the Ontario Disability Support Program Act.[13] The purpose of the Act was to establish a program that would provide income and employment support to eligible people with disabilities. Under this program, an eligible person with a disability can apply to receive directly the funding normally paid to homecare staff. The person is then responsible for hiring, scheduling and monitoring their own personal attendant care.

To be eligible for the program, a person must prove that they are disabled under the Act. The Act includes people with continuous substantial physical or mental impairments that restricts their activities of daily living and impairs their ability to function in the community or workplace. Participants in this program must also prove that they have the ability to manage the financial and personal aspects of employing and managing a staff and meeting other government requirements.

While this program is not suited for everyone, many disabled athletes have found it to be an ideal way to meet their individual needs. For example, some athletes with severe cerebral palsy require assistance to play certain sports. Whereas in the past they would have to rely on volunteers or friends for assistance, with the Ontario Disability Support Program they can build their sport participation into their daily life. The program has allowed elite athletes with disabilities to meet their training and competition needs through personalized attendant care. It has empowered some individuals with disabilities to be in full control of their lives, including participation in sport.

American Legislation

Rehabilitation Act—Overview

In 1973, Congress enacted the first major comprehensive federal law involving rights of people with disabilities (Rothstein, 1997, p. 34). The original purpose of the Rehabilitation Act was to provide rehabilitation services for, and enhance employability of, people with disabilities. However, the provisions of the Act were broad and had a strong impact on the sport and recreation area.

In drafting the Rehabilitation Act, Congress found that "individuals with disabilities constitute one of the most disadvantaged groups in society…[D]isability does not diminish the right of individuals to enjoy full inclusion and integration in the economic, political, social, cultural and educational mainstream of American society… [I]ndividuals with disabilities continually encounter various forms of discrimination in such critical areas as employment, housing, public accommodations, education, transportation communication, recreation, institutionalization, health services, voting, and public services."[14]

Under the Rehabilitation Act, a person with a disability includes any person who:

1. Has a physical or mental impairment which substantially limits one or more of a person's major life activities;
2. Has a record of such an impairment;
3. Is regarded as having such an impairment.

This definition includes individuals with conditions or diseases that may not impede their ability to complete major life activities, but is seen as being disabled (e.g., Acquired Immune Deficiency Syndrome).[15]

Major life activities covered by the Act are defined as: functions such as caring for oneself, performing manual tasks, walking, seeing, hearing, speaking, breathing, learning and working."[16] Courts have reached conflicting decisions when considering whether or not playing intercollegiate sports constitutes a major life activity.[17]

The Section of the Rehabilitation Act most applicable to the sport and recreation field is Section 504, which provides that "no otherwise qualified individual with disabilities…shall, solely by reason of his disability, be excluded from participation in, be denied the benefits of, or be subjected to discrimination under any program activity receiving financial assistance."[18] Unlike other sections of the Rehabilitation Act, which were primarily concerned with employment, Section 504 applies to participation in programs and reaches to schools, higher education and some public facilities (courthouses, transportation and housing). To be protected under the Act, a person must meet the requirements of the definition relating to disability and must also be otherwise qualified (Rothstein, 1997, p. 35).

However, when the act was originally passed, courts differed on the application of the "otherwise qualified" rule. The case of *Southeastern Community College v. Davis* was the first to provide comprehensive guidelines for the term. Although not specifically a sport case, as the first case under the Rehabilitation Act to be heard by the Supreme Court, it played a large role in future court decisions involving disabled student-athletes.

Davis was a deaf nursing student attending Southeastern Community College. She used a hearing aid and lip-reading skills to understand those around her. Southeastern Community College determined that Davis' hearing disability made it unsafe for her to complete the clinical training portion of the program or to practice as a nurse. The College felt that it would be impossible for Davis to participate safely in the clinical training component of the program. In addition, it was felt that the modifications that would be necessary for her complete the program safely would fundamentally alter the program and that without fully participating in the clinical training program she would be unable to develop the knowledge required to be a competent nurse. Davis sued under Section 504, alleging that the school was discriminating against her due to her disability. Davis contended that the school was obliged to take affirmative action to enable her to participate. She suggested that the school provide her with individual supervision during the clinical program or remove the components of the program that she could not complete.

In a unanimous decision, the court concurred with the college, and found that Davis' disability prevented her from performing safely in the training program and as a professional nurse. In finding against Davis, the court determined that Section 504 does not require institutions to disregard disabilities or make substantial modifications to their program to enable people with disabilities to participate. It requires only that people not be excluded *solely* because of their handicap.

In *Davis*, the court found that an "otherwise qualified" person is one who meets *all* of the requirements of a program in spite of their disability. In so finding, the court determined that the clinical requirements of the nursing program were essential and could not be modified to meet Davis' needs. This decision affirmed that Section 504 does not require educational institutions to lower or substantially modify their standards to accommodate people with disabilities. Although the decision went against the plaintiff, the case was a landmark decision for people with disabilities. *Davis* confirmed that people with disabilities should be judged by the same standards as other members of society, affirming a move toward equity for, not special treatment of, people with disabilities.

The decision in *Southeastern Community College v. Davis* and subsequent cases in this area mean that educational institutions must make reasonable accommodations or adjustments for qualified individuals with known disabilities. However, a school is not expected to make modifications for a student with a disability if the disability has not been disclosed to the school. An accommodation is considered unreasonable if it fundamentally alters the program (Tucker, 1998, p. 214).

Student-athletes with disabilities have cited section 504 in numerous cases involving challenges to age-eligibility rules.[19] In *Pottgen v. Missouri State Activities Association*, the court examined the case of a student with a learning disability who was forced to repeat two grades in elementary school. After playing on the baseball team for the first three years of high school, the plaintiff turned nineteen before his senior year. Like most school athletic associations, Missouri had required that all student athletes be under the age of nineteen. Based on this rule, Pottgen was not permitted to play on the baseball team in his senior year.

The District court found that Pottgen was an "otherwise qualified" individual who could meet all of the eligibility requirements of the Missouri State High School Activities Association (MSHAA), except for the age requirement. The court held that the age requirement was not an essential requirement and could be modified for Pottgen to take part.

However, the decision was reversed on appeal. The Court of Appeal decided that the age restriction was an essential eligibility requirement. In their finding, they reasoned that an age limit:

1. Helps reduce the competitive advantage to teams using older athletes;
2. Protects younger athletes from harm;
3. Discourages student athletes from delaying their education to gain athletic maturity and therefore an advantage;
4. Prevents over-zealous coaches from engaging in repeated red-shirting to gain a competitive advantage.

The appeals court found that the only requirement preventing Pottgen from playing on the baseball team was his age, *not* his disability. Therefore, the only possible accommodation that would enable him to play would be to waive the age eligibility requirement. The court rejected this possibility because the age eligibility requirement was deemed essential to the program and waiving the restriction would fundamentally change the program.

One judge in the decision dissented, explaining that each athlete should be assessed on an individual basis. He found that the reason Pottgen did not meet the age requirement had nothing to do with the reasons for the rule being in place. Pottgen did not deliberately miss two years of school to gain an athletic advantage. He was not appreciably larger than his teammates, so there was no concern for the safety of younger players. He was not redshirted by his coach to improve the team's chances.

However, the courts are not completely unanimous on the issue of age eligibility and disability in interscholastic sports. In *Johnson v. Florida High School Activities Association*, a deaf student who was held back in elementary school won the right to compete in football and wrestling even though he exceeded the age eligibility requirement. In this case, the court found that age eligibility was *not* an essential requirement. In particular, the court noted that the plaintiff was not the largest or most experienced football player in his division and the sport of wrestling is divided by weight divisions, so the plaintiff would not enjoy an advantage because of his age in either sport.

In 1987, the Rehabilitation Act was amended by the Civil Rights Restoration Act.[20] The Restoration Act provides that any part of a program or activity receiving financial assistance subjects the entire program to Section 504.[21] The Act also expanded the scope of protection under the Rehabilitation Act to include people with contagious infections and diseases as long as they do not pose a health and safety threat to themselves or to others.[22]

The "health and safety threat" clause also applied to the other groups identified in the Rehabilitation Act. This clause provided a means for programs to exclude people with disabilities if it could be proven that their own health or safety could be threatened. In other words, the right of a person to assume personal risk could be superceded by an organization, agency or program.

While the Rehabilitation Act was a significant improvement in the ability of people with disabilities to assert their rights, there was frustration with the lack of enforcement and practical methods of implementing the legislation (Rothstein, 1997, p. 5). Federal agencies were unwilling to pursue individual complaints, waiting until there were several plaintiffs before becoming involved. Perhaps as a result of this unwillingness, individuals sought redress in federal court.

A significant amendment to the Rehabilitation Act occurred in 1978 when Section 505 declared that the legal remedies available under the Civil Rights Act of 1964 would also be available to people under the protection of the Rehabilitation Act.[23] This amendment meant that plaintiffs who sued under the Rehabilitation Act and were successful could receive attorney fees and monetary damages, thereby giving the Rehabilitation Act some legal strength.

Americans with Disabilities Act (ADA)

The Rehabilitation Act paved the way for the most significant disability rights statute to this day, the Americans with Disabilities Act of 1990 (ADA).[24] While the Rehabilitation Act only covered federal agencies or recipients of federal assistance, the ADA is significant because it broadens the coverage of protection for people with disabilities to include employers, public accommodations, public services, transportation, and telecommunications (Rothstein, p. 14).

Provisions of the ADA

Title II and Title III are the most applicable to the sport and recreation field. Title II provides that no qualified individual with a disability shall, by reason of such disability, be excluded from participation in or be denied the benefits of the services, programs or activities of a public entity, or be subject to discrimination by such an entity.[25]

A *public entity* includes any state or local government, any department or agency of a state or local government and the national railway system.[26]

A *qualified individual with a disability* means an individual with a disability who, with or without reasonable modification to rules, policies or practices, the removal of architectural, communication, or transportation barriers, or the provision of auxiliary aids and services, meets the essential eligibility requirements for the receipt of services or the participation in programs or activities provided by a public entity.[27]

Title II is closely connected with section 504 of the Rehabilitation Act, although the two pieces of legislation do not completely overlap. Unlike the Rehabilitation Act, Title II applies to all state and local government entities, regardless of whether or not they receive federal financial assistance (Tucker, 1998, p. 158). The Rehabilitation Act exempts regulations for companies with less than fifteen employees, while Title II has no such exemption. Title II does exempt historic buildings from accessibility requirements, while section 504 does not.

Title III of ADA provides that "No individual, shall be discriminated against on the basis of disability in the full and equal enjoyment of the goods, services, facilities privileges, advantages, or accommodations of any place of public accommodation by any person who owns, leases (or leases to), or operates a place of public accommodation."[28]

As a general rule, discrimination under the ADA can include a number of areas:

1. Eligibility criteria that screens out people with disabilities.

2. Failure to make reasonable modifications to make goods, services or facilities available to people with disabilities.
3. Failure to take steps to ensure people with disabilities are not excluded or treated differently than other individuals.
4. Failure to remove architectural and communication barriers (e.g. stairs, high countertops) in existing facilities or provide an alternative method of program delivery.[29]

Most ADA cases related to sport deal with the first three areas of discrimination, although there have been some cases challenging the accessibility of sport facilities for disabled fans.[30]

The ADA, with all of its sweeping changes, did not enter quietly into the legislative system. Debate raged over which disabilities should be included and how broad the scope of the Act should be. Critics felt that the Act was an unforgivable trespass on the right of each state to govern their own affairs. There was a concern that small businesses would go bankrupt implementing the mandatory accessibility requirements.[31] In the end, the bill passed with only eight senators opposed.

With its reach into places of public accommodation, the school system and private facilities, the implications of the ADA for sport have been broad. In the area of education, the impact of the ADA has been felt most clearly in interscholastic athletics. Several of the age-eligibility cases previously cited under the Rehabilitation Act also involved the ADA.[32] The ADA has also been used to force the educational institutions and organizations to modify their requirements to meet the needs of disabled athletes. In two cases of note (*Bowers v. the National Collegiate Athletic Association* and *Martin v. PGA Tour*) courts have held the NCAA and the PGA Tour to be places of public accommodation and therefore subject to Title III of the ADA.

In *Bowers v. the National Collegiate Athletic Association*, Michael Bowers, a student with a learning disability, was forced to enroll in special education classes to meet high school requirements. The courses he took were not included in the "core course" requirements of the NCAA and as a result, he was not eligible to participate in college athletics or receive financial aid. The court denied waiving the eligibility requirements and refused to grant a preliminary injunction. However, the court did decide that Title III of the ADA applied to the NCAA as a place of public accommodation and that the NCAA's waiver process and other accommodations for disabled students may not be enough to avoid a claim of discrimination. The case was allowed to proceed to trial on that basis. The court found that through the application of discriminatory standards, the NCAA had regulated itself in such a way to prevent Bowers' full enjoyment of his rights. As a result of Bowers and several other cases, the NCAA made some rule changes in 1997 to make their programs more accessible to student athletes with disabilities.

However, despite the changes, the NCAA was taken to court by the Justice Department in the District of Columbia in *United States v. National Collegiate Athletic Ass'n*. The Justice Department alleged that the NCAA's eligibility standards for student athletes with learning disabilities were too rigid. The Department pointed out that many of the high school courses designed for students with learning disabilities are excluded from the "core course" requirements and the waiver process also puts disabled students athletes at a disadvantage. These policies tend to screen out disabled student athletes, preventing them from enjoying the full spectrum of goods and services of the NCAA.

To avoid a trial and the resulting costs, the NCAA and the Justice Department agreed upon a Consent Decree. Under the Decree, the NCAA agreed to classify courses for students with learning disabilities as "core courses"; include experts on disabilities and take into account high school performance when evaluating waiver requests; allow students the opportunity to earn back a year of eligibility; and designate an ADA Compliance Officer to assist staff and students. The NCAA also paid $35,000 to four disabled student athletes who had been affected by the rules. However, the NCAA never admitted to being a place of public accommodation or being covered by Title III (Anderson, 1999, p. 3).

Casey Martin is a golfer who has a rare circulatory condition that causes his leg to throb and swell to twice its normal size when put under strain for extended periods of time. As a result, he uses a golf cart to travel between holes. The PGA Tour rules require that players walk between holes unless they are permitted to ride by the PGA Tour Rules Committee. The Committee would not grant Martin's request for a cart, so Martin sued under Title III of the ADA, alleging that the PGA Tour was a place of public accommodation and would not make a reasonable accommodation (use of a cart) for him to participate. The PGA Tour did not deny that Martin was disabled, but did not consider themselves to be a public accommodation.

In Casey Martin's case, having the PGA Tour declared to be a place of public accommodation was only the beginning of his legal battle. After the court held that the PGA Tour was subject to the ADA as a place of public accommodation, Martin sued the Tour a second time for the right to use a cart in competition.[33]

The court examined several issues in the Martin case. Firstly, there is no actual rule in the United States Golf Association (USGA) rules of play that prohibits cart use. The rule the PGA Tour was citing is their own, a modification of the USGA rules. Second, the PGA tour asserted that walking was a required element of the game because it requires stamina and that Martin would have an unfair advantage over the other players if allowed to use a cart. On this point the court found that players walk an average of five miles at their own pace during a game, with frequent breaks. This was not determined to be a significant factor. Additionally, even with the use of a cart Martin would still have to walk at least one and a quarter miles which, given his disability, would cause greater fatigue than walking five miles would cause an able bodied golfer. The court also pointed out that if there was any advantage to taking a cart, non-disabled golfers would have challenged the rule long ago. Thus, the court held that the use of a cart by Casey Martin was a reasonable accommodation that would not fundamentally change the nature of the PGA Tour (Anderson, p. 2). However, the PGA Tour appealed and the case continues to progress through the courts.

The publicity surrounding these cases has been in itself beneficial for people with disabilities in sport. The Martin case has been debated in sport bars around the country. Through their discussions, people have become more aware of the systemic discrimination facing disabled athletes and the simple modifications that are required to enable a person with a disability to participate.

Individuals with Disabilities Education Act (IDEA)—Overview

Although both the ADA and the Rehabilitation Act reach into the classroom, no legislation has had more impact on the delivery of education for students with disabilities than the Individuals with Disabilities Education Act (IDEA). Of all disability rights issues, "special" education for students with disabilities has gotten the most attention (Rothstein, 1997, p. 7).

The purpose of IDEA (formerly the Elementary and Secondary Act of 1965) is to "ensure that all children with disabilities have available to them a free appropriate public education that emphasizes special education and related services designed to meet the unique needs and prepare them for employment and independent living; to ensure that the rights of children with disabilities and the parents of such children are protected; and to assist States, localities, educational service agencies and federal agencies to provide for the education of all children." ((20 USC Sect 1400 (d) (1)).

The inclusion of physical education and extracurricular activities in IDEA has important ramifications for student-athletes with disabilities and students wishing to access physical education (Tucker, 1998, p. 361).

Individual Education Plan (IEP)

The cornerstone of IDEA is the requirement of each school district to complete an Individual Education Plan (IEP) for each student with a disability (Tucker, 1998, p.333). The plan must be completed and evaluated annually with the input of parents, and school personnel. The goal of the IEP is to set educational goals for each student on an individual basis and outline strategies to achieve those goals. For example, a student who has underdeveloped physical skills due to developmental or physical disabilities may have physiotherapy included in their IEP. The Rehabilitation Act also requires individual programs similar to the IEP. However, the requirements for physical education under IDEA are more specific and therefore provide more guidance for parents, teachers and the legal system (Dougherty, 1994, p. 82). Schools are also required to submit a plan setting forward their goals, timetables and measures needed to provide full educational opportunities to students with a disability in their system in order to be eligible for federal financial assistance (Tucker, 1998, p. 333).

Least Restrictive Environment (LRE)

In order to facilitate this individualized approach, IDEA mandates that students be placed in the least restrictive learning environment possible. The *least restrictive environment* (LRE) is the setting that minimizes the distinction between students with and without disabilities while permitting students with disabilities the most opportunity to interact with non-disabled students (Dougherty, 1994, p. 84). When segregation can be avoided and appropriate education provided, the Act requires integration (Tucker, 1998, p. 343). The most desirable outcome of placing students in the least restrictive environment appears to be total integration. However, in some cases this may not be the most desirable situation for the student. A school's ability to meet a student's needs also depends greatly on its size and resources. The IEP provides the opportunity for parents and schools to combine the needs of the students with available resources and set attainable goals. Unfortunately, diminishing school resources and increased desire of parents to provide the best possible education for their child do not always make agreeable combinations. Schools have refused requests from parents for additional supports or services, claiming lack of financial resources.

In *West Virginia v. West Virginia Board of Education*, the court held that a school district had to provide an interpreter for a deaf high school student so that she could play on the basketball team. Diana Lambert, an eleventh grade student, had an interpreter for her basic courses, but not for her extracurricular activities. She had participated in athletics since elementary school and played on the basketball team during her first two years of high school without an interpreter. When she began having trouble understanding the coach's directions, her parents requested that the school district provide an interpreter. The school district responded that it could not afford an interpreter for extracurricular activities. The state supreme court concluded that IDEA and the Rehabilitation Act required the school district to provide support services and accommodations for students with disabilities while they participated in non-academic and extracurricular activities.

Protection of Athletic Involvement Through the IEP

The IEP provides a unique opportunity for parents and teachers to ensure that students with disabilities have access to appropriate physical education and extracurricular activities. A student whose IEP includes participation on school sports teams to help develop social and physical skills can claim protection of that right under IDEA as well as the ADA and Rehabilitation Act.

Given that some age-eligibility lawsuits have not been successful under the ADA and the Rehabilitation Act, this may be a way for parents of students with mental or learning disabilities to ensure their child can access athletics throughout their school career. In *Dennin v. Connecticut Interscholastic Athletic Conference, Inc.*, the court found that a nineteen-year-old student with Down syndrome had a federally protected right to participate in interscholastic sports because participation had been recommended as part of his Individual Education Program. Whereas in the *Pottgen* and *Sandison* cases the court found that disability was not an acceptable reason to waive the age eligibility rule, in this case waiving the rule was allowed because participation on the swim team was deemed essential to achieving Dennin's educational goals. Dennin's parents and teachers found that being a member of the team helped him to develop better social skills, improved his knowledge of nutrition and made him feel a part of the high school. In light of these benefits, the special education planning and placement team had strongly recommended that David continue to be an active member of the team. The court found that to deprive David of the opportunity to participate in interscholastic meets and be a member of the team would cause him irreparable harm.

Although IDEA provides protections for some students with disabilities in regards to athletics and physical education, others may still fall between the cracks. IDEA only covers students who, by virtue of their disability, require special education services. Such students are considered "educationally disabled." Educational disabilities include mental disabilities, learning disabilities and physical disabilities or other health impairments that require special education services. Under IDEA, these students are entitled to occupational therapy, recreation, therapeutic recreation and physical therapy. The list is not exhaustive. Any service that can be proven to be of benefit to a child with a disability may be covered under IDEA (Tucker, 1998, p. 336). However, a student requiring no special services is not protected. As a result, some sport cases do not fall under IDEA because they involve students who do not require special education services. For example, a student with an amputated leg who requires no extra services in academics and is not allowed to play on a sports team would have no recourse under IDEA. However, Section 504 of the Rehabilitation Act covers all school-aged children (Tucker, 1998, p. 466).

Risk Management and People with Disabilities

The approach to risk management when dealing with people with disabilities is the same as when approaching people without disabilities. The "reasonable person" standard is applied in a similar manner, with one exception. The actions of a reasonable person when dealing with a person with a disability will be examined under a standard of care that takes the person's disability into account (Barnes, 1996, p. 298).

People with disabilities are considered to be *vulnerable persons* under the law. Although there is no one consistent definition of a vulnerable person in federal or provincial law, the category is generally agreed to include children, youth, seniors and people with physical or mental disabilities. Regardless of how independent a person with a disability considers themselves to be, the court will consider the disability as a mitigating factor in a liability case. Therefore, a teacher who leaves a class of students with mental disabilities unattended for a few minutes may be found liable for negligence if a student is injured, whereas another teacher of students the same age may not.

For example, in *Foster v. Houston General Insurance Company*,[34] a teacher was found negligent when a student with a mental disability was hit by a vehicle while jaywalking en route to a Special Olympics basketball practice. Although the teacher had instructed the group about crossing the street, the court held that the teacher should have realized the information was beyond the capacity of the students to retain. In addition, it was held that the teacher should have foreseen the potential for an impulsive act like running across the street and ensured that there was sufficient supervision to prevent this from happening.

In *Bain v. Calgary Board of Education*, the school board was found negligent for allowing a nineteen-year-old student with a learning disability to go on an unsupervised, unscheduled mountain climb.

These cases show that in designing any program for people with disabilities, the individual needs and abilities of each participant must be considered. Coaches and teachers cannot assume that a person with a disability is able to perform the same tasks with the same degree of skill as other people of the same age or gender. Although the cases reviewed here deal specifically with learning and mental disabilities, there are implications for students with physical disabilities as well. A student with a physical disability like osteogenesis imperfecta (brittle bones syndrome) who is integrated into a physical education class poses some risk management issues for the teacher. It may not be safe for that student to participate in a sport like wrestling, where physical force is involved. These considerations can be effectively managed through the use of an Individual Education Plan.

Just as there is a wide range of disabilities, so there must be a wide range of risk management practices to accommodate those disabilities. Sport and recreation providers may sometimes feel caught between conflicting requirements. On one hand they are required by law not to discriminate against people with disabilities. On the other, they are held to a higher standard of care to these individuals and therefore may feel they cannot treat them equally.

Many cases have arisen against schools who prevented students with disabilities from participating in sports out of a misplaced idea of protecting them from harm. However, courts have held that people with disabilities have the right to enjoy physical activity, with all of its risks, just as anyone else does.[35] However, those involved with providing that activity need to be sure they have taken reasonable steps to ensure the activity is safe in regards to the specific needs of the participants. In some ways, the law is behind the societal developments in this area, so sport providers walk a fine line between meeting the standard of care required and respecting the individual rights of their participants.

Disabled Sport in Canada

Disabled sport in Canada is supervised by a variety of different sport governing bodies. In some sports, such as swimming, swimmers with disabilities are members of the same sport governing body (Swim Nation Canada) as swimmers without disabilities and attend some of the same events. In other sports, such as track and field, the sport is governed nationally and provincially by disabled sport organizations in partnership with Sport Canada. In general, most sports are moving towards a form of integration. The speed at which this happens has traditionally depended on the interest of the non-disabled sport governing body in having disabled athletes as members.

When disabled sports first got started, provincial disability-specific organizations governed competition for a variety of sports. These organizations are still integrally involved in delivering sport opportunities to people with disabilities. In Ontario, Sport for Disabled-Ontario is an umbrella organization for the following provincial sport governing bodies: the Ontario Wheelchair Sports Association, the Ontario Cerebral Palsy Sports Association, the Ontario Blind Sports Association and the Ontario Amputee and Les Autres Sports Association. These provincial associations govern the sports of track and field, boccia (for athletes with cerebral palsy), wheelchair basketball, wheelchair rugby, powerlifting, goalball (for blind athletes) and wheelchair tennis.

To ensure equity in competition as much as possible, athletes with physical disabilities are put into ability classes based on medical evaluations. Thus, an athlete with cerebral palsy would not compete against a blind athlete. Most sports offer competition split by gender as well, although boccia, a sport for athletes with cerebral palsy, is completely co-educational.

For athletes with mental disabilities, sport opportunities are provided by Special Olympics. Special Olympics is also a multi-sport organization, providing training and competition opportunities in the following sports:[36]

Spring	Summer	Winter	Demonstration Sports
Swimming	Soccer	Speed Skating	Curling
5 Pin Bowling	Softball	Nordic Skiing	Rhythmic Gymnastics
10 Pin Bowling	Track and Field	Alpine Skiing	Basketball
Powerlifting		Figure Skating	
Floor Hockey		Snowshoeing	

Competition for athletes with disabilities is available from the regional to international level. The Summer and Winter Special Olympics World Games are held every four years for athletes with mental disabilities, while athletes with physical disabilities may aspire to the Paralympic Games. While the two sport movements are often confused by media and the general public, in reality they are different entities.

The mandate of Ontario Special Olympics is to "provide sport training and competition for athletes with mental disabilities." The philosophy of the organization is inclusionary, and while athletes are placed in divisions, they are not medically classified by mental ability. For example, an athlete who runs the 100m in fifteen seconds will be placed in a division with other athletes with similar times, not with athletes of a similar mental ability. In addition, Special Olympics is an international association with chapters in countries around the world. Each chapter operates sport clubs and programs in a variety of sports, in addition to providing competition.

In contrast, athletes with physical disabilities are placed in classes based on an evaluation of their level of disability, regardless of their competitive results. Therefore, a new below-knee amputee would be placed in a class with other below knee amputees before running their first competitive race. The Paralympics is a set of games that occur every fours years, however as an organization they are modeled on the Olympic Games. They are held following the summer and winter Olympic Games in the same host city. Therefore, unlike Special Olympics, the Paralympic Games have no ongoing involvement in community sport programs or events other than the games themselves. These opportunities are provided by a myriad of international, national and provincial sport bodies.

Both sport movements also use age and gender divisions to provide fair and equitable competition for their athletes. Differences aside, the movements do share an overwhelming commitment to providing sport opportunities for traditionally underserved populations. In addition, there are athletes who belong to both areas. For example, an athlete who has cerebral palsy and uses a wheelchair may also have a mental disability. As of the 1996 Atlanta Paralympic Games, there are also Paralympic events for high-level athletes with a mental disability and a national sport organization (Canadian Association of Athletes with a Mental Handicap) has been established to meet their needs. In recognizing that there are many similarities as well as differences between athletes with mental and those with physical disabilities, the most important thing to remember is that both groups of athletes deserve the same respect for their accomplishments as their non-disabled counterparts.

As the story of Kenny Doyle illustrates, this respect is not always forthcoming. A case in point is the treatment of athletes with disabilities in the United States by the United States Olympic Committee. The USOC assumed responsibility for American Paralympic athletes with a 1998 amendment to the 1978 Amateur Sports Act.[37] However, the USOC provides negligible support to Paralympic athletes in comparison to Olympic athletes. Paralympic athletes are not eligible for the award money set aside for medallists or the training grants for athletes preparing for the games. They are not even able to use the residents' training services at the USOC's San Diego facility. Less than 1.5 percent of the USOC's quadrennial budget for 1996–2000 was allocated to programs for disabled athletes. When it comes to uniforms, disabled athletes receive uniforms of lower quality with fewer pieces than Olympic athletes.

There have been some recent changes made to allow athletes with disabilities greater opportunities. The USOC has added four seats to its Board of Directors for representatives from disabled sport groups and formed a committee to examine integrating athletes with disabilities into non-disabled national sport governing bodies (Byzek, 1999, p. 16–21).

The experiences of athletes with disabilities in Canada have been marked by similar experiences of "different" treatment. However, the general movement has been towards more inclusive programs and events. Swimming and track and field athletes with physical disabilities have been included in a limited way at the Canada and Ontario Summer and Winter Games since 1993. The 1998 Canada Winter Games in Newfoundland marked the debut of wheelchair basketball as a sport with full medal status. The 2001 Summer Games will include swimmers with a mental disability as full members of their provincial teams.[38] Athletes who are not aiming for the elite level of competition can participate in programs in their own communities. However, there is still a long way to go before equity in sport opportunities for people with disabilities will be achieved.

Summary

In general, Canadian and American society as a whole have the best interest of people with disabilities at heart. Organizations that prevent people with disabilities from taking part generally mistakenly feel that they are acting in the individual's best interest. The impact of the ADA and other pieces of legislation is that the decision to participate or not has been taken out of the hands of the organizations and placed into the hands of the individual. Most schools, organizations, clubs and programs make the effort to include people with disabilities in their programs. However, in the event that this does not happen, people with disabilities have several legal avenues through which to challenge discriminatory practices. Society has become more litigious, and people with disabilities have not been immune to this development. People with disabilities, like others in the community, have become more aware of their rights and more willing to challenge instances where they feel these rights have been violated.

Questions for Class Discussion

1. Distinguish between physical, mental and learning disabilities.
2. Should disabled sport organizations be able to exclude people without disabilities from becoming athletes in their programs? What legal support exists for your answer?
3. What was the impact of the *Southeastern Community College v. Davis* decision on sport-related disability cases?
4. How did the Individuals with Disabilities Education Act affect integration in the school system? Discuss the positive and negative implications of classroom integration for teachers and students.
5. A child with cerebral palsy who uses an electric wheelchair wants to participate in an Little Tykes indoor soccer program. Identify what issues would need to be addressed in putting together a risk management plan for the program.
6. You have been asked to do a presentation for a high school class on the differences between Special Olympics and the Paralympics. What will be the main points of your presentation?

Table of Cases

Bain v. Calgary Bd. of Educ., [1994] 2 W.W.R. 468, 18 C.C.L.T. (2d) 249 (Alta. Q.B.).

Bowers v. National Collegiate Athletic Ass'n. 974 F. Supp. 459 (D. NJ 1997) & 9 F. Supp. 2d 460, 1998 U.S. Dist. LEXIS 8552 (D. NJ 1998).

Caruso v. Blockbuster/Sony Music Entertainment Centre at the Waterfront, 174 F. 3d 166 (3rd Cir. , 1999).

Dennin v. Connecticut Interscholastic Athletic Conference, Inc., 94 F. 3d 96, 17 A.D.D. 749, 111 Ed. Law Rep. 1154 (2d Cir. 1996); 913 F. Supp. 663, 16 A.D.D. 416, 106 Ed. Law Rep. 1130 (D.Conn. 1996).

Ganden v. National Collegiate Athletic Ass'n, 1996 U.S. Dist. LEXIS 17368 (N.D. IL 1996).

Hoot by Hoot v. Michigan High School Athletic Ass'n, 853 F. Supp. 243 (E.D. Mich. 1994).

Johnson v. Florida High Sch. Activities Ass'n (FHSAA) 899 F. Supp. 579 (M.D. Fla. 1995).

Martin v. PGA Tour, Inc. 984 F. Supp 1320 (D. Or. 1998) and *Martin v. the PGA Tour, Inc.,* 1998 WL 67529 (D. Or.).

Pottgen v. Missouri State Activities Ass'n, 103 F. 3d 720, 19 A.D.D.763, 115 Ed. Law Rep. 867 (8th Cir. 1994).

Sandison v. Michigan High School Athletic Association, Inc. 64 F.3d 1026 (6thCir. 1995).

Southeastern Community College v. Davis, 442 U.S. 397, 99 S. Ct. 2361, 60 L. Ed. 2d 980, 1 A.D.D. 60 (1979).

Traylor v. West Virginia Bd. of Educ., No. Civ. A. 97-C-2516 (W. Va. Cir. Ct. Dec. 23, 1997).

United States v. National Collegiate Athletic Ass'n. Civ. No. 981 290 (D. D.C. May 27, 1998).

West Virginia v. West Virginia Board of Educ., No. 22225 (W. Va. Sup. Ct. July 20, 1994).

Wright v. Columbia University, 520F. Supp. 789 (E.D. Pa. 1981).

Youth Bowling Council v. McLeod (1990), 75O.R. (2d) 451, 74 D.L.R. (4th) 625 (Div. Ct.); affg. (1988), 9 C.H.R.R. D/5371 (Ont. Bd. of Inq.): affd. (1994), 20 O.R. (3d) 658, 121 D.L.R. (4th) 187 (C.A.).

Endnotes

1. Americans with Disabilities Act [42 USC 1201 2 (a) (1)].
2. The Canadian Charter of Rights and Freedoms, Part I of the Constitution Act, 1982, being Schedule B of the Canada Act 1982, c. 11 (U.K.).
3. Declaration of the Rights of Disabled Persons, 9 December 1975. U.N. G.A. Resolution 34, in Lepofsky, D "Equality Rights for Handicapped Persons in the Charter: Putting the Accent on Individual Ability," *What you need to know about disability law*, p.131.

4 Ibid. Art. 9, p.132.
5 Canadian Bill of Rights S.C. 1960, c.44, R.S.C. 1970.
6 Canadian Charter of Rights and Freedoms, 1982, s.1.
7 Ibid. s. 15(2); Bird, S and Zauhar J. *Recreation and the law*, p. 10.
8 Ontario Human Rights Code R.S.O. 1981, c. 53.
9 Ontario Human Rights Code, R.S.O. 1990, c.H.19 s. 1, 5.
10 Ibid. s. 10.
11 Ontario Human Rights Code, R.S.O. 1990, c.H.19 s17(1).
12 C.H.R.R. D/5371 (Ont. Bd. of Inq.): Youth Bowling Council v. McLeod (1990), 75 O.R. (2d) 451, 74 D.L.R. (4th) 625 (Div. Ct.); (1988), 9 affd. (1994), 20 O.R. (3d) 658, 121 D.L.R. (4th) 187 (C.A.).
13 Ontario Disability Support Program Act, *Statutes of Ontario*, 1997, Chpt. 25 Sched. B.
14 Rehabilitation Act of 1973, [29 USC 701].
15 Rehabilitation Act of 1973, [29 USC 705(8) (b)].
16 34 CFR 104.3 (j)(2)(ii) in Rothstein, L, *Disabilities and the law*, p. 217.
17 *Pahulu v. University of Kansas,* 897 F. Supp. 1387 (D. Kan. 1995). Alani Pahulu was a football player who was hit during practice which caused transient quadriplegia. This condition, combined with a congenitally narrow cervical canal, caused team doctors to disqualify him from participating in football because they believed he was at great risk for injury. Pahulu saw three physicians who cleared him to play and sued the university under Sect. 504 of the Rehabilitation Act, claiming football to be a major life activity that the university was preventing him from enjoying due to his disability. The court found that playing football may be a major life activity in that athletics may be an important component of learning. The court found against Pahulu because he was not disabled within the meaning of Sect. 504 since the university had not substantially limited his opportunity to learn; *Sandison v. Michigan High School Athletic Association, Inc.* 64 F.3d 1026 (6th Cir. 1995). In the case of a student-athlete with a learning disability who did not meet the age eligibility requirement, the court found that participation on intercollegiate sports teams did constitute a major life activity. For a differing opinion, see *Knapp v. Northwestern University* 101 F. 3d 473 (7th Cir. 1996), where the court held that playing intercollegiate basketball is not a major life activity.
18 Rehabilitation Act of 1973, [29 USCA 794].
19 *Sandison v. Michigan High School Athletic Ass'n; Pottgen v. Missouri State Activities Ass'n ; Johnson v. Florida High Sch. Activities Ass'n (FHSAA) ; Traylor v. West Virginia Bd. of Educ.; Hoot by Hoot v. Michigan High School Athletic Ass'n; Dennin v. Connecticut Interscholastic Athletic Conference, Inc.*
20 The Civil Rights Act of 1991, Pub L No 102–166, 105 Stat 1071.
21 [29 USCA Sect. 794 (6)].
22 [29 USCA Sect. 706 (8)(d)].
23 [29 USCA Sect. 785].
24 Americans with Disabilities Act [42 USC 12101].
25 Americans with Disabilities Act [42 USC 12101, 201 (2)].
26 Ibid., 201 (1).
27 Ibid. 201 (2).
28 Americans with Disabilities Act [42 USC 12101, 302].
29 Ibid., 302 (2) (a) (i–v).
30 *Caruso v. Blockbuster/Sony Music Entertainment Centre at the Waterfront,* 174 F. 3d 166 (3rd Cir. , 1999). Attendees in wheelchairs at a concert were unable to see due to standing crowd, or to access the lawn area. A suit was filed under the ADA alleging that the facility was responsible for providing lines of sight over standing patrons and a wheelchair accessible lawn area. The plaintiffs lost in the District Court. On appeal, the court found that the ADA wording on sightlines was too ambiguous to make a decision, but that it was not structurally impractical to provide wheelchair access to the lawn area. This case has implications for grass seating areas in minor league baseball stadiums and other sport facilities. *United Sates v. City of Fargo, North Dakota,* DOJ 204-56-3 (U.S. Department of Justice, Nov. 23, 1993). City of Fargo settled a complaint under the ADA that ticket prices for the Fargodome were discriminatory. The only accessible seating was available in higher-priced seating areas. The City agreed to adjust pricing for people with disabilities requiring special seating.
31 Olsen, S. "Opposition to Disabilities Act OK," *Congressional Record,* Article 12 (Olsen, 1989).
32 *Pottgen v. Missouri State High School Activities Ass'n; Sandison v. Michigan High School Athletic Association, Inc. ; Johnson v. Florida High Sch. Activities Ass'n (FHSAA) ; Dennin v. Connecticut Interscholastic Athletic Conference, Inc.,; Ganden v. National Collegiate Athletic Ass'n.*
33 *Martin v. the PGA Tour, Inc.,* 1998 WL 67529 (D. Or.)
34 *Foster v. Houston General Insurance Company*, in Kozlowski, J. "Handicapped Athlete Fatally Injured en Route to Gym," *National Parks and Recreation Association*, Alexandria, VA.

35 *Wright v. Columbia University*, 520F. Supp. 789 (E.D. Pa. 1981). Joseph Wright was blind in one eye and wanted to play intercollegiate football. School administrators refused him the opportunity to play because it was felt that he might be a danger to himself or to the other players. Under the Rehabilitation Act, the court prohibited the school from excluding Wright from football based on his disability.

36 Sports indicated are available in Ontario. Sport offerings in other provinces or other countries may differ.

37 Amateur Sports Act of 1978, 36 USC s. 371–376.

38 Canada Games News Release, September 28, 1999.

References

Andersen, P. M. (Ed). (1999, Summer). "Entertainment center did not violate the Americans with Disabilities Act by failing to provide wheelchair patrons with lines of sight over standing patrons." *You make the call* (pp. 8–9). Milwaukee, Wisconsin: Marquette University Law School.

Anderson, P. M. (Ed). (1998, Fall). "NCAA found amenable to suit under Title II of the Americans with Disabilities Act and eligibility rules scrutinized." *You make the call* (pp. 1–3). Milwaukee, Wisconsin: Marquette University Law School.

Andersen, P. M. (Ed). (1998, Summer). "Pro-Golf Association ordered to allow disabled golfer the use of a cart for tournament play in accord with the Americans with Disabilities Act." *You make the call* (pp. 1–2). Milwaukee, Wisconsin: Marquette University Law School.

Barnes, J. (1996). *Sports and the law in Canada* (3rd ed.). Toronto: Butterworths.

Bird, S. and Zauhar, J. (1997). *Recreation and the law* (2nd ed.) Toronto: Carswell.

Byzek, J. (1999, September). Bad Sports. *Ragged Edge Magazine*, 16–21.

Colker, R. (1995). *The law of disability discrimination: Cases and materials*. Cincinnati: Anderson Publishing Company.

Dougherty, N., Auxter, D., Goldberger, A. and Heinzeman, G. (1994). *Sport, physical activity and the law*. Champaign, Illinois: Human Kinetics Publishers.

Gregson, I. (1999). *Irresistible force: Disability sport in Canada*. Victoria: Polestar.

Lepofsky, D. (1993). Equality rights for handicapped persons in the Charter: Putting the accent on individual ability. *What you need to know about disability law*. Toronto: Law Society of Upper Canada, Department of Continuing Education.

Moriarty, D., Holman, M., Brown, R. and Moriarty, M. (Eds.)(1993). *Sport, fitness and the law*. Toronto: Canadian Scholars Press Inc.

Thomas, J.L. (1997). "Through the ADA and the Rehabilitation Act, high school athletes are saying 'put me in coach': *Sandison v. Michigan High School Athletics Association*." *University of Cincinnati Law Review, 65*, 727–763.

Tucker, B. P. (1998). *Federal disability law in a nutshell*. St. Paul, Minnesota: West Group.

Raina, P. (1999, Spring). A rose by any other name is not an Ontarians with Disabilities Act. *Abilities, 38*, 32–34.

Rothstein, L. (1997). *Disabilities and the law* (2nd ed.). St. Paul, Minnesota: West Group.

Swanson, L (1997, Spring). "Calling for an Ontarians with Disabilities Act." *Abilities, 30*, 1–6.

Weber, M.C. (1995). "Disability discrimination by State and local government: The relationship between Section 504 of the Rehabilitation Act and Title II of the Americans With Disabilities Act." *William and Mary Law Review, 36*, 1091–1133.

CHAPTER 13

SPORT AND THE LAW OF DEFAMATION

Raymond E. Brown

Introduction

The law of defamation occupies a very special place in the life of the law. It has its immediate origins in the English common law where the courts recognized two distinct causes of action relating to libel and slander. The former protected persons from written defamations while the latter protected them from oral defamations. For historical reasons, which cannot be explored here, the law gave greater protection to a person who was defamed by way of a writing rather than by way of the spoken word. As a result, the distinction continues to be drawn between written and oral defamation in many of the Canadian provinces and American states, although some jurisdictions have abolished the differences and now treat slander the same as libel.[1]

To understand the law of defamation and its implications for those who participate in sports and athletics, I have created the following scenarios.

(1) A coach in the presence of several other players berates one them and says that he is unmotivated, lazy and absolutely inept, and in addition he understands that he and some members of the school band were taking cocaine.

(2) The parents of the player send a blistering letter to the athletic director with a copy to the media calling the coach a tyrant and bully and accuse him of sexually molesting one of his players.

(3) A local columnist in the newspaper calls for the coach's resignation because of his "absolute incompetence" and refers to a series of plays he called during a drive for a touchdown in a losing football game.

(4) The coach is contacted by the local media and asked to comment on the contents of the parent's letter and the article in the newspaper, and he characterizes the letter's charges as an outright fabricated lie and the columnist as an incompetent s.o.b. who knows nothing about sports.

(5) A group of citizens circulate a petition demanding the resignation of the coach for "incompetence" and in contacting members of the public to secure their signatures relate the incidents described in the letter from the parents.

(6) The coach is contacted by a local employer and asked to submit a character reference for the player about whom he was critical and, in response, he characterizes him as a troublemaker.

(7) During legal proceedings in a matter unconnected to these incidents, the coach is subpoenaed to testify and during his testimony he gratuitously refers to the citizens circulating

the petition calling for his dismissal as a bunch of "faggots" and this remark is reported in the local newspaper.

(8) As a result of all the furore, the coach is removed from his position and now sells life insurance where he makes $20,000 less per year.

Prior to 1964, the law in Canada and the United States was remarkably similar. In almost every respect the law imposed a strict liability on those who defamed another. It made no difference whether the defendant intended to defame or injure the plaintiff or even to refer to him or her at all; if he did he was liable. All that a plaintiff had to show in order to recover was that the remarks referred to the plaintiff and were defamatory, that they were published to someone other than the plaintiff, and that the defendant was responsible for the publication. If the defamation was in writing, the case was said to be actionable per se, and there was a presumption that the plaintiff's reputation was injured. No evidence had to be shown as to the extent of that injury, although the plaintiff was free to do so. If, on the other hand, the defamation occurred orally, it was actionable per se only if the publication impugned the reputation of the plaintiff with respect to his or her trade, office, profession or employment, or if it charged him or her with a criminal offense, or imputed to him or her a disease or, in some jurisdictions, imputed unchastity to a woman. In all other cases, a plaintiff in a slander action had to show some special damages, in the form of pecuniary harm, in order to recover.

In 1964, the Supreme Court of the United States in the now famous case of *New York Times Co. v. Sullivan*[2] constitutionalized part of the law of defamation. Because of its concerns about the effect of the law of defamation on First Amendment freedoms of speech and the press, the court held that in cases where a public official was a plaintiff, he or she had to show actual malice in order to recover for defamatory comments and actual malice was defined as knowing or reckless falsity.[3] In subsequent decisions of the Supreme court, the constitutional privilege was extended to publications about public figures as well as public officials (*Curtis Publishing Co. v. Butts*) and a plaintiff who fell into these categories was required to meet a more stringent test in submitting his or her evidence in meeting the appropriate standard of proof.[4] If the defendant was a member of the communications media, the strict liability rules no longer applied and a court could only impose liability if fault was shown by the publisher.[5] In addition, presumed and punitive damages could no longer be awarded without a showing of actual malice. While at one time, the court appeared to provide a constitutional protection for all expressions of opinion, it has since been made clear that expressions of opinion that imply the presence of underlying defamatory facts will not be protected (*Milkovich v. Lorain Journal Co.*). In addition, the court also made it clear that the constitutional protection applies only to publications concerning matters of public concern;[6] all other publications fall within the common law rules of each of the state courts.

Canada has retained its common law rules of strict liability in all cases. The United States has substantially altered the common law rule of strict liability but only where the plaintiff is a public official or public figure or the defendant is a member of the communications media and the defamation involves a matter of public concern. In almost all other respects, the law stands as it did prior to 1964 although several states have modified its common law to create a better balance between the constitutional rules and the state rules governing the law of defamation.

The highest courts of England, Australia and New Zealand have recently provided greater protection for publications on matters of public concern. These may influence the course the Supreme Court of Canada will follow in the future. While these courts have refused to follow the United States decision in *New York Times Co. v. Sullivan*, they have provided greater protection for the communications media, particularly, where they inadvertently defame someone in the process of reporting information to the public. The House of Lords recognized a common law privilege to report matters of public concern to the public generally taking into consideration the seriousness of the allegation, whether it is a matter of public concern, the degree to which it commands respect, the tone of the article in which it appears, the circumstances of the publication including its timing, the source of the information, the steps taken to verify it, including comments by the plaintiff, the urgency of the publication and whether the plaintiff's view is presented.[7] The High Court of Australia has recognized a common law privilege to publish material on governmental and political matters to the public if it is established that the publication was reasonable in the circumstances and that the defendant was not actuated by malice.[8] The New Zealand Court of Appeal has recognized a qualified privilege for generally published statements on matters of public concern touching on the actions and qualities of those currently or formerly elected to Parliament and those aspiring to be members of Parliament.[9] The extent to which these cases might be extended to include reports on sporting matters has not been decided.

Referring to the examples given at the beginning of this article, the common law of strict liability would apply in each of the cases. Assuming that the remarks are defamatory, and there are otherwise no defenses available, the parties would be strictly liable. In the United States, the parties would be strictly liable for the private communications, but fault would have to be shown wherever a decision was made to sue a newspaper. It may be possible that the coach has achieved such a degree of fame that he may qualify as a public figure and, in that case, he may have to show actual malice in order to recover at least where the comments involve matters of public concern. There are some other differences that will be pointed out in the remainder of this paper that may make it more difficult for a coach, athletic director or athlete to recover for any defamatory comments.[10]

In what follows, I intend to explore the elements of a cause of action for defamation, the defenses available to the person sued and the specific application of the law to a coach, athletic director or athlete. It must be emphasized that this chapter is a superficial overview of a complicated area of the law and that any person who feels aggrieved about what may have been said or written about him or her should consult a lawyer before venturing any further.

The Cause of Action for Defamation

What is Defamatory?

In order to establish a cause of action, a plaintiff must show that the words used would be reasonably understood in a defamatory sense. In the majority of cases where a plaintiff has been successful, the words are defamatory because they accuse the plaintiff of a crime of some reprehensible nature. A coach or player may be accused of fixing a game and where that is a crime, it is actionable per se. Thus, Wally Butts, the athletic director at the University of Georgia, was accused of fixing football games while a coach and he recovered $460,000 in a case that was ultimately upheld by the Supreme Court of the United States (*Curtis Publishing Co. v. Butts*). Coaches and athletic directors obviously occupy positions of employment and defamation actions are commonly brought because a person has been accused of incompetence in their office, trade, profession or work. Thus, the accusations used in the illustrative examples may fit into that category. However, there are a large number of accusations that do not fit within either classification but which may be defamatory. Thus a coach, athletic director or player may be accused of racism or prejudice, corruption, cruelty, lack of ethics, falsehood, fraud, dishonesty, hypocrisy, lack of integrity, stupidity, mental incompetence, immorality, insobriety and vulgarity and at one time or another a court has awarded appropriate damages for the loss of reputation caused by these accusations.

In each of these cases the inquiry of the court is rather simple: Does the publication lower the reputation of the plaintiff in the estimation of the community? Does it injuriously affect his or her reputation and good name? Commonly, a court will ask whether it exposes the plaintiff to hatred, contempt or ridicule, although that inquiry may not always disclose the real reason for the court's conclusion.

"Reputation" is formed by the collective judgment of others. We all regard it as a matter of importance as to how persons in the community view us. Therefore, the law will not permit others to injure that reputation with impunity. Nevertheless, the law will not deal with trifles. A publication must appreciably affect a person's reputation. The law of defamation will provide no remedy for inconsequential aspersions on the plaintiff's reputation that merely annoy, embarrass and involve conduct that is at worst foolish, impertinent, meddlesome, silly or unpleasant. Some degree of latitude will be allowed for words of vituperation and insult. There are not enough courts in either country to provide balm to injured feelings for minor unkindnesses.

In the scenarios I have created, the reference to a player taking cocaine might be actionable per se since that may suggest the commission of a crime (Example 1). The same is true with regard to the accusation of sexual molestation (Example 2). It is also generally defamatory to call someone a liar (Example 4), although that conclusion is more likely to be drawn in Canada than in the United States. In the balance of the examples, the results are more questionable since they may be viewed merely as "rhetorical hyperbole" or "insult" not worthy of the protection of the law of defamation. This conclusion is more likely to be drawn in the United States, rather than Canada, and whether they are actionable per se will depend upon whether they were published orally or in writing.

In determining whether the words are defamatory, the court has adopted a number of rules. The words are to be looked at in their plain, obvious and natural meaning since that is how most of us understand language that is used. They are to be looked at as they would be understood by persons generally, that is by reasonable persons of ordinary intelligence and understanding. Courts will avoid an extreme, strained or tortured interpretation of the language. The words will not be distorted to give them an unusual meaning or be evaluated by their extremes. A court will not strain to find them defamatory or non-defamatory. It is to be judged neither by the impact that the words would have on those who are naturally inclined to attribute the worst, nor is it to be judged by those who might naively believe the best about others.

The words will not be considered apart from the context in which they were written or spoken. Words, like individuals, are often judged by the company they keep. A word that has different shades of meaning may derive colour and significance from the nature of the act to which it is applied. Words that may be completely innocent standing alone may be rendered defamatory by the place and circumstances of their publication, and words that are usually defamatory when considered alone may not be actionable when considered in connection with their context.

The court will not seize upon a particular sentence or phrase and detach it from its context. Thus, in an action for slander, the expression on the face or the accompanying gestures, the intonation of the voice, the movement of the body, and the accent or emphasis placed on particular words or phrases may affect the way in which the words will be understood. As an English poet once observed, the accompanying gestures may "convey a libel in a frown and wink a reputation down."[11]

The court does take into consideration changing community values. Community standards change with time. Shifts in public sentiment have allowed different courts at different times to reach different conclusions as to whether certain charges are defamatory. Thus, an untrue accusation that someone is gay (Example 7) may have an entirely different effect on the reputation of someone today than would have been true if it had been published less than a decade ago.[12]

Publication

Because the gist of the action for defamation is injury to reputation, there must be proof that the defamatory words were published. Publication means that the words were communicated to someone other than the person defamed. Thus, if the coach had taken the player aside, he could have said exactly the same things and more and there would be no action for defamation (Example 1). If the parents had sent their letter only to the coach, they could have made even worse accusations without the fear of being sued for defamation (Example 2). The reason is that the law of defamation does not protect the esteem with which the plaintiff regards himself or herself, but rather the opinion or esteem which he or she enjoys in the eyes of others.

A third person for the purpose of publication includes almost everyone. It could be the employee, co-employee, employer, or agent of the defamer or the person defamed. It could be made to their spouses or children, or a complete stranger. However, a communication from one spouse to the other is probably not a publication for the purpose of the tort. And in a minority of American jurisdictions, a communication within a corporation is not considered a publication on the theory that since a corporation is treated as a legal person, a communication within the company must be considered the legal equivalent of talking to oneself.

Everyone who participates in the publication is liable as a publisher. He may be responsible because he authorized, composed or assisted in the composition of the defamation, or because he actually published it or caused it to be published. He may have requested, incited or encouraged someone else to publish it, or he may be responsible because he had the authority to forbid it but permitted it, or he had the responsibility to remove an offending publication but allowed it to remain. Thus, the citizens who signed the petition should have realized that it would later be published and they are as responsible for its circulation as those who actually published it (Example 5). The university may be liable for the publications by the coach if the latter is acting within the scope of his employment (Example 1) and the newspaper may be liable for the column written by the columnist and published in the newspaper (Example 3).

Each person who repeats the defamatory statement is as responsible to the person defamed as though he or she initially put it into circulation. He will not be exonerated on the ground that it is a mere repetition of what someone else has already said. In the law of defamation, talebearers are as bad as talemakers.

A person is liable for a publication only if he or she intended or reasonably should have known that the contents of the defamation would be communicated to a third person. Thus, a defendant would not be liable to the person defamed if the letter was addressed to him and opened and read by someone else unless the defendant knew or was aware of circumstances in which he reasonably should have known that it would be opened and read by someone other than the person to whom the letter was addressed. Thus, if the letter by the parents to the athletic director had been opened and read by a secretary, that would not be a publication to the secretary unless the parents knew that as a matter of course all letters to the athletic director were opened by the secretary (Example 2).

Identification of the Plaintiff

There must be some certainty as to the person defamed. To be actionable, a publication must refer to a specific person and that person must be the plaintiff. The test is whether the ordinary reasonable person to whom the words were published would understand that the words referred to the plaintiff.

There is no requirement that the person defamed be referred to by name. The reference may be made indirectly and shown by extrinsic facts. The plaintiff's identification might be made by physical description, or by association with someone else, or by similarity of name, or by reference to previous or later publications, or by reference to a group to which he or she belongs, or a business or personal relationship which he or she enjoys, or activities in which he or she has engaged. A person may be identified by reference to well known personal characteristics and mannerisms, or by an occupation or profession in which he or she has been engaged or an incident in which he or she was involved. The plaintiff's picture may accompany an article in which he or she is otherwise not named. Thus, if the letter by the parents to the athletic director did not refer to the coach by name, the issue would be whether the person reading the letter would reasonably understand that it referred to the football coach (Example 2).

If the plaintiff is identified, the defendant's innocence is no defence. The question is not whether the defendant aimed the defamation at the plaintiff but whether he hit him. He may not have intended those consequences; he may even have taken every reasonable precaution to insure that those consequences would not occur. If the plaintiff is the one who is hit, the defendant is liable regardless of the innocence of his intent and the reasonableness of his conduct.

The defendant may be liable to an individual even if his or her remarks are directed against a group of persons if the group is small enough so that the remarks can be reasonably understood to apply to each of the persons within that group. The court will look to the intensity of suspicion cast upon the plaintiff as a member of the group. Where the reference is to some of the members of the group, but not all, the question is whether the words point to a sufficient portion of the group so that all the members are defamed by the publication. Thus, the coach referred to "some" members of the band who smoked cocaine (Example 1). Unless the band consisted of only four or five members, it is not likely that any single individual could sue. If the reference had been to all the band members, each individual could sue if the band was relatively small but none could sue if it was relatively large.[13]

Distinction Between Libel and Slander

As previously mentioned, the law distinguishes between libel and slander. Libel is actionable per se; in other words, the law assumes that the publication of a defamation in some written or permanent form necessarily injures the plaintiff in some pecuniary fashion. On the other hand, where the defamation is made orally, no such presumption is made except in four cases; where the plaintiff has been accused of a crime, or where he or she has been disparaged in the way of an office, business, calling, trade or profession, or where he or she has been said to have a particularly loathsome or contagious disease and finally, in most jurisdictions, where a women has been accused of unchastity.[14] In all other cases of slander, the plaintiff, in order to recover for a defamatory statement, must show that he or she suffered some pecuniary loss or damage in order to recover. In the United States, a further distinction has been drawn with respect to libel so that a plaintiff cannot recover without showing special damages where the written defamation is not evident from the writing itself without any reference to extraneous material.

There are a variety of complications. The public gestures of an individual are generally treated as slander while the oral communication of a written script, letter or manuscript is considered a libel. Motion pictures have been treated as a libel while radio broadcasts have been treated as both libel and slander. Television has been treated more like radio than motion pictures. Most of these anomalies have been resolved by statute in many jurisdictions and for the same reason a number of jurisdictions have abolished the distinction between libel and slander and treat both the same as libel was treated at common law.[15]

In the examples provided, the statement of the coach to the players was a slander (Example 1) while the letter from the parents (Example 2), the newspaper column (Example 3), the petition from the citizens (Example 4), and the character reference (Example 6) were libels. The written petition by the citizens is a libel but their oral explanation of the reasons for the petition is a slander (Example 5). Oral testimony in court is a slander but the report by the newspaper is a libel (Example 7). However, if a person orally gives information to a reporter knowing that it will be published in the newspaper, he is liable for that newspaper report as though he or she published a libel.

Defenses to an Action for Defamation

Justification

There are, of course, a number of defenses to an action for defamation. Truth is a complete defense. To be actionable, a publication must be false. Regardless of how callous or malicious a defendant may be, or how disparaging the remarks, if they are substantially true the defendant is not liable. On the other hand, if the information is false, it makes no difference that the defendant may have honestly believed it was true. Thus, if the player and members of the band were taking cocaine (Example 1), or the coach was sexually molesting one of his players (Example 2), the player and coach would have no cause of action for defamation.

Consent

A plaintiff may consent to the defamatory remarks. If so, he or she cannot complain about the damage to his or her reputation from the publication which was invited. Thus, a person may request a defendant to repeat an accusation in the presence of a policeman and he cannot complain if the defendant does so. He or she may agree to some formal channel by which information is to be furnished to a third person. He may ask someone to forward information to someone under circumstances where he knows, or has reason to know, the information is defamatory. He may ask someone to act on his behalf under circumstances where defamatory information is to be discussed. Thus, if the player accused of taking cocaine (Example 1) were to invite his parents to a meeting with the coach and ask him to repeat his charges in their presence, he will be deemed to have consented to that publication to the parents.

Absolute Privilege

There are also occasions which are absolutely privileged. This simply means that the defendant is privileged to publish the defamatory information and the plaintiff has no right to complain. The most common absolute privileges have to do with exchanges between officials occupying some governmental executive office, or a legislative or parliamentary privilege exercised by legislators, or communications made by participants in judicial proceedings. In Canada, the executive privilege is confined to those who occupy some high executive office, while in the United States some jurisdictions extend the privilege to federal, state and municipal offices even though some are of relatively minor stature. It applies only when the official is exercising the functions of his or her office and the communication has some relation to the duties of the executive office. In some jurisdictions, particularly in the United States, the absolute privilege extends to releases to the press where the information is necessary for public consumption.

Legislators enjoy an absolute privilege in communications made during the course of legislative proceedings. This includes defamatory comments made on the floor of the legislature or parliament, or during the course of any legislative inquiry, or that are published in the official organ of that body. However, once the legislator departs from the legislature and repeats the same remarks outside those halls, the cloak of the absolute privilege is removed. In Canada, the privilege applies to both the federal and provincial houses of parliament, while in the United States, some jurisdictions have extended the privilege to such local bodies as a county or municipal council.

An absolute privilege also protects all communications that take place during, or in connection with, or incidental to, judicial or quasi-judicial proceedings. In addition to the regular courts of law, the privilege protects those who appear before various administrative proceedings adjudicating the granting or revocation of licenses, the regulation of labour relations, the peer review of professionals, and the granting of various benefits such as unemployment insurance or workers compensation. It also protects those who appear in arbitration proceedings.

The privilege protects all those who participate in those proceedings including the judge, parties, counsel, jurors and witnesses. Witnesses and parties are protected by the privilege not only for testimony they give in courts, but also for all the information they supply in the form of affidavits or witness statements, or oral information they supply to the parties or their lawyers in contemplation of the litigation. The protection includes not only what they say about the participants, but also whatever they may say about third persons who are not involved in the litigation. However, in the United States the information must be relevant and pertinent to the subject matter of the litigation, while in Canada the information will be protected regardless of its relevancy. Thus, whether the privilege will protect the coach who was subpoenaed to testify (Example 7) may depend whether the case is before a Canadian or American Court, and in the latter case it must be shown that the gratuitous remark was relevant to the proceedings before the court. However, if the testimony is responsive to a question posed by counsel or the court, the law presumes that the information is relevant and material. Once the privilege attaches, the witness is protected even though the testimony is knowingly false and the witness is guilty of perjury.

Protected Reports

In reporting this testimony, a newspaper and other members of the media are protected by a privilege to publish fair and accurate reports of judicial proceedings. So long as it is fair and accurate, the media is protected even though the information is false and defamatory. In some jurisdictions, particularly in Canada, this privilege is absolute and can be defeated only if it is shown that it is not "fair" and "accurate." In other jurisdictions, the privilege can be defeated if there is a showing of actual or express malice. Statutes in most jurisdictions extend the privilege only to the communications media but there is also a common law privilege that protects reports by private citizens if it is made without malice. Thus, the report by the newspaper of the coach's testimony that the citizens were "faggots" is protected by both the statutory and common law privilege (Example 7).

There is a comparable immunity for the report of other matters as well. Legislative proceedings may be reported and if fair and accurate there is no action for defamation. In addition, by statute in both Canada and the United States, the media may be privileged to report such matters as the proceedings of a public meeting, contents of a public document, proceedings of certain governmental or quasi-governmental bodies such as a municipal council, school board, board of education, board of health or hospital board. The publication of any report, bulletin, notice or other document published for the information of the public at the request of a government department or public officer may also be protected in various jurisdictions.

Qualified Privileges

Coaches, athletic directors and players may also be protected by a qualified or conditional privilege. Statements published in discharge of a public or private duty, or in order to advance or pursue a public or private interest are protected if they are published to persons who have a corresponding interest in receiving it and it is made without actual or express malice. The privilege must be exercised at a proper time and on a proper occasion, in a reasonable manner and for a proper purpose. The information must not go beyond that necessary to protect the interest involved and it must be made to someone who has some interest in or duty with respect to the information. A person may communicate information to a third person for the following reasons:

> for the purpose of protecting his or her own private interest,[16]
> the interest of some other third person,[17]
> for the common interest that the speaker or writer has with a third person,[18]
> in order to protect some public interest.[19]

There may be some specific statutory protection for information which is required by law. Thus, a statute may require or encourage the transmission of information on the misuse or misappropriation of drugs or controlled substances,[20] or suspected child abuse,[21] or the presence of venereal disease.[22] In each case, the statute will afford either an absolute or qualified privilege or a court will recognize a qualified privilege.

A qualified privilege must not be abused. It may be lost if the information is communicated to persons not entitled to receive the information, or if the communication contains information that is inappropriate to the occasion and not necessary in order to protect the interest involved.

In the factual scenarios, it is clear that a coach shares a common interest with his players with regard to the motivation of other players and the court will recognize a qualified privilege if he defames one of his players in front of the others because the others are also interested in learning from that behaviour (Example 1). However, the other players may have no interest at all in the fact that either the particular player or members of the band had been taking cocaine. If the coach had informed the band leader, or the school, or the police, the situation might be different and the publication would be protected by a privilege.

In the next scenario (Example 2), the media has no interest in knowing whether the coach is a tyrant or bully (assuming these words are defamatory) or sexually molested one of his players. On the other hand, certainly the parents of the player and the police have an interest in the disclosure of this information and there would be privilege in doing so.

In the fourth scenario, when a coach is attacked in public, he may respond in the same forum to the charges and in the process label the accusation a lie and the accuser a liar. Where the public generally has heard an accusation, it has an interest in its refutation.

In the fifth case, there is a privilege for persons who have a common interest to circulate a petition among each other and to present it to persons who have some control over the hiring or firing of a coach. Thus if the parents of children in a school program or of players on the football team circulated a petition among themselves in order to present it to the proper persons within the school, there may be a privilege protecting them against an action for any defamatory comments. However, if they circulate the petition to the public generally or to persons who have no interest in the school program, the publication may not be privileged.

In the sixth scenario, coaches, athletic directors and school administrators are constantly asked for character references by prospective employers and in providing them they are generally protected by a qualified privilege in any defamatory criticism they may make.[23]

The coach was ultimately removed from his position. If he was a member of a faculty, his removal may have been accomplished through a progression of administrative proceedings and hearings. The exchange of information during these proceedings would have been protected by a qualified privilege. Players, parents, assistant coaches and even fans may have been interviewed and asked to offer their comments. School administrators may have discussed the evidence for and against him and his faculty peers may have been asked to make their assessments. In so far as the discussions and comments were relevant to the proceedings and reasonably necessary to a disposition of the issues, the parties would have been protected by a qualified privilege.

Fair Comment and Expression of Opinion

Generally speaking, expressions that can be identified as comments or opinions are not actionable, while statements that say something factually defamatory about a person are actionable. However, Canada and the United States differ on the treatment of this issue. In Canada, the courts recognize that everyone is entitled to comment fairly on matters of public interest. However, in order to enjoy this right, the expression must be identifiable as comment, the facts upon which the comment is made must be stated or well known, the facts must be true, the comment must be fair and relate to a matter of public interest, and the comment must not be motivated by express malice. In the United States, a person can be liable in an action for defamation only if the publication says something factually defamatory about the plaintiff.[24] Thus, in Canada the law recognizes that a comment and opinion can be defamatory but provides an immunity if it is a fair comment on a matter of public interest made without malice. In the United States, the expression of an opinion on a matter of public concern can never be actionable, regardless of the motivation of the publisher, unless it implies the existence of undisclosed false and defamatory facts.

The protection in Canada extends only to comments made about true facts. The facts upon which the comment is based must be known by those to whom the comment is made. They may be known because they are stated at the same time as the comment, or in advance of the comment, or because they are matters of common knowledge and have received substantial advance or contemporaneous public notoriety.

It is generally recognized that comments are likely to appear in the form of deductions, inferences, conclusions and observations. It is a subjective evaluation that is generally incapable of objective truth. To be protected by privilege, the comment must be expressed in such a way that the listener or reader can readily distinguish and separate what is asserted as fact and what is claimed to be comment.

The comment must also be fair. It is said to be fair if it is conceived in the spirit of fair discussion and based upon facts truly stated by someone who has an honest belief in the opinion he or she is expressing. Comments made about facts that are untrue cannot be fair. If the facts are found not to exist or are not true, the defense will fail since the law will not permit a defendant to create a non-existent state of affairs solely for the purpose of commenting on it.

Honesty of expression has been said to be the cardinal test for the defense. If the publisher acts honestly, there is no requirement that the language be reasonable or temperate. The comment may be acerbic, exaggerated and extravagant and the opinion may be accompanied by sarcasm and ridicule. However, if the comment attacks a person's motives in the form of a personal attack, it will be protected by the defense only if the conclusion drawn by the opinion is one that is warranted by the facts.

The defense applies only to comments on matters of public interest. In that regard, it may be a matter of public interest because of the importance of the person about whom the comment is made, or because of the event, occasion or circumstances giving rise to the comment. It must involve matters that invite public attention or about which the public has a substantial concern. This may include the affairs of government, the administration of justice, public health and safety, educational issues, political events and elections, and artistic and literary affairs. Sports generally are also considered a matter of public interest.[25]

American courts have largely dispensed with the common law defense of fair comment. All expressions of opinion on matters of public concern are protected so long as there is no implication of underlying false and defamatory facts. If the expression is reasonably understood as opinion, it is safeguarded regardless of how insulting, harsh, offensive, outrageous or outlandish the language. The right to criticize includes not only the right to criticize responsibly but to do so irresponsibly as well. In determining whether the publication would be understood as a statement of fact or as an expression of opinion, the court will take into consideration the nature of the medium, the character of the publisher, the type of discourse, its tone and apparent purpose, the form of the language employed, the nature of the audience and its knowledge and understanding.

American courts have recognized that discussions on talk shows directed at a sports-minded audience is a format where comments are likely to be understood as expressions of opinion (*Brooks v. Paige*). In addition, there are certain conventions in professional games, such as baseball, where verbal abuse and harassment are generally regarded as rhetorical hyperbole rather than expressions of fact such as comments made about umpires.[26]

Where the local columnist reviewed a series of plays by the coach during a drive for touchdown and characterizes him as incompetent (Example 3), the latter comment falls within the classic case of a fair comment. The facts have been stated, presumably accurately. Having provided the facts upon which the comment is made, the readers are able to evaluate the merits of the comment and decide for themselves whether the comment is warranted. Given the controversy surrounding the behaviour of the coach and the actions of the parents, the issue has probably become one of public interest. Assuming that the criticism was made honestly and without any malice on the part of the columnist, the comment would be protected in Canada by the defense of fair comment on a matter of public interest. In the United States, it would be seen as an opinion devoid of any factual content and therefore not actionable.

Actual and Express Malice

A qualified or conditional privilege may be defeated by evidence of express malice. A privileged occasion must not be abused by a defendant. It must not be used for a purpose unconnected with the occasion that gave rise to the privilege. A person must not use that privileged occasion for some indirect, improper or dishonest purpose or to gratify some personal animosity, anger, spite or ill will. Nor must a person publish something which he or she knows is untrue, or in reckless or willful disregard of whether it is true or false.

If the judicial proceedings were not protected by an absolute privilege, the gratuitous reference to the citizens as "faggots" (Example 7) might be said to have been spoken maliciously since it was likely motivated by anger and ill will and there does not appear to be any foundation for his belief.

Damages

Where the publication is not actionable per se, a plaintiff can recover only if he or she is able to show special damages in the form of a monetary or pecuniary loss. This may include such things as lost earnings, lost wages, loss of credit, and loss of earning capacity. However, the loss must be a natural and proximate consequence of the defamatory publication. In the scenario described, the coach has definitely suffered the loss of $20,000 per year that is recoverable as special damages and would support a slander that is not actionable per se so long as it can be shown that the loss was the proximate consequence of the publications.

Special damages are just one form of compensatory damages to which a person defamed is entitled. It measures the actual monetary loss which a person has suffered. In addition, he or she is entitled to general damages which the law presumes to be the natural and probable consequence of the publication of the defamation. These damages arise by an inference of law and require no proof. It is assumed that if a person has been defamed, the plaintiff's reputation has been injured. In addition, general damages will compensate the plaintiff for any mental and emotional pain and suffering, injured and wounded feelings and any grief, anguish, embarrassment, humiliation and insult he or she may have suffered. In assessing these damages, the court takes into consideration the nature and character of the defamation, the defendant's bad motive and evil purpose, the plaintiff's reputation and standing in the community, and the extent to which the defamatory remarks were disseminated. In the scenario created, it is a serious charge to suggest that someone was taking cocaine and the damages may reflect the seriousness of that charge (Example 1). However, the publication was made only to a few persons. Sexual molestation is an even more serious charge and the damages will be enhanced by the fact that a copy of the charge was sent to a newspaper where it would be published to the larger community (Example 2). The communication of a character reference to an employer is not likely to be visited with substantial general damages, but if the player is unable to get a job, he may suffer significant special damages (Example 6).

In addition to compensatory damages, both Canadian and American courts permit an award of punitive damages. Punitive damages are awarded as a form of punishment. Compensatory damages address the injuries suffered by the plaintiff; punitive damages are based on the wrongs intended by the defendant. Their purpose is both reparative and admonitory. They are awarded in order to punish the defendant for the injury suffered by the plaintiff, impose some kind of penalty or punishment for the wrong inflicted, and discourage and deter the defendant and others from repeating the same or similar behaviour. It will be assessed only in cases where the conduct of the defendant can be characterized as willful, wanton or malicious. For example, if the parents accused the coach of sexual molestation without any evidence to support the charge, their conduct would warrant an award of punitive damages (Example 2).

A defendant in an action for defamation may take some steps to mitigate the damages. He or she may apologize for or retract the defamatory remarks. It must be suitable and adequate, given the same prominence as the defamatory publication and made promptly. He may show that he was not moved by malice in publishing the defamatory statement but acted in good faith and with honesty of purpose, and that he relied solely on reports from reliable sources that were already in circulation. He may show that he was provoked by the plaintiff and that what was said was done in the heat of passion and in prompt response to the provocation. He or she may show that the publication was made only to persons whose opinion of the plaintiff would not appreciably be affected by the information. He or she may also show that the plaintiff's general reputation in the community relevant to the defamatory remark was bad both before and at the time of the publication.

American Constitutional Considerations

It has already been noted that the law of defamation in the United States has been altered by constitutional considerations. Thus, public officials and public figures can recover in an action for defamation only if they are able to show that the publication was made with actual malice. This rule may be of considerable importance in state run institutions since in a number of jurisdictions it has been held that a public official includes public elementary, high school and university teachers[27] including athletic coaches.[28]

Public figures have been identified by reference to two categories of persons. Some persons may become public figures because they have thrust themselves by their activities into a matter of public controversy in order to influence the resolution of the issues involved. They become public figures for the limited purpose on comments on the issues connected with that controversy. Others have achieved such pervasive fame and notoriety or occupy positions of such extensive power and influence that they are deemed to be public figures for all purposes.

To determine whether a person is a limited purpose public figure, the court will consider the nature, character, purpose and extent of his or her participation in the controversy, whether it was public in nature, whether he actively thrust himself into the forefront of the controversy and whether he or she sought to influence its outcome. A "public" controversy is a public dispute between contending points of view upon which a sizable segment of society have strongly held views. It must be a real dispute, the outcome of which affects the general public or some segment of it in an appreciable way. It has been held that controversies impacting upon education or educational institutions may involve a public controversy. This has included a scandal involving recruiting violations in basketball at a major university which led to the resignation of one coach and the firing of another and the termination of the basketball program (*Barry v. Time,*

Inc.) and the furore caused by a fight during a high school wrestling match and its subsequent investigation (*Milkovich v. News-Herald*). A public controversy was also created among sports fans when the owner of a professional basketball team continuously replaced coaches and players and threatened to move his franchise elsewhere (*Stephen v. Franklin*). A controversy may even be created by an athlete apart from his or her athletic endeavors where, for example, a professional football player is arrested for alleged lewdness at a casino hotel (*Breen v. DeLord*).

A person may achieve such stature and notoriety as a result of his or her prominence in community affairs or personal accomplishments that he or she is considered a public figure for all purposes and in all contexts. This stature is reserved for those who have achieved a celebrity status or pervasive fame and notoriety. The fame may be national in scope or it may be a comparable status within a state or local community. Thus, a person may be the prominent owner of a professional sports team (*Stephen v. Franklin*), a prominent athletic director at a major university (*Curtis Publishing Co. v. Butts*), or a basketball coach at a major public university (*Grayson v. Curtis Publishing Co.*). He or she may be a professional football, basketball, or soccer player, a professional horse jockey, or a former championship boxer.[29] Even local community sports figures may be all purpose public figures such as a tennis professional attached to a country club,[30] and a high school wrestling coach who had achieved considerable honours and accomplishments on a local level (*Milkovich v. News-Herald*).

Where the plaintiff is a public official or a public figure, and the subject of the defamation involves a matter of public concern, he or she must show that the defamatory falsehood was published with knowledge of its falsity or with reckless disregard for the truth. Reckless falsity means that the defendant published the information with a high degree of awareness of probable falsity,[31] or that he or she entertained serious doubts as to the truth of the defamatory statement.[32] It is a matter of public concern if it touches upon issues in which the public generally has an interest. Almost anything having to do with education and sports is generally considered to be a matter of public concern.

In Example 2 of the scenarios, whether the coach is a public figure depends upon his or her prominence as a coach. A nationally renowned coach in football at Notre Dame or Miami, or in basketball at Duke or Indiana, may have to show actual malice in order to recover for the defamatory comments while a less prominent coach at some other college or university may not have the same burden of proof. The leader of the citizens who circulated a petition demanding the resignation of the coach (Example 5) may be a limited person public figure for purposes of an action for defamation when the coach refers to them as "faggots" (Example 7) while those who merely sign the petition will not be considered public figures and will not have the same burden of proof. It is not likely that an athlete on the high school or university level would be considered a public figure since they would not have yet achieved the kind of prominence necessary for that purpose.

If the defendant is a member of the media, the plaintiff in *every* case must show at least that the media was at fault in publishing the defamatory material. In addition, no presumed or punitive damages can be awarded without a showing of actual malice at least where the defamatory publication involves a matter of public concern. Most jurisdictions have adopted the minimum standard of care and impose liability on a media publisher where there is a showing of negligence in publishing the defamatory material. Negligence in this regard is conduct that creates an unreasonable risk of harm and constitutes a failure to use the amount of care that a reasonably prudent person would use under the same or similar circumstances to prevent the plaintiff from being defamed. Some states provide greater protection for the media and require that the plaintiff show actual malice in order to recover for any publication appearing in the media.

Where a private person is suing another private person, most American courts have retained the strict liability rule imposed under the common law and, like their Canadian counterparts, the defendant will be held liable regardless of their innocence in publishing the defamatory remarks. However, there are a few courts that require at least a finding of negligence in order for the plaintiff to recover.

In the United States, a plaintiff cannot recover for comments made on matters of public concern unless it can be shown that the statement contains a false statement of fact. In other words, expressions of comment or opinion on matters of public concern are protected so long as there is no implication of underlying false and defamatory facts. Thus, in Example 3 it is clear that the columnist's characterization of the coach as incompetent is based upon the plays called by the coach during a drive for a touchdown in the losing football game. On the basis of this factual information, the public is capable of assessing the merits of the opinion that the coach is incompetent. Under these circumstances, the opinion would have been protected. Had the columnist labelled the coach incompetent without referring to any factual scenario, the public would have had to speculate on the reasons for the opinion and might have drawn the conclusion that it was based upon undisclosed false and defamatory facts that supported the columnist's opinion. In that case, the columnist would have been liable for defamation.

In determining whether a statement is one of fact or opinion, a court will take into consideration the nature of the medium, the character of the publisher, the nature and type of discourse, the form of the language employed, its tone and apparent purpose and whether it is capable of verification, the character of the audience and its knowledge and understanding. Thus newspaper and television columnists are noted for expressions of comments and opinion, radio and television talk shows usually involve the airing of divergent viewpoints, reader's column's are places where the public expects expressions of opinions, sports pages are noted for their cajoling, invective and hyperbole, cartoons are seldom taken in a literal sense and reviews by critics are recognized as places where comment rather than facts are expressed. In the midst of a heated debate or exchange, persons use words or phrases that are not intended to be applied literally or understood in that sense.

With regard to the scenarios, a court is likely to find the comments by the coach that a player is unmotivated, lazy and absolutely inept as an expression of hyperbole on his part (Example 1). The same is true when the coach refers to the columnist as an incompetent s.o.b. who knows nothing about sports (Example 4).

Conclusion

This is a superficial review of a very complicated area of the law. The lessons, however, are clear. It is safest to criticize persons, whether a coach, athlete or athletic director in private. If the criticism must be made in the presence of others, it should be made only when those present have some interest in the criticism. If statements of fact are made about others, they should be true or substantially true. If in doubt, investigate further before commenting. In the meantime, silence is golden. If you are not one to heed sensible advice, find yourself a competent lawyer. Eventually, you will need one.

Questions for Class Discussion

1. Historically, what is the distinction between libel and slander and which has been given the greater protection?
   a) What is the situation today and what forms of media fall under each category?
2. Prior to 1964 Canada and the USA were strikingly similar in that both applied strict liability in defamation.
   a) What does strict liability mean and what four things did the plaintiff have to prove?
   b) Were there any differences in libel and slander prosecution?
   c) What does "per se" mean and what were the five things which could make a slander "actionable per se"?
3. What is Constitutional Protection?
   a) Why, when, where and to whom does it apply?
4. What are the grounds under which a coach may sue for defamation for media comments?
   a) Go to the library and secure *Curtis Publishing Co. v. Butts*, 388 U.S. 130 (1967) and report the facts of the case, the judgement and the rationale of the Supreme Court of the United States.
5. What do we mean when we say words like "people are judged by the company they keep," or that you

can "convey a libel in a frown and wink a reputation down"?
6. In publication to a third party, who can be a publisher? Who is a third party?
    a) Can a group be defamed?
    b) Relate these questions to the opening seven scenarios.
    c) Which scenarios were libelous and which were slanderous?
7. List the six defenses to an action of defamation, define and explain each and relate them to the seven scenarios in the introduction. Remember to make the distinctions between the United States and Canada.
8. What is the difference between compensatory damages (general damages and special damages) and punitive damages?
    a) Relate the actions in the introductory seven scenarios to these types of damages.
9. What is the difference between a limited versus an all-purpose public figure?
    a) Give some examples from the scenarios and then from professional athletic and amateur sports in Canada and the USA.
10. Look up the cases listed in the footnotes under the section on American Constitutional concerns. Give the facts, judgements and relate them to the content of this Chapter.
11. What are four rules of thumb to avoid slander and what should you do if you fail to heed them?

Relevant Cases

Barry v. Time Inc., 584 F supp. 1110 (N.D. Calif. 1984).
Scandal involving recruiting violation at a major university led to resignation of one coach, firing of another and termination of the program.

Breen v. DeLord, 723 S.W. 2d 166 (Tex. App. 1986).
A professional football player is arrested for alleged lewdness at a casino hotel.

Brooks v. Paige, 773 P 2d 1098 (Colo. App. 1989).
Case of professional horse jockey.

Chuy v. Philadelphia Eagles Football Club, 592 F, 2d 1265 (3rd Cir. 1979).
Case of professional football player.

Conyd v. Brekelmens (1971) 3 W.W.R. 107 (B.C.S.C.).
Conyd, an amateur fencer of some note, sued Brekelmens, a member of the British Columbia Physical Fitness and Amateur Sport Fund, claiming damages for slander. Conyd had applied for and been approved for $3,500 from the fund for a personal program of fencing training and competition in Cuba, U.S.A., Canada and France.

When it became known that the grant was forthcoming, there was criticism in fencing circles and a meeting was called to review the grant. At this meeting attended by Conyd, Brekelmens, Zahara, Executive Director of the B.C. Sport Assoc., and James H. Phanton, secretary of the Fund, it is alleged the defendant said of Conyd "Everybody knows that he did not make an honest living in the last couple of years and if he gets the money, he will pocket it." The initial grant decision was rescinded and instead three fencers (including the plaintiff) each received $500 to go to Cuba. Conyd sued for slander.

The court raised the following questions (1) were the words spoken by the defendant and, if so, were they defamatory? (2) If so, was there malice? Since slander is not actionable per se, special damages must be proven before answering these questions. (3) Did the defendant have qualified privilege? and (4) Did the words, if spoken, materially affect the final decision regarding the grant?

Plaintiff's counsel argued special damages were suffered, namely, the loss of the $3,500 grant and/or further that the words fall into one of four categories where special damages need not be proven, namely, "words which impute to the plaintiff commission of a crime for which he can be made to suffer 'corporally— i.e. physically—' by way of punishment" (Gatley on *Libel and Slander* 6th ed. para 148). Plaintiff's counsel claimed the defendant accused Conyd of "criminal breach of trust" under s.282 of the Criminal Code, 1953–54 (Can), c 51, or that the imputed crime was an attempt to get money by way of grant by a "false pretence." (Section 303 (1) and 304 (1) of the criminal code respectively) Section 304 (1) states a "false pretence is a representation of a matter of fact either *present* or *past* made by words or otherwise, that is known by the person who makes it to be false and that is made with fraudulent intent to induce the person to whom it is made to act upon." Since the word allegedly spoken refer neither to present nor past behaviour but merely intention they are not actionable. Gatley points out in *Libel and Slander*, 6th ed. para 163:

> Words which merely impute an intention or inclination to commit a crime are not actionable without proof of special damage, for a criminal intention does not amount to a crime. But to impute an attempt to commit an indictable offense is actionable without proof of special damage, for an attempt to commit an indictable offense is an offense punishable corporally.

Defendant's Counsel argued successfully the words were not spoken as stated but merely referred to "visible means of support," that the decision wasn't made on the basis of these words, and, therefore, the plaintiff suffered no special damage as a result of the alleged slander.

Curtis Publishing Co. v. Butts, 388 U.S. 130 (1967).

Wally Butts Athletic Director at University of Georgia recovered $460,000 in a case where he was accused of fixing a game.

From v. Tallahassee Democrat, Inc., 400 So. 2d 52 (Fla. App. 1981).

Case of tennis professional attached to a country club.

Grayson v. Curtis Publishing Co., 436 P. 2d 756 (Wash. 1967).

Basketball coach at a major university sues for libel.

Mahoney v. Adirondack Publishing Co., Doing Business as Adirondack Daily Enterprise et. al. 71 N.Y.S. 2d 3F, 523 N.Y.S. 2d 480 (Ct. App. 1987).

Mahoney, a high school football coach, brought suit against sports reporter and Editor Bengston for an article that he claimed "harmed his reputation as a coach and educator. In an article following a 31–7 loss by Mahoney's winless St. Lawrence H.S. to previously winless Upper Lake H.S. an article appeared that said in part Mahoney "cursed and belittled his players from the sidelines throughout the game" and "screamed at his players so loudly in the locker room after the game that he easily could be heard by embarrassed fans outside the school using vulgar abuse mired with profanity." Mahoney admitted saying "hell," "damn," and "goddam," but vehemently denied saying to his quarterback who was intercepted six times, "Get your head out of your @#!? and play the game!" This was substantiated by the quarterback and his father, the coach's wife and the coach of the St. Lawrence cheer leading squad.

Initially a jury and Supreme court returned a verdict in favour of the plaintiff for compensatory damages ($10,000) on the grounds parts of the article were false, defamatory and published with malice either knowing it was false or with reckless disregard for whether it was false, and punitive damages ($5,000) finding the defendant acted in common-law malice i.e. with a desire to harm the plaintiff or reckless disregard for the injurious effect of the article upon him. The Supreme Court, Appellate Division, modified disallowing the punitive damages but endorsing the compensatory damages. (123 A.D. 2d 10,509 N.Y.S. 2d 193).

Finally, on appeal with permission (64 NY 2d 609, 509 NE 2d 360) C.J. Wachtler held the coach had failed to carry his burden of establishing actual malice and maintained that if there was falsity in the defendants' newspaper report it was "more a product of misperception and misunderstanding rather than fabrication" by the reporter.

Proving the story false and defamatory is not enough to sustain plaintiff's claim in view of constitutionally bases protection to assure "robust, uninhibited wide open debate on public issues." These rules are grounded in the First and Fourteenth Amendments assuring free speech and press reporting on public figures by members of the media. Since plaintiff conceded he was a public figure he needed to prove (1) defamatory statement was published with actual malice (2) actual malice had to be established by clear and convincing evident and (3) appellate review must include independent review to determine clear and convincing evidence. Falsity and malice are distinct concepts. It is one thing to publish false statements but another to do so knowingly or recklessly. Evidence supports the finding Bengston's report was inaccurate but doesn't support the conclusion he knew it was false simply because he was an eye witness. There was no evidence to negate the possibility that he simply misunderstood and the falsity was the product of misperception rather than fabrication.

Milkovich v. News-Herald, 15 Ohio St. 3d 292, 473 N.E. 2d 1191 (1984); *Milkovich v Lorain Journal Co.*, 497 U.S.-, III L. Ed. 2d 1,110 S.Ct.- 1990).

Furore over a fight during a high school wrestling match led to probation for the team and in a subsequent hearing which overturned the ruling, the plaintiff coach made a statement that was reported in the newspaper account as "a lie under oath." Plaintiff sued on grounds the article accused him of committing the crime of perjury, damaged his reputation or occupation as coach and educator and constituted a libel *per. se.* Instead, judgement for defense on grounds "no actual malice." Court of Appeal reversed and returned for retrial where summary judgement was for the defendant on grounds article opinion protected from libel action and the coach as a public figure failed to make a case. Court of Ohio reversed and remanded for retrial on the grounds coach was not a public figure and statements were of fact, not opinion. At retrial the defense prevailed when court ruled article was constitutionally protected opinion in a column entitled "TD (Theodore Diaclum) Says" and was on the sport page "a traditional haven for cajoling" where even the most gullible readers "know it is opinion." Milkovich appealed to the U.S. Supreme Court which, after discussing fair comment and legal immunity, ruled in favour of the coach saying "This is not the sort of loose figurative or hyperbolic language which would negate the impression that the writer was seriously maintaining (Milkovich) committed the crime of perjury."

Orlando Cepeda v. Cowles Magazines and Casting Inc., 328 F 2d 869 (1964).

National League championship baseball player sued for libel when a nationally known sportswriter magazine article referred to him as "temperamental, uncooperative and unproductive," "not a team player" who "when things go wrong, blames everyone else" and had "doghouse status" with management.

In the initial trial, judgement was for the defendant, however, in appeal on summary judgement, the decision was reversed with judgement for Cepeda.

Defense counsel arguments for acquittal on the doctrine of qualified privilege of fair comment and criticism were denied since the writer did not give readers the benefit of his analysis and comment of "l'affaire Cepeda" but merely passed along what he purported to hear "listening at the keyhole of the Giant's front office." One cannot escape libel by showing he was merely repeating defamatory language used by another, *a fortiori* he may not escape by falsely attributing to others the ideas to which he gives expression.

Judge Madden cited Sec. 45 of the Civil Code of California defining libel as:

> A false and unprivileged publication by writing, printing, picture, effigy or other fixed representation which exposes a person to hatred, contempt, ridicule, or obloquy, or which caused him to be shunned or avoided, or which has a tendency to injure him in his occupation.

The Judge felt Cepeda would suffer in his occupation since management of baseball, if they read and believed the articles, might shun him as a troublemaker. He also quoted Civil Code Section 45 which says:

> a libel which is defamatory of the plaintiff without the necessity of explanatory matter, such as inducement, innuendo, of other extrinsic fact, is said to be a libel on its face.

Since the article could not have any effect but to hurt the reputation of Cepeda, it was "if false and unprivileged, libelous on its face, i.e. per se and there was no necessity for any allegation or proof of special damages resulting from it." (p.371).

The judge rejected defense reliance on the California Code relating to qualified privilege, section 47 (3) of the Civil Code.

> A privileged publication or broadcast is one made... In a communication without malice to a person interested therein, (1) by one who is also interested, or (2) by one who stands in such relation to the person interested as to afford a reasonable ground for supporting the motive for the communication innocent... (p. 372).

The Judge maintains this only applies to fair comment and criticism and quotes Prosser in *Torts*, 2nd ed. p. 621: "Three-quarters of the states hold that the qualified privilege on account of public interest does not extend to any false assertion of fact. The 'Snively doctrine' which extends qualified privilege to 'non-malicious untrue statements as well as to criticism and opinion' ...did not extend...to a statement published with knowledge of its falsity or without an honest belief in its truth."

The circuit judge both concurred and dissented stating "I do not believe the libel laws of California oblige us to police the general run of sportswriter's fantasy and horsefeathers" but agreed "we do have a possible Little League Libel here!" (However, in his opinion, not one worth 10 million dollars!).

Pep v. Newsweek Inc., 553 F. Supp. 1000 (S.D.N.Y. 1983).
Case of former champion boxer.

Stephen v. Franklin, 39 Ohio App.3d 47, 528 N.E 2d 1324 (1988).
Public controversy when the owner of a professional basketball team constantly replaces players and coaches, and threatens to move the franchise.

Time Inc. v. Johnson, 448 F. 2d 378 (4th Cir. 1971).
Case of professional soccer player.

Endnotes

1. In Canada, the provinces of Alberta, Manitoba, New Brunswick, Newfoundland and Prince Edward Island, and to a limited extent Nova Scotia, have abolished the distinction. In the United States, the distinction is no longer drawn in Illinois, New Mexico, Tennessee, Virginia and Washington. Both Quebec and Louisiana are civil law jurisdictions and never embraced the distinction in the first place.
2. 376 U.S. 254 (1964).
3. Specifically, Brennan J. said that actual malice was a statement that was made "with knowledge that it was false or with reckless disregard of whether it was false or not." *Ibid.*, at 280.
4. Proof of actual malice must be made with "convincing clarity."
5. *Gertz v. Robert Welch Inc.*, 418 U.S. 323 (1974).
6. *Dun & Bradstreet Inc. v. Greenmoss Builders Inc.*, 105 S. Ct. 2939 (1985).
7. *Reynolds v. Times Newspapers Ltd.*, [1999] 4 All E.R. 609 (H.L.).
8. *Lange v. Australian Broadcasting Corp.* (1997), 143 Aust. L.R. 96 (H.C.).
9. *Lange v. Atkinson*, [1998] 3 N.Z.L.R. 424 (C.A.) This was affirmed by the Privy Council but remanded for further consideration in light of the House of Lords' decision in *Reynolds v. Times Newspapers Ltd.*
10. There has been an additional development in Canada that is especially important to coaches or athletic personnel covered by collective agreements. It has been held by the Supreme Court of Canada that all differences between the parties arising either expressly or impliedly out of the collective agreement fall exclusively within the grievance and arbitration provisions of that agreement and a court is precluded from exercising any jurisdiction over the matter. *Weber v. Ontario Hydro* (1995), 24 C.C.L.T. (2d) 217 (S.C.C.), noted in (1996), 4 Can.

Lav. & Employment Law J. 183. This includes any issues of defamation., *Venneri v. Bascom* (1996), 28 O.R. (3d) 281 (Gen. Div.). Thus, in the scenario provided, if the coach who is fired is covered by a collective agreement, any defamatory remarks made by fellow employees or players leading to the dismissal would fall within the jurisdiction of the arbitrator and not the courts, although presumably the coach would have separate actions against the parents, citizens and media.

11 Dean Smith, quoted in *Grubb v. Bristol United Press Ltd.*, [1963] 1 Q.B. 309 at 328 (C.A.) by Pearce L.J. from "Journal of a Modern Lady."

12 For example, charges of communism were defamatory at the time of the Hitler-Stalin pact and after the Second World War. The same charges were not defamatory after the invasion of Russia by Germany and probably would not be defamatory today. Comparable changes have affected the word "papist" and "witch." It was once defamatory to refer to a person as a "Wesleyan" in England and as a Mormon in the United States. In the southern United States, it was defamatory per se to mistakenly refer to a caucasian as a negro.

13 Occasionally a court will permit a single person to sue where the reference is to the entire group and the group is relatively large. Thus, a magazine ran an article on the Oklahoma national championship football team and claimed they were on drugs. It was held that an alternate fullback on that team, which had 60 to 70 members, could sue for defamation. *Fawcett Publications, Inc. v. Morris*, 377 P. 2d 42 (Okl. 1962).

14 The first three exceptions were created by common law courts over the centuries. The imputation of unchastity to a woman, where that exception exists, is largely of statutory origin in each of the provinces and states. However, there is some question whether statutes creating this exception to the common law can survive a constitutional or charter of rights challenge since they draw a distinction on the basis of sex. For this reason, the exception was removed from the Ontario statute. In some states, the statute was drawn gender free while at least one court has reinterpreted its state statutory provision to read that way. *Wardlaw v. Peck*, 318 S.E. 2d 270 (S.C. App. 1984).

15 *Supra*, footnote 1.

16 For example, if someone took the personal property of a player or coach, they could report their suspicions to the police and the information would be privileged.

17 The same privilege would apply if a player witnessed the theft of the coach's property and reported his or her suspicions to the coach or the police. The parents of the players have an interest in the well being of their children and may communicate information to or receive information from the coach, athletic director or school officials.

18 For example, a coach and the players have a common interest in the well being of the team or the school for whom they coach or play. A coach has a comparable common interest in matters relating to the team with assistant coaches, the athletic director and certain officers of a university.

19 Communication of information to law enforcement officials is also in the public interest and is protected for that reason as well. There may be other public officials who should be informed and in turn it may be in the public interest for those same officials to communicate information to the public generally. In each of these cases, the parties may be protected by a qualified privilege.

20 See, for example, Illinois Nursing Act, Ill. Rev. Stat. 1985, ch. 111, par. 3435.1.

21 See, for example, South Dakota C.L. 26-10-14.

22 See, for example, Mass. Laws, ch. 112, section 12.

23 Under the traditional common law doctrine, a character reference is protected by a qualified privilege that can be defeated only by showing that the writer was moved by actual or express malice. Under the common law, negligence on the part of the writer was not considered malicious conduct, However, the House of Lords has recently held that the plaintiff defamed in a character reference may proceed in an action for negligence, rather than defamation, and recover damages for any injury received as a result of the negligence of the writer of the character reference. *Spring v. Guardian Assurance Plc.*, [1994] 3 W.L.R. 354 (H.L.).

24 *Milkovich v. Lorain Journal Co.* Prior to 1974, the law in the United States was comparable to Canada and expressions of opinion were actionable unless they were fair comment on a matter of public interest published without malice.

25 See, for example, *Hoeppner v. Dunkirk Printing Co.*, 227 A.D. 130, 237 N.Y.S. 123 (1929), reversed in part on other grounds 254 N.Y. 95, 172 N.E. 139 (1930) (high school football coach).

26 *Parks v. Steinbrenner*, 131 A.D. 2d 60, 520 N.Y.S. 2d 374 (1987).

27 See, e.g., *Stevens v. Tillman*, 855 F. 2d 394 (7th Cir. 1988); *Kapiloff v. Dunn*, 27 Md. App. 514, 343 A. 2d 251 (1975); *Reaves v. Foster*, 200 So. 2d 453 (Miss. 1967).

28 See, e.g., *Basarich v. Rodeghero*, 24 Ill. App. 3d 905, 321 N.E. 2d 739 (1974); *Johnston v. Corinthian Television Corp.*, 583 P. 2d 1101 (Okl. 1978).
29 Professional football, *Chuy v. Philadelphia Eagles Football Club*; professional basketball player, *Time Inc. v. Johnston*; professional soccer player, *Brooks v. Paige*; professional horse jockey, *Gomez v. Murdock*, 193 N.J. Super. 595, 475 A. 2d 622 (1984); former championship boxer, *Pep v. Newsweek, Inc.*
30 *From v. Tallahassee Democrat, Inc.*, 400 So. 2d 52 (Fla. App. 1981).
31 *Garrison v. Louisiana*, 379 U.S. 64 (1964).
32 *St. Amant v. Thompson*, 390 U.S. 727 (1968).

CHAPTER 14

INSURANCE FOR SPORT AND FITNESS ORGANIZATIONS

Gina M. Jefferson and David L. LaBute

Introduction

The theoretical need for insurance is easy to comprehend. Organizations are frequently exposed to losses, some of them potentially devastating. In order to reduce the financial burden of these losses, an agreement is struck with an *insurer*, who agrees to assume the losses on behalf of the organization. The insurer then disperses the losses to members of a group who are exposed to similar losses. This agreement is known as an *insurance contract*. In order to provide this service to its members, the insurance company charges each member an amount or *premium*, from which it can recover a portion of the loss it is required to pay out. Many factors affect premium rates, some positively, some negatively. Due to increased exposure to liability lawsuits, the insurance cost associated with running recreational or sporting activities is sometimes very high. Still, now more than ever, it is imperative that organizations are properly insured against all unexpected events.

The Insurance Crisis

Because possessing insurance is imperative for most sport and recreation organizations, insurance companies can essentially control what activities can be run by these organizations and indeed, how the organizations run them. Some sport associations, fitness centres, parks and recreation departments, and school boards have considered closing their doors and/or dropping certain activities because of a potential lack of liability protection.

In 1998, a volunteer track coach for Snow Canyon High School in Utah died when he hit his head after landing while pole vaulting ("Pole Vault," 1998). The Utah High School Activities Association, as well as the agency that provided the track and field facilities with liability insurance, wanted to ban pole vaulting for safety concerns (Wyatt, 1998).

Other sport associations have had difficulty securing insurance protection at all:

> In 1983 the Canadian Ski Association paid $7,700 [CDN$] in premiums for eleven million dollars in liability coverage. In 1984 the CSA was forced to find a new insurer who agreed to provide the same coverage for $47,000 [CDN$] in premiums. When that policy expired in December of 1985, that association could not find liability insurance at any price. Across Canada news reports carried stories of our national alpine ski team who would have to return home if coverage could not be secured soon. A prime example of how the insurance companies are often unwilling to provide coverage for a team, facility, organization, or when they are willing, the premiums will be astronomical. (Hanna, 1986, p. 164)

One of the most significant factors affecting high insurance rates is the increase in large compensatory awards given out by the judicial system. Recently there has been a gradual and deliberate change in society's view towards compensation.

James A. Baley and David L. Matthews (1988) cite a case in which

> a Florida jury ordered Riddell, Inc., manufacturers of football helmets, to pay $4,000,000 [US$] to Greg Stead who was paralyzed after being struck in the spine with the back of Riddell's TK2 helmet. (p. 10)

According to Riddell's attorney, other settlements have included a $5,300,000 [US$] judgement in Florida and a $600,000 [US$] judgement in Philadelphia. The expense of just preparing for a single case (of which there may be several going to trial concurrently) often runs over $100,000 [US$], and in some cases may be double or triple that amount.

Liability insurance is being asked to play a very convenient and essential role in today's social welfare scheme. This was never the intention of, and in fact is completely contrary to the basis and fundamental concepts of the tort system. (A *tort* is "a civil wrong or injury" (Insurance Institute of Canada [IIC], 1997a, p. 1–2).) Under the tort system, the victim of a loss is compensated by shifting the burden of that loss to the party that causes the loss. That party had a responsibility to the victim, and was negligent in carrying out that responsibility. That party would be, therefore, liable. Rather than assuming it themselves, however, the financial burden of that loss then gets shifted to the insurance company. Damage awards can be very high, which may stretch the resources of the affected insurance companies. To offset these costs, the insurance companies raise their premiums. The more the insurance companies have to pay, the higher the rates will get, resulting in an escalating spiral.

Brian W. Robertson and Brenda J. Robertson (1988) have described what they refer to as a crisis in recreation and sport, consisting of three major components:

1. The *liability crisis* is based partly on the perception that injured parties are increasingly inclined to sue to receive compensation for their injuries, rather than accepting their injuries as a natural hazard of the activity in which they were participating. Baley and Matthews agree (1988), and cite many reasons why the number of lawsuits has increased (see *Table 14.1: The Liability Crisis – Reasons for an Increase in the Number of Lawsuits*).
2. The *insurance crisis* follows from the liability crisis. Larger payouts and more frequent losses lead to exorbitant premiums or the need to drop certain high-risk activities. For some activities, the risk may be so great that no coverage may be available.
3. Organizations may be more willing to closely examine the ins and outs of legal liability due to its increased importance, but many other organizations may be afraid of drowning under the complexities of the law. Robertson and Robertson (1988) call this the *information crisis*. They continue, "Unfortunately, good, clear, understandable information on the law is a rare commodity. At the very least, it is fair to say that demand far exceeds supply" (p. 6).

Liability for Negligence

Liability can be described as the responsibility that falls upon a party or parties by virtue of their actions or arising from their ownership or use of something (IIC, 1997a, 1–2). *Negligence* is the failure to fulfill a duty of care, resulting in damage or injury to another. While negligence and liability are related, they are not necessarily the same. It is possible for someone to be negligent but not liable for that negligence. For example, an employer has an obligation to tell their employees about rules of business. If an employee doesn't know the rules and because of this ignorance causes injury to a customer, the employee would be negligent but the employer would be liable.

The Determination of Negligence

The tort system specifies four factors used to establish the degree of negligence of a defendant towards a

---

Table 14.1
THE LIABILITY CRISIS: REASONS FOR AN INCREASE IN THE NUMBER OF LAWSUITS[1]

In their book *Law and Liability in Athletics, Physical Education, and Recreation* (1988, pp. 2-11), James A. Baley and David L. Matthews provide several reasons to explain the increasing number of liability suits in today's society. They include:

1. *Increased Leisure*
   Individuals tend to have increased leisure time and thus have more time to participate in recreational activities.
2. *The Female Sports Boom*
   More and more females are participating in sport activities, requiring new teaching techniques and new equipment.
3. *Television*
   Television has an ever-increasing influence on how we spend our leisure time. Increased sport coverage encourages participation from the audience.
4. *Lifetime Sports*
   The popularity of lifetime sports (i.e., tennis, bowling, skiing, et cetera) increases the potential of injury at some point during the participant's life.
5. *Legal Negligence*
   Consumers tend to have a greater awareness of negligence issues. What were once considered to be reasonable precautions are often seen today to be inadequate.
6. *Increased Accessibility of Legal Services*
   The number of small claims courts has dramatically increased in the last several years.
7. *Increased Transportation of Athletes*
   People have greater access to recreational programs.
8. *Comparative Negligence*
   Since fault or responsibility can be apportioned between the plaintiff and the defendant in a finding of comparative negligence, the possibility of compensation of some type may be increased.
9. *Increased Valuing of Individual Rights*
   It is becoming more commonplace to see lawsuits, therefore consumers are more willing to accept the possibility of participating in a lawsuit themselves should something happen.
10. *Consumerism*
    With the increase in the number of lawsuits comes the increased number of large monetary judgements. The more consumers hear of these judgements, the more they are likely to award them as jurors.
11. *Libel and Slander*
    Individuals empowered by an increased awareness of their rights are more apt to sue to protect their reputation.
12. *Player Suits Charging Excessive Violence*
    It is becoming more common to see lawsuits filed by athletes for incidents occurring during the course of the contest in which they were participating.
13. *Product Liability*
    Equipment manufacturers are being asked to take more responsibility in ensuring that their products are rigorously tested.

---

plaintiff. A defendant will be found guilty of negligence only if all of the following conditions are satisfied:

1. *The defendant owed a duty of protection to the plaintiff against unreasonable risk.*
2. *There was a breach of duty on the part of the defendant to provide a reasonable standard of care toward the plaintiff.*
3. *The plaintiff suffered injury, loss or damage as a result of the defendant's conduct.*
4. *The conduct of the defendant had a close causal connection to the injury, loss or damage incurred.*

The plaintiff also has a responsibility to themselves and to the defendant. By entering into a contract (written, verbal, or gestural) with the organization, the individual assumes this responsibility and accepts the consequences for failing to handle it properly. The individual must avoid any unnecessary risks, and comply with all rules and regulations.

In assessing the responsibility of the plaintiff and the negligence of the defendant, the *reasonable person standard* is applied. The reasonable personal standard may be defined as "how a person of ordinary sense using ordinary care and skill would react under similar circumstances" (Wong, 1998, p. 307). In other words, a reasonable person would use prudence and care. One person owes a *duty of reasonable care* to another person and to their property.

In a website addressing physical education teacher resources, the provincial government of Saskatchewan notes

> Negligence [within the context of the school setting] exists only if the teacher or the school board has failed to meet the standard of care which the law prescribes under those circumstances. The standard of care the courts are most likely to apply is that exercised by "the careful parent" (although in some cases lower courts have applied the standard of the competent coach or qualified instructor.) There are less rigorous standards related to the duty of an owner or occupier of property toward an invitee or with the duty a driver of a motor vehicle owes to a gratuitous passenger. Depending on the circumstances, these standards might be held appropriate by the courts; however, it would be prudent to expect the courts to apply the higher standard because of the vulnerability of children and due to the teacher's professional qualifications (Saskatchewan, 1996).

See Appendix 14.1: Tort Laws and Negligence for additional information.

Negligence Suits

A negligence suit could be decided in one of four ways, differing in the degree of negligence incurred by the defendant:

1. *No negligence.* If the defendant did not have a duty to the plaintiff then they would not be found negligent. On the other hand, if the defendant did have a duty to the plaintiff, but was not found to have breached it, then they would not be negligent.
2. *Contributory negligence.* Contributory negligence is a result of a deviation from the standard of reasonableness required of all individuals. This standard is held for both the defendant and plaintiff. If the plaintiff does not exercise due care for their own safety then this lack of care at least to some degree leads to contributory negligence. The plaintiff may be responsible to some degree for their own loss/injuries.
3. *Comparative negligence.* A decision of comparative negligence (or *apportionment of negligence*) means that both parties are to some degree negligent. Comparative negligence divides the responsibility among the negligent parties. "Apportionment under the *Ontario Negligence Act* is made where damages have been caused or contributed to by the fault or negligence of two or more persons" (Barnes, 1983, p. 295).
4. *Assumption of risk.* If the plaintiff gives consent prior to participating in an event which could potentially cause injury, the defendant is relieved of a certain standard of conduct toward the plaintiff. Wong (1988) adds,

> Assumption of risk requires that the plaintiff knows and fully appreciates the risks involved in pursuing the cause of action to which he is committed. In addition to knowing and appreciating the risk, the plaintiff must also carefully and reasonably agree to assume whatever risk is involved (p. 313).

This assumption of risk may take place in many ways, but it usually is in the form of a signed document of some type, such as a waiver.

Negligence in Sport

Sport and recreation activities are by their very nature characterized by social interaction, especially in the context of organized sport. Certainly part of the mass appeal of sport activities are the dynamics between coaches, teachers, owners, players, and spectators. With interaction, however, comes responsibility. Each party owes the other parties their respect and care. Therefore, when accidents occur, many parties may share in the liability for its occurrence.

Liability of Coaches and Teachers

When coaches and teachers take on their positions they are not shielded by the defenses of consent, privilege, and immunity from liability by virtue of their position. They are responsible for any intentional tort they commit in their capacity as coaches or teachers. Providing reasonable supervision to the students/athletes under their direction is the responsibility of the coaches and teachers involved in the program. The coach and teacher must properly instruct the athletes on the activities, rules of the game, and safety procedures. Proper pre-season conditioning programs and training should also be provided to the athletes. Coaches must be careful on how they instruct and supervise their athletes.

When an injury to an athlete or spectator occurs coaches are held to a standard of reasonable care to render medical assistance to the injured individual. The coach may be sued for unintentional or intentional tort (Berry & Wong, 1993). The coach or instructor should not, however, fail to render assistance on the basis that a lawsuit may arise. Robertson and Robertson (1988) write,

> Negligence, which means failure to meet the reasonable standard of care, should not be confused with bad judgement. It is not negligence if you make the wrong decision – it is negligence to make decisions wrongly. If any reasonable person would have taken the same course of action, it was not negligently taken (p. 45).

Adequate first aid supplies should be visible and available, and coaches should be proficient at administering them. An accident procedure policy should be in place. Coaches and instructors should hold all proper qualifications. If these precautions have all been considered, it would be very difficult to prove negligence on the part of the coach.

Liability of Participants

Over the years there has been a change in attitude with respect to sport injuries. In the past, injuries were viewed as a part of the competitive and physical nature of the sport. Participants assumed the inherent dangers of the sport and were reluctant to sue other participants. Participants today do not necessarily assume the risk of all injuries resulting from gross recklessness on the part of another player. Because professional sports and intercollegiate and amateur athletics are viewed as big business, a lawsuit is a much more viable option than it has been in the past. The judicial system is being used more frequently to resolve disputes related to sport injuries. As such, legal precedents have been set which allow more and more athletes to recover lost wages, medical costs, and pain and suffering damages. In order to prevent injuries and protect players, safety rules have been implemented in many sports, including football, soccer, and softball.

> In cases involving the alleged violation of a safety rule, the courts have held that a player is liable for tort action only if his or her conduct displays deliberate, willful, or reckless disregard for the safety of other participants and results in injury to another participant (Berry & Wong, 1993, p. 449).

Liability of Clubs and Teams

Most sports leagues are incorporated, which results in the creation of separate legal entities. Many clubs have by-laws that are included in its rules. The members of the club are subject to the club rules, while the shareholders and administration of the company are subject to the incorporated documents and general company law. An incorporated club can be sued or may sue in the name of the corporation (Barnes, 1993, pp. 322–324).

Liability of Players to Spectators

When spectators attend an event they assume the ordinary risks associated with the sport. These risks are inevitable and are an incidental part of attending the game. However, the risk of injury caused by improper player conduct or the negligent organization of an event is not assumed risks, and the spectator does not accept them merely by his/her attendance at the event (Barnes, 1993, p. 298).

Negligence Case Studies

The following examples provide some insight into the evidence presented and decisions rendered in typical negligence hearings:

1. *Nganga v. College of Wooster*, 557 N.E. 2d 152 (Ohio App. 1989)

    In this case the plaintiff was playing an intramural soccer game against a team with a reputation for rough play. During the game, the plaintiff was slide-tackled after he had passed the ball. The plaintiff sued the college and player who tackled him. The trial court granted summary judgement for the college based on the primary assumption of risk. Soccer is a high-contact sport and the plaintiff testified that he himself often used the sliding tackle to obtain the ball from an opponent.

2. *Aldridge v. Van Patter*, (1952) O.R. 595, (1952) O.W.N. 516, (1952) 4 D.L.R. 93 (Ont. H.C.)

    A spectator at a stock car race was injured when a car left the track. This particular track was a former harness racing track, and was surrounded by a light fence. It was also therefore not properly banked for auto racing. The driver, the organizer of the race, and the local fair association from which the property was rented were all found liable; the driver, for participating in a dangerous event, the organizer, for putting it on, and the fair association, for allowing the property to be used for such an activity.

3. *Regina v. Ciccarelli*, (1988) 5 W.C.B. (2d) 310, aff'g (1990) 54 C.C.C (3d) 121 (Ont. D.C.)

    After the whistle was blown and the play stopped during a professional hockey game, the accused struck the victim in the head with his stick three times. There was no bodily harm done, but the conduct was beyond the activity implicitly consented to by the players. The accused pleaded not guilty. The defendant was charged with assault, common assault, and mistaken belief in consent due to the following:
    a. The accused applied force intentionally;
    b. The force was applied directly or indirectly; and
    c. The victim did not consent to the intentional application for force.

    The defendant was found guilty as charged.

4. *McFatridge v. Harlem Globetrotters*, 69 N.M. 271, 365 Pa. (2d) 918 (N.M. 1961)

    In the spirit of fun, the defendant faked a pass to a player and deliberately threw the basketball into the stands, injuring the plaintiff. The defendant denied negligence on the grounds that
    a. The plaintiff assumed the risk by sitting in the stands;
    b. The accident was unavoidable;
    c. The injuries were unforeseeable; and
    d. By contributory negligence, the plaintiff was responsible for the injury.

    The court held that because the plaintiff had no choice between a protected and an unprotected seat, and that because there is no real danger in a basketball game of spectator injury due to errant balls, the defendant would be liable if in fact he threw the ball negligently into the crowd.

Tort law has as its focus, one purpose: fair compensation of the victim. The courts often seek this compensation not through the party most liable, but through the defendant most capable of paying the damages. Consider, for example, the case of *Thornton v. Board of School Trustees of School District No. 57* (1975, 1976, and 1978), as cited by McNulty (1975). A teacher was attempting to mark report cards and supervise three activities at the same time. Gary Thornton, attempting a gymnastics move, fell and broke his neck.

Although the teacher was negligent in his duty and therefore at least theoretically liable, the board, not the teacher, was forced to pay the damages. The board was found to be *vicariously liable* because the teacher was acting within the context of his employment. The employer is wealthier, and in a better position to fulfill its responsibilities to compensate the victim.

Several provinces have statutes requiring the purchase of insurance and recognizing the existence of vicarious liability. For example, the *Education Act* of Ontario (1991), R.S.O. 1980, c. 129, item 154, states:
A board may,

1. Provide, by contract with an insurer licensed under the *Insurance Act*,
    i. Group accident insurance to indemnify a member of a board or of an advisory committee appointed by a board or his estate against loss in case he is accidentally injured or killed, and
    ii. Group public liability and property damage insurance to indemnify a member of a board or of an advisory committee appointed by a board or his estate in respect of loss or damage for which he has become liable by reason of injury to persons or property or in respect of loss or damage suffered by him by reason of injury to his own property,
while travelling on the business of the board or in the performance of his duties as a member of the board or of an advisory committee either within or outside the area over which the board has jurisdiction...

The *Education Act* of Saskatchewan (c. 228) provides

that a teacher or any other person responsible for the conduct of pupils shall not be liable for injuries suffered by pupils or property damage caused by pupils during activities approved or sponsored by the school board, principal or teacher during school hours or at other times (Saskatchewan, 1996).

It further states, however, that this provision does not exempt teachers from being sued for negligence or being held responsible for an accident; however, it should prevent a court from levying damages against a teacher personally (Saskatchewan, 1996).

As mentioned above, negligence is determined using four simple conditions. In practice, however, due to the complexities of the legal system and the accountability of potentially several parties involved, liability for negligence is almost never simple. In any case, as expressed by Robertson and Robertson (1988),

[liability] for negligence ... is a completely separate issue from the issue of who will eventually end up paying for that liability. Any of the [defendants] found liable in a given case may have an indemnification agreement with someone else, under which [that] party agrees to indemnify that defendant for any liability incurred (p. 39).

In short, most often the question is not who is liable for negligence, but rather who is responsible for compensation because of it.

Risk Management

Negligence is not always the primary cause of an accident. Thus, not every injury serves as the basis of a lawsuit. Litigation involving negligence and breech of duty of care is, however, frequent and becoming more popular. As a result, a *risk management program* is proving to be a necessity for any organization or facility. Within the area of sport and recreation activities this is even more so. In Canada, thirty percent of all injuries to adults arise from recreation-related activities, and this number rises to forty percent for those fifteen to twenty-four years old (Corbett & Findlay, 1993). Many of these injuries could have been prevented with a proactive risk management program in place.

Risk management can be described as the process of recognizing potential risks that might occur during an activity, then taking appropriate steps to avoid or minimize them. On paper, a risk management program can look fairly simple. Putting it into practice usually proves to be more difficult. For example, a risk management plan may need to be altered and revised to abide by the policies and practices of the organization itself. One of the most critical factors of the success of any risk management program is that it fits into the established "company style," the way that a company is structured and managed (Crockford, 1980, p. 102). If the program is contrary to the company style, the program will fail or, at the very least, meet with some obstacles.

It is important to remember that a risk management program must be continuously developed and updated frequently. Ideally, an efficient program will allow an organization to operate free from most liability concerns. While risk management programs should be in effect for all organizations, be they recreational, commercial, industrial, et cetera, they are of paramount importance to organizations involved with athletic activities, as they are held to a higher standard of care because of the nature of their enterprise.

Baley and Matthews (1988, p. 303) list a few mandatory components of a successful athletic-based risk management program, including:

- *Safety consciousness:* It is the instructor's duty to teach, assist, and protect their charges. The instructor should "practice, teach, and preach" safety.
- *Supervision*: All school-sponsored events as well as events sponsored by organizations renting facilities should be supervised adequately.
- *Adequate insurance coverage*: Employees and volunteers should be covered for liability if they are acting within the scope of their duties.
- *Physical prerequisites for athletics*: It is the instructor's duty to ensure that the activities being engaged in are appropriate for the participant's age level, and that participants are sufficiently fit.
- *Safe premises*: Of course, equipment should be properly maintained and inspected regularly, but it should also be noted that bleachers and other seating arrangements are common subjects for spectator litigation.

Betty Van der Smissen (1990) groups these concerns and others into two categories: *operations control* (training and education, enforcement of rules and procedures, monitoring and maintaining equipment and facilities, adequate supervision of all activities, proper documentation of meetings and decisions, et cetera) and *financial risk management* (insurance).

The Retention of Risk

Insurance, while an effective means of absorbing financial losses, does not by itself constitute risk management. As outlined above, it is but one aspect of a complete and well-balanced program. Not every risk and potential loss has to be insured against. Because of the rising costs of insurance premiums, the increase of inflation and interest rates, and a general trend towards efficient spending and cost-consciousness, it is sometimes more convenient to absorb a loss. The risk potential and frequency of a particular loss need to be determined. In addition, the cost of insurance should be contrasted against the cost of absorbing the loss. Some alternatives to purchasing insurance from brokerages include self-insurance, expensing, and the use of deductibles.

Self-Insurance: Sometimes called *funded reserves*, self-insurance usually involves the formation of joint insurance pools with similar organizations in a particular area. Smaller businesses usually find this an effective way of protecting against major, but infrequent losses. The more participants in the pool, the greater the spread of costs. Individual members may absorb a portion of the loss themselves before turning to the pool (serving as a deductible, in essence.) Several universities in Canada have pooled their resources to carry their own insurance under the *Canadian Universities Reciprocal Insurance Exchange (CURIE)* with the mandate to:

stabilize insurance premiums; broaden liability exposure coverage; add catastrophe and earthquake coverage; offer higher and more flexible policy limit and deductible options; and coordinate and promote an improved and coordinated approach to risk management with a focus on addressing the specific needs of universities (CURIE Internet).

The United States Olympic Committee has also turned to self-insurance:

> Turned down in January 1986 by all 31 insurance companies it approached to underwrite liability insurance for the United States Olympic teams, although it never had a suit, the USOC created *Panol*, its own "captive insurance company" (Lubell, 1987, p. 196).

Expensing: Smaller losses may be charged as expense items rather than setting aside funds. Usually these losses are budgeted for yearly. While certainly not used for major payouts, expensing can be an effective risk management technique in that it can dramatically cut down the number of claims processed and thereby keep premiums to a minimum.

Deductibles: Organizations may decide to assume financial losses up to a certain amount before seeking insurance. Usually deductibles are incorporated into the insurance policy itself, however an organization may make a conscious decision not to rely on insurance until a particular loss figure has been reached. This figure may change depending on the nature of the loss, or may represent a cumulative yearly total.

The Transfer Of Risk

In most cases, organizations choose not to absorb losses on their own, but transfer the responsibility of compensation to another party. This is commonly done in two ways, by *contract* and by *insurance*. These agreements do not necessarily transfer blame or liability from any party, but rather shift the financial burdens to parties that are willing to take them on.

Transfer of Financial Risk by Contract

Through an *indemnity agreement*, one party agrees to assume or address the claims against another party that would under normal circumstances be considered liable. As expressed by Betty Van der Smissen (1990, p. 25–63):

> if an organization was using the facilities of another and there was [an indemnity agreement between the two parties], if injury occurred during [an] activity in the facility and the facility owner was assessed damages for such injury, the organization which signed the use contract ... would have to pay or "indemnify" the facility owner.

Because most school boards possess facilities that can be accessed by the public in some fashion, usage contracts are quite common. An example is provided in *Appendix 14.2: Contract For Use Of School Facilities – School District Of Owen-Withee [WI]*.

In Canada, common law recognizes the existence of vicarious liability, that is, the liability of one party for the misconduct of another, although the former is not directly at fault. An employer could be found to be vicariously liable if an employee displays negligence while acting within the scope of their employment. Since an employer-employee relationship (in insurance terms, a *master-servant* relationship) exists between a school board and a teacher, the school board is under an obligation to ensure the proper performance of the teacher's duty. For example, the school board is liable in law for injuries to a pupil due to a teacher's negligence if it deals with a matter that may reasonably be regarded as falling within the scope of their employment.

The master-servant relationship also exists between fitness businesses and the instructors they employ. This implicit indemnity agreement gives a teacher or fitness instructor some security because they assume a great deal of risk in many of the activities they undertake daily in the performance of their duties.

An *exculpatory clause* (also called a *waiver* or *release*), rather than transferring liability, waives liability (usually of a facility or equipment owner or manufacturer).

Exculpatory clauses are most commonly used on registration and participation forms, admission tickets, and rental agreements (see *Appendix 3: Release Form – 2000 USA Cycling*). They tend to be overused, however, and many would probably not hold up to legal scrutiny.

Transfer of Financial Risk by Insurance

Insurance is seen by many as the only active component of a risk management program. While certainly one of the most important, it is easy to lose sight of alternative methods in which to "insure" against losses. Rachel Corbett (1995) argues that in fact,

> for a sport or recreation organization, insurance is a risk management technique which should be reserved for the most critical and crippling potential financial losses – those events which would put your organization right out of business (p. 7).

High judgements and/or faulty claims, limited markets, and excessively high risk areas have led to inaccessible insurance and/or exorbitant premiums in some areas of sport, physical activity and recreation. While it is crucial that organizations carry enough insurance to protect against losses, it is also advisable, in these times of fiscal restraint, to evaluate and determine exactly from what types of insurance an organization would truly benefit. According to Corbett (1995), "insurance can be effective and valuable if it is designed to meet ... specific risk management needs, and if it is used in conjunction with other appropriate risk management techniques" (p. 41).

The Importance of Insurance

Insurance has been defined as "a method of hedging one's bet against foreseeable but uncertain occurrences involving financial loss" (McNulty, 1975, p. 103). The benefits of insurance coverage, while mostly intangible, are numerous:

1. Insurance protects an organization against serious financial loss, which helps in eliminating the possibly of bankruptcy. While insurance premiums are potentially costly in their own right, "an ounce of prevention is worth a pound of cure."
2. Insurance passes on the expenses associated with investigating claims, securing legal counsel, and attempting settlement with the plaintiff's insurance carrier.
3. A regular premium payment is easier to budget than are an erratic number of claims.
4. Insurance coverage meets a moral obligation to give redress for injury, which an organization might not otherwise be capable of doing. It is unfortunate, yet inevitable that a substantial number of claims go before the courts, but it is necessary to ensure that any monetary damages are fairly assessed. Of course, money cannot compensate for personal losses, but it can aid in making life a little more comfortable for the injured.

The Insurance Contract

A contract is usually defined as a binding agreement made between two parties. Insurance is then, by definition, a contract. According to the Insurance Institute of Canada (IIC, 1998, p. 1–17), insurance is the undertaking by one party (the *insurer*) to indemnify another party (the *insured*) against loss or liability for loss with respect to a certain risk (or *peril*) or danger (or *hazard*). A peril is an event that may cause a loss, such as fire, theft, or vandalism. A hazard is a condition that may cause a peril to occur, such as poorly maintained premises. Depending on the nature of the loss or to whom this loss may occur, the insurer may be required to compensate a third party who may have been injured or whose property may have been damaged by the insured.

For any contract (insurance or otherwise) to be valid in a court of law, five elements must be present (IIC, 1998):

1. An *agreement* is made up of an offer and an acceptance. The offer must be well-defined

and it must be communicated orally, in writing or by a recognized gesture. The acceptance must also be definite and communicated. The acceptance must be based on the terms of the offer. Any change to the offer amends the acceptance into a counter-offer. The original offer is then no longer valid.

2. *Consideration* is what one party gives or promises to give in exchange for a product or service form the other party. Consideration must have some value, however, an equitable exchange is not necessary. Consideration is not required if the contract has been sealed. Consideration must include only present or future services, and not be based upon the past to be legally binding.

3. *Genuine intent* must be present in order for a contract to be legally binding. All parties must enter into a contract by mutual consent and not under duress of any type.

4. The capacity of all parties connected with the contract must be considered for it to be valid. Not all individuals have the capacity (mental, physical, financial, or otherwise) to enter into contracts that are binding. Insurance contracts can only be made with individuals having the *capacity to contract* or with legal entities only.

5. The object of the contract must be *legal*. The judicial system will not enforce an illegal contract.

In addition to these five elements, there are three additional requirements for an insurance contract to be considered legally binding (IIC, 1998):

Insurable interest: Before a party can purchase insurance, they must stand to lose if the insured event happens. The insured must possess an insurable interest. For example, an individual has an insurable interest (i.e., legal liability) to pay for damages for which the individual is responsible.

Indemnity: There are two types of risk, pure and speculative (IIC, 1998, p. 1–5). Pure risk involves only a chance of loss; there is no chance of profit. Speculative risk involves a chance of loss in addition to a chance of profit. Only pure risks can be insured against. This is called indemnity. The insured cannot profit from a loss, but can only be put back in the same financial position as they were before the loss. Insurance contracts indemnify the insured on an actual cash value (the value of an equivalent piece of property of the same age and condition, and subject to the same wear and tear as the property that was lost or destroyed), or a replacement cost (an assessment based on the cost of the item at the time of the loss, repaired or replaced with like kind and quality, without any deduction for depreciation).

Utmost good faith: The agreement between the insured and the insurer must be made with utmost good faith. All material facts that would influence a prudent underwriter in accepting or rejecting the risk must be given by the insured to the insurer. The insurer in turn must also act with utmost good faith, by providing the insured with all the information necessary to make educated decisions.

Reading an Insurance Policy

Virtually all insurance policies contain five parts (IIC, 1997c):

1. The *declaration* is sometimes referred to as the cover page of the policy. It provides the details of the insurance policy, including the insured's name and address, the insurer, the broker, policy number, policy term (effective and expiry date including the times), limits of insurance and deductibles.

2. The *insuring agreement* describes what is covered by the policy. The agreement will describe the property which is insured (for example, the building, contents, equipment, and machinery). It will also describe the perils (or events) which the property is insured for example, (fire, theft, lightning, explosion, smoke, falling object, riot, vandalism or malicious acts, windstorm or hail).

3. The *exclusions* state what is not covered by the policy, or in other words, what property and perils are not insured. For example, in a typical homeowner's policy, motorized vehicles such as cars and motorcycles are excluded, but lawn movers, snow blowers and garden tractors are insured. *Overcash v. Statesville City Board of Education*, 348 S.E. (2d) 524 (N.C. App. 1986) is a case based on an athletic injury exclusion in an insurance policy. Martin Overcash was a member of his high school baseball team. He was struck by a pitch, and was jogging to first base, when he fell and broke his leg. He claimed that his fall was caused by a metal spike on the baseline, hidden by the dirt and chalk. The lawsuit was against the negligent maintenance of the field by the employees of the Statesville Board of Education. The board's insurance policy specifically excluded injuries arising out of participation in athletic contests sponsored by the school board. The board was therefore immune from liability.

4. *Conditions* (or *statutory conditions*) state what the insured must do, or refrain from doing, in order to be covered by the insurance policy. For example, the insured must notify the insurer of any material change increasing the chance of loss promptly, such as converting a garage into a woodworking shop. Termination of the insurance policy, to give another example, is a cancellation condition. This condition states what parties may give notice and the number of days of notice required in order to cancel the policy. An insured can cancel at any time without having to give a specified number of days notice. The insurer, on the other hand, must give a specified number of days notice by registered mail or personal delivery.

5. *Endorsements* are changes made to the policy. These changes may be amended on the policy itself or on a separate attachment to the policy. Endorsements can change any aspect of the policy and therefore must be applied very carefully.

Distribution of Insurance

Insurance may be secured through independent agents/brokers, exclusive agents, directly through an insurance company, through associations, or by self-insurance. As mentioned previously (see *The Retention of Risk*), *self-insurance* usually involves the formation of joint insurance pools with other organizations faced with similar risks.

Insurance agents or *brokers* represent many insurance companies, such as (in Canada) the Royal & SunAlliance Insurance Company, the Zurich Insurance Company, the Lombard Insurance Company, and Economical Insurance. Insurance companies appoint independent agents or brokers to market and sell their products. Because a broker is not restricted to one company, they are better equipped to supply the customer with a policy best suited to their needs at the most competitive rates.

Exclusive agents represent one company only. While the agents are not employees of the insurance company, the company markets their policies exclusively through these agents. The State Farm Insurance Company, for example, markets their policies through exclusive agents. Because of the visibility of their franchises, these insurance companies have an increased amount of exposure and recognition, thus enabling them to create competitive rates for their policies.

Direct writing companies deal directly with the public. The Allstate Insurance Company and the Co-operators General Insurance Company are examples of direct writing insurance companies. By eliminating overhead expenses, these companies can keep their rates competitive.

Associations: Because of the nature of the insurance business and its reluctance to insure athletic activities, many organizations which offer sport and fitness programs have been forced to seek a new avenue of insurance. *Associations* present a practical avenue for organizations in the sport and fitness fields, who might not otherwise be able to secure insurance at a reasonable rate, if at all.

The Canadian Ski Association, as related by Hanna (1986),

> indemnifies downhill and cross country ski instructors, coaches and tour leaders, the Canadian Association of Nordic Ski Instructors insures cross country ski instructors, and the Coaching Association of Canada has purchased policies to offer to certified individuals functioning as coaches in any sanctioned sport (p. 172).

Sometimes athletes themselves are insured by associations. The National Federation of State High School Associations in the United States had to create its own national insurance program. Athletes pay a small fee annually to secure lifetime catastrophe insurance. For example, a Tacoma, Washington student covered under the 1982–83 pilot program in that state, became a paraplegic as a result of a wrestling injury. The plan paid his medical expenses. The plan also protected the national and state associations, and the member school and its employees from liability suits ("Associations," 1983).

General Liability and Accident Insurance

Comprehensive General Liability

As stated by Hugh Morand (1987), "liability insurance especially in sport organizations and more recently fitness businesses has never been popular with underwriters" (p. 14). Depending on the nature of the activity or organization, the potential for large or frequent claims can be great. Morand offers other reasons, as summarized in *Table 14.2: Liability Insurance and Sport*. (See *The Insurance Crisis*, above, for further reference.)

The *comprehensive general liability* policy provides coverage for liability arising from the premises, operations, products and completed operations of the insured. It covers costs awarded by courts, including legal defense costs, and legal damages (up to determined limit). It could also pay out settlement costs. Most are designed to protect against liability to the public or to third parties (IIC, 1997a). Comprehensive general liability is the most important type of insurance, and therefore an organization should purchase as much as is possible, as damage awards can easily render it destitute.

Comprehensive general liability policies cover four distinct areas of liability exposures: bodily injury and property damage liability, personal injury liability, medical payments, and tenants' legal liability. Each coverage carries with it its own set of exclusions, most of which can be supplemented by endorsements. These coverages can also be purchased separately, as it is sometimes not necessary to purchase each type. A consultant, for example, would not need bodily injury and property damage coverage. A standard liability insurance contract does not exist, but the described coverages are essentially the same.

Bodily Injury and Property Damage Liability
Bodily injury is defined as any physical injury, sickness, disease, or death that is suffered as a result of the insured's negligence. The policy pertains only to those damages for which the insured is legally obligated to pay. In other words, damages are limited to those that are compensatory in nature. This precludes the payment of punitive or exemplary damages. Sympathy or gratuitous payments cannot be made through a bodily injury policy.

In a sport or recreation context, the possibility for bodily injury is enormous. At particular risk are spectators. Spectators are, in many instances, more at risk of being injured than are the participants themselves. Facing the average spectator are participatory dangers (balls or pucks hit into the stands, basketball or football players running out of bounds), crowd control dangers (rowdyism and disorderliness, fighting and assaults), and building and premises dangers (bleachers and other seating arrangements, parking lots, steps and walkways).

Property damage is defined as the loss or damage of property and the resulting losses of use of

TABLE 14.2
LIABILITY INSURANCE AND SPORT[2]

Hugh Morand, in his article *The Sports World—How To Obtain Insurance* (1987), writes, "liability insurance especially in sport organizations and more recently fitness businesses has never been popular with underwriters" (p. 14).

Morand provides several reasons to back up his claim:

1. Those involved in sport tend to have a high public profile. Sport and fitness accidents make the press.
2. Underwriters are ignorant of the risks involved and only assume what the risks are.
3. It is not, according to underwriters, economically justifiable to devote resources and expertise to areas such as sport and fitness that are hard to place.
4. Sports and fitness organizations don't collect claims statistics. Therefore, there is a lack of these statistics in the insurance industry.
5. Poorly constructed hold harmless agreements. In many cases teams using municipal facilities have to hold harmless the municipality for damages.
6. Owners of facilities make ridiculous demands on the users, thereby making liability limits out of reach. The City of Toronto, for example,

> originally required the sponsors of the Indy race to carry $100,000,000 [CDN$] of liability insurance, at a time when any informed person in the insurance industry could have told Toronto such coverage was unobtainable. At the same time the City of Toronto itself was having difficulty in buying 1/10 of that limit. (p. 5)

that property. It should be noted that this coverage pertains to the property of a third party, and not the property of the insured. Not only would insurance cover the replacement value of any property lost or damaged by the insured, but it would also cover the costs of lost revenue due to the loss or damage of this property.

Some common exclusions from this liability coverage include injuries to employees (usually covered by worker's compensation laws), losses assumed by contract (see indemnity agreements above), use of automobiles (usually covered by as separate automotive policy), damage of the insured's property or equipment (covered by property insurance), consumption or service of alcohol, wrongful dismissal, environmental pollution or contamination (which may concern marina and stable owners), and complaints or proceedings under any human rights code (such as discrimination and sexual harassment).

Personal Injury Liability
Personal injury, in an insurance context, refers to injury or damage to the character or reputation of a third party. Libel, slander, and false arrest, detention, or confinement are all covered under the terms of this policy. The most significant exclusion from this coverage relates to the use of media by the insured causing slander or libel (covered under advertisers' liability).

Medical Payments
First aid, X-ray and dental services, medical and surgical costs, and ambulatory expenses are all payable under this coverage. This part of the policy covers reasonable medical expenses. Significantly, this coverage does not include employees, nor does it include participants in athletic events (covered by sports accident liability).

Tenants' Legal Liability
Tenants' legal liability coverage provides that the insured is covered if they should negligently cause any damage to facilities that they rent for

their activities. Most sporting organizations would carry tenants' legal liability insurance due to the fact that they rent space in a third party's facilities, although this is not necessarily the case in professional sports (baseball, football, hockey, and basketball in particular). Usually one party owns both the sporting venue and the team itself, although they may be incorporated under separate names.

Although excluded from the standard coverage offered by the comprehensive general liability policy, many risks may be protected against through endorsements (supplementary policies). Common endorsements relevant to sport and recreation include:

Watercraft Liability: A watercraft liability endorsement would cover payments for injuries or damages resulting from the ownership, maintenance, or use of both owned and non-owned watercraft. (This may pertain to rowing or sailing organizations.)

Saddle Animal Liability: A saddle animal liability endorsement handles claims due to negligence arising out of the ownership or use of saddle animals, primarily horses (of concern to equestrian or polo teams).

Liquor Liability: Any facility serving alcohol to an individual whom subsequently commits a negligent act causing injury or damage could be found liable for those damages. Curling rinks, racquet and fitness clubs, and golf and country clubs would typically carry liquor liability insurance.

Products Liability: Products liability insurance covers losses resulting from the possession, use, existence, or consumption of products manufactured or sold by insured. It gives protection to the insured against lawsuits where it is alleged that the insured's product caused injury or damage to a third party's person or property. Products liability would cover defective workmanship or materials, failure to warn of potential dangers of use, hazardous design, and breach of warranty.

In 1983, the United States Senate considered a bill that would have radically altered product liability laws ("Bill Would Limit," 1983). This bill would have shifted some of the legal liability for some sports injuries from the equipment manufacturers to school officials. It would have assigned a "percentage of responsibility" to any individual involved with the use of the product. This individual would then share in the legal liability in the event of a lawsuit. The manufacturer would be solely liable only if relevant warnings were not posted on the product, or if the product was not manufactured properly. This bill failed to pass, but its introduction could point to the future of product liability legislation.

Advertisers' Liability: Personal injury liability typically excludes the use of media to libel, slander, or otherwise damage the character of a third party. Advertisers' liability covers offenses such as misappropriation of ideas, pictures, copyrights, and rights of privacy relating to advertising, publishing, broadcasting, or telecasting.

Cross Liability: The comprehensive general liability policy protects the insured against claims from a third party. It does not cover claims from one named insured against another (such as coaches or volunteers vs. an organization). Cross liability treats these claims as if each named insured had a separate policy. Cross liability coverage is also referred to as a *severability of interests* or a *separation of insureds* clause. The policy outlined in *Appendix 4: HPAC Liability Insurance Coverage Summary* addresses many issues surrounding cross liability coverage.

Other Liability Insurance

Sports Teams Liability: Sports teams insurance is a type of comprehensive policy that is currently available through a few insurance companies (including Lloyd's Underwriters and All Sport

Insurance Marketing Ltd.). It was designed to meet the basic needs of sport teams, organizations, and associations without the athletic sports participant exclusion. Companies such as SportsInsurance.com cater almost exclusively to this market. They offer insurance packages for soccer, baseball, hockey, football, and other team sports. Premiums would of course depend of the nature of the activity. Table 14.3: Sport Classification Chart, provided by All Sport Insurance Marketing Ltd., ranks sports from least risky (Class A) to most risky (Class C).

As stated above, most liability policies protect organizations or individuals that, in the course of their operation or performance, injure a third party or damage their property. Separate policies are needed to protect an organization against claims from their employees.

Sports Accident Liability: Accident insurance provides extra coverage over and above the benefits paid under public health care programs or private insurance. It covers medical and dental care, medical equipment, transportation costs, supplies, drugs, and rehabilitation expenses, as well as compensatory damages in the event of the loss of a hand, foot, eye, or even the loss of life. While most sport organizations possess accident insurance, payouts are not common, because this coverage comes into effect only after other benefits are paid. Two sports accident policies are outlined in *Appendix 14.5: Softball Manitoba – Liability and Sports Accident Insurance Policy* and *Appendix 14.6: Indiana University Club Sport Liability Policy*.

Professional Liability: A teacher/coach has many duties with regard to the well-being and safety of their athletes. Coaches, for example, must supervise players, manage behaviour problems, assess the developmental level of their athletes, and ensure that equipment is safe (to name but a few), in addition to providing adequate instruction and training. Regardless of the pressure inherent in performing these duties, if a coach owes a duty of care to a player, and through the coach's failure to meet a reasonable standard of care, the player is harmed, the coach will be found liable, whether or not the coach was acting within the scope of their duty.

Insurance does not allow a teacher/instructor to disregard standards of conduct and safety. Few would construe it as such. An employee or volunteer would most probably not be protected by the sponsor of an activity if the individual acts in excess of assigned authority, or exhibits blatant negligence. The master-servant relationship may even be nullified if an employee or volunteer acts outside the scope of their duty. Thus, professional liability insurance is usually carried by the individual professional on the grounds that the organization may not cover them.

Robertson and Robertson (1988) state, somewhat cynically,

> Usually, someone who starts a legal action is more interested in money than justice, so if he or she is confident that liability can be established on the part of the organization he or she might not think it worth bothering to sue the individual as well. However, the more common approach taken is to cast the net wide and sue any party who might possibly be held responsible (p. 42).

This is commonly referred to as the *deep-pocket syndrome*.

Directors and Officers Liability: Under common law, directors and officers (managers) are charged with acting in a responsible manner, in accordance with three duties of conduct. As summarized by Corbett (1995, p. 31), they include the duty of *diligence* (to act in the best interests of the corporation), the duty of *loyalty* (to not use a position of responsibility to further private interests), and the duty of *obedience* (to act within the law and the bylaws of the corporation).

Directors and officers liability covers the damage caused by misleading statements or acts, and

TABLE 14.3
SPORT CLASSIFICATION CHART[3]

CLASS A

Badminton	Horseshoes
Bowling	Orienteering
Curling	Table Tennis
Golf	

CLASS B

Archery	Netball
Baseball	Racquetball
Basketball	Rowing
Bicycling	Sailing
Canoeing	Shooting
Cross-Country Skiing	Soccer
	Softball
Cricket	Speed Skating
Fencing	Squash
Field Hockey	Swimming
Figure Skating	Tennis
Football	Track and Field
Gymnastics	Volleyball
Handball	Water Polo
Judo	Water Skiing
Karate	Weightlifting
Lacrosse	Wheelchair Sports
Lawn Bowling	Wrestling

CLASS C

Alpine Skiing	Hockey
Boxing	Rugby
Diving	

neglect or breach of duty. In short, this coverage protects against mismanagement. As an example, a coach may sue a general manager for wrongful dismissal. A player may sue due to the failure on the part of an organization to abide by the terms of their contract. Corbett (1995) writes, "when an organization makes decisions which affect the rights and privileges of its members, such as selection or discipline decisions for athletes, [its directors may be sued for] having improperly authorized, rendered, or implemented [these decisions]" (p. 29).

Errors and Omissions Liability: Errors and omissions liability (also called *malpractice liability*) protects the insured from the repercussions of an oversight or error within the scope of their professional area or activity. Doctors, lawyers, and accountants typically purchase errors and omissions insurance, but trainers, physiotherapists, and sport consultants, might also require this coverage.

Workers' Compensation Insurance

Workers' compensation insurance provides financial reimbursement to employees for any job-related injuries. It is administered and regulated by individual state and provincial governments. Each state and province has its own schedule of benefits, but compensation is usually limited to actual medical and hospital expenses, and does not usually include compensation for pain and suffering.

Each state and province has its own worker's compensation board, whose task it is to verify and validate the many claims it receives daily. Decisions are often disputed, as in the following case.

William Merchant, a physical education teacher, was required in his job to participate in vigorous racquetball activities for twenty hours each week. After three months on the job, he began to experience pain in his knee, which eventually led to orthopedic surgery. Having missed a day of work to undergo the surgery, Merchant sought compensation for medical expenses, but the state insurance fund denied coverage on the grounds that the knee problem was the result of a progressive ailment and not an accident at work. Merchant sued and the administrative law judge ordered the fund to pay Merchant because similar injuries had been compensated in the past ("P. E. Teacher," 1987).

Depending on the declarations and conditions contained in each state or province's respective Workers' Compensation Act, extra insurance may be necessary.

Medical Insurance

Medical insurance is usually carried only if an employee cannot benefit from health care packages such as the Ontario Health Insurance Plan (OHIP). Even public health plans have their limitations, especially in the area of out-of-country medical expenses. Supplementary coverage may be necessary. Usually excluded from medical insurance policies are soft-tissue and overuse injuries, replacement of glasses or contact lenses, massage therapy, and physiotherapy beyond a certain limit.

Protection of Property, Finances, and Operations

Property Insurance

Whereas a *property damage liability insurance policy* covers the costs of damages or replacement of a third party's property, a *property insurance policy* covers the replacement value of property owned by the insured or for which the insured is responsible. Basic policies cover fire and theft, but extended coverage is available for specifically named perils. All-risk policies cover losses by whatever means. Exclusions to property insurance policies include money, vehicles, personal property, landscaping, mechanical and electrical breakdown, and damage from heat, cold, dryness, or dampness. Most of these exclusions are covered by all-risk policies.

Crime and Fidelity Insurance

Crime insurance covers the loss of property through burglary, robbery, or theft. (For the precise definitions of these terms, see *Table 14.4: Crime Insurance*.) Usually, this coverage also extends to any damages to the premises caused as a result of the crime. Crime insurance can be purchased separately or as an endorsement to a property insurance policy. The most common exclusion is loss or damage due to any fraudulent, dishonest, or criminal act committed by the insured or employees of the insured, alone or in collusion with others. This exclusion can be covered, however, through a *fidelity* or *employee dishonesty insurance* endorsement or policy. Fidelity insurance coverage may also include stock pilferage, embezzlement, forgery, and computer or bookkeeping fraud (IIC, 1995).

**TABLE 14.4
CRIME INSURANCE**[4]

The Insurance Institute of Canada (1995) makes distinctions between the terms burglary, robbery, and theft, defining them as follows:

Burglary means the unlawful taking of insured property from within the premises by a person unlawfully entering or leaving the premises as evidenced by marks of forcible entry or exit.

Robbery means the taking of insured property from a custodian by a person or persons who have

i. caused or threatened to cause the custodian bodily harm; or
ii. committed an overt unlawful act witnessed by the custodian; or
iii. taken such property from a custodian who has been killed or rendered unconscious.

Theft is the felonious taking of property with or without force or violence while the premises are open or closed. The essential element is the *felonious* taking without any strictures as to how it is done; it does not include the mere misplacing of property. It is much broader in its implications than either burglary or robbery, therefore it embraces both of them as well as the ordinary stealing of property.

Vehicle Insurance

Liability arising out of the use of an automobile is perhaps the most common concern of teachers and coaches, due in part to the exposure that vehicular accidents receive from the media. Instructors might also be wary because accidents are often the result of someone else's negligence, and thus totally out of the instructor's control. Numerous liability suits have been brought against teachers/instructors, coaches, and recreational personnel stemming from the transportation of school teams or special groups associated with sport, fitness, or recreation.

There will exist a need for transportation so long as extracurricular activities are run by school districts. It is imperative, therefore, that proper insurance coverage is obtained, as illustrated by the following case, cited by Baley and Matthews (1988, p. 271). Forest Naggle was hired as teacher and coach. He received permission to drive his car to a tournament at the board's expense. Mr. Naggle brought with him two participants. On the return trip, Mr. Naggle was killed in a serious accident. Both of the student participants in the vehicle were injured. Under the board's insurance policy, death benefits were sought for Mr. Naggle, and medical benefits were sought for the students. The automobile policy specifically covered buses owned by district, but allowed for substitution of personal vehicles when the buses weren't used, so Mr. Naggle's car was covered under the policy. The students' medical expenses were therefore reimbursed. However, the insurance rider had a specifically worded disclaimer of coverage for the owner of the substitute auto, so no death benefits could be granted to Mrs. Naggle.

Automobile insurance is governed by statute in each province and state, and each automobile owner is required by law to insure against liability arising out of the use of that automobile.

As described by the Insurance Institute of Canada (IIC, 1996a, p. 7–2), there are three primary sections of the vehicle insurance policy:

1. *Third party liability*: Third party liability insurance covers bodily injury or property damage suffered by third parties for which the insured is legally liable.
2. *Accident benefits*: The accident benefits portion of the policy provides reimbursement for injuries to the driver, passengers or pedestrians, including medical and death benefits, without regard to liability.
3. *Loss of or damage to the insured automobile:* This coverage compensates the insured for the loss of or damage to their vehicle. Available coverage includes *specified perils* (such as fire, theft, hail, et cetera), *collision or upset* (striking or being struck by another object, including the surface of the ground), *comprehensive* (specified perils, plus vandalism, and falling or flying objects), and *all-perils* (which combines the coverage provided by collision and comprehensive policies).

Organizations that own their own vehicles usually insure them minimally, or as Corbett (1995) writes, "to the extent that the vehicles are used for conducting the business of the organization" (p. 26). Generally, the policy does not apply to the personal use of organization vehicles, nor to the business use of personal vehicles. (This coverage, however, could be included as an endorsement of a personal vehicle policy.)

Liability coverage for leased or rented vehicles (as for every vehicle) is mandatory by law. Collision coverage is not. In some cases,

> organizations and businesses self-insure collision damage to their vehicles, as do individuals who drive older vehicles. They do this because the cost of premiums is high in relation to the cost to repair or replace a damaged vehicle (Corbett, 1995, p. 25).

More often that not, if extra coverage is needed organizations will purchase a *non-owned automobile liability* policy. A non-owned automobile liability policy protects the board, business, or organization from liability arising out of the use of an automobile not owned by the board, organization, or business. Through a non-owned insurance policy, the employer assumes the liability of employees or volunteers, but only in excess of existing insurance carried by the owner of the vehicle. In other words, once a teacher's or a coach's personal automobile insurance (or for that matter, the rental organization's insurance) is exhausted, there remains some additional protection under this assumption of liability by the employer. The memo summarized in *Appendix 14.7: Non-Owned Automobile Insurance – Windsor-Essex Catholic District School Board [ON]* defines for local school board employees a non-owned automobile insurance policy as it pertains to their daily operations.

Business Interruption Insurance

A business is said to experience a *direct* loss when property is damaged or destroyed. These losses are usually covered by a property insurance policy. Business interruption insurance protects organizations against *indirect* losses, i.e., losses of earnings that occur while a business is shut down so that lost or damaged property can by repaired or replaced (IIC, 1996b). This coverage allows a business to avoid further debt or drain by providing income that it normally provides for itself through revenues.

Key Person Insurance

Suppose a famous individual (i.e., a Michael Jordan or a Wayne Gretzky) founds a sport organization and names it after herself/himself. When that individual later passes away, a key person will have been lost. The morale and confidence of the business may suffer, creating potentially substantial financial hardships. While rare, this case illustrates the possible need for key person insurance.

Summary

As described by Barnes (1983), the contract of insurance transfers the risk and burden of bearing a loss to the many subscribers of an insurance company; in effect, sharing the risk among many. In exchange for the payment of a premium by the insured, the insurer undertakes to pay for the financial loss incurred by the insured, subject to the maximum limits specified in the policy.

Risk management is the process of recognizing potential risks inherent in an activity, then taking the appropriate steps to avoid them or to minimize their impact. Risk management programs can opt to retain these risks, or to transfer them through contractual or insured means. Thus, insurance is an integral part of risk management control. It is not feasible to believe that a risk management program will be completely effective, so the need for insurance is practical and necessary for its full implementation.

In the determination of insurance needs, there should be a thorough examination and understanding of the risks to which the insured will be exposed. A few principles to follow in establishing an effective insurance program (adapted from Gray (1996)) include:

- *Identify your risks.*
- *Decide how to protect for each risk.*
- *Insure risks only if deemed necessary.*
- *Cover the largest risk first.*
- *Seek good advice.*
- *Use brokers, as they have a larger pool of insurance.*
- *Always try to reduce your insurance cost.*
- *Risks and needs change; review the insurance policy regularly.*

In a sport and recreation context, insurance allows instructors and coaches the opportunity to perform the duties for which they were hired without living under the fear of making a mistake. However, as Corbett (1995) notes, "insurance does not eliminate liability, does not help an organization avoid negligence, and does not make staff or volunteers more responsible" (p. 41). Thus, insurance will protect you or your association from extensive financial loss, but it will not reduce the likelihood of a lawsuit; in fact, it has been postulated that possessing good insurance coverage actually increases the possibility of being sued (Van der Smissen, 1990).

Although insurance does provide some security to coaches and teachers, it does not provide a license to act irresponsibly. Safety must always be their primary concern, and proper instruction must always be their primary focus.

Insurance does not negate the need for a risk management program. It should not be considered a substitute for risk management. Rather, it is an integral part of an effective program which on its own, may actually be overrated. It is less costly and more practical to find ways to avoid risks. Corbett (1995) agrees: "when confronted with a risk management problem, insurance will rarely be the best solution ... the most widely available, effective and inexpensive risk management technique is common sense" (p. 41).

Questions for Class Discussion

1. Explain the theoretical need for insurance.
2. Define the term *tort*.
3. Describe the crisis that exists in recreation and sport.
4. Explain the difference between *liability* and *negligence*.
5. How is negligence determined in a court of law?
6. What is the *reasonable person standard*? Discuss the advantages and disadvantage of applying the reasonable person standard when deciding negligence cases.
7. Explain the need for a risk management program. List five components of a successful athletic-based risk management program.
8. Define and contrast the terms *indemnity agreement* and *exculpatory clause*.
9. List and explain the five elements of any valid contract.
10. Name the three additional elements required of a valid insurance contract.
11. Define the terms *declaration*, *insuring agreement*, *exclusion*, *condition*, and *endorsement*.
12. List and explain the four liability exposures covered by a comprehensive general liability policy.
13. Explain why a business would require products liability insurance and give an example of a business that might require this coverage.
14. Explain the *deep-pocket syndrome*.
15. Explain the difference between *property damage insurance* and *property insurance*.
16. List the three primary sections of a vehicle insurance policy.
17. Explain the difference between *collision* and *comprehensive* vehicle insurance coverage. If a shopping cart was to run into a parked car, which coverage would apply?
18. What is *non-owned vehicle insurance* and what does it cover?
19. Discuss the postulate that possessing good insurance coverage actually increases the possibility of being sued.
20. Do you agree with the categorization of each of the sports listed in *Table 14.3: Sport Classification Chart*? Choose one sport not listed in the table and place it in the class you feel most appropriate.

Relevant Cases

Canadian Cases
Aldridge v. Van Patter, (1952) O.R. 595, (1952) O.W.N. 516, (1952) 4 D.L.R. 93 (Ont. H.C.).

Regina v. Ciccarelli, (1988) 5 W.C.B. (2d) 310, aff'g (1990) 54 C.C.C (3d) 121 (Ont. D.C.).

Thornton v. Board of School Trustees of School District No. 57 (Prince George), (1975) 3 W.W.R. 622, 57 D.L.R. (3d) 438, varied: (1976) 5 W.W.R. 240, 73 D.L.R. (3d) 35 (B.C.C.A.) varied: (1978) 1 W.W.R. 607, 83 D.L.R. (3d) 480, 3 C.C.L.T. 257, 2 S.C.R. 267.

American Cases
McFatridge v. Harlem Globetrotters, 69 N.M. 271, 365 Pa. (2d) 918 (N.M. 1961).

Nganga v. College of Wooster, (1989) 557 N.E. (2d) 152 (Ohio App.).

Overcash v. Statesville City Board of Education, 348 S.E. (2d) 524 (N.C. App. 1986).

Southern Farm Bureau v. Naggle, 437 S.W. 2d 215 (Arkansas 1969).

Endnotes

1. Baley, J. A., & Matthews, D. L. (1988). *Law and liability in athletics, physical education, and recreation.* Dubuque, IA: Wm. C. Brown Publishers.
2. Morand, H. (1987, January 16). The sports world – How to obtain insurance. *Sports in the courts.* Toronto: Canadian Bar Association, Ontario Branch, Continuing Legal Education.
3. All Sport Insurance Marketing Ltd. Sport accident classifications. [fax] (rec'd 1999, December 1).
4. Insurance Institute of Canada. (1995). *Insurance against crime.* Toronto: Insurance Institute of Canada.

References

* Since 1990, *Athletic Director and Coach* has been incorporated into the periodical *Your School And The Law*, published by LRP Publications, Horsham, PA.

All Sport Insurance Marketing Ltd. *Sport accident classifications*. [fax] (rec'd 1999, December 1).

Appenzeller, H., & Ross, C. T. (Eds.) (1987, Summer). North Carolina – Athletic injury exclusion in insurance policy protects school board. *Sports and the courts, 8*, 7–8. Dallas, TX.

Baley, J. A., & Matthews, D. L. (1988). *Law and liability in athletics, physical education, and recreation*. Dubuque, IA: Wm. C. Brown Publishers.

Barnes, J. (1983). *Sports and the law in Canada*. Toronto: Butterworths & Co. (Canada) Ltd.

Berry, R. C., & Wong, G. M. (1993). *Law and business of the sports industries*. Westport, CN: Prager.

Campbell, T. (1998, June 5). *Re: Banning pole vaulting*. [online]. Available: http://www.polevault.com/wwwvault/messages/4024.html. [2000, April 2].

Canadian Universities Reciprocal Insurance Exchange. (no date). *CURIE Internet*. [online]. Available: http://www.curie.org. [2000, July 5].

Center for Effective Collaboration and Practice. (1999). [online]. Available: http://cecp.air.org. [2000, June 20].

Corbett, R. (1995). *Insurance in sport & recreation: A risk management approach*. Edmonton, AB: Centre for Sport and Law.

Corbett, R., & Findlay, H. (1993). *Managing risks: A guide book for the recreation and sport professional*. Edmonton, AB: Centre for Sport and Law.

Crockford, N. (1980). *An introduction to risk management*. Cambridge, England: Woodhead-Faulkner Ltd.

Decof, L. & Godesky, R. (1979). *Sports injury litigation*. New York: Practicing Law Institute.

Gray, D. A. (1996). *Start and run a profitable consulting business: A step-by-step business plan*. 5th ed.. North Vancouver, BC: Self-Counsel Press.

* Haight, W. (Ed.) (1983, July). Associations see catastrophe insurance plan as the answer to injury, liability problems. *Athletic director and coach, 1*(7). Madison, WI: Professional Publications.

* Haight, W. (Ed.) (1983, May). Bill would limit manufacturer's liability. *Athletic director and coach, 1*(5). Madison, WI: Professional Publications.

* Haight, W. (Ed.) (1987, July). P.E. teacher claims worker's compensation for knee injury. *Athletic director and coach, 5*(7). Madison, WI: Professional Publications.

Hanna, G. (1986). *Legal liability in outdoor education recreation*. Edmonton, AB: University of Alberta Press.

Humphreys, G. (1999, May 20). *Details of our insurance renewal for 1999*. [online]. Available: http://www.hpac.ca/insurance.html. [2000, March 27].

Insurance Institute of Canada. (1998). *Principles and practice of insurance*. Toronto: Insurance Institute of Canada.

Insurance Institute of Canada. (1997a). *Insurance against liability*. Toronto: Insurance Institute of Canada.

Insurance Institute of Canada. (1997b). *Insurance on property – Part 1*. Toronto: Insurance Institute of Canada.

Insurance Institute of Canada. (1997c). *Introduction to personal lines insurance*. Toronto: Insurance Institute of Canada.

Insurance Institute of Canada. (1996a). *Automobile insurance – Part 1 (Ontario)*. Toronto: Insurance Institute of Canada.

Insurance Institute of Canada. (1996b). *Business interruption insurance*. Toronto: Insurance Institute of Canada.

Insurance Institute of Canada. (1995). *Insurance against crime*. Toronto: Insurance Institute of Canada.

Lubell, A. (1987, September). Insurance liability and the American way of sport. *The physician and sport medicine, 15*, 192–200.

Manitoba Softball Association. (no date). *Insurance policy*. [online]. Available:
http://www.softball.mb.ca/sbinsure.htm. [2000, March 27].

McNulty, P. (1975). Legal liability in physical education and recreation. *Canadian coach, 6*(3), 8.

Morand, H. (1987, January 16). The sports world – How to obtain insurance. *Sports in the courts*. Toronto: Canadian Bar Association, Ontario Branch, Continuing Legal Education.

Ontario. (1991, April). *Education Act*. R.S.O. 1980, c. 129, (154, 1). Toronto: Ministry of the Attorney General.

Pole vault fall kills Snow Canyon track coach. (1998, March 5). *Salt Lake Tribune: Utah Online*. [online]. Available: http://www.sltrib.com/1998/mar/03051998/sports/26198.htm. [2000, April 2].

Robertson, B. W. & Robertson, B. J. (1988). *Sport and recreation liability and you!* North Vancouver, BC: Self-Counsel Press.

Saskatchewan, Department of Education. (1996). *Teacher resources*. [online]. Available: http://www.sasked.gov.sk.ca/docs/physed/physed2030/tresources.html. [2000, March 27].

School District of Owen-Withee. (1999). *School district of Owen-Withee contract for use of school facilities*. [online]. Available: http://www.telebotics.com/clark/owen/schools/oschpol/dfda.html. [2000, April 2].

SportsInsurance.com. (no date). [online]. Available: http://www.sportsinsurance.com/insurance/programs.html. [2000, March 27].

Superintendents' general insurance agent advisory committee. (1980). *Introduction to general insurance*. Toronto: The Insurance Institute of Canada.

Trustees of Indiana University. (2000, January 10). *Club sport liability coverage*. [online]. Available: http://www.recsport.indiana.edu/~public/clubs/liabilityins.htm. [2000, March 27].

USA Cycling. (2000). *Standard Athlete's Entry Blank and Release Form*. [online]. Available: http://www.usacycling.org/membership/docs/std_release.html. [2000, April 17].

Van der Smissen, B. (1990). *Legal liability and risk management for public and private entities*. Cincinnati: Anderson Publishing Co.

Windsor-Essex Catholic District School Board. (2000, March 30). *Caution: Use of private vehicles for field trips*. [memorandum].

Wong, G. M. (1988). *Essentials of amateur sports law*. Dover, Mass: Auburn House Publishing Company.

Wyatt. (1998, May 16). *Banning pole vault in Utah. Need help!!* [online]. Available: http://www.vaultworld.com/wwwvault/messages/3838.html. [2000, April 2].

Appendix 14.1: Tort Laws and Negligence

Source: Center for Effective Collaboration and Practice. (1999). [online]. Available: http://cecp.air.org. [2000, June 20].

The Center for Effective Collaboration and Practice (CECP) provides resources, including articles, reports, monographs, statistics, and web-sites related to emotional and behavioral problems in such areas as education, families, mental health, juvenile justice, child welfare, early intervention, school safety, and legislation.

The CECP provides on its home page a summary of tort laws as they pertain to negligence. The following is an excerpt from that summary.

WHAT ARE TORT LAWS?

Tort laws are laws that offer remedies to individuals harmed by the unreasonable actions of others. Tort claims usually involve state law and are based on the legal premise that individuals are liable for the consequences of their conduct if it results in injury to others (McCarthy & Cambron-McCabe, 1992). Tort laws involve civil suits, which are actions brought to protect an individual's private rights. There are two major categories of torts typically seen in education-related cases: intentional and negligence.

INTENTIONAL TORTS

Intentional torts are usually offences committed by a person who attempts or intends to do harm. For intent to exist, the individual must be aware that injury will be the result of the act. A common type of intentional tort is assault. Assault refers to an overt attempt to physically injure a person or create a feeling of fear and apprehension of injury. No actual physical contact need take place for an assault to occur. Battery, on the other hand, is an intentional tort that results from physical contact. For example, if a person picks up a chair and threatens to hit another person, assault has occurred; if the person then actually hits the second person, battery has occurred. Both assault and battery can occur if a person threatens another, causing apprehension and fear, and then actually strikes the other, resulting in actual injury.

Teachers accused of assault and battery are typically given considerable leeway by the courts (Alexander & Alexander, 1992). This is because assault and battery cases often result from attempts to discipline a student or stop a student from injuring someone. Courts are generally reluctant to interfere with a teacher's authority to discipline students (Valente, 1994). Courts have found teachers guilty of assault and battery, however, when a teacher's discipline has been cruel, brutal, excessive, or administered with malice, anger, or intent to injure.

In determining if a teacher's discipline constitutes excessive and unreasonable punishment, courts will often examine the age of the student, the instrument, if any, used to administer the discipline, the extent of the discipline, the nature and gravity of the student's offence, the history of the student's previous conduct, and the temper and conduct of the teacher. For example, a teacher in Louisiana was sued and lost a case for assault and battery for picking up a student and slamming him against bleachers. The teacher then dropped the student to the floor resulting in the student's arm being broken (*Frank v. New Orleans Parish School Board*, 1967). In Connecticut, a student was awarded damages when a teacher slammed the student against a chalkboard and then a wall, breaking the student's clavicle (*Sansone v. Bechtel*, 1980). Clearly, both of these actions were excessive and indicate that in such situations teachers may be held personally liable for injuries that occur to students because of the teacher's behaviour.

NEGLIGENCE TORTS

The second type of tort seen most frequently in education related cases is negligence. The difference between negligence and an intentional tort is that in negligence the acts leading to injury are neither expected nor intended. Students who bring negligence claims must prove that school personnel should have foreseen and prevented the injury by exercising proper care. Accidents that could not have been prevented by reasonable care do not constitute negligence (McCarthy & Cambron-McCabe, 1992).

There are four elements that must be present for negligence to occur: (1) the teacher must have a duty to protect students from unreasonable risks, (2) the teacher must have failed in that duty by not exercising a reasonable standard of care, (3) there must be a causal connection between the breach of the duty to care and the resulting injury, and (4) there must be an actual physical or mental injury resulting from the negligence. In a court, all four elements must be proven before damages will be awarded for negligence.

Duty to Protect

The first element, the duty to protect, is clearly part of a teacher's responsibilities. Teachers have a duty to anticipate foreseeable dangers and take necessary precautions to protect students in their care (McCarthy & Cambron-McCabe, 1992). Specifically, teacher duties include: adequate supervision, maintenance of equipment and facilities, and heightened supervision of high-risk activities. In the majority of negligence cases against teachers, the duty to protect is easily proven (Fischer et al., 1994). Clearly this duty applies to activities during the school day, however, courts have also held that this duty may extend beyond regular school hours and away from school grounds (e.g., after-school activities, summer activities, field trips, bus rides).

Failing to Exercise a Reasonable Standard of Care

The second element that must be proven in cases of negligence occurs when teachers fail to exercise a reasonable standard of care in their duties to students. If a teacher fails to exercise reasonable care to protect students from injury, then the teacher is negligent. Courts, in negligence cases, will gauge a teacher's conduct on how a "reasonable" teacher in a similar situation would have acted. The degree of care exercised by a "reasonable" teacher is determined by factors such as: (a) the training and experience of the teacher in charge, (b) the student's age, (c) the environment in which the injury occurred, (d) the type of instructional activity, (e) the presence or absence of the supervising teacher, and (f) a student's disability, if one exists (Mawdsley, 1993; McCarthy & Cambron-McCabe, 1992). For example, a primary grade student will require closer supervision than a secondary student; a physical education class in a gymnasium or a industrial arts class in a school woodshop will require closer supervision than a reading class in the school library; and a student with a mental or behavioural disability will require closer supervision that a student with average intelligence.

A number of cases have held that the student's IEP [individual education plan], disability, and unique needs are all relevant factors in determining the level of supervision that is reasonable (Daggett, 1995). Additionally, school officials may be liable for damage claims resulting from a failure to supervise a student with disabilities when that student injures another student.

Proximate Cause

The third element that must be proven in a negligence case is whether there was a connection between the breach of duty by the teacher and the student's injury; that is, the teacher failed to exercise a reasonable standard of care (element two) and this breach of duty resulted in the subsequent injury to the student (element four). This element, referred to as proximate cause, often hinges on the concept of foreseeability. That is, was the student's injury something that could have been anticipated by a teacher? If the injury could have been foreseen and prevented by a teacher if a reasonable standard of care had been exercised, a logical connection and, therefore, negligence may exist. To answer questions regarding proximate cause, courts will attempt to ascertain "was the injury a natural and probable cause of the wrongful act (i.e., failure to supervise), and ought to have been foreseen in light of the attendant circumstances?" (*Scott v. Greenville*, 1965).

Negligence claims will not be successful if the accident could not have been prevented through the exercise of reasonable care.

Actual Injury
The final element that must be proven in negligence cases is that there was an actual physical or mental injury. Moreover, although the injury does not have to be physical, it must be real as opposed to imaginary (Mawdsley, 1993). Even in instances where there is negligence, damage suits will not be successful unless there is provable injury.

CONTRIBUTORY NEGLIGENCE
If it can be shown that a student contributed to the injury, the teacher may use a defence of contributory negligence. If the court finds that contributory negligence was present, the teacher will not be held liable. With younger students (i.e., under the age of 6), it is difficult to prove contributory negligence because the tort laws in many states hold that young children are incapable of contributory negligence. In these instances, therefore, students can collect damages even if they did contribute to the injury. If students are between 7 and 14, unless it can be shown that they are quite intelligent and mature, contributory negligence is also difficult to prove.

REFERENCES
Alexander. K. & Alexander, M.D. (1992). *American public school law*. St. Paul, MN: West Publishing Company.

Daggett, L.M. (1995). *Reasonable schools and special students: Tort liability of school districts and employees for injuries to, or caused by, students with disabilities*. Paper presented at the International Conference of the Council for Exceptional Children, Indianapolis, IN.

Fischer, L., Schimmel, D., & Kelly, C (1994). *Teachers and the law* (3rd ed.). White Plains, NY: Longman.

Frank v. New Orleans Parish School Board, 195 So. 2d 451 (L.A. Ct. App. 1967).

Mawdsley, R.D. (1993). Supervisory standard of care for students with disabilities. *Education Law Reporter, 80*, 779-791.

McCarthy, M.M. & Cambron-McCabe, N.H. (1992). *Public school law: Teachers' and students' rights*. (3rd ed.). Boston: Allyn and Bacon.

Sansone v. Bechtel, 429 A.2d 820 (Conn. 1980).

Scott v. Greenville, 48 S.E. 2d 324, (1965).

Valente, W.D. (1994). *Law in the schools* (3rd ed.). New York: Merrill.

Appendix 14.2: Contract for Use of School Facilities: School District of Owen-Withee (WI)

Source: School District of Owen-Withee. (1999). School district of Owen-Withee contract for use of school facilities. [online]. Available: http://www.telebotics.com/ clark/owen/schools/oschpol/dfda.html. [2000, April 2].

The following contract outlines the conditions under which the Owen-Withee Board of Education (in Wisconsin) will allow the use of its facilities. The contract includes sections on illegal activities, supervision, property loss or damage, and indemnity from liability.

SCHOOL DISTRICT OF OWEN-WITHEE CONTRACT FOR USE OF SCHOOL FACILITIES

1. The Owen-Withee Board of Education encourages the use of school facilities by residents of the school district. The Board has established Board policies for rental charges and nominal fees to cover costs of labor, heat, and lights.
2. Some restrictions are necessary to protect the facilities and equipment which in reality belongs to all the people of the school district. The Board has an established policy with detailed regulations pertaining to public use of the facilities and equipment.
3. It is hereby understood that school activities have priority for use of any building and a scheduling change, et cetera, may result in the cancellation of this agreement or a necessary change in date/time.
4. It is understood that full responsibility rests with the organization, group, or individual using the facilities and equipment, to maintain adequate security and to leave the facilities and equipment in the same condition as they were before usage.
5. It is understood that drugs, alcoholic beverages, or gambling, will not be permitted in the school facilities or on school district property at any time, and smoking will be allowed only in specific areas.
6. It is understood that any organization, group, or individual using school facilities shall designate one individual as being in charge and responsible for the program or activity. That individual shall in turn be responsible to the district administrator or building principal.
7. It is understood that a custodian, or other school employee, as designated by the district administrator, must be maintained in the building at all times during the period of use. The Board of Education will pay for all services out of the total fee as assessed in this agreement.
8. It is understood that any key(s) that are given to the undersigned are not to be given to any other individual for use or duplication.
9. It is understood that application for any use of the school facilities must be filed with, and approved by, the district administrator or his/her designee.
10. In the event that property loss or damage is incurred during such use, or occupancy of district facilities, the amount of damage shall be decided by the District Administrator and approved by the Board, and a bill for damages will be presented to the organization, group or individual using or occupying the facilities during the time the loss or damage was sustained.
11. Where permitted by law, the applicant, organization, or group using the school facilities shall agree to indemnify, save and hold free and harmless, the School District of Owen-Withee, their officers, agents and employees, from and against all claims, demands, loss, liability, cost or expense of any kind or nature whatsoever, which the school district, their officers, agents or employees may sustain or incur, or that may be imposed upon; or injury to, or death of, persons; or damages to property arising out of, connected with, or attributable to rental, use, and occupancy of the public school building or facilities as provided herein.

12. The Board of Education has liability insurance which covers only the Board of Education. Users of the facilities are encouraged to see that they are properly insured for liability, accidents and injuries.
13. The undersigned do hereby acknowledge that they have read and understand the responsibilities of this agreement, and assume all and responsibilities for the proper use of the facilities and equipment, and if any damages occur from this use, will be responsible for payment of such damages.

Adopted: February 11, 1985
Legal References: Wisconsin Statutes: 120.12 (9)(10), 120.13 (17)(19)(21)

APPENDIX 14.3: RELEASE FORM: 2000 USA CYCLING

Source: USA Cycling. (2000). Standard Athlete's Entry Blank and Release Form. [online]. Available: http://www.usacycling.org/membership/docs/std_release.html. [2000, April 17].

The following is the release or waiver portion of a standard entry form for USA Cycling. Note that the rider acknowledges the dangers inherent in the sport, and releases the organizers and sponsors of any liability arising from his or her negligence.

2000 USA CYCLING
STANDARD ATHLETE'S ENTRY BLANK AND RELEASE FORM

I ACKNOWLEDGE THAT BY SIGNING THIS DOCUMENT, I AM RELEASING USA CYCLING, INC. (USAC), THE UNITED STATES CYCLING FEDERATION (USCF), NATIONAL OFF ROAD BICYCLE ASSOCIATION (NORBA), NATIONAL COLLEGIATE CYCLING ASSOCIATION (NCCA), AND U.S. PROFESSIONAL RACING ORGANIZATION (USPRO) AND THEIR RESPECTIVE AGENTS, EMPLOYEES, MEMBERS, SPONSORS, PROMOTERS AND AFFILIATES (COLLECTIVELY "RELEASEES") FROM LIABILITY. THIS ENTRY BLANK AND RELEASE IS A CONTRACT WITH LEGAL CONSEQUENCES. I HAVE BEEN ADVISED TO READ IT CAREFULLY BEFORE SIGNING.

In consideration of the Releasees or USAC's issuance of a license to me or the acceptance of my application for entry in the above event, I hereby freely agree to and make the following contractual representations and agreements. I acknowledge that cycling is an inherently dangerous sport and fully realize the dangers of participating in a bicycle race and FULLY ASSUME THE RISKS ASSOCIATED WITH SUCH PARTICIPATION INCLUDING, by way of example, and not limitation, the following: the dangers of collision with pedestrians, vehicles, other racers, and fixed or moving objects; the dangers arising from surface hazards, equipment failure, inadequate safety equipment, THE RELEASEES' OWN NEGLIGENCE, and weather conditions; and the possibility of serious physical and/or mental trauma or injury associated with athletic cycling competition.

For myself, my heirs, executors, administrators, legal representatives, assignees, and successors in interest (collectively "Successors"). I HEREBY WAIVE, RELEASE, DISCHARGE, HOLD HARMLESS, AND PROMISE TO INDEMNIFY AND NOT TO SUE the Releasees and the sponsors of this event, the organizer and any promoting organizations, property owners, law enforcement agencies, all public entities, special districts and properties, and their respective agents, officials, and employees through or by which the events will be held, (the foregoing are also collectively deemed to be Releasees), FROM ANY and all rights and CLAIMS INCLUDING CLAIMS ARISING FROM THE RELEASEES' OWN NEGLIGENCE, which I have or which may hereafter accrue to me and from any and all damages which may be sustained by me directly or indirectly in connection with, or arising out of, my participation in or association with the event, or travel to or return from the event.

I agree it is my sole responsibility to be familiar with the race course, the Releasees' rules, and any special regulations for the event. I understand and agree that situations may arise during the race which may be beyond the immediate control of the race officials or organizers, and I must continually ride so as to neither endanger myself nor others. I accept responsibility for the condition and adequacy of my competition equipment. I will compete wearing a helmet which satisfies the requirements of the Releasees' racing rules or regulations and that can protect against serious head injury, and assume all responsibility and liability for the selection of such a helmet. I have no physical or medical condition which to my knowledge, would endanger myself or others if I participate in this event, or would interfere with my ability to participate in this event.

I understand that drug testing may be conducted for athletes registered for this event and that the use of blood boosting or substances prohibited by Releasees' rules would make me subject to penalties including, but not limited to, disqualification and suspension. I agree to be subject to drug testing if selected, and its penalties if I fail to comply with the testing or am found positive for the use of a banned substance.

I agree, for myself and my successors, that the above representations are contractually binding, and are not mere recitals, and that should I or my successors assert my claim in contravention of this agreement, the asserting party shall be liable for the expenses (including legal fees) incurred by the other party or parties in defending, unless the other party or parties are finally adjudged liable on such claim for willful and wanton negligence. This agreement may not be modified orally, and a waiver of any provision shall not be construed as a modification of any other provision herein or as a consent to any other provision herein or as a consent to any subsequent waiver or modification.

Every term and provision of this agreement is intended to be severable. If any one or more of them is found to be unenforceable or invalid, that shall not affect the other terms and provisions, which shall remain binding and enforceable.

Parents or guardians of younger children are also required to release the organizers from any liability:

My child is fit for the race, and I consent to my child's participation. I HAVE READ AND I UNDERSTAND THE ATHLETE'S COMPETITION AND RELEASE AGREEMENT. In consideration of allowing my child to participate, I consent to it and agree that ITS TERMS SHALL LIKEWISE BIND ME, MY CHILD, my heirs, legal representatives, and assignees. I HEREBY RELEASE AND SHALL DEFEND, INDEMNIFY AND HOLD HARMLESS THE RELEASEES FROM EVERY CLAIM AND ANY LIABILITY that I or my child may allege against the

Releasees (including reasonable attorney's fees or costs) as a direct or indirect result of injury to me or my child because of my child's participation in the race, WHETHER CAUSED BY THE NEGLIGENCE OF THE RELEASEES or others. I PROMISE NOT TO SUE RELEASEES on my behalf or on behalf of my child regarding any claim arising from my child's participation in the race.

APPENDIX 14.4: HPAC LIABILITY INSURANCE COVERAGE SUMMARY

Source: Humphreys, G. (1999, May 20). Details of our insurance renewal for 1999. [online]. Available: http://www.hpac.ca/insurance.html. [2000, March 27].

The following is an excerpt from a memo by Gregg Humphreys, Insurance Director of the Hang-Gliding and Para-Gliding Association of Canada (HPAC), summarizing their 1999 liability coverage. The liability coverage includes cross liability for all insureds, except in the case of a potential claim by pilots against landowners. This exception is made possible through the use of a waiver. Mr. Humphreys concludes the memo with some good advice on the reporting of claims.

> The basic policy is known as a Commercial General Liability policy. It promises to protect us (we are referred to as "the insureds") for claims brought against us by others. The claim may be for either personal injury to the claimant or for damage to their property.
>
> **WHO IS INSURED?**
> "The insureds" include you, if you are a paid-up member of the HPAC. Other insureds are our association, our member clubs, certified schools and students of the schools. Perhaps most importantly, additional insureds are "owners of land who have granted permission for the use of property for hang-gliding or para-gliding activities." These landowners have the full protection of our policy, if they fit this definition. [Because] they are insured on this policy and because you are insured on this policy, it follows that if you sue them, it is like suing yourself and this policy can't respond. Some landowners have been worried that a pilot, referred to as a "participant" in the policy, might suffer injury or death and then sue the landowner. To solve this we have attempted to arrange insurance where the landowners would be protected from us suing them. This is not easy to arrange since, if the insurance company let participants claim

against other insureds, you could claim for an injury which you sustained while participating in our sport, for example, when another pilot flew into you. This was accomplished, under the condition that the pilots sign a release acceptable to the insurance company. In other words, you will be asked to agree not to bring a claim against the landowner. You might ask why, if you sign a release saying you won't sue a landowner, do they need insurance. Because in the 1990s, lawyers will gladly sue people, alleging that the release is invalid. If they do, and you have signed a release, the owner of your favourite flying site is protected by our insurance and you get to keep flying there.

A new feature this year is that we have added "volunteers" to the coverage. People working at a meet were previously excluded from this policy. Now, if they are sued for something to do with an incident and this arises from their activities involving hang-gliding or para-gliding, they too are protected.

COVERAGE

In addition to the general liability coverage mentioned above, this year we were able to add coverage to include liability arising from gliders while under tow. Please note that, because of the fact that damage or injury to participants is not covered, as with the rest of our policy, damage caused while under tow is for that to third parties only. This means of course, that damage to the tow plane or tug, is not covered in any way. Similarly, the tug pilot and owner should have their own insurance. This policy does not protect them, only the glider pilot. Our policy also covers us for defence costs; if someone sues you and it is groundless, you are still covered for the cost of lawyers. The territory of our policy has also been improved. Our coverage now applies not only in Canada and the U.S.A. but anywhere in the world.

DEDUCTIBLE

If a claim is paid on your behalf, regardless of the size of it, you will be responsible for up to $1,000 [CDN$]. After that, the insurance company pays.

LIMITS

The insurance company is at risk to a maximum of $3,000,000 [CDN$]. This should be adequate for most situations but, if you are found liable for a loss greater than this, there is no coverage beyond this amount.

CLAIMS

If you are involved in any incident where you cause damage to someone or you injure someone, it is important that you notify our insurance company at once. There is no down side to advising them of something that later turns out to be nothing. There is however, a down side to not telling them. If we don't give them an opportunity to start investigating an incident early on, they can say that we put them in a bad position by failing to inform them of the incident while circumstances are fresh. They can then refuse coverage. Therefore, especially if you injure someone, report the incident promptly.

APPENDIX 14.5: LIABILITY AND SPORTS ACCIDENT INSURANCE POLICY: SOFTBALL MANITOBA

Source: Manitoba Softball Association. (no date). Insurance policy. [online]. Available: http://www.softball.mb.ca/sbinsure.htm. [2000, March 27].

The following is an excerpt from a summary of the general liability and sports accident policies offered by Softball Manitoba. Also included are all relevant exclusions, and the procedures needed to submit claims. (All dollar amounts in CDN$.)

INSURANCE POLICY

Who is insured?
Any association or league registered with the provincial governing body is insured under the liability program offered through All Sport Insurance Marketing Ltd.. The only requirement is that 100% of members within each association must participate.

Why liability insurance?
Because of your operations, or actions, you are open for possible suit from third parties. You may not be liable but you will need to be defended in court. A liability policy pays for this defence as well as any costs found against you. Legal fees can be very expensive and this can be an affordable way to have them covered. This policy covers your legal liability for bodily injury to or damage to property of others such as spectators, passers-by, property owners, and others resulting from your activity. In addition your legal liability for injury to participants is covered.

Who is covered?
All members collectively including executives, managers, coaches, trainers, officials, and volunteers while acting within the scope of their duties on your behalf.

GENERAL LIABILITY
Limit: as negotiated
Includes the following extensions:

- *Premises Property and Operations*
- *Products and Completed Operations*
- *Blanket contractual*
- *Personal Injury (libel and slander)*
- *Employees, as Additional Insureds*
- *Cross Liability*
- *Non-Owned Automobile (in most cases)*
- *Employers Liability*
- *Occurrence Basis Property Damage*
- *Medical Payments*
- *Incidental Malpractice*
- *Tenants' Legal Liability ($100,000)*

N.B.: Costs and coverage vary according to needs.

SPORTS INJURY INSURANCE
Coverage extends to practices, games, and team travel. One plan covers all participants, managers, coaches, executives, and field officials throughout the entire season.

For each separate accident the plan pays:

Dental
Up to $5,000 for dental treatment resulting from injury to whole and sound natural teeth and received within 52 weeks of the accident.

Blanket Accident Reimbursement
Up to $10,000 for cost of prescription drugs, ambulance, hospital services in excess of standard ward accommodations, physiotherapy, private duty nurses (R.N.), crutches, splints, medical braces, trusses, incurred within 52 weeks of the accident.

Principal Sum Benefits
Up to $20,000 in the event of the loss of use of hands, arms, or legs (quadriplegia, paraplegia, hemiplegia), or the loss of speech and hearing or dismemberment occurring within 52 weeks of the accident.

Accidental Death
Up to $10,000 in the event of accidental death occurring within 52 weeks of the accident.

Fracture Indemnity Benefit
Up to $300 paid for the fracture of bone or bones (including chip and linear fractures).

Rehabilitation Indemnity Benefit
Up to $3,000 for special occupational training required due to an accident.

Tuition Fees Reimbursement
Up to $2,000 for tutorial services made necessary by post-accident confinements.

Emergency Transportation Benefit
Up to $50 for transportation from an arena or field to the nearest hospital or doctor's office.

Eyeglasses and Contact Lenses Expense
Up to $100 for the repair or replacement of eyeglasses or contact lenses when damage results from an accident which required the insured person to receive treatment by a physician or dentist.

LIMITATIONS AND EXCLUSIONS
No benefit shall be payable for any loss resulting directly or indirectly, wholly or partially from any of the following causes:

a. purchase, repair, or replacement of eyeglasses, contact lenses or prescriptions thereof (except as otherwise provided);
b. sickness or disease either as a cause or effect;
c. any intentionally self-inflicted injury;
d. any of the hazards of aviation except while riding as a fare paying passenger in a licensed aircraft operating on a regular scheduled service between airports.
e. declared or undeclared war, invasion or civil war, or any act thereof;
f. service in the armed forces of any country;
g. any benefits that are available under any government health insurance plan, whether enrolled in such a plan or not;
h. dental and/or other expense benefits shall be for the excess of expenses payable under any other benefit plan or policy;
i. and insured person who is not a resident of any Canadian province that has enacted medical care legislation unless stated specifically in this policy.

This document of insurance is subject to and shall not contravene any federal or provincial statutory requirements with respect to hospital or medical plans, nor shall it duplicate any benefits which are provided under any federal or provincial hospital or medical plans, or any other policy providing a reimbursement indemnity.

ATHLETIC ACCIDENT CLAIM PROCEDURES
1. It is the responsibility of the insured to get an Athletic Accident Claim Form from the association or club executive.
2. The insured or parent/guardian shall complete fully the front portion concerning the accident particulars.
3. The insured shall submit the completed claim form to the association or club executive for their signed certification.
4. The insured shall be responsible to forward to All Sport Insurance Marketing Ltd. the completed claim form for payment.
5. For dental claims the insured shall have the attending dentist complete applicable portions.
6. For claims requiring a report from a doctor, chiropractor, osteopath, et cetera, the insurer will forward the necessary forms to you on receipt of the completed Athletic Accident Claim Form.
7. *The insurer should be notified within 30 days and proof of claim, including a report from the attending dentist or doctor, must be submitted within 90 days of the date of the accident.*

8. This form and all insured accounts which you are required to pay should be forwarded without delay to:
   All Sport Insurance Marketing Ltd.
   107–1367 West Broadway
   Vancouver, B.C., V6H 4A9

APPENDIX 14.6: CLUB SPORT LIABILITY POLICY: INDIANA UNIVERSITY

Source: Trustees of Indiana University. (2000, January 10). Club sport liability coverage. [online]. Available: http://www.recsport.indiana.edu/~public/clubs/liabilityins.htm. [2000, March 27].

The Trustees of Indiana University issued this summary of their liability insurance policy for club sports. Note the attention to detail regarding team rosters and vehicular accident reports. (All dollar amounts in US$.)

CLUB SPORT LIABILITY INSURANCE

I. Coverage

The policy covers all members of the club, including coaches, instructors, and advisors against claims from anyone, except participants, due to alleged acts of negligence during the activities.

Liability insurance is not medical insurance. It does not cover club members and opponents injured while participating in a club function. Also, travel in personally-owned vehicles is not covered. The driver's automobile insurance will cover claims associated with an accident.

The limits of the insurance policy are as follows:

- *General Aggregate limit: $1,000,000*
- *Products Completed Operations Aggregate limit: $1,000,000*
- *Personal and Advertising Injury limit: $1,000,000*
- *Each Occurrence limit: $1,000,000*
- *Fire Damage limit: $50,000*
- *Medical Expense limit: $5,000*

The cost of the liability coverage will be based on the number of members involved in each club sport.

The coverage period is from March to March.

II. Procedures for Implementation

Each club sport is responsible for documenting each club member on the Club Sport Membership Roster Form before he or she attends a club practice, tournament or activity. In addition, each member must sign an Acknowledgement of Responsibility Form. New members should be added to the roster form before the next club practice, tournament or activity. The date the individual became a club member must be listed on the Club Sport Membership Roster Form.

All club members should be informed of the extent of club insurance coverage. This information may be discussed during a club meeting (this information should be recorded in the club meeting minutes), club newsletter or special mailing.

III. On-going Responsibilities

New members are to be added to the club roster forms and responsibility forms completed before the next club practice, tournament or activity. Process the appropriate payments at the beginning of each semester and as members are added.

IV. Claims

Clubs must inform the Assistant Director of Club Sports of all accidents or injuries. Accident injury information must be recorded on an Accident Report Form. An Accident Report Form may be obtained from an Informal Sport Supervisor/Lifeguard or the Assistant Director of Club Sports.

Should a serious accident occur during a club practice, tournament or activity, the Assistant Director of Club Sports and/or the Program Director of Club Sports must be contacted immediately. In addition to the accident report and list of members present, witnesses' names, addresses, phone numbers and statements must be documented immediately.

Club members should not speak to anyone concerning the accident, including lawyers or insurance representatives, unless the Assistant Director of Club Sports or a designated university representative is present.

The injured individual should not be informed that the club sports insurance policy will automatically cover the claim. Refer to the extent of the insurance coverage explained in Section I.

V. Cost and Payments

The cost of the liability insurance is $2.95 per person.

APPENDIX 14.7: NON-OWNED AUTOMOBILE INSURANCE: WINDSOR-ESSEX CATHOLIC DISTRICT SCHOOL BOARD [ON]

Source: Windsor-Essex Catholic District School Board. (2000, March 30). Caution: Use of private vehicles for field trips. [memorandum].

In this memo, the Windsor-Essex Catholic District School Board (in Ontario) outlines its policies regarding the use of private vehicles for school board business, and describes for its staff non-owned liability insurance. (All dollar amounts in CDN$.)

USE OF PRIVATE VEHICLES TO TRANSPORT STUDENTS

As part of the procedures and guidelines for field trips, it is understood that persons who use a privately owned vehicle in the transportation of students shall have the principal's authorization. This authorization is dependent upon the driver having current and valid public liability insurance.

It is also understood by the owner of the vehicle that his or her own public liability insurance policy bears the initial liability for property damage and/or personal injury to self and passengers.

The Windsor-Essex Catholic District School Board maintains an excess liability insurance policy which covers all employees and volunteers who are transporting students within Canada on behalf of the board. This coverage comes into effect only in the event that a judgement arises against that employee or volunteer resulting from use of his/her vehicle and is in excess of the limit carried by the individual on his/her personal policy.

The number of students per vehicle cannot exceed the available, working seat-belts, which must be worn by each student/adult in the vehicle. In the case of vehicles equipped with air bags, students under 12 years of age shall be seated in the back seat(s) only.

NON-OWNED AUTOMOBILE INSURANCE

Purpose

Non-owned automobile liability insurance is designed primarily to pay claims in excess of the insurance carried on a vehicle not owned by the board or another insured while being used or operated on board business. In all cases, the Insurance Act stipulates that a vehicle owner's insurance is primary to any non-owned automobile liability insurance policy. For example, if the limit of liability coverage on the owner's vehicle were $500,000 and a claim cost a total of $2 million, the automobile insurer would pay the first $500,000 and the non-owned automobile liability policy would pay the next $1.5 million.

Coverage for School Boards

Non-owned automobile liability insurance provides protection to a school board against liability imposed by law upon the school board for loss or damage arising out of the use of or operation of any automobile not owned in whole or in part or licensed in the name of the school board on school board business.

Coverage is also provided to protect school boards which have, by resolution or contract, assumed responsibility on behalf of employees, volunteers, trustees, and other for the legal liability for losses arising out of the use of their own vehicles or another person's vehicle on board business.

Such coverage is excess of insurance carried by the owner of the vehicle or $200,000, whichever is higher.

Coverage for Individuals

Employees, trustees, volunteers, parents, students, and other individuals are protected while operating a vehicle not owned by them on board business. Further, they are protected while operating their own vehicles on board business, such as field trips. Driving to and from work is not considered board business. Again, coverage is excess of any vehicle owner's insurance coverage.

Insurance on Personal Vehicles Uses for School Trips

If the use of a personal vehicle to transport students to school activities is infrequent or occasional, the personal automobile insurance policy automatically extends coverage to the vehicle owner and authorized drivers.

If the personal vehicle is used regularly to transport students, then the vehicle owner should notify his agent, broker or insurer and ask that a rider be added to the policy to extend coverage for such usage.

Individuals will be protected by school boards which have assumed responsibility for loss or damages exceeding the limit of insurance carried on their own vehicle or $200,000, whichever is higher, while transporting students on school trips.

CHAPTER 15

TURNING CONFLICT INTO COOPERATION: ALTERNATIVE DISPUTE RESOLUTION

Margery Holman, Rebecca Mowrey, and Dan Bondy

The sport environment is replete with scenarios of conflict. It is the nature of competition. However, there are situations where it is in the best interests of all involved to solve conflict in a more cooperative way than moving towards litigation. Most of these situations occur within the organizational structure of sport as opposed to the competition itself. Cases may involve conflicts around such issues as: due process, as in the instance of disciplinary action; fair treatment, as in the designation of facilities, coaching expertise or competitive schedules; personal relations, such as harassment; alcohol or drug use; and, interpretation of rules and regulations. The issue remains the same in each of these examples. It is important to find the best way for organizations to solve differences in a manner that is fair and mutually satisfactory to the parties involved. Alternative Dispute Resolution (ADR) is a technique that may serve this objective.

The essence of sport often makes it difficult for people to address conflicts with a cooperative strategy. Sport participants learn to value winning and, when they view that they have not won, the only position remaining is that they have lost. This win-loss dichotomy influences the method by which conflict resolution is viewed.

Traditionally, power relationships in sport are both autocratic and hierarchical. People within the organizational structure have recognized their position within the hierarchy and have accepted decisions determined by someone else on their behalf. Even in the presence of a perceived negotiation, the relationship of those involved distorts the negotiating strategies. As a result, conflict often remains unresolved and antagonisms intensify. At this point the dysfunction is embedded, not only in the conflict itself, but also, in the method used for conflict resolution.

The characteristics of conflict resolution in sport issues can result in one of the parties experiencing dissatisfaction with the process and its outcome. At some point, it is this alienation that prompts individuals or groups to challenge through litigation. However, litigation maintains the win-loss dichotomy. It injects another level of power that dictates an outcome which may be unsatisfactory to everyone. It almost ensures that hostilities will linger and conflict will surface again in the future. An intermediary step would be alternative dispute resolution.

This chapter will provide a brief analysis of conflict, followed by an overview of the relationship between ADR and the law. It will then present the concept of ADR and how it can function within the sport setting. The question section and the case scenarios proposed as group tasks at the end of the chapter are either hypothetical or actual disputes that have gone through litigation. They are intended to foster your thinking about ADR approaches for sport conflicts.

Conflict

"In general terms, most conflicts arise from the perception of one party that the other party's behaviors/actions have been inappropriate and unacceptable" (Arbitration and Mediation Institute of Canada Inc., 1998, p. 3–7). Individuals bring their own experiences to professional relationships and to an organization. Consequently, their beliefs, values and attitudes influence their interactions within the organization. It is, therefore, inevitable that they will encounter opposition that challenges their views. The Arbitration and Mediation Institute of Canada Inc. (1998) identifies a number of catalysts that may contribute to the conflict: emotions; communication dynamics; cultural dynamics; assumptions, perceptions, expectations; power imbalances; stress; behavior, perceived or real; environment/setting; and, time demands (p. 3–6). The human orientation of conflict demands that attention be given to the catalysts that influence the conflict in attempts to arrive at a successful resolution.

In the past, individuals have been relatively tolerant of the risks involved in sport and the decision making processes that govern sport. In order for conflict to arise, this tolerance must be transformed into a perceived injustice. Once an injustice has been determined, it will be viewed as a wrong that needs remediation. This determination is the initial stage of identifying the dispute and seeking a resolution.

Past tolerance was coupled with the assumption of some responsibility for the undesired outcome on the part of the individual or group. When a decision is viewed as an injustice, the responsibility for the outcome shifts from the individual to the organization and those agents within the organization who determined the outcome. A disputant may identify a coach, an athletic director, or other individuals or groups within the organizational structure as responsible for an injustice.

When the identification of a person or persons responsible for an injustice is coupled with dismissal of a request for remedial action, a dispute has been fully established. At this point, it is important to recognize the possibility of a dispute escalating, potentially leading to legal action. Conflict resolution through ADR strategies may be useful in managing the dispute and avoiding litigation. This process is identified by Felstiner, Abel and Sarat (1981) as the emergence and transformation of disputes and incorporates the naming, blaming and claiming stages of conflict.

The presence of conflict is not necessarily a negative component of an organization unless that conflict is dysfunctional. With proper management, functional conflict will promote positive growth and development. A disregard for properly managing conflict will contribute to an organization that fails to realize its potential and risks organizational destruction.

ADR and the Law

Society is becoming more litigious, a trend from which sport is not immune. Further, there are some disputes where litigation is required. However, in most disputes, when there is a sincere desire by the parties involved to resolve the conflict, and a motivation to do so in a collaborative manner, ADR provides a non-litigious alternative.

Alternative dispute resolution offers a number of procedures by which conflict may be resolved without litigation. It is a process that is intended to intervene at an early stage within a dispute prior to parties becoming entrenched in their positions and viewing litigation as the only alternative remaining. In contrast to the confrontational approach routinely employed in the litigation process, it demands a collaborative style that generates cooperation in problem solving. Alternative dispute resolution can be a more economical approach to conflict resolution than legal recourse financially, emotionally and morally.

What is ADR?

Alternative Dispute Resolution (ADR) represents a vision for settling conflict in a more effective manner than the typical confrontational, win-loss approach referred to earlier. The courts and its litigation process will always need to exist for settlements in the more difficult and serious matters. However, when athletic organizations consider the costs of litigation, both financially and interpersonally, the alternatives to the legal adversarial system may become a preferred method for dealing with conflict.

For many years, sport organizations have used the adversarial methods for solving disputes. Hard bargaining for contracts, litigation for infractions of the law, or the tactics of posturing, rule manipulation, dirty tricks, or bribery in negotiations are representative of the confrontational approach commonly followed. The adversarial system also uses strategies like sabotage, lobbying and marketing to sell their positions. These strategies and tactics only serve to increase the hostile nature and the costs attached to settling the problem.

In this new vision, ADR, people in athletic organizations will become accustomed to dealing with conflict. They will understand that conflict is inevitable in all relationships, and that they should employ a proactive method to solve the dispute, rather than avoid or fight it. The ADR approach requires a change of focus for the people in the organization. The education and training of all organizational members in the skills of ADR is the immediate, and necessary goal for this new vision.

The template (see Figure 1) adapted from Slaskieu and Hasson (1998) will be used here to describe the alternative strategies of the ADR approach. Their model outlines the information in four areas and will provide the structure for describing these alternative conflict processes.

The first step is labelled "Site-based Resolution" (p. 57). This represents the ideal, or the ultimate goal for dealing with conflict. All of the people associated with a particular athletic organization (instructors, coaches, players, administrators, and others) have the potential to experience conflict. The template outlines that it is most desirable for anyone in conflict to use their own initiative to confront the problem and to work out a solution. Going to a superior in the organization, or a higher authority, is described as the last resort or the backup process in this first step of the process.

In the first step, individuals within the organization and those involved in a dispute must acquire the skills necessary for successful conflict resolution. These skills include active listening, reframing, and positive inquiry, among others. Active listening involves the checking of any personal bias when listening. It requires repeating and clarifying information and identifying underlying interests rather than only stating a personal position. You know what you believe and may know how you would handle the conflict. You now must listen for what the disputants believe and help them to solve the conflict in a manner which is useful to their needs.

The skill of reframing a statement is to restate the information provided in an alternate way to confirm an understanding of what has been said about the dispute. This strategy also serves to remove or diminish the emotion. The technique of positive inquiry has the individual start with open ended questions to get the greater picture, and eventually proceed to very specific, leading questions to focus on the central issues. These are examples of the ADR techniques that people will use in conflict resolution.

The second step is labelled "Internal Support" (p. 57), and represents the various roles that a sport organization can assign to individuals to help deal with conflict. The intent here is that a third party, whether serving as an institution's Ombudsperson, Human Resources Manager or an Internal Mediator, has been assigned, for the benefit of the organization, the task of dealing with conflicts that cannot be settled in the first step. Within this phase of the process, a third, neutral party who is highly trained in ADR techniques, will guide the process with the disputant with the goal of arriving at a solution.

The third step, "Convening for External ADR" (p. 57), describes the next or preferred course of action to follow if the conflict cannot be settled within the organization. The template identifies four techniques, Mediation, Arbitration, Minitrials, and Fact Finding, that could be used to solve the disputes. The third party in each case is someone who is not part of the organization. The process and solution provided by each of these ADR techniques is meant to be neutral and more desirable than any settlement obtained by using the legal system.

The fourth step, "External Higher Authority" (p. 57), is the final and last resort available to organizations for settlement of conflicts. This generally involves a legal or quasi-legal process. Although individuals are encouraged to settle disputes without using this option, it is absolutely necessary that the option of litigation and government agency involvement be identified as an available alternative.

Slaskieu and Hasson use arrows in their template to show what they call the preferred path to solve conflicts.

Figure 15.1. ADR Process for Sport/Physical Activity Organizations

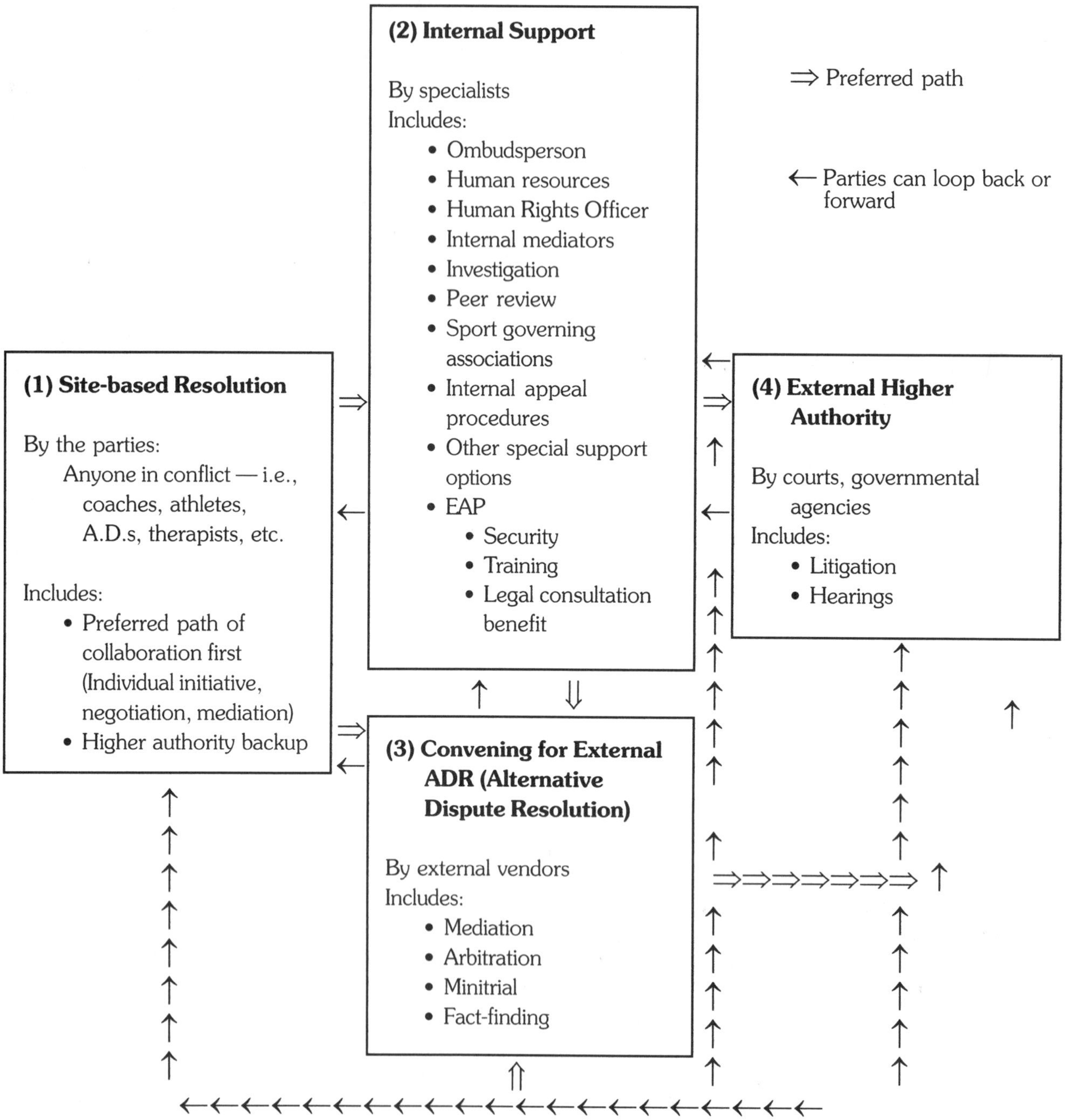

$\Rightarrow$ Preferred path

$\leftarrow$ Parties can loop back or forward

(1) Site-based Resolution

By the parties:
  Anyone in conflict — i.e., coaches, athletes, A.D.s, therapists, etc.

Includes:
- Preferred path of collaboration first (Individual initiative, negotiation, mediation)
- Higher authority backup

(2) Internal Support

By specialists
Includes:
- Ombudsperson
- Human resources
- Human Rights Officer
- Internal mediators
- Investigation
- Peer review
- Sport governing associations
- Internal appeal procedures
- Other special support options
- EAP
  - Security
  - Training
  - Legal consultation benefit

(3) Convening for External ADR (Alternative Dispute Resolution)

By external vendors
Includes:
- Mediation
- Arbitration
- Minitrial
- Fact-finding

(4) External Higher Authority

By courts, governmental agencies
Includes:
- Litigation
- Hearings

Adapted from Slaikeu & Hasson, 1998, p. 56

Logically, a dispute should go from step 1 to 2 to 3 to 4, until solved. However, the template also shows that a conflict does not necessarily follow a preferred path and can jump ahead, or loop back, to any area when desirable.

It is inevitable that conflict will exist in all institutions, including sport. The process described here demonstrates a typical approach to conflict resolution. ADR provides organizations with an efficient and effective method to resolving conflict. Those in athletic organizations who use ADR skills, are more likely to maintain collegiality and less likely to fuel their adversarial positions.

ADR and Sport/Physical Activity

As previously discussed, it is inherent that there will be conflicts within and among sport organizations due to the diversity of individuals who comprise these groups. These conflicts typically have a negative effect upon productivity. Thus, a fair and quick resolution is in the best interest of all parties. When disagreements arise, if there is a violation of law *per se* i.e., assault, negligence, or contract violation, the individual claiming injury has the option of pursuing formal litigation or an alternative resolution process as outlined earlier in this chapter. Filing a lawsuit might not be a viable option nor a suitable remedy when there is a desire to preserve an on-going relationship such as that between team members, coaching staff, or organization personnel. ADR techniques are uniquely appropriate in these types of situations as tools for addressing the dispute for the following reasons:

a) matters of conflict that are not covered by formal legal action can be resolved;
b) issues that must be resolved quickly are typically expedited faster through an ADR approach;
c) ADR procedures allow for more flexibility in the remedy than traditional litigation; and,
d) when there is a desire to maintain an on-going relationship, the less-adversarial ADR approach supports that desired outcome.

An example provides the best method of demonstrating the benefits of applying ADR procedures to address sport organization disputes. The following is a fictitious example of such a situation. Mary is a first year (ninth grade) student who tried out and was selected to play on the intercollegiate ice hockey team. Mary is one of only three first year students selected for the varsity team. It is tradition on this team that the student-athletes in the lowest grade on the team are responsible for completing "team chores" such as collecting the dirty uniforms and taking them to the laundry area daily, collecting all equipment from the ice and bleacher areas, and placing all team gear onto the bus for transportation to and from away contests. While Mary is not thrilled about this situation, she realizes that it is tradition and completes her chores with the two other first year players. During the fifth week of the season a junior member of the team approaches Mary and demands that she also begins to clean the "ice house." The ice house is a large home off campus where upper-class members of the ice hockey team reside. Mary resists at first but is warned that if she does not want trouble from the upper-class players, she should do as she is told. Mary considers this and the information regarding hazing that she received during the Athletic Department's orientation meeting for all new student-athletes. She decides to stay away from the "ice house" and not comply with her teammate's request. While Mary realizes that hazing could take a much more violent and hostile form, she believes that this is harassment and a form of hazing and she does not wish to get involved. After this altercation, a series of incidents occur to Mary, i.e., her residence is trashed, her team locker is vandalized and graffiti is spray painted on her personally owned skates, stick, and practice gear. Her coach notices the graffiti and tells Mary to "work it out with your teammates or get off the team because I don't want to get involved. Besides, cleaning the 'ice house' is not as bad as what they could do to you."

Hearing this comment from her coach makes Mary realize that the team behavior towards her is not only known by her coach, but the coach condones it. Mary left practice and went directly to the Athletic Director's (AD) Office where the AD met with her and recorded all of the incidents previously mentioned. The AD, who was trained in ADR procedures and had established an internal approach for department disputes, was disappointed and surprised by the behavior of the ice hockey coach and team members. The AD indicated that she would do some more fact gathering and meet with the other parties, but she talked with Mary about possible approaches to the dispute. The AD asked Mary to think about how she would ideally like to have the conflict be resolved or how she would like to have the situation change. The fact finding confirmed each of the complaints. Mary indicated that she really wanted to remain a member of the team and she primarily wanted an apology from the coach and the members of the team who had been involved. Additionally, she wanted safeguards established to protect her from possible retaliation, and she was willing to continue her "team chores" as a first year team member. She also indicated that she did not want any coaches or members of the team to be dismissed, but she did want those responsible to pay for the restoration of items that had been vandalized. Through mediation, written agreements were reached between all of the parties to establish Mary's wishes. The AD also required remedial and corrective action from the coaching staff and student-athletes involved in the incident.

At several points of this example, Mary could have pursued legal recourse for the harassment, battery, and threats upon her safety, perhaps resulting in a guilty verdict and compensatory damages. This lengthy and adversarial approach is designed to determine guilt or innocence and to award damages accordingly. It is not the objective of the trial court process to maintain or improve any relationship the plaintiff and defendants might have, a key element of significant relevance to the sport context. Nor would the court system invest its resources towards gaining an apology as it cannot be demanded as a form of compensation in many court systems. The internal mediation process was better suited to obtain the true satisfaction that Mary was seeking and to do so in a timely manner with the least amount of disruption to the team cohesion.

Current Sport Use of ADR

The international sport community provides an example within sport where alternatives to traditional legal approaches to resolve conflicts have been embraced. Disputes between athletes and governing bodies are not limited to domestic sport situations. World championship and Olympic athletes have contested the results of drug tests and rule interpretations (Rochat, 1997). Disputes in international sport settings raise several unique dilemmas. For example, when crossing national boundaries, do you follow the legal system of the host country or that of the athlete? When decisions need to be made prior to the final heat of competition how is a remedy established in a short time-span?

To address these unique situations, the Court of Arbitration for Sport (CAS) was established by the International Olympic Committee (IOC) to provide a process of arbitration for Olympic sport organizations (Thoma and Chalip, 1996). The CAS is organized into the following three divisions: the Appeals Arbitration Division; the Olympic Division; and, the Ordinary Arbitration Division. Athletes competing internationally typically take their disputes to the sport federation that serves as the liaison for their sport to the IOC. Athletes competing internationally, who disagree with the decisions of their sport federation or sport regulation body, with the exclusion of the Olympic Games, would seek arbitration through the Appeals Division. When the conflict occurs during the Olympic Games, the CAS Olympic Division is charged with resolving disputes that actually occur at this time. The CAS Ordinary Arbitration Division is charged with addressing commercial contract disputes. The CAS currently has established courts in three locations worldwide: Lausanne, Switzerland; Denver, USA; and, Sydney, Australia. The CAS courts use Swiss law or the law of the country where the sport federation involved is located, unless the involved parties agree to abide by the law of another country (Thoma and Chalip, 1996).

Originally, the CAS members were closely associated with the IOC, the National Governing Bodies and the International Federations. In 1994 The International Council of Arbitration for Sport (ICAS) was established to provide a process for arbitration that is neutral and independent of the IOC and to administer the CAS. The objectives of the ICAS are to provide a fair environment, to protect the rights of all parties, and to assure that neutral and appropriate arbitrators are assigned to hear and review disputes (Rochat, 1997).

The use of ADR for resolving conflict can be used at other levels of sport as well. The Canadian Interuniversity

Athletic Union (CIAU) encourages its members to seek assistance through ADR techniques (see Table 1) with the inclusion of a clause in their Operations Manual. At the time of this writing, the process had not been used so its effectiveness could not be evaluated. However, organizations are encouraged to incorporate similar policy within their guidelines.

Table 1. CIAU Guideline for Alternative Dispute Resolution

ALTERNATIVE DISPUTE RESOLUTION (ADR)

A. CIAU supports the principles of Alternative Dispute Resolution (ADR) and is committed to the techniques of mediation and arbitration as effective ways to resolve disputes with its members, and avoid the harm of litigation.

B. Accordingly, opportunities for mediation may be pursued at any point in a dispute where it is appropriate for the dispute in question and where the disputing parties each agree that such a course of action would be mutually beneficial.

C. In the event that a dispute persists after internal avenues of decision-making and appeals have been exhausted opportunities for arbitration may be pursued. Where the continuing dispute relates to an appeal panel having made a decision which was outside its jurisdiction, having failed to follow proper procedures, or having made a decision which was influenced by bias, such a dispute may be dealt with through binding arbitration before an independent arbitrator who is acceptable to the parties in the dispute.

D. No action or other legal proceeding shall be commenced by a member against CIAU in respect of a dispute, unless CIAU has failed to participate in arbitration in accordance with this policy.

CIAU Operations Manual (1999, September), p. 117

The implementation of ADR techniques can be used for dispute resolution in recreational through elite environments and for disputes that involve any combinations of organizational roles. Yet many disputes remain unresolved. They may simply dissipate over time or they may lie dormant until frustrations mount and are expressed as an accumulation of issues. In this case, small conflicts become large conflicts. Further, sport managers may never know how many coaches, therapists, officials, athletes or others may quit contributing to sport programs because of unresolved conflicts. Effective conflict management using ADR as an alternative to the adversarial or litigation process that now exists, requires a transformation in people and in organizations. Both disputants and leaders must learn how to settle conflict in a productive way and apply this learning to the inevitable discord within their organization. A professional or volunteer staff can be strengthened and maintained with effective dispute resolution.

Questions for Class Discussion

Part A
The following two fictitious cases serve as examples of typical disputes in sport/physical activity. Work through these cases as a class activity by discussing the questions at the end of each case.

Case A.
The first case is one where the dispute arose from the overlapping of consecutive seasons of play in high school sport. The dispute revolves around the regulation governing a high school sport's season of play for Girl's Basketball and for Girl's Volleyball. A regulation exists to prevent one sport from taking time away from another sport and also to equalize the number of games in which a team can play. For example, a team competing in 50 games in a four month season was considered to have too great an advantage over a team playing 15 games in a two month season. The location of the school and its financial resources usually dictated the number of games a team could play in a season. This regulation evolved

from a need to equalize opportunities and competition. It allowed schools to encourage a greater variety of sporting activities for a greater number of students.

The specific regulation governing the seasons of play state that Senior Girl's Basketball must end by the 15th week after Labour Day, or whenever the team is eliminated from post season play, whichever comes first. In this particular dispute, the basketball team's season was over on November 18th. As of this date, volleyball may begin.

The school basketball coach, whose season ended November 18 without making playoffs, arranged for his team to play in a tournament in a warm vacation climate during the Christmas break. The volleyball coach, whose season started November 18 and did not finish until early March, was planning on playing in several exhibition matches during the holiday break. This extra practice and competition was a critical element in the team's bid for the State Championship.

The girls on the basketball team were of course very excited about the idea of going to a warm climate to play basketball during the holidays. This creates a conflict, however, because many of the players participate in both sports, a common occurrence in high school. The volleyball coach is upset with the tournament plans, which interfere with the volleyball training program.

The dispute went to the principal of the school, who decided that he would support the decision of the athletic department head on the matter. The department head ruled that the basketball trip was out of season and therefore would not be allowed.

This top-down decision ended the plans for a basketball Christmas tournament, but did not settle the dispute. The basketball players and their parents were unhappy, several players decided not to tryout for the volleyball team, and the basketball coach carried a grudge against the department head and volleyball coach. This type of decision making is common practice in sport organizations (higher authority makes the final ruling).

Questions:
1. What other problems can you identify as a result of this decision?
2. Was there any form of litigation that could have been started as a result of this decision?
3. What benefits can you suggest that an ADR process would have given in this case?
4. Role play an ADR approach to be used to facilitate a more acceptable resolution for everyone concerned.

Case B.

The second case involves a dispute between school and club sport. A track and field coach at one local high school (A) has a dispute with a track and field coach (B) from another local high school, who is also the coach of a community club team. Two of the athletes from the first school (A) have decided to compete for a community club team and not for their high school. The club/school coach (B) will not allow students from her own school to compete on the community team.

The aggrieved coach (A) brings the dispute to the attention of the local high school coaches association. The association decides that their members will not compete in track and field events where the club/school coach (B) has athletes entered. This decision became public knowledge and was covered at length in the local newspaper.

In an interview with the local newspaper the coach (A), who raised the issue initially, was quoted as saying that the community coach (B) had recruited two of A's athletes for the club team but would not allow any of her own school's athletes to leave the school team to tryout for the club team. The local media then proceeded to investigate and report the story with an overtone of sensationalism that magnified the dispute.

The director of education was eventually consulted for a solution. He ruled that the community coach (B) could no longer coach the high school team. This position contributed to a decision on the part of coach (B) to file a lawsuit against coach (A) who initiated the debate, and to a public protest on the part of the parents and athletes of the community/school coach. Ultimately, with pressures from a variety of sources, the decision made by the director was reversed and the coach (B) was reinstated to serve as the school coach while continuing to coach the community team.

The dispute between the two coaches remained unresolved with the continuation of the lawsuit, and with the local coaches association which still faced the dilemma about what to do.

Questions:
1. What type of an ADR approach could be used here to facilitate a better resolution to this dispute?

2. When should the ADR process have been initiated?
3. What do you think would result from a lawsuit?
4. Can litigation prevent this from reoccurring in the future?

Part B

The following scenarios will outline some actual cases that went to litigation in which ADR might have served as an option to litigation for resolution of the conflict. Discuss the advantages of using ADR techniques and the ways in which they might be used, before referring to the court decisions that are presented at the end of the scenarios.

Court scenarios:

Dispute #1 — Teacher-coach

A tenured physical education teacher, who also spent twenty four years coaching basketball for an additional stipend, was upset when the Superintendent assigned the coaching responsibilities to another individual. This decision had no implications for the teacher in his classroom appointment.

Porrell v. School Committee of Wayland, 694 N.E.2d 399 (Mass. App. 1998).

Questions:
1. What benefit would be realized if an ADR process was followed in this case?
2. Develop an ADR scenario that would be of value to the coach and the school.

Dispute #2 — Unbecoming teacher behaviour

A tenured physical education teacher was terminated by the School District for conduct unbecoming a teacher and insubordination. It was found that the teacher engaged in repeated contact with fourth and fifth grade girls by nudging and poking them in the back and snapping their bra straps during physical education class. Upon verbal and written warnings, the conduct continued. The teacher claimed justification citing motivational and instructional techniques for the behaviour. Following a hearing by the School District, the teacher was terminated. The teacher's appeal to the Commissioner of Education was denied. The teacher pursued the matter with a lawsuit.

Forte v. Mills, 672 N.Y.S.2d 497 (App. Div. 1998)

Questions:
1. When should an ADR process have been started in this case?
2. When should litigation rather than ADR be used?

Dispute #3 — Abuse of officials

During a basketball game, a coach berated an official for a call and proceeded to bump his body into the official. Following the game, the official resisted the escort of security officers from the facility, intending to discuss possible legal action with the coach for his conduct. The official subsequently brought action against the coach, the Board of Education, the Principal and the security officers. The claims were that the safety of the official had not been ensured, the coach had been abusive and the security officers had used excessive force.

Darnell v. Houston County Board of Education, 506 S.E.2d. 385 (Ga. App. 1998).

Questions:
1. What type of policy should the league and officials' association have in place to deal with this type of conflict?
2. What will happen if there is no policy in a similar type of conflict in the future?

Dispute #4 — Team selection

An athlete who has met the qualifying standards to compete internationally is initially named to the National team complement. However, without warning or explanation, the athlete was removed from the team. This was followed by a directive that the athlete compete in head to head competition with another athlete who was ranked behind him and who he had out performed consistently throughout the selection process. When the case was filed with the court, the courts ordered the Association and the coach to put the plaintiff on the team. His name was eventually put on the recommended list, however, a third governing body not involved in the original lawsuit, did not follow the recommendation provided, excluding the athlete from the team complement and denying him the opportunity to compete in this particular international event.

Garrett v. Canadian Weightlifting Federation, unreported decision, January 18, 1990, J.D. of Edmonton.

Questions:
1. If an ADR process is to be effective, who (what levels) must accept and understand this approach?
2. How can an ADR procedure in a sport governing body improve dispute resolution for athletes?

Court decisions:

Dispute #1 — Teacher-coach
The courts dismissed the lawsuit brought forward by the teacher-coach. It was decided that he was not entitled to tenure protection in his position as head basketball coach since the position does not parallel the process used in granting tenure to a teacher. Since positions were granted separately, the Superintendent was free to make a decision at his discretion.

Dispute #2 — Unbecoming teacher behaviour
The courts upheld the teacher's termination, declaring that the teacher had been informed that the behaviour was inappropriate and that it made the students feel uncomfortable. It was determined that such behaviour was a reasonable cause for dismissal.

Dispute #3 — Abuse of officials
The Superior Court granted Summary Judgment and the case was dismissed. Upon appeal, the courts did allow the case against the coach for willful or malicious actions to be heard.

Dispute #4 — Team selection
Since the third party association that made the ultimate decision was not named as a defendant in the lawsuit, the athlete had no further recourse.

References

Arbitration and Mediation Institute of Canada Inc. (1998). *The commercial mediation practice handbook*. Ottawa, ON: Published by author.

Canadian Inter-university Athletic Union. (1999, September). Alternate Dispute Resolution. *Operations Manual*. Ottawa, ON: Published by author.

Felstiner, W.L.F., R.L. Abel, & A. Sarat. (1981). The emergence and transformation of disputes: Naming, blaming, claiming... *Law and Society (15)*, 42–65.

Moriarty, Dick. (1980). A curriculum for conflict and change. In Frank. J. Hayden (Ed.), *Mind and body in the '90s* (pp. 410–427). Ottawa, ON: Canadian Council of University Physical Education Administrators, Health and Welfare Canada and Fitness and Amateur Sport.

Rochat, J.P. (1997). The court of arbitration for sport. *Olympic Review, 26*, 73–74.

Slaikeu, K. A. (1998). *Controlling the costs of conflict: How to design a system for your organization*. San Francisco: Jossey-Bass Publishers.

Stitt, Allan J. (1998). *Alternative Dispute Resolution for organizations: How to design a system for effective conflict resolution*. Etobicoke, ON: John Wiley & Sons Canada Limited.

Thoma, J.E. & L. Chalip. (1996). *Sport governance in the global community*. Morgantown, WV: Fitness Information Technology, Inc.

CITATIONS

Canadian

CIVIL

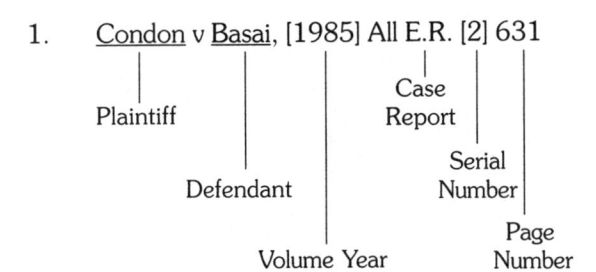

1. Condon v Basai, [1985] All E.R. [2] 631

   - Condon — Plaintiff
   - Basai — Defendant
   - 1985 — Volume Year
   - All E.R. — Case Report
   - [2] — Serial Number
   - 631 — Page Number

2. Crocker v. Sundance (1985), 33 C.C.L.T. (3d) 73 (Ont. C.A.)

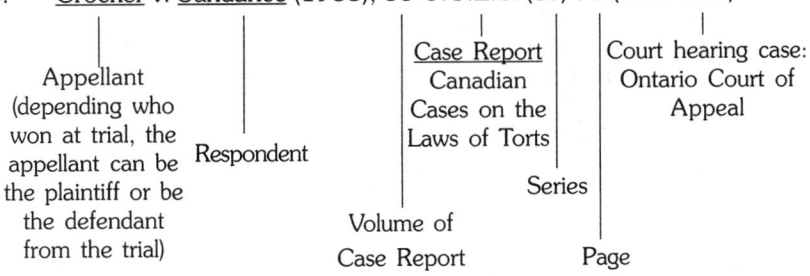

   - Crocker — Appellant (depending who won at trial, the appellant can be the plaintiff or be the defendant from the trial)
   - Sundance — Respondent
   - 1985 — Volume of Case Report
   - C.C.L.T. — Case Report: Canadian Cases on the Laws of Torts
   - (3d) — Series
   - 73 — Page
   - (Ont. C.A.) — Court hearing case: Ontario Court of Appeal

   Note: look for the series first, then for the volume when locating a case.

3. McKay v. Govan, [1968] S.C.R. 589

247

CRIMINAL

4. R v. Kanhai (1981), 60 C.C.C. (2d) 71

    - R → Crown (Regina)
    - Kanhai → Accused
    - 1981 → Year case heard
    - 60 → Volume of case report
    - C.C.C. → Canadian Criminal Cases
    - (2d) → Series
    - 71 → Page

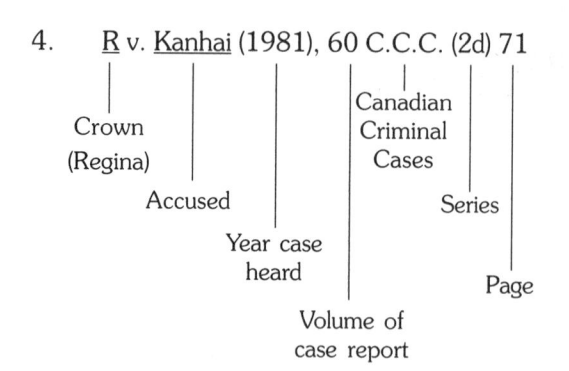

United States

CIVIL

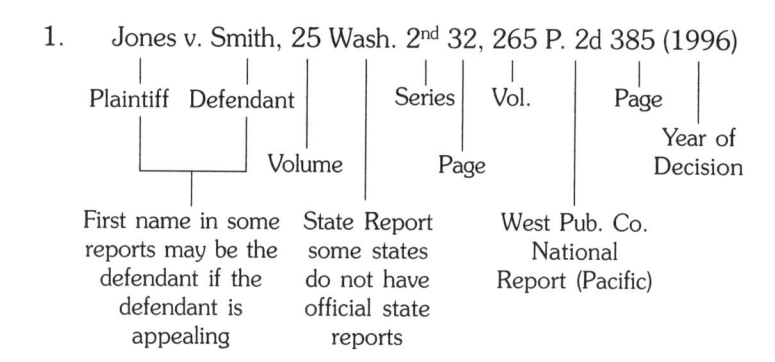

1. Jones v. Smith, 25 Wash. 2nd 32, 265 P. 2d 385 (1996)

    - Jones → Plaintiff
    - Smith → Defendant
    - 25 → Volume
    - Wash. → Series
    - 2nd → Vol.
    - 32 → Page
    - 265 → Page
    - P. → West Pub. Co. National Report (Pacific)
    - 385 → Page
    - (1996) → Year of Decision

    First name in some reports may be the defendant if the defendant is appealing.

    State Report — some states do not have official state reports.

CRIMINAL

2. United States v. Johnson, 14 Wash. (3d) 17, 281 (1998)

    This is used in federal cases. State cases are usually State v., sometimes People v. or occasionally Michigan v.

ABBREVIATIONS

Admin.L.Rev.	Administrative Law Review.	N.Y.S.	New York Supplement Reporter.
App.	Appendix; Court of Appeals.		
Cir.Ct.	Circuit Court (state).	N.Y.S.2d.	New York Supplement Reporter, Second Series.
Ct.App.	Court of Appeal[s] (state).		
Dist.Ct.	District Court (state).	Ohio St.2d.	Ohio State Reports, Second Series.
F.Supp.	Federal Supplement.		
J.L. & Educ.	Journal of Law & Education.	P.	Pacific Reporter.
J.L. & Health	Journal of Law & Health.	S.E.	South Eastern Reporter.
J.Prod.Liab.	Journal of Products Liability.	So.2d.	Southern Reporter, Second Series.
Law & Hist.Rev.	Law and History Review.		
Loy.L.A.Ent.L.J.	Loyola Entertainment Law Journal.	Sup.	Supplement.
		Sup.Ct.	Supreme Court.
N.E.2d	North Eastern Reporter, Second Series.	Super.Ct.	Superior Court.
		Supp.	Supplement.
Notre Dame J.L. Ethics & Pub. Pol'y	Notre Dame Journal of Law, Ethics, & Public Policy.	S.W.	South Western Reporter.
		T.M.R.	Trade Mark Reports.
		Trademark Rep.	Trademark Reporter.
		Women Law.J.	Women Lawyers Journal.

GLOSSARY OF TERMS

The authors have defined some of the more common terms used in this book. For a more exhaustive, accurate and technical definition of these terms the reader is referred to *Blacks Law Dictionary* (West Publishing Company), and *The Legal Environment of Business* (McGraw Hill, Inc., 1984 and Dryden Press, 1987).

A fortiori Even more clearly; said of a conclusion that follows with even greater logical necessity from another which is already included in the argument.

A priori (From first principles.) From the cause to the effect.

Abuse of discretion The failure of a judge or administrator to use sound or reasonable judgment in arriving at a decision.

Acceptance In contract law, the agreement of the offeree to the proposal or offer of the offeror.

Accused The person against whom a charge is laid in a criminal case. For a civil suit, see **defendant**.

Act of God An extraordinary natural event, such as an earthquake, occurring without the intervention or assistance of any human agency.

Action at law A suit in which the plaintiff is seeking a legal remedy (such as damages), as distinguished from an equitable remedy (such as an injunction).

Action in equity A civil suit in which the plaintiff is seeking an equitable remedy, such as an injunction or decree of specific performance.

Actual authority The express and implied authority of an agent.

Actus reus Criminal act, as distinct from ***mens rea***, criminal intent.

Adjudication The judicial determination of a legal proceeding.

Adjudicatory power In administrative agency law, the right of an administrative agency to initiate actions as both prosecutor and judge against those thought to be in violation of the law (including agency rules and regulations) under the jurisdiction of the administrative agency—referred to as the quasi-judicial function of an agency.

Administrative law Public law administered and/or formulated by a government unit such as a board, agency, or commission to govern the conduct of an individual, association, or corporation.

Administrative agency A board, commission, agency, or service authorized by a legislative enactment to implement specific laws on either the local, state/provincial, or national level.

Affidavit A sworn written statement made before an officer authorized by law to administer oaths.

Affirmative action In employment law, any voluntary or required program or action designed to remedy discriminatory practices in hiring, training, and promoting of protected class members. Such programs attempt to eliminate existing and continuing discrimination, to remedy lingering effects of past discrimination, and to create procedures to prevent future discrimination.

Agency A relationship created by contract, agreement, or law between a principal and an agent whereby the principal is bound by the authorized actions of the agent.

Agent One who is authorized to act for another (called a "principal"), whose acts bind the principal to his or her actions.

Answer In pleadings, the defendant's response to the plaintiff's complaint or petition. In Canada the pleading is referred to as "the Statement of Defense."

Appellant The person who files an appeal from the decision of a lower court.

Appellee The person against whom an appeal is filed (usually the successful litigant in the lower court). Also known as "respondent."

Arbitration The submission of a dispute to a third party or parties for settlement.

Arguendo For the sake of argument.

Articles of incorporation A legal document, meeting the legal requirements of a given state/province, filed with a designated official as an application for a certificate of incorporation.

Articles of partnership The agreement of the partners that forms and governs the operation of the partnership.

Assault In tort law an assault is defined as an act by which one person causes in another an imminent apprehension of a harmful or offensive contact, or **battery**. In criminal law, an assault consists either of the application of force against another or the attempt to use force, when both the intention and the apparent present ability to perform the act are present. See Canadian Criminal Code, Section 244.

Assumption of risk A defence to negligent conduct where it is found that the plaintiff has agreed, expressly or impliedly, to waive any claim he or she may have against the defendant for the latter's failure to live up to the standard of care required by law toward the plaintiff.

Award In arbitration proceedings, the decision or determination rendered by an arbitrator on a controversy submitted for settlement. In general usage, to grant, assign or give by sentence or judicial determination. For example, the court *awards* an injunction; the arbitration *award* is equitable.

Banc French for "Bench." When an appellate court sits "en banc," it means that all of the appellate judges of the court are sitting together.

Bankruptcy A court procedure by which a person who is unable to pay his or her debts may be declared bankrupt, have nonexempt assets distributed to his or her creditors, and thereupon be given a release from any further payment of the balance due on most of these debts.

Barrister In England, lawyers are divided between "barristers" and "solicitors." Historically, a barrister argued a case before the higher courts, although that distinction is now being eroded.

Battery An act which is intended to and does cause a harmful or offensive contact with another. In criminal law, such conduct is defined as an **assault**.

Beyond a reasonable doubt This is the burden which the crown must meet in establishing the guilt of an accused. If there is any serious reasonable doubt as to the accused's guilt, he must be acquitted.

Bilateral mistake A mistake in which both parties to a contract are in error as to the terms of or performance expected under the contract. Also called mutual mistake.

Bilateral contract A contract formed by the mutual exchange of promises by the offeror and the offeree.

Board of directors A body composed of persons elected by the corporation's shareholders and entrusted with the responsibility of managing the corporation.

Bona fide In good faith; innocently; without fraud or deceit.

Boycott In antitrust law, an agreement between two or more parties to not deal with a third party. When the purpose is to exclude a firm or firms from a market, such an agreement is *per se* illegal under Section 1 of the Sherman Act. In labor law, action by a union to prevent others from doing business with the employer. A primary boycott, directed at the employer with whom the union has a labor dispute, is usually legal. A **secondary boycott**, aimed at a connected employer with whom the union does not have a labor dispute, is usually an unfair labor practice.

Burden of proof In every lawsuit, one party has the burden of producing sufficient evidence to establish his or her case. This is known as the "burden of proof." Generally the burden is on the party bringing the civil suit or prosecuting the criminal charge. For burden in civil cases, see **preponderance of evidence**. In criminal cases, see **beyond a reasonable doubt.**

"But for" rule In order to establish liability in a negligence action, it must be shown that the negligent conduct was a **cause-in-fact** of the injury or damage about which the plaintiff complains. This requirement is commonly referred to as the "but for" or "*sine qua non*" rule; the defendant's conduct is not considered a cause of the event if that event would have occurred without it. See also the **substantial factor** test.

Bylaws The internal rules made to regulate and govern the actions and affairs of a corporation.

Capacity The legal ability to perform an act, especially an act from which legal consequences flow, such as the making of a contract.

Case law Essentially synonymous with **common law**.

Cause of action The assertion of a fact or facts that are sufficient to support a lawsuit. In the area of sports liability, these would include an action in **battery**, **assault**, and **negligence**.

Cause-in-fact In a negligence action, it must be shown that the defendant's negligent conduct was a cause-in-fact of the plaintiff's injury. For the tests used by the court in determining factual causation, see the **but for** rule and **substantial factor** test.

Caveat emptor (Let the buyer beware); rule imposing on a purchaser the duty to inform him or herself as to defects in the property being sold.

Cease and desist order An administrative agency order directing a party to refrain from doing a specified act.

Certificate of incorporation A document of a state/province that grants permission to do business as a corporate entity—sometimes called a "charter."

Certification The process by which a union is selected by employees as their official bargaining representative. Certification via supervised elections protects the union from rival union challenges for a period of one year.

Circumstantial evidence Facts which indirectly prove the existence of another fact in dispute. For example, the identity of a person who stole an article from a house may be shown by footprints on the floor which match the defendant's shoes. Circumstantial evidence is contrasted with direct evidence, where in the same case someone would testify that she saw the defendant steal the article.

Civil action This is a lawsuit brought by a private individual to vindicate purely personal and private rights and redress personal grievances.

Civil law That area of law dealing with the rights and duties of private parties as individual entities, to be distinguished from **criminal law**. The phrase also refers to the Quebec, Louisiana, and European system of codified law.

Civil Rights Act A comprehensive 1964 U.S. congressional enactment that prohibits discrimination in housing, public accommodations, education, and employment.

Civil rights law That body of statutory and constitutional law defining and enforcing the privileges and freedoms belonging to every person in the U.S. The objective of civil rights law is to secure equality of opportunity for all persons.

Class action A legal proceeding initiated by one or more members of a similarly-situated group or class of persons on behalf of themselves and other group members.

Collateral estoppel The doctrine which bars further inquiry into factual matters which have been conclusively adjudicated at a previous trial or hearing.

Collective bargaining The process of good-faith negotiation between employers and employee representatives concerning issues of mutual interest.

Commercial contract A contract between two or more persons (merchants) engaged in trade or commerce.

Common law The law as articulated and administered by judges rather than by statute, which began in England and was subsequently adopted and continued in such countries as the U.S., Canada, Australia, and New Zealand.

Comparative negligence The ability of a court to assess liability in a negligence case between a plaintiff and defendant according to the comparative fault of each party.

Competency In the law of evidence, this refers to the ability of a witness to perceive, recollect, or communicate pertinent information in a court of law.

Competition The condition of economic and noneconomic rivalry among firms for consumers' business.

Complaint In legal practice and pleading, the first written statement of the plaintiff's contentions, which initiates the lawsuit. In Canada, the pleading is referred to as a "Statement of claim."

Consent order An administrative agency order, the terms of which are arrived at by agreement between the agency and the charged party.

Consent decree A court injunction, the terms of which are arrived at by agreement of the parties.

Consent In tort law, consent is a willingness expressed overtly or tacitly by one party that another party may engage in conduct which would otherwise constitute a tort. Thus consent to a touching would relieve defendant of any responsibility for that touching. While lack of consent has generally been considered to be an element of a cause of action in an intentional tort, which the plaintiff must plead and prove, there is recent authority in Canada that consent is a defence which the defendant has the burden of proving.

Consignment A delivery of goods by the owner to another, usually by sale.

Conspiracy A combination or agreement between two or more persons for the commission of a criminal act.

Constitutional law Those provisions of the provincial/state and federal constitutions that prescribe the structure and functions of the respective governments and the basic limitations upon these governments, as well as the courts' interpretation of these provisions.

Consumer products Goods that are used or bought primarily for personal, family, or household purposes.

Consumerism The movement that has led to increased protection for the consumer and substantial burdens on the manufacturer and merchant.

Contingent fee An arrangement whereby an attorney is compensated for services in a lawsuit according to an agreed percentage of the amount of money recovered.

Contributory negligence An act or omission amounting to want of reasonable care on the part of the plaintiff which has contributed to the injury about which he or she complains. Perhaps more accurately known as "contributory fault."

Corporation An association of persons created by statute as a legal entity (artificial person) with authority to act and to have liability separate and apart from its owners.

Counteroffer A proposal made by an offeree in response to the offer extended him or her, the terms varying appreciably from the terms of the offer. Such a proposal by the offeree constitutes a rejection of the offer.

Covenant An agreement or promise in writing by which a party pledges that something has been done or is being done. The term is often used in connection with real estate to describe the promises of the grantor of the property.

Criminal law That area of law dealing with the prosecution of crimes, or wrongs against the state as representative of the community at large, to be distinguished from civil law which hears cases of wrongs against persons.

Criminal prosecution A proceeding instituted by the Crown on behalf of the public for the determination of guilt where one has been accused of a crime.

Culpable A person who is blameworthy or at fault with regard to a particular act or conduct.

Custom The usual and regular behavior of a community under the same or similar circumstances may be shown as evidence of reasonable conduct on the part of those who comport themselves in accordance with the customary community standards or as evidence of unreasonable conduct for those who fail to do so.

Damages Monetary compensation recoverable in a court of law.

De facto corporation A corporation not formed in substantial compliance with the laws of a given state but which has sufficiently complied to be a corporation in fact, not right. Only the state can challenge the corporation's existence.

De jure corporation A corporation formed in substantial compliance with laws of a given province/state; a corporation by right.

De novo To start anew. A trial *de novo* is a completely new trial requiring the same degree of proof as if the case were being heard for the first time.

Decree The decision of a court of equity.

Defamation A false imputation on the character or reputation of another either in some written or permanent form (generally "libel") or orally ("slander").

Defendant The person against whom a civil action is brought. For a criminal case, see **accused**.

Delegation In contract law, the transfer of the power or right to represent or act for another; usually referred to as the delegation of duties, to a third party.

Delegation of authority In administrative law, a grant of authority from a legislative body to an administrative agency.

Demurrer In common law pleading, a formal statement by the defendant that the facts alleged by the plaintiff are insufficient to support a claim for legal relief.

Deposition Sworn written testimony of a witness taken outside of court; a discovery procedure. In the U.S. an oral examination may also be known as a deposition.

Dicta (Singular: **dictum**) Those comments or remarks in a written appellate opinion which are not necessary or essential to a determination of the issue.

Direct evidence Proof of a fact without the intervention of the proof of any preliminary fact. For example, it is direct evidence if A testifies that he saw B stab C where the issue is who stabbed C. Compare this to **circumstantial evidence** where evidence of B's fingerprints on the knife that killed C is evidence that B killed C.

Direct examination In the U.S. the side that questions its own witness is said to be engaged in "direct examination." In Canada, this is referred to as **examination-in-chief**.

Directed verdict Where the evidence adduced at trial is so clear and convincing that no reasonable jury could reach a different conclusion, a judge may take the matter out of the hands of the jury and require them to enter a given verdict.

Disclaimer A provision in a sales contract which attempts to prevent the creation of a warranty.

Discovery A formal process whereby one party is obligated to disclose certain information in his or her possession relevant to a lawsuit. This may take the form of production of certain documents or an oral examination of either party to the lawsuit. In the U.S. an oral examination may also be known as a **deposition**.

Discretionary powers The right of an administrative agency to exercise judgment and discretion in carrying out the law, as opposed to ministerial powers (the routine day-to-day duty to enforce the law).

Discrimination Any failure to treat all persons equally, where no reasonable distinction can be made between those favored and those not favored.

Dissent The objection of a judge who disagrees wholly or partially with the decision of the majority of judges in a lawsuit. If put into written form, it is known as the "dissenting opinion."

Dissolution Termination of the existence of a business entity.

Divestiture The antitrust remedy which forces a company to get rid of assets acquired through illegal mergers or monopolistic practices.

Docket (1) A list of causes for trial. (2) A book containing a brief summary of all procedural steps taken in court in the conduct of each case.

Domicile (1) The place that a person intends as his or her fixed and permanent legal residence, or place of permanent abode. This is contrasted with a residence, which may be temporary; a person can have a number of residences but only one domicile. (2) Province or state of incorporation of a corporation.

Double jeopardy A constitutional doctrine which prohibits an individual from being prosecuted twice in the same tribunal for the same criminal offense.

Due process Fundamental fairness. As applied to judicial proceedings, adequate notice of a hearing and an opportunity to appear and defend in an orderly tribunal.

Duty A legal obligation owed by one person to another. In negligence, the duty is to conform to a standard of conduct that is reasonable in light of the apparent risk.

Easement The right of a person other than the owner of land to some use of that land.

Embezzlement The fraudulent appropriation by one person, acting in a fiduciary capacity, of the money or property of another.

Eminent domain The power of the government to take private property for public use by paying just compensation.

Enjoin To require performance or abstention from some act through issuance of an injunction.

Equal protection A principle of the Fifth and Fourteenth Amendments to the Constitution that individuals under like circumstances shall be accorded the same benefits and burdens under the law.

Equity A body of law, formerly administered by the Chancery courts, which seeks to supplement common law rules and procedures on the basis of fairness and good conscience. For example, principles of equity may require or prohibit specific acts where monetary damages at common law will not afford complete relief. Equity and common law were amalgamated in 1873.

Escrow A deed, bond, or deposit which one party delivers for safekeeping by a second party who is obligated to deliver it to a third party upon the fulfilment of some condition.

Ex parte On one side only. For example, an *ex parte* proceeding is held on the application of one party only, without notice to the other party; and an *ex parte* order is made at the request of one party when the other party fails to show up in court, when the other party's presence is not needed, or when there is no other party.

Examination-in-chief See **direct examination**.

Exclusive-dealing contract A contract under which a buyer agrees to purchase a certain product exclusively from the seller or in which the seller agrees to sell all his product production to the buyer.

Exculpatory clause Generally refers to a clause in favour of a trustee in a will which excuses him of all responsibility for any loss so long as he or she acts in good faith.

Exemplary damages Damages awarded over and above those necessary to compensate the plaintiff for actual loss and awarded under circumstances where defendant's conduct has been arrogant, high-handed, malicious or socially reprehensible. The purpose of such an award is to punish the defendant for such conduct and deter him or her and others from engaging in such conduct in the future. While exemplary damages are generally confined to cases involving intentional misconduct, in the U.S. and the province of British Columbia they have also been awarded in negligence actions. Also known as "punitive" or "vindictive" and, colloquially, as "smart-money" damages.

Express warranty In sales law, a guarantee or assurance as to the quality or performance of goods that arises from the words or conduct of the seller.

Express contract Authority specifically given by the principal to the agent.

Fair comment In defamation law, the right of someone to comment fairly on a matter of public interest. In such a case a fair comment is a defence to an action for libel and slander even though the comment is defamatory if it is based upon facts truly stated, does not contain imputations of corrupt and dishonourable motives, and is an honest expression of the speaker's or writer's real opinion.

False imprisonment The intentional and total confinement, however momentary, of one person, without consent, by another. Such confinement may be physical, psychological or by the assertion of authority to which another accedes. Where such imprisonment is made unlawfully by a police officer, it is known as "false arrest."

Fault When used in tort law, fault refers to any want of care, omission, or neglect of duty for which the party is responsible.

Felony In American criminal law, a serious crime. In Canada, this is known as an **indictable offense**.

Fiduciary A person to whom a trust or confidence has been entrusted by another and for whom he or she has undertaken to act in connection with some matter.

Foreseeability "You must take reasonable care to avoid acts or omissions which you can reasonably foresee would injure your neighbour." (per Lord Atkin in *Donoghue v. Stevenson*, 1932.) The test of reasonable foreseeability is used in determining tortious liability, as well as in contract, and in murder cases.

Forum non conveniens The doctrine under which a court may dismiss a lawsuit in which it appears that for the convenience of the parties and in the interests of justice, the action should have been brought in another court.

Franchise (1) A business conducted under someone else's trademark or tradename. The owner of the business, which may be a sole proprietorship, partnership, corporation, or other form of organization, is usually referred as the franchisee. The owner of the trademark or tradename, who contractually permits use of the mark or name, in return for a fee and usually subject to various restrictions, is ordinarily referred to as the franchisor. The permission to use the mark or name, which is part of the franchising agreement, is called a trademark license. (2) The term can also be used to refer to a privilege granted by a governmental body, such as the exclusive right granted to someone by a city to provide cable TV service in that city.

Fraud A false representation of fact made with intent to deceive another, which is justifiably relied upon to the injury of that person.

Garnishee A person who holds money owed to or property of a debtor subject to a garnishment action.

Garnishment A legal proceeding whereby a creditor may collect directly from a third party who is obligated to the debtor.

Good faith Honesty in dealing; innocence; without fraud or deceit.

Guardian One charged with the duty of care and maintenance of another person such as a minor or incompetent under the law.

Guilty One who has been found to have committed a crime. Occasionally, it is also used to describe someone who has committed a tortious act.

Habeas corpus The name of a writ which orders one holding custody of another to produce that individual before the court for the purpose of determining whether such custody is proper.

Hearsay Refers to evidence given by one person based upon information related to him or her by another. Since the probative value of such evidence depends upon the veracity and competency of persons not before the court, it is generally not admissible except in narrowly defined circumstances.

Homicide The killing of another person. The word does not necessarily suggest that a crime has been committed.

Illegal In violation of a penal or criminal law.

Immunity Status of exemption from lawsuits or other legal obligations.

In loco parentis In the place of a parent.

In re In the matter (of).

In rem The jurisdiction of a court to affect property rights with respect to a specific thing.

In camera A hearing in the privacy of the Judge's chambers or in court with the public excluded.

Inadmissible In the law of evidence this refers to facts or documents which cannot be received in evidence at trial.

Incapacity Lacking the legal power or ability to act in certain matters. For example, a child may lack the capacity to make a contract.

Incompetency Lacking the physical or mental ability to care for or manage his or her own affairs or discharge his or her responsibilities. For example, a person who is insane or feeble-minded is incompetent and a committee or guardian may be appointed to manage his or her affairs.

Incorporation The act or process of forming or creating a corporation. This is generally prescribed by statute.

Incriminate To expose oneself or another to a charge of a crime.

Indemnify To reimburse another for a loss suffered.

Indictable offence See **felony**.

Indictment A document issued by a grand jury formally charging a person with a felony.

Indirect evidence See **circumstantial evidence**.

Informed consent A term generally used in medical negligence cases describing that information which must be made available by a doctor to a patient before the latter is presumed to have consented to a medical or surgical procedure. In general, this should include information regarding all material risks, which includes those risks which a doctor knows or ought to know will likely influence the patient's decision whether to submit to the prescribed treatment or operation. It also includes the benefits to be gained, consequences of foregoing treatment, and the advantages and disadvantages of alternative procedures, together with responses to specific questions posed by the patient. See also **consent**.

Infra Below.

Injunction An order of the court requiring a party to do or refrain from doing some act.

Injure (1) To transgress or violate the legal rights of another. (2) To physically harm another or his property.

Insanity In tort law, a person who is insane is not legally responsible for his or her conduct. The question in each case is whether a person has become so disabled mentally that he or she cannot form the requisite intent to commit an intentional tort or cannot understand or appreciate the duty to take care where the allegation is one of negligence.

Insolvency In bankruptcy law, the financial condition of a debtor when his or her assets at fair market value are less than his or her debts and liabilities.

Intangible property Something which represents value but has no intrinsic value of its own, such as a note or bond.

Intent In tort law, intent describes the desire to bring about a result which will invade the legal interests of another. Intentional misconduct and negligent conduct describe the principal categories of intent in tort law. The principal common law torts that are intentional in nature are **battery**, **assault**, **false imprisonment**, and **trespass** to property or land.

Inter se Between themselves.

Interrogatory A written question propounded by one party to a lawsuit to another; a type of discovery procedure.

Intervening cause An independent event which occurs or agency which acts after an original wrongdoer has acted, setting into motion certain events and producing certain results for which the original wrongdoer will no longer be held responsible. For example, someone who negligently injures another in a locker room will not be responsible for the injuries intentionally inflicted by a third party who finds the injured person on the floor.

Intestate A person who dies without a will.

Intra vires Within the powers.

Investigative power In administrative agency law, the statutory right of an administrative agency to hold hearings, subpoena witnesses, examine persons under oath, and require that records be submitted to it in order to determine violations and to do research for future rule making.

Invitee In the tort law defining the obligations of occupiers of property to those coming onto his or her property, an invitee is one whose entry provides some business or economic advantage to the occupier. At common law, an occupier owes to such an invitee an obligation not to create unusual dangers in the condition of the premises, about which the occupier knows or should have known. Some jurisdictions have adopted Occupiers' Liability Acts, which establish a general duty to make premises reasonably safe for lawful entry. See also **licensee**, and **trespasser**.

Ipso facto By the very fact.

Joint venture A pooling of resources by two or more firms to achieve a common objective.

Judgment The official decision of a court determining the merits of a claim between contesting parties.

Judgment notwithstanding the verdict The decision of a court which sets aside the verdict of a jury and reaches the opposite result.

Judicial Matters relating to the office of a judge or the administration of his or her office.

Judicial restraint The principle that controversies must be settled, insofar as possible, in conformity with previously established legal principles and decisions.

Judicial review The process by which the courts oversee and determine the legitimacy or validity of executive, legislative, or administrative agency action.

Jurisdiction Identifies the geographic area and subject matter over which, and the persons against whom, a court may exercise its judicial authority.

Jurisprudence The philosophy, or science, of the law.

Justification An excuse recognized by the law exempting someone from liability for acting or falling to act. For example, self defence may be a justification for the taking of human life.

Laissez-faire doctrine The doctrine whereby business is permitted to operate without interference by government.

Last clear chance A principle of tort law which states that the person having the last opportunity to avoid injuring another must do so at his or her peril. This doctrine was devised to avoid the impact of the common law rule that contributory fault would bar recovery on the part of the plaintiff. If the defendant is aware of the plaintiff's peril and his inability to extricate himself and defendant can, by the exercise of reasonable care, avoid that peril he must do so, otherwise he will be considered wholly at fault. In Canada this rule is known as the **last opportunity** principle and has been largely, though not completely, discredited by comparative negligence statutes.

Last opportunity rule See **last clear chance**.

Latent Something hidden or concealed and which is not apparent on the face or surface of a thing. For example, a written contract may contain a latent ambiguity or an article may have a latent defect.

Lawful Legal; that which is authorized or at least not forbidden by the law.

Legacy Personal property disposed of by a will. Sometimes the term is synonymous with "bequest." The word "devise" is used in connection with real property distributed by will.

Legal entity An association recognized by law as having the legal rights and duties of a person.

Legal See **lawful**.

Legal environment A broad, imprecise term referring generally to those judicial, legislative, and administrative processes and rules that have particular application to the business world.

Lex Latin for "law."

Liability Denotes some legal obligation or responsibility in the broadest sense.

Libel Generally refers to a defamatory imputation on the reputation of another, in written or permanent form. See also **Slander**.

License Authority or permission to engage in or forebear from engaging in a particular act, as well as the document which evidences it.

Licensee In tort law defining the obligation of occupiers of property to those coming onto his or her property, a licensee is someone who enters with the permission of the occupier, express or implied, but without any economic or business advantage to that occupier. The duty owed to a licensee at common law was not to create any hidden traps or concealed dangers about which the occupiers knew or had reason to know. Some jurisdictions have adopted Occupiers' Liability Acts which have established a general duty to make the premises reasonably safe for lawful entry. See also **invitee** and **trespasser**.

Lien A claim to an interest in property in satisfaction of a debt or claim.

Limited partnership A partnership in which one or more individuals are general partners and one or more individuals are limited partners. The limited partners contribute assets to the partnership without taking part in the conduct of the business. The limited partner's liability to third persons is restricted to his or her capital contributions.

Litigant A party to a lawsuit.

Litigation A lawsuit.

Lockout The withholding of employment by an employer as a means of coercing concessions from or resisting demands of employees.

Mala fide In bad faith.

Malfeasance The doing of some wrongful or unlawful act.

Malice An act motivated by evil intent or marked by an utter disregard for the rights and interests of another.

Malpractice Any misconduct which does not meet the reasonable standards or skills of a particular profession such as doctors or lawyers.

Mandamus "We command" (opening words of a writ). A court order directing the holder of an office to perform his or her legal duty.

Matter of law Those rules or principles discoverable by reference to statute or the decisions of previously-decided cases.

Mens rea A guilty mind or criminal intent. See also *actus reus*.

Merger The combining of two corporate entities, and hence the extinguishment of one by the transfer of its assets and liabilities to the other.

Ministerial duty An example of a definite duty or act where nothing is left to discretion or judgment.

Misdemeanor A relatively minor criminal offence. In Canada, this is known as a **summary offence**.

Misfeasance The improper performance of an act which one is otherwise lawfully entitled to perform.

Misrepresentation An assertion, either by words or conduct, which does not comport with the facts.

Mistrial A trial which is invalidated because of some fundamental procedural irregularity.

Mitigating circumstances Circumstances accompanying the conduct of a party which, while not operating as an excuse, may serve as basis for reducing the criminal penalty or civil damages assessed.

Modus operandi Mode of operating.

Monopoly Exclusive control of a market by a business entity.

Mutual mistake A situation in which parties to a contract reach a bargain on the basis of an incorrect assumption common to each party.

National Labor Relations Act (NLRA) A 1935 congressional enactment regulating labor-management relations. This Act (1) established methods for selecting a labor union that would represent a particular group of employees, (2) required the employer to bargain with that union, (3) prescribed certain fundamental employee rights, (4) prohibited several "unfair labor practices" by employers, and (5) created the Nation Labor Relations Board to administer and enforce the NLRA. Also known as the Wagner Act.

Negligence The omission to do something which a reasonable person ordinarily would do or doing something which a reasonable and prudent person would not do which causes damage or injury to another. The elements of this cause of action have been described as follows: (1) A duty or obligation recognized by the law requiring a person to conform to a certain standard of conduct for the protection of others against unreasonable risks. (2) A failure to conform to this standard. (3) A reasonably close causal connection between the conduct and the resulting injury. (4) Actual loss or damage resulting to the interests of another. See Prosser, *Torts* (4th ed., 1971).

Nexus A logical connection.

No-fault laws Laws barring tort actions by injured persons against third-party tortfeasors and requiring such persons to obtain recovery from their own insurers.

Nolo contendere A plea entered by the defendant in a criminal case which neither admits nor denies the crime allegedly committed but which if accepted by the court permits the judge to treat the defendant as guilty.

Non-feasance The omission or failure to act for the benefit of another.

Non sequitur It does not follow (it is a logical fallacy).

Noscitur a sociis The principle that the scope of general words is delimited by specific accompanying words; a doctrine of legislative interpretation.

Notary public A public officer authorized to administer oaths and certify certain documents.

Notice Communication sufficient to charge a reasonable person with knowledge of some fact.

Nuisance In tort law, this is an action brought by the Crown to protect the public from activity which causes discomfort, injury, or inconvenience to the public generally in their enjoyment of life or property (public nuisance), or by a private person to protect his or her use and enjoyment of property from unreasonable interference by another (private nuisance).

Occupational Safety and Health Act (OSHA) In the USA, a 1970 congressional enactment creating the Occupational Safety and Health Administration as part of the Labor Department, and requiring that agency to develop and enforce occupational safety and health standards for American industries. In Ontario, referred to as the Health and Safety Act.

Offence Any violation of a criminal law.

Offer In contract law, a proposal made by an offeror which manifests a present intent to be legally bound and expresses the proposed terms with reasonable definiteness.

Offeree The person to whom an offer is made.

Offeror A person who makes a proposal to another, with the view in mind that if it is accepted, it will create a legally enforceable agreement between the parties.

Oligopoly Control of a commodity or service in a given market by a small number of companies or suppliers.

Omission The failure to perform a certain act.

Onus Burden of proof.

Opinion A judge's statement of the decision he or she has reached in a contested case, setting out the law, facts, and reasons upon which his or her decision was based.

Opinion evidence The conclusions drawn by a witness with regard to certain facts in dispute. Generally, opinion evidence is limited to experts.

Option A contractual arrangement under which one party has for a specified time the right to buy certain property from or sell certain property to the other party.

Ordinance The legislative enactment of a city, county, or other municipal corporation.

Ownership The right to exclusive enjoyment of a thing (Austin) because of having title to it.

Parol evidence Legal proof based on oral statements; with regard to a document, any evidence which is extrinsic to the document itself.

Partnership An association of two or more persons who by agreement carry on a business for profit as co-owners.

Party A person who is involved in a lawsuit either as a plaintiff or defendant or who otherwise might be directly affected by the disposition of the lawsuit.

Patent Something open and obvious and readily apparent on the face or surface of a thing. For example, the difference between the written figure and numbered figure on a check is a patent defect. Compare to **latent**.

Penal That which is punishable, or concerning punishment.

Per capita By or for each individual.

Per curiam By the court; said of an opinion expressing the view of the court as a whole as opposed to an opinion authored by any single member of the court.

Peremptory challenge The right of the parties to a proceeding to have a specified number of prospective jurors stricken without a showing of cause.

Perjury The giving of false testimony under oath.

Per se In itself.

Personal injury Any physical or emotional hurt or damage done to a person.

Personal property Physical or intangible property other than real estate.

Plaintiff A person who starts a lawsuit against another in a civil action.

Pleading The formal process of submitting in written form the contentions of the plaintiff and defendant in a lawsuit.

Plenary Entire, absolute.

Position of trust (1) A situation in which someone has a significant degree of authority or decision-making power over another, or unsupervised access to another person and to his/her property. (2) A situation where the success of the service depends on the development of a close, personal relationship between the individuals as in mentoring or friendly visiting programs.

Possession The control over or custody of anything that may be the subject of ownership.

Power The right or ability to do something.

Precedent A legal decision will serve as an authority for future cases in lower courts within the same jurisdiction if the material facts of both cases are the same or substantially similar—the basis of the principle of **stare decisis**.

Prejudicial error An error in judicial proceedings which may have affected the result in the case.

Preponderance of evidence The greater weight of credible and convincing evidence.

Presumption A conclusion drawn as to a disputed fact by the process of reasoning from other facts which are known to be true.

Prima facie case The introduction of sufficient evidence at trial that will enable a party to succeed if there is no evidence submitted by the opposing party to the contrary.

Private corporation A corporation formed by individuals, as compared to one formed by the government.

Privilege A particular advantage which a person enjoys exempting him or her from a liability or releasing him or her from some duty or obligation which he or she otherwise would be obligated to perform.

Pro tanto So far as it goes.

Probability Having the appearance of truth on the basis that there is more evidence in favour of the proposition than there is against it.

Probative Tending to prove something.

Procedural law The rules for carrying on a lawsuit (pleading, evidence, jurisdiction), as opposed to **substantive law**.

Procedure The form or manner by which the parties are regulated in processing or advancing their interests through a judicial proceeding.

Product liability Refers to the liability of manufacturers, distributors, and others for injuries or damages caused by a defect in a product. In the U.S., liability is generally strict while in Canada negligence must be shown.

Property Generally includes anything which is the subject of ownership, whether tangible or intangible.

Prosecute Formally proceeding against a person charged with a criminal offense.

Provocation An act or conduct by one person which incites another to engage in certain conduct in response. While provocation is generally not a defence to any illegal or unlawful behavior, it may be considered by a court in reducing the severity of the punishment meted out for the unlawful behavior.

Proximate cause That which a court will recognize as the legally responsible cause of the injury or damage about which a plaintiff complains.

Publication In the law of defamation, the communication of the defamatory matter to someone other than the person defamed.

Public policy That which is perceived by a court as having some bearing on the public interest or tending to affect the public good.

Punitive damages See **exemplary damages**.

Quash To vacate, annul, or void the action or decision of another judge or administrative officer.

Quasi-contract A contract imposed upon the parties by law to prevent unjust enrichment, even though the parties did not intend to enter into a contract (sometimes referred to as an "implied-in-law contract").

Quasi-judicial Administrative actions involving factual determinations and the discretionary application of rules and regulations.

Quid pro quo Something given or received for something else.

Quo warranto Latin for "By what authority are you acting?" An action brought by the government to test the validity of some franchise, such as the privilege of doing business as a corporation.

Ratio decidendi (Reason for deciding.) The principal point in a decision which effectively determines the case.

Real property Land and fixtures to land.

Reasonable man In a negligence action, a fictional character of judicial contrivance whose behavior, knowledge, and perception ought to serve as a model to a jury or court in determining whether someone has acted reasonably. For example, "Would the reasonable man think that this was a risky course of action?"

Redshirt to keep a college athlete out of varsity competition for a year to develop his or her skills.

Release Relinquishment of a right or claim against another party.

Relevancy In the law of evidence, something is relevant, and thus admissible, if it tends to prove or disprove a question in issue.

Remand (1) To return a prisoner to custody pending further enquiries, or while awaiting trial. (2) The act of a higher court in sending a case back to a lower court for further proceedings.

Remedy The means employed by the court to enforce the rights of one individual against that of another or to redress any injury which someone may have received.

Res A thing, object, or status.

Res ipsa loquitur (The thing speaks for itself.) In tort law, where a person is injured by something under the control of another under circumstances where the event normally would not occur without negligence on the part of that person, the court may draw an inference of negligence against him or her. The defendant has the burden of disproving negligence.

Res judicata (A thing adjudged.) Once a court of competent jurisdiction has finally entered a judgment on the merits of a dispute between parties, those matters in dispute may not be the subject of any new lawsuit between the persons involved.

Rescind To cancel or annul a contract and return the parties to their original positions.

Rescission Annulment or cancellation of an obligation so as to return the parties to their status prior to the origin of the obligation.

Respondeat superior (Latin for "Let the master answer.") Under this doctrine, an employer is responsible for all the acts of his employees done in the course of their employment.

Respondent See **appellee**.

Restraint of trade Any contract, agreement, or combination which eliminates or restricts competition (usually held to be against public policy and therefore illegal).

Reverse discrimination The unequal treatment of non-minorities arising from affirmative action programs. Subject to certain conditions, the courts permit such discrimination where court-ordered affirmative action is aimed at eliminating specific discriminatory practices or where affirmative action is strictly voluntary and temporary in nature.

Reverse The action of a higher court in setting aside the decision of a lower court.

Right of action The legal ability to bring a lawsuit.

Ruling A decision of a court affecting the legal position of parties during the course of a trial.

Sanctions Penalties imposed for violation of a law.

Scienter With knowledge; particularly, guilty knowledge.

Secondary boycott Conspiracy or combination to cause the customers or suppliers of an employer to cease doing business with that employer.

Self-defence The right of an individual to use reasonable force against another where his or her own physical well-being, or that of a third person, is threatened.

Separation of powers The doctrine which holds that the legislative, executive, and judicial branches of government function independently of one another and that each branch serves as a check on the others.

Sherman Antitrust Act An 1890 congressional enactment that (1) made illegal every contract, combination in the form of trust or otherwise, or conspiracy in restraint of trade or commerce among the several states, and (2) made it illegal for any person to monopolize, or attempt or conspire to monopolize, any part of the trade or commerce among the several states.

Sine qua non See **but for** rule.

Slander Generally refers to a defamatory imputation on the reputation of another orally or in some impermanent form. See also **libel**.

"Smart money" See **exemplary damages**.

Standing The right to sue.

Stare decisis ("Stand by the decision.") The principle that once a decision has been made by a court, it serves as a **precedent** for future decisions of similar cases in lower courts.

Statement of claim See **complaint**.

Statement of defense See **answer**.

Status quo The conditions or state of affairs at a given time.

Statute of limitations A law that sets forth a maximum time period, from the happening of an event, for a legal action to be properly filed in or taken to court. The statute bars the use of the courts for recovery if such action is not filed during the specified time.

Statute A legislative enactment.

Strict liability A legal principle by which a person can be held liable for damage or injury even if not at fault or negligent. Basically, any seller of a defective product that is unreasonably dangerous is liable for any damage or injury caused by the product, provided that the seller is a merchant and the product has not been modified or substantially changed since leaving the seller's possession. This rule applies even if there is no sale of the product and even if the seller exercised due care.

Subpoena A court order directing a witness to appear or to produce documents in his or her possession.

Subrogation After a party secondarily liable for a debt has made payment to the creditor, he or she then has the right to stand in the place of the creditor and to enforce the creditor's right against the party primarily liable in order to obtain indemnity from that party.

Substantial factor An event is considered a cause of another event if it is a substantial factor in producing that result. This is a test used in determining whether one event is a **cause-in-fact** of another event in the law of negligence. See also **But for** rule.

Substantive law The actual law, the basic rights and duties of parties as provided for in any field of law. Compare with **procedural law,** under which these rights and duties are determined in a lawsuit.

Sue The process of starting or commencing a lawsuit.

Summary judgment A judicial determination that no genuine factual dispute exists and that one party to the lawsuit is entitled to judgment as a matter of law.

Summary offence See **misdemeanour**.

Summons An official notice to a person that a lawsuit has been commenced against him or her and that he or she must appear in court to answer the charges.

Supra Above.

Tangible property Physical property.

Testator One who has made a will.

Testimony Evidence given by a witness in court while under oath.

Textual context The court's reading of a statute in its entirety rather than a single section or part; a principle of statutory interpretation.

Title Legal evidence of ownership.

Tort A civil wrong by one person against another for which the wrongdoer may be liable in damages. For examples of torts in the area of sports, see **assault**, **battery** and **negligence**.

Tortfeasor A person who commits a tort (sometimes referred to as a wrongdoer).

Trademark A distinctive mark, sign, or motto that a business can reserve by law for its exclusive use in identifying itself or its product.

Training A learning process, during which time an individual is taught specific skills, which will assist them in performing their duties.

Trespass At early common law, this was a form of action whereby one could sue for damages for some injury caused by an act of the defendant that was forceful, immediate and direct. Today, the term refers to the wrongful entry upon another's land (trespass to real property) or the wrongful interference in the possessory rights of another's chattel (trespass to chattel).

Trespasser Someone who unlawfully enters upon the land of another.

Trespass on the case At early common law, this was a form of action by which damages could be awarded for acts injurious to others where they were indirect or consequential. This form of action has largely been displaced by **negligence**.

Trust A fiduciary relationship whereby one party (**trustee**) holds legal title for the benefit of another (beneficiary).

Trustee One who holds legal title to property for the benefit of another.

Ultra vires Beyond the scope of corporate powers granted in the charter.

Unconscionable In the law of contracts, provisions which are oppressive, overreaching, or shocking to the conscience.

Unilateral contract An offer or promise of the offeror which can become binding only by the completed performance of the offeree; an act for a promise, whereby the offeree's act is not only his or her acceptance but also the completed performance under the contract.

Usury A loan of money at interest above the legal rate.

Verbatim Word for word.

Verdict Findings of fact by the jury.

Vicarious liability The liability of a person, not himself or herself at fault, for the actions of others. For example, an employer is vicariously liable for the work-related actions of his or her employees.

Void Without any legal effect.

Voidable contract A contract having legal effect but capable of being avoided by one party; for example, because of fraud. The non-fraudulent party may, however, take steps to affirm the contract, in which case it will be legally enforceable by both parties.

Voir dire The preliminary examination of prospective jurors for the purpose of ascertaining bias or interest in the lawsuit.

Volenti non fit injuria No legal injury occurs to one who is willing.

Volunteer An individual: (1) who chooses to undertake a service or activity, who is not coerced or compelled to do it; (2) who does this activity in service to an individual or an organization, or to assist the community-at-large; (3) who does not receive a salary or wage for this service or activity.

Vulnerable person An individual who has difficulty protecting him- or herself from harm temporarily or permanently and is at risk because of age, disability, or handicap.

Waiver Intentionally or voluntarily relinquishing a legal right.

Wanton Conduct which is characterized by a recklessness indifference to human life or a total disregard of the consequences.

Warranty An assurance or guaranty, expressly or impliedly made, that certain actions or rights can take place, that information given is correct, or that performance will conform to certain standards.

Warranty of fitness for a particular purpose In sales law, an implied warranty imposed by law on a seller, who has reason to know of the buyer's intended use of the goods (where the buyer relies on the seller's skill and judgment), that the goods are suitable for the buyer's intended use.

Warranty of merchantability In sales law, an implied warranty imposed by law upon a merchant seller of goods that the goods are fit for the ordinary purposes for which goods of that kind are used.

Wilful A conscious act of the will. An act done intentionally or with some design or purpose.

Writ In early common law, a writ was a writing issuing from a court in the name of the King and directed to a person in commencement of some proceeding or requiring the performance of certain acts. For writs relevant to actions in tort, see **trespass** and **trespass on the case**.

Writ of certiorari A discretionary proceeding by which an appellate court may review the ruling of an inferior tribunal.

AGMV Marquis

MEMBER OF THE SCABRINI GROUP
Quebec, Canada
2001